About the Author

Jennifer R. Prince is a youth services librarian at a public library in North Carolina. She holds a bachelor's degree in literature from UNC at Asheville and a master's in library and information science from UNC at Greensboro. A long-time book reviewer for local newspapers and professional journals, including a weekly column about books for children and teens in the *Asheville Citizen-Times* and reviews in the *School Library Journal,* Ms. Prince has made a lifelong habit of reading and studying the Bible and participating in many in-depth Bible studies. She is excited that her first book is *The Handy Bible Answer Book.* Ms. Prince lives in North Carolina.

Also from Visible Ink Press

The Handy African American History Answer Book
by Jessie Carnie Smith
ISBN: 978-1-57859-452-8

The Handy American History Answer Book
by David Hudson
ISBN: 978-1-57859-471-9

The Handy Anatomy Answer Book
by James Bobick and Naomi Balaban
ISBN: 978-1-57859-190-9

The Handy Answer Book for Kids (and Parents), 2nd
    edition
by Gina Misiroglu
ISBN: 978-1-57859-219-7

The Handy Art History Answer Book
by Madelynn Dickerson
ISBN: 978-1-57859-417-7

The Handy Astronomy Answer Book, 3rd edition
by Charles Liu
ISBN: 978-1-57859-190-9

The Handy Biology Answer Book, 2nd edition
by Patricia Barnes Svarney
ISBN: 978-1-57859-490-0

The Handy Civil War Answer Book
by Samuel Willard Crompton
ISBN: 978-1-57859-476-4

The Handy Dinosaur Answer Book, 2nd edition
by Patricia Barnes-Svarney and Thomas E. Svarney
ISBN: 978-1-57859-218-0

The Handy Geography Answer Book, 2nd edition
by Paul A. Tucci
ISBN: 978-1-57859-215-9

The Handy Geology Answer Book
by Patricia Barnes-Svarney and Thomas E. Svarney
ISBN: 978-1-57859-156-5

The Handy History Answer Book, 3rd edition
by David L. Hudson, Jr.
ISBN: 978-1-57859-372-9

The Handy Investing Answer Book
by Paul A. Tucci
ISBN: 978-1-57859-486-3

The Handy Law Answer Book
by David L. Hudson Jr.
ISBN: 978-1-57859-217-3

The Handy Math Answer Book, 2nd edition
by Patricia Barnes-Svarney and Thomas E. Svarney
ISBN: 978-1-57859-373-6

The Handy Mythology Answer Book
by David A. Leeming
ISBN: 978-1-57859-475-7

The Handy Ocean Answer Book
by Patricia Barnes-Svarney and Thomas E. Svarney
ISBN: 978-1-57859-063-6

The Handy Personal Finance Answer Book
by Paul A. Tucci
ISBN: 978-1-57859-322-4

The Handy Philosophy Answer Book
by Naomi Zack
ISBN: 978-1-57859-226-5

The Handy Physics Answer Book, 2nd edition
By Paul W. Zitzewitz, Ph.D.
ISBN: 978-1-57859-305-7

The Handy Politics Answer Book
by Gina Misiroglu
ISBN: 978-1-57859-139-8

The Handy Presidents Answer Book, 2nd edition
by David L. Hudson
ISB N: 978-1-57859-317-0

The Handy Psychology Answer Book
by Lisa J. Cohen
ISBN: 978-1-57859-223-4

The Handy Religion Answer Book, 2nd edition
by John Renard
ISBN: 978-1-57859-379-8

The Handy Science Answer Book®, 4th edition
by The Science and Technology Department Carnegie
    Library of Pittsburgh, James E. Bobick, and Naomi
    E. Balaban
ISBN: 978-1-57859-140-4

The Handy Sports Answer Book
by Kevin Hillstrom, Laurie Hillstrom, and Roger
    Matuz
ISBN: 978-1-57859-075-9

The Handy Supreme Court Answer Book
by David L Hudson, Jr.
ISBN: 978-1-57859-196-1

The Handy Weather Answer Book, 2nd edition
by Kevin S. Hile
ISBN: 978-1-57859-221-0

Please visit the "Handy" series website at www.handyanswers.com.

THE
HANDY
BIBLE
ANSWER
BOOK

THE HANDY BIBLE ANSWER BOOK

Visible Ink Press®
43311 Joy Rd., #414
Canton, MI 48187–2075

Visible Ink Press is a registered trademark of Visible Ink Press LLC.

Most Visible Ink Press books are available at special quantity discounts when purchased in bulk by corporations, organizations, or groups. Customized printings, special imprints, messages, and excerpts can be produced to meet your needs. For more information, contact Special Markets Director, Visible Ink Press, www.visibleink.com, or 734–667–3211.

Managing Editor: Kevin S. Hile
Art Director: Mary Claire Krzewinski
Typesetting: Marco Di Vita
Proofreaders: Paul Cain and Sharon Gunton
Indexer: Shoshana Hurwitz

Library of Congress Cataloging–in–Publication Data

Prince, Jennifer Rebecca.
    The handy Bible answer book / by Jennifer Rebecca Prince.
        pages cm
Includes bibliographical references and index.
ISBN 978-1-57859-478-8 (pbk. : alk. paper)
    1.   Bible–Miscellanea. 2.   Bible–Introductions.   I. Title.
BS612.P67 2014
220.6'1–dc23   2013044595

10 9 8 7 6 5 4 3 2 1

THE
HANDY
BIBLE
ANSWER
BOOK

**Understanding
the World's
All-Time
Bestseller**

Jennifer R. Prince

VISIBLE
INK
PRESS

Detroit

Contents

Photo Credits

Introduction

What is in this book?

A Jewish saying goes, "There are 70 ways to interpret the Torah and all of them are correct." The same thing can be said for the entire Bible. No one book can provide all of the variations on thoughts about and interpretations of the Bible. The purpose of *The Handy Bible Answer Book* is to provide the casual reader with an introduction to the people, places, and events in the Bible.

This is not a project I undertook lightly. Every day before I sat down to work on this book, I prayed. I prayed for God to enlarge my understanding of the Bible and grant me the ability to write about it in a meaningful, accessible way.

My name appears as the author of this book, but really there are so many people who helped make this possible. First, I thank Scott and Rookie. Also, I thank Abby, Ann, Ariel, Avery, Carolyn, Debbie, Etta, Gerald, Jane, John, Karen, Katie, Laura, Maggie, Marge, Meg, Rocky, Ruth Ann, Sally, Sallyanne, Shellie, Sherie, Sharon, and Tricia for their invaluable insights, ideas, proofreading abilities, and encouragements. Some of these folks are clergy; some are not. All of them helped immeasurably.

I used several translations of the Bible throughout the book in order to provide the reader with an idea of how the translations are similar and different. Each translation has its own flavor, so to speak. They are cited in quotes with the following abbreviations:

- NRSV: *The New Oxford Annotated Bible: New Revised Standard Version with the Apocrypha,* third edition, edited by Michael D. Coogan, Oxford University Press, 2007. This is the translation I used most frequently.

- NIV: *The Life Application Study Bible: New International Version,* Tyndale House Publishers and Zondervan, 1997.

- NLT: *The Life Application Study Bible: The New Living Translation,* Tyndale House Publishers, 1996.

- The Message: *The Message: The Bible in Contemporary Lanuage,* by Eugene H. Peterson, NAVPress, 2002.
- KJV: *The Holy Bible: Authorized King James Version,* Holman Bible Publishers, 1987.

The Message does not have the content of chapters divided into verses, so the verse numbers are approximations based on verse numbers in other translations.

Also, in this book the terms BCE (Before the Common Era) and CE (Common Era) are used to designate the years before and after the birth of Jesus.

BUILDING THE BIBLE

What is the Bible?

The Bible is the most widely distributed book in history. It has been translated more times and into more languages than any other book. The word "bible" comes from the Latin word "biblia", which means books. So the Bible is a collection of books. More precisely, the Bible is a collection made up of sixty-six separate books. The books are grouped into the Old and New Testaments. Within those books there is history, law, prophecy, song, and poetry, all of which have their special role in imparting inspiration, comfort, wisdom, and directions for living. While the Old Testament is sacred in Judaism and Christianity, the New Testament is sacred only in Christianity. Within the testaments, the books are divided into historical books, poetic books, prophetic books, and letters.

What are the names of the books in the Bible?

The names of the books in the Bible are as follows:

Old Testament	New Testament
Historical Books	**Historical Books**
Genesis	Matthew
Exodus	Mark
Leviticus	Luke
Numbers	John
Deuteronomy	Acts
Joshua	
Judges	**Letters**
Ruth	Romans
I and II Samuel	I and II Corinthians
I and II Kings	Galatians
I and II Chronicles	Ephesians

Old Testament	New Testament
Historical Books	Letters
Ezra	Philippians
Nehemiah	Colossians
Esther	I and II Thessalonians
	I and II Timothy
Poetic Books	Titus
Job	Philemon
Psalms	Hebrews
Proverbs	James
Ecclesiastes	I and II Peter
Song of Songs (Song of Solomon)	I, II, and III John
	Jude
Prophetic Books	
Isaiah	**Prophetic Books**
Jeremiah	Revelation
Lamentations	
Ezekiel	
Daniel	
Hosea	
Joel	
Amos	
Obadiah	
Jonah	
Micah	
Nahum	
Habakkuk	
Zephaniah	
Haggai	
Zechariah	
Malachi	

What language was the Bible written in originally?

The Old Testament was written in Hebrew mostly, with a few portions being written in Aramaic, a group of related languages of the Middle East. The New Testament was written in Greek, which at the time was the language not just of Greece, but of the entire region (much in the same way that English is not spoken only in England but in many other countries as well).

What are some other names for the Bible?

Some other names for the Bible are: Holy Bible, Holy Scripture, Scripture, Good Book, Word of God, the Word.

Aramaic was the language of Semitic peoples in the time of Jesus and is likely the language he spoke. The script of the language (a written example shown here) was adopted by many cultures and is the precuror of modern Hebrew and Arabic.

What are some other names for God in the Bible?

God goes by many names in the Bible. "El" and "Yahweh" mean God in Hebrew. When each of these two words is combined with other words or phrases, a little bit of God's nature is revealed. Below are a just a few examples:

- El Shadday—God Almighty
- Elohim—God, Mighty Creator
- Yahweh Nissi—The Lord is My Banner or Protector
- Yahweh Roi—The Lord is My Shepherd
- Yahweh Rophe—The Lord who Heals
- Yahweh Shalom—The Lord is Peace

What makes the Bible holy?

Christians believe that the content in the Bible was written and assembled by men, but that the whole process was led by God.

How is the Bible used?

In public worship, church leaders or lay leaders read a portion of scripture out loud to the congregation. Then the church leader delivers a sermon about that scripture. In some churches, the church leader builds his or her sermon around the prompts in a Lectionary, a schedule for reading Scripture. For example, at a Christmas service the leader could read thematically or topically related passages from Isaiah, Psalms, and Matthew.

Sometimes, small groups of believers meet regularly and study the Bible using a study guide or related curriculum. In private worship, individuals read from the Bible on their own time. As in the group studies, individuals can use study guides or other aides.

Who wrote the Bible?

The authorship of the Bible has a long, complex history going back thousands of years. For centuries, stories and songs were spread and passed down to succeeding generations by word of mouth. Authors include kings, prophets, fishermen, farmers, and others.

How old is the Bible?

Scholars continue to debate this. Some suggest that the oldest parts of the Old Testament were written in the sixth century B.C.E., though some say the oldest parts were written as early as the fourteenth century B.C.E. Some say the oldest book is Job, while some say the oldest books are the first five books of the Bible.

Like the Old Testament, the New Testament was not written all at once. For generations, Christians used only the Hebrew Bible. It was not until the second century C.E.

that Christians began to set apart writings that were specifically Christian and treat them as equal to the Hebrew Scriptures. Generally speaking, the New Testament was written in the decades following the death and resurrection of Jesus, making it roughly two thousand years old.

When was the Bible first known as the Bible?

Most likely, the name stuck around 400 C.E.. It was about this time that Christians referred to the Old Testament and the New Testament as "the book."

What is the Torah?

The Torah is the first five books of the Old Testament: Genesis, Exodus, Leviticus, Numbers, and Deuteronomy. For Chris-

The Torah consists of the first five books of the Old Testament.

> ## Was the Bible always divided into chapters?
>
> The Bible has not always been divided into chapters and verses. The practice of dividing the Bible into chapters was the brainchild of archbishop of Canterbury, Stephen Langton (1150–1228). The practice of dividing the Bible into verses was accomplished by Robert Estienne (1503–1559).

tians, this collection of books has the same status as other Old Testament books. For Jews, however, the Torah is the most important part of the Scriptures because it not only contains the history of the Israelite people, but also the laws and instructions for daily living according to God's will.

What is the Septuagint?

This is the name given to the first Greek translation of the Hebrew Bible, or Old Testament. Originally the Hebrew Scriptures were written in Hebrew, but around the third century B.C.E., the scriptures started being translated into Greek. In addition to being written in a different language, the Septuagint differs from the Hebrew Scriptures in its order of books and its inclusion of books from the Apocrypha. The term Septuagint comes from the Latin "septuaginta," which means "seventy." According to tradition, Ptolemy II asked seventy (some sources say seventy-two) Jewish scholars to start with translating the Torah. The other books in the Hebrew Bible were translated into Greek in the ensuing years.

What are some of the differences between the Old Testament and New Testament?

In Judaism, only the Old Testament is holy, and it is not known as the Old Testament; rather, it is called the Tanakh, or Hebrew Bible. Among the things covered in these thirty-nine books are the creation of the world and the formation of Israel. The Hebrew Bible is divided into three sections: Torah, Prophets, and Writings. Writings is subdivided further into three sections: Poetic Books, Festival of Scrolls, and Historical Books. In the Hebrew Bible, the books are in a different order than in the Christian Old Testament as follows:

Torah
  Genesis, Exodus, Leviticus, Numbers, Deuteronomy

Prophets
  Joshua, Judges, I and II Samuel, I and II Kings

Latter Prophets
  Isaiah, Jeremiah, Ezekiel

The Twelve Minor Prophets (called "minor" not because they are less important, but because there are fewer of their writings)
  Hosea, Joel, Amos, Obadiah, Jonah, Micah, Nahum, Habakkuk, Zephaniah, Haggai, Zechariah, Malachi

The Writings
Psalms, Proverbs, Job

Scrolls
Song of Songs, Ruth, Lamentations, Ecclesiastes, Esther

Then:
Daniel, Ezra, Nehemiah, I and II Chronicles

In Christianity, both the Old and New Testaments are holy. Christians believe parts of the Old Testament point to the coming of Jesus. The New Testament is made up of twenty-seven books, and is holy in Christianity. The New Testament recounts the arrival of Jesus, his life on earth, and what happened in the years right after his death and resurrection. God is present throughout the whole Bible—sometimes as an observer, sometimes as an active participant.

What is the oldest surviving complete Old Testament?

This distinction belongs to the Leningrad Codex, which dates from 1008 C.E. It was written in Hebrew. The Leningrad Codex is so called because it has been part of the collection at the National Library of Russia in St. Petersburg since 1863. In 1924, the city's name was changed to Leningrad, so the Codex's name was changed accordingly. When the city's name was changed back to St. Petersburg in 1991, the Codex retained its Leningrad prefix. The Allepo Codex is slightly older than the Leningrad Codex, but it has been missing some pages since 1947.

What is the oldest surviving complete New Testament?

It is the Codex Sinaiticus or Sinai Book. Discovered in the Monastery of St. Catherine at the foot of Mount Sinai in 1859 by Count Constantin von Tischendorg, the copy dates from around 350 C.E., and is written in Greek. As the story goes, the count found the pages in a basket of leaves waiting to be burned.

Why are Jews referred to by so many different names in the Bible?

Sometimes the Jews are referred to as Hebrews. Abraham was the first one to be called a Hebrew. Most scholars think the

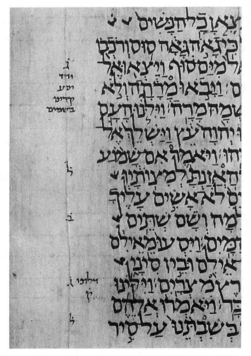

A page from the Leningrad codex, which is the oldest surviving complete copy of the Old Testament.

What is a codex?

A codex consists of papers bound in a book as opposed to loose manuscripts rolled into scrolls.

---

word derives from the name Eber, who was one of Abraham's ancestors (Genesis 14:13). The use of the name Hebrews set Abraham and his family apart. Sometimes Jews are referred to as Israelites, a term that came into use when God changed Jacob's name to Israel (Genesis 32:28). The use of the name Israelite marks the beginning of nationhood for Jacob and his family. When the Jews are referred to as Jews it refers to the fact that they are people from Judah.

THE INTERTESTAMENTAL PERIOD

How much time passed between the last events recorded in the Old Testament and the first events recorded in the New Testament?

Malachi, the final prophet to appear in the Old Testament, lived around 450 B.C.E.. The birth of Jesus at around 4 B.C.E. marks the beginning of the New Testament. So, roughly 400 years passed between the Old and New Testaments. This in-between time is known as the Intertestamental Period.

What happened during the Intertestamental Period?

Jewish writings flourished. Many of these writings formed what would later be called the Apocrypha. See the chapter on the Apocrypha for more details on these writings.

THE FIRST AND SECOND CENTURIES C.E.

What happened that changed the course of Jewish history?

The fall of Jerusalem to the Romans in 70 C.E. forever changed the course of Jewish history. The temple, which had been the focus of Jewish worship and the Jewish priesthood for centuries, was in ruins. In addition, Romans continued to persecute the Jewish population. As a result, the Jewish priesthood was nearly wiped out.

With a population spread over many countries, how did the Jewish people retain their religion and culture?

A small group of rabbis, or teachers, set about to shift the focus of Jewish worship from the temple to the Torah. They did this by deciding on a canon for the Tanakh, or Hebrew Scriptures, and by organizing the lengthy oral law into a systematic, written form.

What does "vulgate" mean?

The word "vulgate" means "written in the language of the people." The Apocrypha was included in the Vulgate translation. The Latin Vulgate was the most popular Bible translation for a thousand years, on up to the Protestant Reformation. By that time, Latin as a language spoken by everyday people was outmoded. Incidentally, the words "vulgate" and "vulgar" are derived from the same Latin word "vulgaris."

What is the Diaspora?

After the destruction of the temple by the Romans, Jewish people fled to other countries and settled there. This dispersion of the Jewish population became known as the Diaspora.

What is the oral law?

Along with the written Ten Commandments, God gave Moses a set of laws that were not written down, but transmitted orally. In addition to the laws transmitted by God, the oral law consisted of centuries of rulings and interpretations of the Torah. Up to the time of the destruction of the temple, these laws, too, were passed down from generation to generation by word of mouth.

What is the codified, written collection of oral law called?

It is called the Mishnah. So massive was the oral law that it took top Jewish scholars twenty years—from about 200 C.E. to about 220 C.E.— to complete the compilation. The group of scholars was led by Judah Ha-Nasi, a revered scholar and teacher.

What kinds of laws are in the Mishnah?

The Mishnah prescribes laws and regulations for numerous real-life situations. Judah Ha-Nasi and his colleagues organized the Mishnah into six sections:

1. Agriculture—This section contains laws on land use and other farming issues.
2. Appointed Times—This section lays out the Hebrew calendar and describes the observances associated with it, including the proper way to observe the Sabbath.
3. Women—This section describes laws on marriage and the role of women.
4. Damages—This section explains civil and criminal laws and ethics.
5. Holy Things—This section describes the regulations associated with temple worship.
6. Purities—This section covers issues of ritual purity and impurity.

What were some of the other Jewish writings of this time?

Following the completion of the Mishnah in 200 C.E., Jewish scholars and teachers continued to discuss and debate the laws. These discussions and debates were codified into

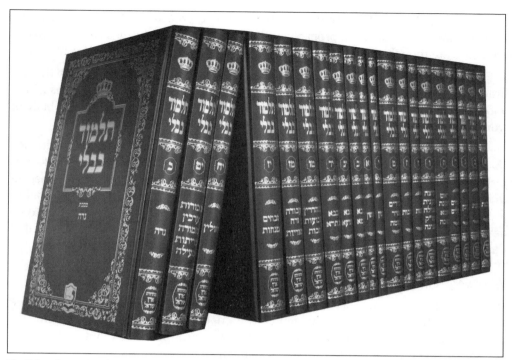

The Talmud contains the central teachings used in Rabbinic Judaism.

a collection of writings known as the Gemara. The Gemara contains stories by and about rabbis, some of which supplement accounts in the Tanakh.

So the Jewish people use the Tanakh, the Mishnah and the Talmud?

Yes. Eventually, the Gemara and the Mishna were combined to create one big collection, the Talmud. The study of the Talmud continues to be very important in Orthodox Judaism.

THE THIRD AND FOURTH CENTURIES C.E.: FORMING THE CANON

What is the canon?

The word canon derives from the Greek word that was used for cane, or reed. Canes were used as measuring devices. Today, canon refers to the books that were approved, or measured as being appropriate, as Holy Scripture, and thus suitable for inclusion in the Bible.

How was the canon determined?

Little is known for certain about the canonization of the Old Testament books. Opinions differ, but, generally, scholars think that the Old Testament was canonized in stages over

9

several hundred years. The Torah was canonized first, probably in the 600s B.C.E.. The Prophets was canonized next, probably in the 200s B.C.E.. The Writings and the remaining books are thought to have been canonized in the 100s B.C.E. or the first century C.E.

When early Christians spoke of Scriptures, they were referring to the texts of the Hebrew Bible—the Old Testament. As Christians began to record accounts of Jesus' life and teachings, and as Paul's letters circulated to an ever-growing audience, a body of work that was completely Christian began to take shape.

For writings to appear in the final canon of the New Testament, church leaders decided that they had to meet certain criteria. First, the writings had to have widespread—not just regional—acceptance among the churches. Second, the writings must be connected to one of Jesus' apostles by authorship or direct association. Third, the writings had to prove beneficial to the churches that heard them read. Fourth, the writings had to be deemed suitable for the reading public. In 397 C.E., church leaders met at the Council of Carthage and officially approved the twenty-seven books for the New Testament canon.

Who were some of the people influential in shaping the canon?

In the second century C.E., a man named Marcion received people's attention (and the attention of the church) when he denied the importance of the Old Testament. He claimed that Old Testament books might have been inspired by God, but that the Old Testament God was inferior to the New Testament God. Also, he denied Jesus' humanity, going so far as to excise all references to Jesus' incarnation and suffering in the small canon he developed. Marcion's increasing popularity spurred the church to decide in earnest which scriptures should be in the New Testament canon.

In the fourth century C.E., Eusebius of Caesarea was asked by Emperor Constantine to come up with a standard Bible. As Eusebius pored over the wealth of Christian writings, he learned about what writings had been accepted by various churches. By determining which writings were most widely accepted and which were least accepted, Eusebius developed a standard by which he judged the writings canonical or not. The framework of this standard was used in the final canonization of the Bible.

Athanasius, a contemporary of Eusebius, was the Bishop of Alexandria. The first known reference to a list that mirrors the New Testament canon as it is known today appeared in his Easter letter to Christians in 367 C.E.. In the letter, Athanasius declared that some Christian writings should be read as Holy Scripture; other writings were suitable for understanding the faith, but should not be classified as holy.

EARLY TRANSLATIONS AND TRANSCRIPTIONS

Who was St. Jerome?

St. Jerome (c. 347–420 C.E.) was a priest, historian, and theologian. In the Roman Catholic Church, he is the saint of encyclopedists, translators, and librarians. Around

405 C.E., Jerome finished his translation of the Bible into Latin, the version which is known as the Vulgate.

What is the Vulgate?

This is the Latin translation of the Bible done (mostly, some scholars say) by St. Jerome around 400 C.E. The Old Testament was translated from the original Hebrew. The New Testament was translated from the original Greek. Because Jerome translated the Old Testament from the original Hebrew and not from a later Greek translation, he determined that certain books were not found in the Hebrew Scriptures of the Jews. Jerome believed that if Jews did not see the necessity of adding books to the Old Testament canon, then neither should Christians. Accordingly, people started arguing about which books were canonical. In 1546, at the Council of Trent, the Vulgate was deemed the official Bible of the Church.

How were copies of the Bible made?

Manuscripts were copied by hand. Scribes who were called the Masoretes were key in seeing to it that this arduous task was done.

Who were the Masoretes?

Active between the sixth and eleventh century, the Masoretes were a group of respected scribes who devoted themselves to sorting, compiling, and copying manuscripts to form an authoritative text of the Old Testament. The manuscripts with which they worked were considered inviolable. So as centuries passed, Masoretes took great care with their work to ensure that as few alterations were made as possible.

Was transcribing by hand a reliable way to preserve the original content of the Bible?

Yes. The Masoretes and other scribes who copied manuscripts were meticulous about their work. Over the centuries, as Jewish scribes worked to preserve and pass down the Old Testament to future generations, they observed rituals. These rituals involved counting the words and letters in final copy and making sure those numbers matched the number of appearances of those same words and letters in the original manuscript. In effect, the rituals compelled the scribes to be mindful about their work and not make mistakes.

As the gospel spread and the Church grew, what happened when disagreements sprang up among believers?

After Jesus' crucifixion and resurrection, the church and its teaching founded in his name did not gain widespread popularity until 500 C.E. Around this time, Christianity in the form of the Roman Catholic Church became the state religion of the Roman Empire, and later the Holy Roman Empire. Sometimes, church leaders met to try and resolve disagreements. Other times, individuals or groups broke from the Church and formed their own church. One such break involved John Wycliffe.

Who was John Wycliffe?

Wycliffe (1320–1384) was an English scholar. He was a philosopher, theologian, translator, and teacher. Wycliffe criticized the Church for what he saw as false teachings. He believed that God's law was found in the Bible and in the Bible only. He did not approve of the hierarchy of Church leaders. Furthermore, Church leaders maintained that the Bible should be in Latin only and that only Church leaders should be allowed to read it and interpret it for laypeople. Wycliffe disagreed. He believed that all people had the right to read the Bible in their own language.

The fourteenth-century scholar John Wycliffe translated the Bible from the vulgate into English.

What did Wycliffe do to address this conflict?

In 1382, Wycliffe translated the Latin Vulgate Bible into English (some scholars think Wycliffe had no part in the translation, some think he translated a little of it, some think he translated all of it). At any rate, this was the first complete English translation of the Bible. It became known as the Wycliffe Bible. The Church forbade English translations, thus many copies of the Wycliffe Bible were destroyed. However, enough copies survived that the English translation gained a foothold among not just the learned, upper class, but among the common people.

The pope disliked Wycliffe immensely. Four decades after Wycliffe died, the pope declared Wycliffe a heretic and had his body exhumed and burned. Wycliffe was a man ahead of his time. Church reform did come about, but did not begin in earnest for another two hundred years. That is why Wycliffe is known as the Morning Star of the Reformation.

Did anyone carry on Wycliffe's work after he died?

Yes. Wycliffe had devoted followers, one of whom was Jan Hus (written sometimes as John Hus).

Who was Jan Hus?

Hus (c. 1369–1415) was a theologian in Bohemia (modern-day Czech Republic). When Wycliffe's teachings spread across Europe, Hus learned of them and was influenced in his own theology by them. Hus, like Wycliffe, disagreed with the Church hierarchy of leaders, and he believed the focus of Christianity should be on the teachings in the Bible. In 1415, because Hus refused to acknowledge the authority of the pope, he was charged with heresy. As a result of this charge, he was burned at the stake.

In the Middles Ages, how did people obtain copies of the Bible?

In the Middles Ages, every aspect of putting together a copy of the Bible was time-consuming, labor-intensive, and expensive. Ink and parchment were made by hand. Scribes copied the text by hand. In some copies, artists filled margins with elaborate, colorful images called illuminations. The copied manuscripts were bound by bookbinders. So, copies of the Bible were expensive but demand was high. Because there was so much poverty and books were expensive, owning an entire Bible was out of the question for most people. Besides this, the Church prohibited Bibles from being written in any language except Latin, even though Latin was no longer the language of regular people. There is evidence, however, that some people ignored the prohibition. Bibles dating from this era have been found in which, between the Latin text, someone wrote literal translations in another language. Some scholars think that this might be the origin of the modern-day saying "reading between the lines."

Also, illiteracy was widespread. Consequently, profusely illustrated versions of the Bible with condensed texts became popular. In this way, the basic beliefs of Christianity

In the Middle Ages, artists sometimes added illuminations (elaborate illustrations) to the hand-copied pages of the Bible.

13

were shared and spread. Biblia Paupernum, or "Poor Man's Bibles", were small picture-books in which events from the Bible were told through a series of panels, something like today's comic books. Florilegia, Latin for "to gather flowers," were small books containing Bible quotations. They spread from the Middle East to all over Europe then beyond.

Was language a barrier to the spread of the Bible?

Yes, but not for long. In a few European cultures, written language did not exist. Because it was thought important that these cultures have access to the Bible, alphabets were invented. For instance, a bishop named Ulfilas (c. 310 C.E.–?) was committed to spreading Christianity among his people, the Visigoths (the Visigoths lived in the area of what is present-day Romania). As part of his mission, Ulfilas set about to produce a Gothic Bible in 350 C.E., but Ulfilas ran into three problems. First, there was no written component to the Gothic language. It was only spoken. Not one to be discouraged by the lack of an alphabet, Ulfilas set about to invent one. Second, the Goth language did not have words to express some Christian concepts such as Holy Spirit. So Ulfilas set about to remedy that, as well. Third, the Goths had a reputation of being warmongers. Consequently, Ulfilas excluded I and II Kings from the Goth Bible because he did not think it would behoove them to read about a bunch of wars and killings. Because none of his manuscripts exist today, no one is sure how much of his ambitious project Ulfilas accomplished. What is certain is that Ulfilas linked the ancient and medieval worlds by his steady efforts to introduce Christianity to the people of central Europe.

THE 1400S AND THE PRINTING PRESS

What happened in the 1400s that revolutionized the way the Bible was copied and distributed?

In 1456, Johannes Gutenberg (c. 1395–1468) printed, in Latin, the first Bible using his movable type printing press. The result was twofold. For centuries, Bible manuscripts had been transcribed painstakingly by hand. Copies were few and expensive. The printing press made copies of the Bible easier and cheaper to produce, making more copies available to more people. In the next twenty years, Gutenberg and his colleagues created more Bibles than had been created in the previous 1,400 years. Forty-eight of the nearly two hundred original Gutenberg Bibles exist today.

When was the printing press used to print the Bible in its original languages of Hebrew and Greek?

In Spain, Francisco Jiménez de Cisneros (1436–1517) initiated the project for the Complutensian Polyglot in 1502, but the translation was not complete until 1522. It was a six-volume set. Six hundred copies were made. Only 123 are known to have survived to the present day. The adjective Complutensian derives from Complutense, the name of the university that published the translation. A polyglot is book in which the text is presented is several different languages arranged side by side in columns. In the case of the Complutensian Polyglot, the languages used were Greek, Hebrew, and Latin in the Old Testament and Greek and Latin in the New Testament.

THE 1500S: THE PROTESTANT REFORMATION

What major religious movement was helped by the invention of the printing press?

The Protestant Reformation was spurred by the availability of Bibles to more people.

What was the Protestant Reformation?

For centuries, the Church was ruled by the papacy in Rome. By the sixteenth century, however, some Christians were frustrated by the rites and rituals that were not biblically based, such as papal indulgences (papal claims that forgiveness of sins could be purchased). The Christians who disliked the status quo and fought to change became protesters—hence the name Protestant. Also, those seeking reform sought to get back to the original sources of the Bible. They were concerned that centuries of translations had muddied the ideas in the Bible.

Who was one of the forerunners of this "back to the sources" movement?

In the early 1500s, Dutch humanist, theologian, and scholar Desiderius Erasmus (1466–1536) became committed to translating and publishing the New Testament from the original Greek.

Who was one of the most influential Protestant reformers?

Martin Luther (1483–1546) was a German priest, monk, scholar, and theologian. He is known best for his 95 Theses.

What are the 95 Theses?

The 95 Theses are a collection of Luther's ideas criticizing some of the Church's practices, particularly the selling of indulgences (selling forgiveness of sins). In Wittenberg, Germany, on October 31, 1517, Luther nailed a copy of his theses on the door of All Saints Church. Within weeks of Luther posting the 95 Theses in Germany, copies were seen all over Europe, thereby

The German priest Martin Luther started the Protestant Reformation with his 95 Theses criticizing the practices of the Catholic Church.

15

marking the Protestant Reformation the first religious movement to be facilitated by the invention of the printing press. In a move that angered the Church even more, Luther translated the Bible into German. This translation became known as the Luther Bible.

William Tyndale was executed for heresy in 1536 for publishing translations of the Bible.

How did the Church respond to Luther's actions?

To the Church, Luther's words were heretical. As a result, the Church excommunicated him. Still, Luther continued to dispute practices of the Church. Luther died in 1546 of natural causes.

While Luther was working on Bible translations in Germany, who was the key figure working on Bible translations in England?

William Tyndale (c. 1490–1536). Tyndale, an English scholar, priest, and theologian, translated various biblical manuscripts into English. Like Luther, he believed that the Bible should be available for people to read in their own language. In 1526, while in France, Tyndale and his assistant, William Roye, translated a 1516 Greek translation of the New Testament into English. Thanks to the efficiency of the printing press, Tyndale's New Testament translations spread throughout England quickly. Tyndale translated several books of the Old Testament into English, but he did not live to see them published. In 1536, because of what the Church saw as his heresy, Tyndale was sentenced to death by strangling. After he was strangled, his body was burned at the stake.

What did the Church think of Tyndale's translations?

The Church did not like Tyndale's translations. Copies were smuggled into England in bolts of cloth. The copies were burned as soon as they were found by Church authorities. Anyone caught with a Tyndale Bible risked being burned at the stake in Belgium. Today, it is believed that only a handful of Tyndale Bibles are in existence.

What happened to the Reform movement after Tyndale's death?

It was carried on by other reformers. One of the most influential of these was Miles Coverdale.

Who was Miles Coverdale?

Miles Coverdale (c.1488-1569), whose name is sometimes written as Myles Coverdale, was an Englishman, who, like Tyndale, fled England and sought refuge in Belgium. There, he helped Tyndale translate parts of the Old Testament into English. In 1535 he published the first complete translation of the Bible in English.

What did the Church think about Coverdale's translation?

The Church did not like it, unsurprisingly. However, the King of England, Henry VIII (1491–1547) turned a blind eye to its publication.

Why did King Henry VIII allow, albeit unofficially, the publication of Coverdale's translation when prior to this he had been against the Bible being printed in English?

Henry VIII wanted to divorce his wife Catherine of Aragon (1485–1536), so he could marry his mistress, Anne Boleyn (1501–1536). The papacy refused to grant King Henry VIII a divorce. So in a shocking move the king separated the centuries-old Church of England from the Roman Catholic Church. The Church of England had existed since the time when Christianity first entered England.

What did the break mean for the Church of England?

It meant that the Church of England no longer was under the authority of the pope. In 1533, after years of arguing with the Roman Catholic Church, King Henry VIII got his divorce. Essentially, the king authorized the publication of Coverdale's translation to emphasize the distinction between the Roman Catholic Church and the Church of England.

Which Bible was printed after the Coverdale Bible?

The Matthew's Bible was published in 1537, two years after the publication of the Coverdale Bible. The title page of this version reads that the translation was done by Thomas Matthew. However, most scholars think this was a pseudonym for John Rogers.

Who was John Rogers?

Rogers (1500–1555) was an English chaplain who went to Belgium. In Belgium, he became friends with William Tyndale and was influenced by his theology and his Bible translations.

Which Bible was printed soon after the Matthew's Bible?

The Great Bible was published in 1539. This was the first officially authorized English Bible. Thomas Cromwell (1485–1540), chief minister to King Henry VIII, assigned Miles Coverdale the job of completing this translation. Throughout the project,

Miles Coverdale used the Tyndale Bible and original Greek and Hebrew texts to create the authorized English Bible.

Coverdale used Tyndale's Bible and the best Hebrew and Greek texts that he could find. By 1541, seven editions of the Great Bible were published.

What did Cromwell do to get word out about the Great Bible?

Cromwell encouraged King Henry VIII to issue an injunction stating that a copy of the Great Bible be placed in every single church in England. Parishioners were free to look at it and read it. For the first time in the history of England, the Bible could be read from the pulpits in the English language instead of Latin. In 1543 an act of Parliament rescinded this movement by restricting the reading of the English Bible to the upper class.

How did the Catholic Church respond to Reformation efforts?

Leaders of the Catholic Church did not like the reforms at all. One way they combatted the reforms was by issuing new laws. Some of the new laws were issued at the Council of Trent.

What was the Council of Trent?

Catholic Church leaders met in a series of meetings, or councils, between 1545 and 1563 in Trento, Italy, to address the Reformation and other concerns. Also, it was in these councils that the Catholic Church's leaders determined that certain Apocryphal books were canonical and others were not.

What happened to the Reformation movement after Henry VIII died in 1547?

Henry VIII's son, Edward VI, became king. Edward was made king when he was only nine years old. During his brief reign, Protestant reforms continued. The Archbishop of Canterbury, Thomas Cranmer (1489–1556), was a trusted adviser of Edward's and proponent of Protestant reforms. When Edward died in 1553 at the age of fifteen due to a lung ailment, most of the reforms of the past several years were shattered.

What happened to shatter the reforms?

Henry VIII's daughter, Mary Tudor (1515–1558) became queen. Devoted to Catholicism, Queen Mary I wasted no time in trying to erase Protestantism in England.

How did Queen Mary I do that?

She married King Philip II of Spain. That made King Philip II, a devout Catholic, King of England. She revived the laws against heresy. She had hundreds of Protestants burned at the stake, including the Archbishop of Canterbury, Thomas Cramner. Her harsh tactics earned her the name Bloody Mary. Fearing for their lives, many other English Protestants fled to Protestant-friendly Geneva, Switzerland. There, the exiles were helped by French Protestant reformer John Calvin (1509–1564).

What did the English Protestants do in Geneva?

They set about to publish a new Bible, one that they and their families could use while in exile. The Geneva translators used text from several sources, including Tyndale's Bible and the Great Bible. The resulting Bible came to be known as the Geneva Bible. At first it was published in parts, but then it was published in its entirety in 1560. The first edition was dedicated to Queen Elizabeth I (1533–1603).

1558: ENTER QUEEN ELIZABETH I

Why was the Geneva Bible dedicated to Queen Elizabeth I?

When Elizabeth ascended the throne in 1558, she continued the work of her father, King Henry VIII, in turning England away from Catholicism and towards Protestantism. Catholicism lost favor completely in England when King Philip II of Spain sent the ill-fated Spanish Armada to England in 1588 in order to use overthrow Queen Elizabeth I and, thus, end the Protestant Reformation in England and the other areas where Queen Elizabeth I had influence such as the Netherlands. Queen Elizabeth sent the English fleet to meet the Spanish and destroyed nearly half its ships. This significant defeat for Spain contributed significantly to the decline of the Spanish Empire, and by 1604 England had won the war and secured its position as a Protestant nation.

Was the Geneva Bible popular?

Yes. At least 140 editions of it were printed. It was the favorite translation for the home and continued to be so for decades. The Geneva Bible was the Bible of William Shakespeare, John Bunyan, the Puritans, and the Pilgrims. It was the first Bible taken to America.

How did Queen Elizabeth I influence the publication of other Bible translations?

In 1559 Queen Elizabeth ordered that a copy of the entire Bible be placed in every church in England. The Great Bible was reprinted for this purpose, but the Archbishop of Canterbury, Matthew Parker, was not satisfied. In 1566 he assigned portions of the Great Bible to members of a team, most of whom were bishops. This team's job was not to just keep the essentials of the Great Bible intact, but also to correct inaccuracies that

Why do some translations of the Bible capitalize all the letters in LORD?

In many translations of the Old Testament, the word "lord" is written in two different ways: LORD and Lord. When "LORD" appears in scripture it means that in the original Hebrew the word "YHWH" or "Yahweh" was used. "YHWH" is believed to be God's proper name and means roughly, "he creates" or "he causes to be." When "Lord" is used in scripture it means that in the original Hebrew language, the word "YHWH' was to be understood as "Adonai" or "Elohim", words which mean "Lord" and "God" respectively.

had come to light since its publication. The resulting Bible was published in 1568 and came to be known as the Bishop's Bible.

Was the Bishop's Bible popular?

Yes. It was the Bible of the Church of England and it went through numerous editions. In addition, it served as the starting point for translators of the subsequent King James Version of the Bible.

When was the King James Version of the Bible published?

It was published in 1611. By this point, Queen Elizabeth I was dead and King James VI of Scotland was made King James I of England. To create a sense of unity among the religious factions of his realm, he ordered a translation of the Bible that was to appeal to everyone and be used by all churches. The King James Version proved to be the most popular translation of the Bible for centuries to come.

In 2011, the King James Version had its four-hundredth birthday. To honor the importance of the translation, every public primary and secondary school in England received a free copy of the KJV.

Why was the King James Version so popular?

The translators who worked on the King James Version were scholars. Striving for accuracy, they examined minutely the original Greek and Hebrew texts of the Bible. Striving for beauty, they fashioned the original texts into English that was filled with lyricism and elegance yet was still written so that people who were not scholars could understand it.

AN ENGLISH BIBLE FOR ENGLISH CATHOLICS

When did the leaders of the Catholic Church change their minds about allowing the publication of an English Bible for their parishioners?

The Catholic Church authorized an English translation of the Latin Vulgate in the late 1570s. Under persecution by Queen Elizabeth I, many English Catholics fled England and went to Douay, France.

What happened to the English Catholics in France?

They established a Catholic college in Douay (now Douai) that was later moved to Rheims, France. The New Testament was translated from the Latin Vulgate by Gregory Martin, an Oxford scholar who specialized in Hebrew studies. The New Testament was published in 1578. Because of a lack of funds, the Old Testament was not published until 1609. By this time, the college had moved back to Douay. This Bible translation became known as the Douay-Rheims Bible.

POST–KING JAMES TRANSLATIONS AND ADAPTATIONS

How many Bible translations are there?

Hundreds, maybe thousands of translations exist today. After the King James Version became the standard Bible in English, it was translated into many languages. Because trade routes expanded greatly in the 1500s, the Bible was taken to places all over the world, which increased demand for copies. Since then, it has been translated and published countless times.

What are some of the most notable Bible translations through the ages?

Some translations are notable because they are the first of their kind. John Wycliffe's translation, the Wycliffe Bible (1384 C.E.), is credited with being the first complete Bible in the English language. Because it was written in English, more people could read it for themselves and not rely on church officials.

What is the Red Letter Bible?

The Red Letter Bible (1928 C.E.) refers to the first Bible in which Jesus' words are printed in red.

When did the King James Version of the Bible appear in the Colonies?

The Crown held exclusive copyright of the King James Version. It was printed only in England. Copies of it were shipped to the Colonies. However, after the American Revolution broke out, Colonial publishers began to publish the King James Version, as well.

What is an adaptation?

A biblical adaptation is a version of the Bible in which the changes are made not by translating it from one language to another, but by condensing the text or changing some key aspect such as the setting.

What was the first Bible printed in the United States?

The Geneva Bible was brought to America by the Puritans in the 1600s, but it was not the first translation to be printed in America. The first Bible to be printed on American soil was the Algonquin Bible. It was published in 1663 under the title *Mamuse Wunneetapanatamwe Up-Biblum God*. It was in the language of Massachuset, a dialect of Algonquin, and was spoken by the Massachusetts Bay Indians. Before the printing of the Algonquin Bible, the Massachuset language had never been written down.

Other Native American translations followed, including a Mohawk translation of the Gospel of Mark in 1787 and a Cherokee translation of the New Testament in 1857.

What are some examples of Bible adaptations published in the United States?

Thomas Jefferson (1743–1826), in his *The Life and Morals of Jesus of Nazareth,* or the so-called Jeffersonian Bible (1820), rewrote the New Testament with drastic results. Using the original cut-and-paste method, Jefferson cut up a copy of the New Testament, excising all mentions of the Trinity and Jesus' miracles, divinity, and resurrection. Also, he streamlined Matthew, Mark, Luke, and John into one narrative.

Nineteenth-century feminist Elizabeth Cady Stanton (1815–1902) and a committee of her colleagues published a revised English version. Their version, the Women's Bible, changed the text so that women were seen as more independent of men and less subservient. The

There have been many adaptations of the Bible, some more radical than others. One of the United States' founding fathers and presidents, Thomas Jefferson, published *The Life and Morals of Jesus of Nazareth,* in which he cut out all mention of Jesus' miracles.

Women's Bible was published in two parts. The first five books of the Bible were published in 1895. The rest of the Old Testament and all of the New Testament were published in 1898.

For his Cotton Patch Gospels, published between 1968 and 1973, Clarence Jordan (1912–1969) rewrote parts of the New Testament so that the setting is the American South of the 1950s and 1960s. So when Jesus was crucified, for instance, it was referred to as a lynching and reads like this: "They crucified him in Judea and they strung him up in Georgia, with a noose tied to a pine tree."

Other versions, such as the 2011 New International Version Bible, reflect concern for twenty-first-century sensibilities by replacing masculine pronouns such as "he" and "him" with neutral pronouns such as "they" and "them."

Not all versions of the Bible are bound in a book, however. Some versions, such as the ones available for download on iPad and Kindle, are digital. Some versions are audio recordings of actors and actresses reading the text.

What are some notable illustrated versions of the Bible?

The Book of Kells from around 800 C.E. features a Latin translation of the four Gospels. The pages are filled with vibrant illustrations—or illuminations—depicting Christian iconography and elaborate patterns. Since the mid-1800s, the Book of Kells has been on display at Trinity College Dublin.

A critically acclaimed version by Siku, *The Manga Bible: From Genesis to Revelation* (2008), uses the popular, highly stylized Japanese art style of manga, and twenty-first-century speech patterns to convey the content of the Bible.

Artist and author Brendan Powell Smith is the creator of "The Brick Bible" book series. In these books, Smith uses elaborate Lego vignettes to retell portions of the Old and New Testaments.

Are there versions of the Bible tailored for children?

Yes. The language and subject matter of most Bible translations makes it hard for children to read and comprehend. Accordingly, numerous Bible versions for children have been published over the years. In some cases, the adaptation features a select group of dramatic events in the Bible, such as Adam and Eve in the Garden of Eden or Daniel in the lions' den.

For example, first published in 1953, the Arthur S. Maxwell (1896–1970) "Bible Story" series features easy-to-understand retellings and lush, full-color illustrations. Other books feature one biblical event at a time such as the account of Noah's Ark. *On Noah's Ark* by children's author and illustrator Jan Brett, and *Noah's Ark* by children's author Peter Spier, feature gentle, engaging accounts of the biblical text and colorful, imaginative illustrations.

Old Testament

THE PENTATEUCH

GENESIS

What is the Pentateuch?

This is the term Christians use to refer to the first five books of the Old Testament. The term Pentateuch come from two Greek words that mean "five books" or "five scrolls."

What is the setting for events in the Bible?

Events in the Bible are set in what is now known as Israel. Because so many events in the Bible are expansive and epic, it is easy to imagine that the events are set over a wide area of land. Actually, the opposite is true. Over the centuries, the names and borders of the region have changed many times, so determining an exact extent of the land area is difficult, if not impossible, to do. The events described in the Bible were set in an area of roughly 6,000 square miles— about the size of the state of Connecticut.

What is the book of Genesis about?

The word "genesis" means beginning or source. The book of Genesis is about that—all kinds of beginnings. It is about how God began a relationship with people. It is about the beginning of the earth, the sun and moon, people, marriage, families, animals, agriculture, music, and sin.

When was Genesis written?

The events recorded in Genesis were part of oral tradition long before they were written. Tradition holds that Moses wrote Genesis, Exodus, Leviticus, Numbers, and Deuteronomy. Most scholars place Moses' life around 1400 B.C.E.

"In the beginning ..." happened twice?

No, creation did not happen twice, but it is described twice in the Bible. Essentially, there are two separate creation accounts. The first creation account is the one in the first chapter of Genesis. "In the beginning when God created the heavens and the earth, the earth was a formless void and darkness covered the face of the deep, while a wind from God swept over the face of the waters." (Genesis 1:1–2) In this account, God created day, night, sky, dry land, seas, vegetation, the sun, the moon, animals, and people. The second account is told immediately following the first:"In the day that the Lord God made the earth and the heavens, when no plant of the field was yet in the earth and no herb of the field had yet sprung up ... " (Genesis 2:4–5). While this account can be read as a summation and expansion of the first account, generally it is viewed as altogether separate. In this account, creation was a more personal event. The order of events differs from the first creation account. God created a man, planted a garden, established rivers, created animals, then created a woman.

When did creation happen?

No one knows for sure, but that does not stop people from trying to figure it out. Irish bishop James Ussher (1581–1656) came up with a theory. Using the Jewish calendar and astronomical charts, Ussher theorized that creation began early in the morning on October 23, 4004 B.C.E. This date was accepted widely until the nineteenth century.

What sources did the author of Genesis use?

No one knows for sure, but many scholars support the documentary theory. The documentary theory states that the author of not only Genesis, but Exodus, Leviticus, Numbers and Deuteronomy as well, used at least four independent sources. These hypothetical sources are referred to as the Yahwist source, the Elohist source, the Deuteronomist, and the Priestly source. It is common to see these sources referred to as J, E, D, and P, respectively. According to the documentary theory, the sources were written over a period of centuries, and hailed from different parts of Israel and surrounding regions.

Is Jesus mentioned in Genesis?

Maybe. When God contemplated making humans, God said, "Let us make humankind in our image, according to our likeness ... " (NRSV, Genesis 1:26). Why does God use the plural first person? The Bible does not address this directly. One possibility is that God was addressing God's heavenly court. Another possibility is that God was referring to the Holy Trinity of the Father, Son, and the Holy Spirit—in which case, yes, Jesus *is* mentioned in Genesis.

Where is the modern-day location of Eden?

Its exact location is unknown, but the Bible offers a couple of clues. "A river flows out of Eden to water the garden, and from there it divides and becomes four branches. The

Back in the seventeenth century, Irish bishop James Ussher estimated that God created the universe and the world in 4004 B.C.E.

name of the first is Pishon; it is the one that flows around the whole land of Havilah, where there is gold; bdellium and onyx stone are there. The name of the second river is Gihon; it is the one that flows around the whole land of Cush. The name of the third river is Tigris, which flows out of Assyria. And the fourth river is the Euphrates." (NRSV, Genesis 2:10–14) Because the Tigris and Euphrates are known by those names still, their locations are known. Accordingly, many Bible scholars believe Eden was located somewhere in what is now Iraq.

If God is all-knowing, all-powerful, eternal, and ever-present, why did God rest on the seventh day of creation?

The Bible does not say why God made a point of resting. God could have instructed people to observe a day of rest and not done so himself. After all, God is God. Perhaps, though, God rested on the seventh day to emphasize the importanceof the behavior. God modeled the behavior for people.

29

ADAM, EVE, AND FAMILY

Why did God forbid Adam and Eve to eat from the tree of the knowledge of good and evil?

The Bible does not say why this tree is off limits. It just is. Also, the possibility exists that there were two special trees in Eden. "Out of the ground the Lord God made to grow every tree that is pleasant to the sight and good for food, the tree of life also in the midst of the garden, and the tree of the knowledge of good and evil." (NRSV, Genesis 2:9) Some Bible scholars think this means that there were two important trees in Eden, while other Bible scholars think that the two names refer to one tree.

What kind of fruit did Eve give Adam?

An apple, right? Actually, no. Oftentimes the fruit is depicted as an apple in art. The Bible, however, does not specify what kind of fruit it is. Eve explained to the serpent, "We may eat of the fruit of the trees in the garden; but God said, 'You shall not eat of the fruit of the tree that is in the middle of the garden, nor shall you touch it, or you shall die.'" (NRSV, Genesis 3:2–3) The fruit might be an apricot, pomegranate, or fig. Or it might be a fruit that people of today have never had, a fruit that is now extinct.

What were the jobs of Cain and Abel?

Cain and Abel were the sons of Adam and Eve. Cain was a farmer and Abel was a shepherd.

Why did God reject Cain's offering?

The Bible does not say specifically why God rejected Cain's offering. "And the Lord had regard for Abel and his offering, but for Cain and his offering he had no regard. So Cain was very angry and his countenance fell. The Lord said to Cain, 'Why are you angry, and why has your countenance fallen? If you do well, will you not be accepted? And if you do not do well, sin is lurking at the door; its desire is for you, but you must master it.'" (NRSV, Genesis 4: 4–7) Some readers of the Bible take this to mean that the actual offering Cain gave was not the issue. God was not making a preference of shepherds over farmers. Perhaps Cain's motivation for offering the sacrifice or his attitude in general did not please God.

After committing the original sin of disobeying God, Adam and Even were thrown out of the paradise of the Garden of Eden.

What was the mark of Cain?

This phrase is often used incorrectly to suggest that someone bears stigma or punishment inflicted by God because of sin. Biblically, however, the mark of Cain was a symbol of God's protection. After Cain killed his brother, Abel, God confronted him. "And the Lord said, 'What have you done? Listen; your brother's blood is crying out to me from the ground! And now you are cursed from the ground, which has opened its mouth to receive your brother's blood from your hand. When you till the ground, it will no longer yield to you its strength; you will be a fugitive and a wanderer on the earth. Cain said to the Lord, 'My punishment is greater than I can bear! Today you have driven me away from the soil, and I shall be hidden from your face; I shall be a fugitive and a wanderer on the earth, and anyone who meets me may kill me.' Then the Lord said to him, 'Not so! Whoever kills Cain will suffer a sevenfold vengeance.' And the Lord put a mark on Cain, so that no one who came upon him would kill him. Then Cain went away from the presence of the Lord, and settled in the land of Nod, east of Eden." (NRSV, Genesis 4:10–16) As God did with Adam and Eve, so did God with Cain. God tempered justice with mercy.

If the only people created at this point are Adam, Eve, Cain, and Abel, of whom was Cain afraid? How did Cain get a wife if the only people alive were he and his parents?

Readers have speculated about this for centuries. One theory is that Cain married a sister whose birth is not mentioned. Another theory is that God created other people shortly after he created Adam and Eve.

Were there hybrid people in the Bible?

Maybe. "The Nephilim were on the earth in those days—and also afterward—when the sons of God went in to the daughters of humans, who bore children to them. These were the heroes that were of old, warriors of renown." (NRSV, Genesis 6:4) Some readers of the Bible take this to mean that angels from Heaven came to Earth and mated with human women. Their offspring, the Nephilim, were giants by human standards. Later, when Moses sent a group of men to spy on Canaan, the spies reported back to him, "The land that we have gone through as spies is a land that devours its inhabitants; and all the people that we saw in it are of great size. There we saw the Nephilim (the Anakites come from the Nephilim); and to ourselves we seemed like grasshoppers, and so we seemed to them." (NRSV, Numbers 13:32–33)

NOAH AND FAMILY

Why did God get so mad that he destroyed the earth?

God became mad because people were rotten through and through. "The LORD saw how great man's wickedness on the earth had become, and that every inclination of the thoughts of his heart was only evil all the time. The LORD was grieved that he had made man on the earth, and his heart was filled with pain. So the LORD said, ' I will wipe mankind, whom I have created from the face of the earth—men and animals and creatures that move along the ground, and birds of the air—for I am grieved that I have made them.'" (NIV, Genesis 6:5–7)

Whom did God save from the flood?

In all, God saved eight people: Noah; Noah's wife; Shem; Ham; Japheth (Noah's sons); and the sons' three wives.

How many of each animal did God tell Noah to put on the ark?

Two, right? Well, sort of. As with the creation accounts, there are two different flood accounts. God did instruct Noah to bring two of every living creature onto the ark and keep them alive. In addition, God instructed, "Take with you seven of every kind of clean animal, a male and its mate, and two of every kind of unclean animal, a male and its mae, and also seven of every kind of bird, male and female, to keep their various kinds alive throughout the earth" (NIV, Genesis 7:2–3). Presumably, these "surplus" clean animals were needed so Noah and his family could make sacrifices to God.

How big was the ark?

The ark was three hundred cubits long, fifty cubits wide, and thirty cubits high. A cubit is about eighteen inches long. Translating those measurements into United States cus-

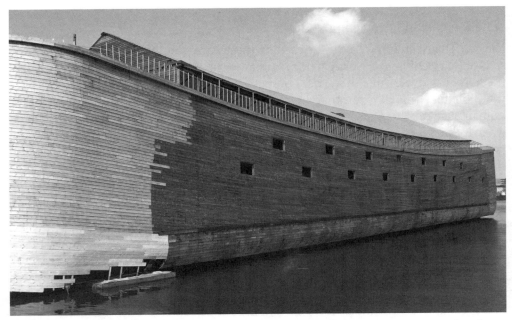

Based on the biblical description, engineers in Dordrecht, Netherlands, constructed a full-size recreation of Noah's ark.

tomary units means that the ark was 450 feet long, seventy-five feet wide, and forty-five feet high, roughly making it the size of the *Mississippi Queen* steamboat. So the ark was about half the size of a Carnival cruise ship, minus the all-you-can-eat buffet and Broadway-style shows.

What is the first thing Noah did after he got off the ark?

He honored God. This might be where all of those extra pairs of clean animals came in use. "Then Noah built an altar to the LORD and taking some of all the clean animals and clean birds, he sacrificed burnt offerings on it." (NIV, Genesis 8:20)

God promised to establish a covenant with Noah. What is a covenant?

A covenant is a formal agreement. In this case, God said, "As for me, I am establishing my covenant with you and your descendants after you, and with every living creature that is with you, the birds, the domestic animals, and every animal of the earth with you, as many as came out of the ark. I establish my covenant with you that never again shall all flesh be cut off by the waters of a flood, and never again shall there be a flood to destroy the earth." (NRSV, Genesis 9:8–11)

What sign did God offer Noah to seal the deal?

The rainbow.

Besides being a sailor and zookeeper, what other interests did Noah have?

Noah is described as a "man of the soil." (NIV, Genesis 9:20) He was the first to plant a vineyard and make wine. Noah's pleasant occupation had disastrous results.

How did Noah's wine making have disastrous results?

One day, Noah imbibed a little too much. "He drank some the wine and became drunk, and he lay uncovered in his tent." (NRSV, Genesis 9:21) Ham, one of Noah's sons, saw Noah naked, and told his two brothers, Shem and Japheth. Shem and Japheth were not amused. They took a garment of some sort and, walking backwards, into the tent, covered up their father without looking at him. When Noah woke up and learned what Ham did, he cursed Ham's son, Canaan: "Cursed be Canaan; lowest of slaves shall he be to his brothers." This particular Bible passage does not say why it was that Ham's son—and not Ham himself—who was cursed. One theory is that Canaan was there and saw what Ham did, yet did nothing to protect his grandfather's dignity. Another theory is that Noah cursed Ham's son because while Ham might have endured his own punishment, it was more painful to see his innocent son and descendants punished.

A MULTILINGUAL WORLD

What was the Tower of Babel?

At this time, people spoke with one language—and liked it that way. In a movement of solidarity, they began to build a tower. "Come, let us build ourselves a city, and a tower with its top in the heavens, and let us make a name for ourselves; otherwise we shall be scattered abroad upon the face of the whole earth." (NRSV, Genesis 11:4) God did not like this. So, again invoking the plural first person, God said, "Come, let us go down, and confuse their language there, so that they will not understand one another's speech." (NRSV, Genesis 11:7) In this, what many Bible scholars see as his final step in creating civilized humanity, God established a variety of territorial groups and a variety of languages by scattering these people all over the earth.

34 This 1563 painting by Pieter Brueghel the Elder depicts the Tower of Babel.

ABRAHAM, THE FIRST PATRIARCH

Who was Abraham?

The name Abraham means "father of many." In the Bible, Abraham lived up to his name. Abraham's story begins in Chapter 11 of Genesis. It is not clear why God singled out Abraham, but he did. God entered into another covenant, or formal agreement, with humankind. God commanded Abraham to pack up and leave his hometown Ur, the thriving port city along the Euphrates River, and cross some six hundred miles of desert to Canaan. If Abraham obeyed, God promised to make Abraham "the father of a great nation." (NLT, Genesis 12:2) God expanded on the promise: "I will bless those who bless you and curse those who curse you. All the families of the earth will be blessed through you." (NLT, Genesis 12:3)

What did God's promise involve?

God made this promise to Abraham several times. At one point, God linked the promise with two key things: a name change, and circumcision. Abraham, who had been known as Abram, was given his new name. Abraham's wife, Sarah, who had been known as Sarai, was given her new name. Circumcision, the surgical removal of the foreskin of the penis, became for all of Abraham's male descendants an indication of commitment to the one and only God. God specified that from that point forward, all male descendants of Abraham should be circumcised at eight days old. Abraham and the other males who were already past eight days old had their circumcisions retroactively.

What kind of person was Abraham?

Abraham was handpicked by God to become the father of many nations. So Abraham must have been a pretty upright guy, right? Actually, Abraham was no saint. He was a human being, complete with flaws and inconsistences in character. Abraham tended to lie when he felt cornered. When Abraham and Sarah were ready to enter Egypt, Abraham instructed the beautiful Sarah to tell the Egyptians that the two of them were brother and sister, not husband and wife. Abraham was afraid the Egyptians would kill him if they knew he was Sarah's husband.

What is the reason for circumcision?

With Abraham, circumcision became an indication of Israelite faith. However, the Israelites were not the only ones who practiced circumcision. According to various passages in the Bible, Egyptians, Edomites, Ammonites, and Moabites practiced circumcision. Some reasons for the practice were that it was for hygiene, that it was a rite of passage, and that it was a tribal mark.

Did this ruse work?

At first it did. The Pharaoh did not know that Sarah was already married and took her as his wife, but soon afterwards God afflicted the Egyptians with plagues. Bewildered, Pharaoh summoned Abraham: "What is this you have done to me? Why did you not tell me that she was your wife? Why did you say, 'She is my sister,' so that I took her for my wife?" (NRSV, Genesis 12:19) Without further ado, Pharaoh sent Abraham and his entire household away.

Abraham tried the she's-my-sister bit again sometime later when they settled in Gerar. Abimilech, the king of Gerar, took Sarah as his own. God warned Abimilech in a dream that if he made Sarah his wife, he and his family would die. Bewildered and frightened by God's message, Abimilech sent Sarah back to Abraham.

What was one of Abraham's positive traits?

He was big-hearted. Abraham traveled for a long time with his nephew, Lot. Both of them accumulated livestock, silver, and gold. Their livestock grew so numerous that the land would not support both Abraham's livestock and Lot's livestock. So, in a gesture of humility and generosity, Abraham told Lot, "This arguing between our herdsmen has got to stop.... After all, we are close relatives! I'll tell you what we'll do. Take your choice of any section of the land you want, and we will separate. If you want that area over there, then I'll stay here. If you want to stay in this area then I'll move on to another place." (NLT, Genesis 13:8–9) Lot chose Sodom (bad idea). Abraham chose Canaan.

What happened to Abraham in Canaan?

God reminded Abraham, "I will make your offspring like the dust of the earth; so that if anyone could count the dust then your offspring could be counted. Go, walk through the length and breadth of the land, for I am giving it to you." (NIV, Genesis 13:16–17) God repeated this promise in Genesis 15. Most scholars estimate the year of Abraham's arrival in Canaan at 2090 B.C.E.

SODOM AND GOMORRAH, TWIN CITIES OF SIN

Where were Sodom and Gomorrah?

Sodom and Gomorrah were located in the southern part of Canaan. Robbery, deceit, violence, and blasphemy were rampant in these cities.

What happened to Lot in Sodom?

Two angels visited Lot, and he welcomed them inside. The men of Sodom, both young and old, surrounded Lot's house, and insisted that Lot turn the angels (they appeared to be ordinary men) out so that they could "know" them ("know" being a veiled way of saying "have sex"). Instead, Lot offered to send out his two daughters. Lot pleaded with the men of Sodom, "Do to them as you please; only do nothing to these men, for they have come under the shelter of my roof." (NRSV, Genesis 19:8) Most scholars contend that Lot was concerned about his reputation as a host. When the men of the town threatened Lot, the angels struck the townsmen blind so they couldn't find the door.

What was the purpose of the angels' visit to Lot?

The angels visited Lot so they could warn him that they were sent by God to destroy Sodom and Gomorrah. The angels warned Lot to get his family and leave immediately without looking back. Lot hemmed and hawed a bit, but finally left. God told them not to look back or they would be consumed. Lot's wife, hurrying along with Lot, looked back and was turned into a pillar of salt.

Why did God save Lot, who offered his daughters to be gang-raped, and not his wife, who was guilty only of looking back?

The Bible is silent on this. One theory is that Lot was spared because it was through his line that Ruth was born, and Ruth was an ancestor of Jesus.

How did God destroy Sodom and Gomorrah?

God caused a rain of sulfur and fire to come down on the two cities. Some scholars think that sulfur and fire were the results of a massive volcano.

What happened to Lot after Sodom and Gomorrah were destroyed?

Lot and his two daughters took shelter in a cave. The daughters, in their eagerness to extend the family line, came up with a terrible idea.

Legend has it that this pillar of salt by the Dead Sea is the remains of Lot's wife.

What was Lot's daughters' bad idea?

The daughters got Lot drunk, so drunk that he was not aware when they took turns "knowing" him. Both daughters became pregnant. The first daughter had a son, Moab. The second daughter had a son, Ben-ammi. This is another instance of God finding a way to work his will despite the mistakes of people. Moab becomes the father of the Moabites. Ruth is a Moabite. Jesus is a descendant of Ruth.

FAMILY PLANNING

How did Sarah rush God's plan along?

Sarah had no children and feared she never would, despite God's promise to her husband. Sarah did, however, have a slave girl named Hagar. According to the custom of the day, it was appropriate for a wife to encourage her husband to sleep with the slave girls and claim any resulting offspring as her own. That is just what Sarah did. She encouraged Abraham to sleep with Hagar. If Hagar got pregnant, then the baby would be Sarah's.

What did Hagar think about being forced to sleep with Abraham?

The Bible does not say. However, Hagar became pregnant and viewed Sarah with disdain. Sarah got mad at both Abraham and Hagar, and then turned Hagar out of the house.

What happened to Hagar after Sarah kicked her out?

The Bible says that an angel of God visited her. Because Hagar said after the encounter that God visited her, some scholars think this angel was actually God in human form. As such, God encouraged

After giving birth to Ishmael, Hagar was told to leave when Sarah became mad at her and Abraham.

Hagar to go back home, and promised to give her many children. Also, God told Hagar to name the baby in her womb Ishmael.

What does the name Ishmael mean?

Ishmael means "God hears." There was more, though. God added an ominous note. God told Hagar that Ishmael "shall be a wild ass of a man, with his hand against everyone, and everyone's hand against him; and he shall live at odds with all of his kin." (Genesis 16:12)

Did Sarah ever have a child of her own?

Yes. Sarah had a son, Isaac.

What does the name Isaac mean?

Isaac means "he laughs." Isaac was named that because Sarah laughed when she overheard God tell Abraham that even though she was old and passed the age of bearing children, she would have a child. God questioned Sarah, "Is anything too wonderful for the Lord?" (NRSV, Genesis 18:14)

Were Ishmael and Isaac raised together as brothers?

At first they were raised together. When Isaac was at the age to be weaned, Sarah saw him playing with Ishmael. She got angry and told Abraham, "Get rid of that servant and her son. He is not going to share the family inheritance with my son, Isaac. I won't have it!" Abraham was reluctant to do so but God reassured him, "Do not be upset over the boy and your servant wife. Do just as Sarah says, for Isaac is the son through whom your descendants will be counted. But I will make a nation of the descendants of Hagar's son because he also is you son." (NLT, Genesis 21:10–13)

Were Hagar and Ishmael kicked out again?

Yes. This time, Hagar and Ishmael wandered about in the wilderness of Beersheba. When their water was gone, Hagar put Ishmael under a bush and began to weep. God heard her and sent an angel to

The seventeenth-century Dutch artist Rembrandt's painting "The Sacrifice of Abraham" shows an angel stopping Abraham from carrying through with God's order to sacrifice his own son.

39

her. The angel showed her where to find water. Ishmael's mother found a wife for him in Egypt.

Why did God command Abraham to sacrifice Isaac?

Why did God do it? Scholars continue to debate this. Abraham was quick to obey God. God said, "Go," and Abraham said, "OK." This suggests that Abraham was a man of amazingly strong faith. Though the account does not say so, Abraham might have been thinking of God's promise to him that it would be through Isaac that offspring would be named for him. Another indication of Abraham's strong faith is that when he and Isaac left their traveling companions to go up on the mountain, Abraham said, "Stay here with the donkey; the boy and I will go over there; we will worship, and then we will come back to you." (NRSV, Genesis 22:5) "We" is the operative word here. Abraham's use of this word (instead of "I") suggests that he anticipated that God would provide an alternate sacrifice, which is exactly what God did. The Bible does not say what Isaac and Sarah thought about all of this.

THE SECOND PATRIARCH, ISAAC

How did Isaac meet his wife, Rebekah?

Abraham's servant went to Aram-naharaim to find a wife for Isaac among their relations. The servant prayed to God, "Let the girl to whom I shall say, 'Please offer your jar that I may drink,' and who shall say, 'Drink, and I will water your camels'—let her be the one whom you have appointed for your servant Isaac." (NRSV, Genesis 24:14) It happened just as the servant prayed. Rebekah came out and gave the servant water, and offered to water his camels. After some bargaining with her father, the servant took Rebekah back to Isaac. Isaac loved Rebekah and was comforted after his mother, Sarah, died.

Did Abraham get married again after Sarah died?

Yes. He married Keturah and had several sons by her. Abraham wanted Isaac to be his only heir, so he gave these other sons some parting gifts and sent them away.

Did Isaac and Rebekah have children?

Yes, but not at first. Rebekah was barren. Isaac prayed to God to help Rebekah. God listened to Isaac, and Rebekah conceived twins. The twins struggled within her so

A servant brought Rebekah to Isaac, who fell in love her. She was barren at first but later bore Isaac children.

much that she cried, "If it is to be this way, why do I live?" (NRSV, Genesis 25:22) God explained to her, "Two nations are in your womb, and two peoples born of you shall be divided; the one shall be stronger than the other, the elder shall serve the younger." (NRSV, Genesis 25:23) When the twins were born, the first one came out red and hairy. He was named Esau, which is a playful term for "red." The second one came out with his hand gripping Esau's heel. This twin was named Jacob, which means "heel grabber."

THE POWER OF A GOOD STEW

How did God's plan of the younger twin serving the elder twin come to pass?

Jacob, a homebody, cooked a red lentil stew one day. Esau, an outdoorsman, came back from hunting and was very hungry. Esau asked his brother for some stew. Jacob said he would give Esau some stew if Esau sold him his birthright. Esau, impatient and thoughtless, agreed. Thus, Jacob, the younger brother, got in line to inherit more and be the head of the family after Isaac died.

What did Isaac think about this plan?

It is likely he never learned about it. On his deathbed, Isaac, blind and feeble, called Esau to him. Isaac told Esau to go out and hunt game and prepare a meal for him so he could bless Esau before he died. Rebekah overheard this. She urged her favorite son, Jacob, to act in Isaac's stead. So Jacob dressed as Esau, even going so far as to put goatskin on his hands and neck to mimic his brother's hairiness. Isaac said, "How is that you have found it so quickly my son?" Jacob answered, "Because the Lord your God granted me success." (NRSV, Genesis 27:20) Jacob's wording suggested that he did not believe in God yet, or at any rate, he believed in other gods as well. That was about to change.

Isaac thought Jacob was Esau, and gave Jacob the blessing that belonged to the oldest son. Esau, when he learned this, wailed, "Have you only one blessing, father? Bless me, also, father!" (NRSV, Genesis 27:38)

Isaac realized that Jacob had deceived him, but according to the custom of the time, could not retract the blessing he had given. Isaac blessed Esau as well, but it was bittersweet: "Your dwelling will be away from the earth's richness, away from the dew of heaven above. You will live by the sword and you will serve your brother. But when you grow restless, you will throw his yoke from off your neck." (NIV, Genesis 27:39–40) After that, Esau planned to murder Jacob, so Jacob left the area.

THE THIRD PATRIARCH, JACOB

What was Jacob's ladder?

The event involving Jacob's ladder marked Jacob's first personal interaction with God. After Jacob received his father's blessing and learned of his brother's deadly intentions toward him, he went toward Haran to find a wife. One night he set up camp. He placed

41

a stone under his head, and settled down to sleep. As Jacob slept, he dreamed of a ladder that reached to heaven. Angels went up and down the ladder while God stood beside Jacob. In the dream, God made a promise to Jacob as he had made to his grandfather, Abraham. God promised Jacob all of the land around him, and countless descendants. God promised Jacob that he would always be with him. When Jacob woke up, he placed a rock upright on the spot where he had slept. He called the rock Bethel, which means House of God. Jacob declared, "Surely the Lord is in this place—and I did not know it! And he was afraid, and said, 'How awesome is this place! This is none other than the house of God, and this is the gate of heaven.'" (NRSV, Genesis 28:16–17) The rock served as a physical testament to Jacob's newfound resolve to serve God and only God. In addition, Jacob promised to give God one-tenth of all he owned.

How did Jacob meet his wife, Rachel?

It was love at first sight—at least for Jacob. Jacob saw Rachel as she came to water her father's sheep. Jacob removed the stone from the mouth of the well. Then Jacob did two things that were unusual for the time and place. First, he kissed Rachel. Second, he cried. Presumably Jacob kissed Rachel because he was smitten with her, and cried because he was so overcome with happiness.

What kept Jacob from marrying Rachel right away?

Rachel's father, Laban, saw to it that the course of true love did not run smoothly. Jacob agreed to work for Laban for seven years in exchange for Rachel's hand in marriage. Jacob loved Rachel so much that he worked the seven years cheerfully and without complaint. When the seven years ended, Jacob married Laban's daughter all right, only it was not Rachel he married, but Leah wearing a veil! It is up for speculation as to how Jacob could not realize he was marrying the wrong sister, veil or not. "And Jacob said to Laban,

'What is this you have done to me? Did I not serve with you for Rachel? Why then have you deceived me?'" (NIV, Genesis 29:25) Jacob, the one who deceived his father and brother, found himself on the receiving end of deception.

Then, perhaps to spare Leah's feelings, Jacob agreed to work for Laban another seven years in order to marry Rachel. In the process, Jacob acquired Leah and Rachel's maids, Bilhah and Zilpah, as concubines.

Did Jacob ever see his brother Esau again?

Yes. Years passed. Jacob married and had several children. He was wealthy and suc-

Jacob prayed to God to rescue him from his brother, Esau, and to protect him.

cessful. When his wealth and property became so great that his interests conflicted with Laban's, he took his family and left. At one point during their travels, angels of God met him. The Bible does not say exactly why the angels are there, but what follows suggests they might have been there to herald a big change for Jacob.

Jacob sent messengers to Esau to find out if Esau would be receptive to meeting him. The messengers came back with this worrisome announcement: "We went to your brother Esau, and now he is coming to meet you, and four hundred men are with him." (NIV, Genesis 32:6) Jacob, fearing the worst, split his group in two. That way, if Esau harmed one group, the other group could escape.

How did Jacob change over the years

Jacob was no longer the selfish, dishonest man he had been in his youth. He was humble, and knew his own wiliness would not help matters with Esau. So he prayed to God: "I am not worthy of all the faithfulness and unfailing love you have shown to me, your servant. When I left home, I owned nothing but a walking stick, and now my household fills two camps! O LORD, please rescue me from my brother, Esau. I am afraid that he is coming to kill me, along with my wives and children. But you promised to treat me kindly and to multiply my descendants until they become as numerous as the sands along the seashore." (NLT, Genesis 32:10–12)

What happened when Jacob and Esau met again?

Like two gunslingers on a dusty road in front of a saloon, Jacob and Esau eyed each other from a distance. The reader knows Jacob's thoughts and feelings, but can only guess at Esau's. Was Esau still angry with Jacob for his past treacheries? In what has to be one of the most exhilarating reunion scenes ever, the Bible explains: "But Esau ran to meet him, and embraced him, and fell on his neck and kissed him, and they wept." (NRSV, Genesis 33:4)

JACOB AND SONS (AND DAUGHTER)

Who are the Twelve Tribes of Israel?

Leah, Rachel, Bilhah, and Zilpah bore a total of twelve sons. Each of these twelve sons became the father of a tribe of Israel. Leah had Reuben, Simeon, Levi, Judah, Issachar, and Zebulun. Bilhah had Dan and Naphtali. Zilpah had Gad and Asher. Rachel

Brothers Esau and Jacob eventually met again and reconciled.

43

had Joseph and Benjamin. Collectively, the sons are known as the twelve tribes of Israel because all Israelite people come from them.

Did Jacob have any daughters?

He had one. Her name was Dinah. Leah was her mother.

What does the Bible say about Dinah?

Not a lot, and what little is said is tragic. Dinah's story is described in Genesis 34. Dinah went to visit some friends. While away from home, she was raped by Shechem, "a prince of the region."

What did Dinah's family think of her rape?

Jacob was concerned about relations with other tribes. Jacob's sons were concerned with family honor. After Shechem raped Dinah, he wanted to marry her. Shechem's father, Hamor, tried to smooth things over with Jacob and Jacob's sons by offering a high bride price. Jacob's sons pretended to agree to the deal on the condition that all of Hamor's men, including Shechem, would be circumcised. Hamor agreed to that. While Hamor and his men recovered from their circumcisions, Simeon and Levi ransacked Hamor's town and killed all of the men, including Hamor and Shemech. Dinah, who had been staying in Shechem's house, was retrieved by Simeon and Levi, and taken back home. Jacob got angry at Simeon and Levi, and said, "'You have brought trouble on me by making me odious to the inhabitants of the land, the Canaanites and the Perizites; my numbers are few, and if they gather themselves against me and attack me, I shall be destroyed, both I and my household.' But they said, 'Should our sister be treated like a whore?'" (NRSV, Genesis 34:30–31) Dinah's thoughts are never described. She is mentioned only once more, when Jacob packs his family up and moves to Egypt (Genesis 46).

JACOB WRESTLED WITH GOD

Why did God change Jacob's name to Israel?

The name Israel means, "The one who strives with God," or "God strives." God changed Jacob's name to mark a turning point. It was as if Jacob had been in training up to this point. Now, with the new name, he had to get down to the business of being a patriarch.

As with the account of creation and the flood, Jacob's name change is described twice. The first instance happened when Jacob was fearful of reuniting with Esau. One night, after Jacob ferried his family across the river to put them out of harm's way, Jacob found himself alone. The Bible explains, "A man wrestled with him until daybreak. When the man saw that he did not prevail against Jacob, he struck him on the hip socket; and Jacob's hip was out of joint as he wrestled with him. Then he said, 'Let me go, for the day is breaking.' But Jacob said, 'I will not let you go, unless you bless me.' So he said to him, 'What is your name?' And he said, 'Jacob.' Then the man said, 'You shall no longer be called Jacob, but Israel, for you have striven with God and with humans, and have prevailed.'" The Bible does not say exactly why Jacob and God wrestled. One possibility is that the wrestling was a physical manifestation of anguished prayer.

The second time Jacob's name was changed happened after Dinah was raped. God told Jacob to take his family and settle in Bethel. Once there, "God appeared to Jacob again when he came from Paddan-aram, and he blessed him. God said to him, 'Your name is Jacob; no longer shall you be called Jacob, but Israel shall be your name.' So he was called Israel. God said to him, 'I am God Almighty: be fruitful and multiply; a nation and a company of nations shall come from you, and kings shall spring from you. The land that I gave to Abraham and Isaac I will give to you, and I will give the land to your offspring after.'" (NRSV, Genesis 35:9–13)

The story of Jacob wrestling with the angel might be symbolic of Jacob's fervent and anguished prayers to God.

CHANGES

What important events happened in Jacob's family after his name was changed?

After Jacob and his family had a reunion with Esau, Jacob and Esau went their separate ways again. As Jacob and his family traveled, Rachel, who was pregnant, went into labor. "After a very hard delivery, the midwife finally exclaimed, 'Don't be afraid—you have another son!' Rachel was about to die, but with her last breath she named him Ben-oni; the baby's father, however, called him Benjamin." (NLT, Genesis 35:17) So Jacob lost his beloved wife and gained a new son.

Also, it was during this time that Isaac died. "Then he breathed his last and died and was gathered to his people, old and full of years." (NIV, Genesis 35:29)

Something else happened. One verse sums it up: "While Israel lived in that land, Reuben went and lay with Bilhah his father's concubine; and Israel heard of it." (NRSV, Genesis 35:22) Israel heard of it—and then what? That is it. That is all that is said about the incident—right then, anyway. The incident came back to haunt Reuben when Israel doled out blessings to his sons on his deathbed: "Reuben, you are my firstborn, my might and the first fruits of my vigor, excelling in rank and excelling in power. Unstable as water, you shall no longer excel because you went up unto your father's bed; then you defiled it—you went up onto my couch!" (NRSV, Genesis 49:3–4)

Why did Jacob not call Benjamin the name his mother gave him?

The name Ben-oni means "son of my sorrow" or "son of my pain." The name Benjamin means "son of my right hand." So perhaps Jacob used the name Benjamin to honor Rachel, who was his favorite wife, or to make a statement about power (the right hand being considered stronger than the left), or to downplay the sadness surrounding Benjamin's birth.

Before the narrative shifts focus from Israel to his son, Joseph, the Bible lists extensive genealogies. Why are there so many genealogical lists in the Bible?

The family lists are important because it was through family ties that individuals received rights of inheritance. Also, the genealogies were important in establishing a strong sense of community and kinship.

JACOB'S SON, JOSEPH

What special gift did Jacob (Israel) give Joseph?

Jacob gave him a coat with long sleeves because of a mistranslation in the King James Version of the Bible: "coat with long sleeves" was translated incorrectly as "coat of many colors." Long-sleeved or many-colored, the significance was the same. Joseph was the favorite son, and his brothers resented him for it.

What sort of young man was Joseph?

When the narrative shifts from Jacob to Joseph (Genesis 37), Joseph is seventeen years old. The characteristics that inspire his brothers' dislike are highlighted. First, Joseph was a tattletale (why he told on his brothers is not clear). Second, in his youthful pride, Joseph boasted about dreams he had in which his brothers and father were subject to him. Favorite son or not, even Jacob got a little riled at Joseph for this. "When [Joseph] told it to his father and brothers, his father reprimanded him, 'What's all this dreaming? Am I and your mother and your brothers all supposed to bow down to you?'" (The Message, Genesis 37:10)

What did Joseph dream?

Joseph described the first dream like this: "There we were, binding sheaves in the field. Suddenly my sheaf rose and stood upright; then your sheaves gathered around it, and bowed down to my sheaf." (NRSV, Genesis 37:5–7) In the second dream, "the sun, the moon, and eleven stars were bowing down to me." (NRSV, Genesis 37:9).The sheaves and celestial creations were symbolic, but the meaning was pretty clear.

How did the brothers handle their resentment?

The brothers considered killing Joseph, but Reuben persuaded them to throw Joseph in a pit instead. (Reuben planned to retrieve him later.) So the brothers tossed Joseph into a pit. Then Judah came up with the idea to get a little money out of the escapade and sell Joseph as a slave. Some Midianite traders who happened by pulled Joseph out of the pit and sold him to a band of Ishmaelites for twenty pieces of silver. The Ishmaelites (descendants of Abraham and Hagar's son, Ishmael) took Joseph to Egypt. Because they wished to cover their tracks, the brothers dipped Joseph's coat in goat blood and showed the coat to Jacob. Upon seeing the bloody garment, Jacob recognized it, and said, "'It is my son's robe! A wild animal has devoured him; Joseph is without doubt torn to pieces.' Then Jacob tore his garments, and put sackcloth on his loins, and mourned for his son many days. All his sons and all his daughters sought to comfort him; but he refused to be comforted, and said, 'No, I shall go down to Sheol to my son, mourning.' Thus his father bewailed him." (NRSV, Genesis 37:33–35)

Why did Jacob tear his own garments?

Tearing one's own clothes was a common expression of grief.

What is sackcloth and why did Jacob put it on his loins?

Sackcloth is a rough fabric, sometimes made of goat hair. Jacob wore a loincloth made of rough fabric as an outward sign of his despair.

JOSEPH IN EGYPT

What happened to Joseph after the Ishmaelites took him to Egypt?

The Ishmaelites sold Joseph to Potiphar, an officer of the Pharaoh. The LORD blessed everything that Joseph did and gave him success. Potiphar saw that the LORD was with Joseph and put him in charge of his household. As a result, "The LORD blessed the Egyptian's house for Joseph's sake." (NIV, Genesis 39:5)

How long was Joseph at Potiphar's house?

The Bible does not say how long Joseph was there. At some point, however, Potiphar's wife tried several times to seduce Joseph. He refused her advances, saying, "Look, with

---

What was Sheol?

At that time, there was no concept of heaven. When people died, it was believed they went to Sheol, the underworld. Sheol was a dim, shadowy place—not a place for rejoicing. So Jacob reuniting with Joseph there was not a happy prospect.

47

me here, my master doesn't give a second thought to anything that goes on here—he's put me in charge of everything he owns. He treats me as an equal. The only thing he hasn't turned over to me is you. You're his wife, after all! How could I violate his trust and sin against God?" (The Message, Genesis 39:8–9) Joseph's response to Potiphar's wife demonstrated how he had matured since he left his father's house. He showed concern for Potiphar's integrity, and respect for God. Joseph's refusal made Potiphar's wife angry, so she framed him for rape. Potiphar believed his wife, and had Joseph put in prison.

What happened to Joseph in prison?

The chief jailer came to trust Joseph, and put him in charge of the care of the other prisoners: "The head jailer gave Joseph free rein, never even checked on him, because God was with him; whatever he did GOD made sure it worked out for the best." (The Message, Genesis 39:23)

Who were some of the other prisoners?

Pharaoh's cupbearer and baker were there. One night, both the cupbearer and the baker had dreams. Joseph, dusting off a skill that had gotten him into trouble when he was at home, interpreted the dreams for him.

What did the cupbearer dream?

The cupbearer dreamed of a vine with three branches. When the branches budded, they blossomed and the blooms ripened into grapes. In the dream, he pressed the grapes into Pharaoh's cup, which he held in his hand.

What meaning did Joseph give to the cupbearer's dream?

Joseph said that the three branches represented three days, and that within three days Pharaoh would "lift up your head and restore you to your office; and you shall place pharaoh's cup in his hand, just as you used to do when you were his cupbearer." (NRSV, Genesis 40:13) Joseph explained to the cupbearer that he, Joseph, was in the prison unjustly, and he asked the cupbearer to mention him to Pharaoh.

What did the baker dream?

The baker dreamed that he had three baskets on his head. In the topmost basket were all kinds of baked goods for Pharaoh, but birds snatched up all of it.

What meaning did Joseph give to the baker's dream?

Joseph said that the three baskets represented three days. Then, without tact but plenty of honesty, Joseph explained, "Within three days Pharaoh will lift up your head—from you!—and hang you on a pole; and the birds will eat the flesh from you." (NRSV, Genesis 40:19) Showing forbearance, Joseph did not ask any favors of the baker.

Did the cupbearer remember to mention Joseph to Pharaoh?

He did remember, but it was two years after the fact. The cupbearer remembered Joseph when Pharaoh himself had puzzling dreams.

What did Pharaoh dream?

Pharaoh had two dreams. In one dream Pharaoh stood on the banks of the Nile. As he stood there, seven healthy, fat cows came up out of the river and fed in the river grass. Then seven ugly, scrawny cows came up out of the river and ate the healthy cows. The scrawny cows looked no better afterwards. In the second dream, Pharaoh saw seven ears of full, healthy grain growing on one stalk. Then seven withered, blighted ears of grain sprouted after them. The withered ears ate the healthy ears.

No one else could explain the dreams to Pharaoh. Did Joseph?

Yes. Joseph, showing humility, acknowledged that God worked through him to interpret dreams. Joseph explained to Pharaoh that the two dreams meant the same thing. "Seven years of plenty are on their way throughout Egypt. But on their heels will come seven years of famine, leaving no trace of Egyptian plenty. As the country is emptied by famine, there won't be even a scrap left of the previous plenty—the famine will be total." (The Message, Genesis 41:29–31) Joseph added that because Pharaoh had two dreams that meant the same thing, that in itself was significant. That meant that God's mind was made up about the matter.

Did Pharaoh reward Joseph for interpreting the dreams, or punish him for giving a grim prediction?

Joseph, in a bit of chancy self-promotion, advised Pharaoh "to select a man who is discerning and wise, and set him over the land of Egypt." (NRSV, Genesis 41:33) Surprise! Pharaoh selected Joseph. Pharaoh changed Joseph's name to Zaphenath-paneah. Also, Pharaoh gave Joseph Asenath, daughter of Potiphera, priest of On, as his wife. In this way, Joseph became the most influential, powerful man in Egypt, next to Pharaoh. Joseph was thirty years old.

What was Joseph's plan for dealing with the upcoming famine?

Joseph had overseers collect one-fifth of the land's produce during the prosperous years and store it. The stored food would

Joseph was the only person who could interpret Pharaoh's dreams, and he predicted Egypt would have years of plenty followed by a famine.

be a reserve for when the famine came. When the famine came, Joseph sold the food to the Egyptians. Because the severity of the famine was widespread, people came from other countries to buy food as well.

JOSEPH'S BROTHERS BACK IN THE PICTURE

Did the famine affect Joseph's family back in Canaan?

Yes. When Joseph's father, Jacob, heard that there was food in Egypt, he fretted and complained to his sons, "Why do you sit around here and look at one another?" (The Message, Genesis 42:1) He sent ten of his sons there to buy some. He kept Joseph's full brother, Benjamin, with him because he feared for his safety.

What happened when Joseph's brothers got to Egypt?

Joseph had two key advantages. First, he recognized his brothers, but they did not recognize him. Second, he remembered the dreams he had about them when he was younger. So, Joseph came up with a plan—a test.

What was Joseph's plan to test his brothers?

Joseph pretended that he thought his brothers were spies. The brothers denied it, but Joseph insisted. In trying to establish their identity for Joseph, the brothers told him that they were ten of twelve brothers belonging to a man in Canaan. One brother was dead, and the other was still with their father. Joseph decreed that unless one of the brothers brought the absent brother to Egypt, all of them would die in an Egyptian prison. A few days later, Joseph changed his mind and came up with a different plan. He had Simeon stay imprisoned in Egypt while the other brothers went back to Canaan with food, and the understanding that they were to bring Benjamin back. Reuben, Joseph's lukewarm champion back in the old days, scolded his brothers, "Spake I not unto you, saying, Do not sin against the child; and ye would not hear? Therefore, behold, also his blood is required." (KJV, Genesis 42:22)

What happened when the brothers went back to Canaan?

On the way home, one of the brothers opened his sack to get food for his donkey, only to discover that in addition to the food, the money was still there. Joseph had slipped the money back in while the brothers were not looking. Fearing they would be taken for thieves, "they lost heart and turned trembling to one another, saying, 'What is this that God has done to us?'" (NRSV, Genesis 42:28) When the brothers told Jacob what happened, and that they were expected to take Benjamin back, Jacob cried, "I am the one you have bereaved of children: Joseph is no more, and Simeon is no more, and now you would take Benjamin. All this has happened to me!" (NRSV, Genesis 42:36) Reuben tried to console Jacob (but probably alarmed his own sons) when he said, "You may kill my two sons if I do not bring him back to you. Put him in my hands, and I will bring him back to you." (NRSV, Genesis 42:37) Jacob refused.

So Jacob and his sons just left Simeon in Egypt?

It looks that way for a while. When the food ran out again, Jacob agreed to let the brothers take Benjamin to Egypt and get more food.

What happened when the brothers got back to Egypt?

Joseph had a feast prepared for his brothers. The brothers, summoned to Joseph's house without knowing why, were afraid. They explained to the steward of Joseph's house what happened the last time with the money being found in their sacks on the way home. The steward told them not to worry, and that their payment had been received. Simeon was reunited with his brothers, and they were treated as guests. When Joseph arrived, his brothers bowed down to him. Sound familiar? When Joseph saw Benjamin, he was overcome with emotion and left the room.

Did the brothers make it back to Canaan without incident this time?

No. As the brothers prepared for their trip home, no one saw Joseph plant his silver cup in Benjamin's sack. When the brothers were not far from Egypt, Joseph had his steward overtake them and search for the cup. The brothers swore they did not steal it. Of course, Joseph's cup was found in Benjamin's sack. Judah, shaken and contrite, was afraid to turn Benjamin over to Joseph. Judah explained to Joseph how important Ben-

jamin was to Jacob: "It shall come to pass, when he seeth that the lad is not with us, that he will die: and thy servants shall bring down the gray hairs of thy servant our father with sorrow to the grave." (KJV, Genesis 44:31)

How could Joseph keep his identity secret in the presence of this honest, emotional plea?

He did not keep his identity a secret any longer. He wept. He revealed his identity to his brothers. At first, the brothers were fearful of his retaliation. Joseph, however, showed mercy and compassion when he reassured them, "And now do not be distressed, or angry with yourselves, because you sold me here; for God sent me before you to preserve life." (KJV, Genesis 45:5).

Despite their bad treatment of him, Joseph forgave his brothers and promised to take care of them.

51

Joseph saw a larger purpose in what happened to him. He saw how God used his great misfortune for ultimate good.

AFTER THE FAMILY REUNION

What happened to Jacob's other sons after the family was reunited?

It is not clear at what point this happened in the family history, but at one point, Judah left home and settled near Adullam, a village near Bethlehem. While there, Judah married a Canaanite woman named Shua. Together they had three sons: Er, Onan, and Shelah. Er married a woman named Tamar, but the LORD put Er to death because he was wicked. Judah said to his next oldest son, Onan, "Go in to your brother's wife and perform the duty of a brother-in-law to her; raise up offspring for your brother." (NRSV, Genesis 38:8)

What was the duty of a brother-in-law to his sister-in-law?

According to Hebrew law (Deuteronomy 25:5–10), the duty of the brother-in-law was to father a male child for his deceased brother, thereby continuing his brother's family line.

Did Onan do as he was told?

No. As a result, he had a sin named after him—the Sin of Onan. Onan knew that any children he had with Tamar would not be his, so "he spilled his semen on the ground whenever he went in to his brother's wife, so that he would not give offspring to his brother." (NSRV; Genesis 38:9) The Lord put Onan to death as well. For years, the Sin of Onan was used as an injunction against masturbation. However, most modern scholarship contends that what Onan practiced was not masturbation, but coitus interruptus.

What happened to Tamar?

Judah promised Tamar that she could marry Shelah when he got old enough. Shelah grew up, and no wedding came to pass. Tamar, intent on having a son, dressed as a prostitute, and tricked Judah into sleeping with her. In payment, he gave her his signet, cord, and staff to keep until he could send her the agreed-upon goat. Judah sent a friend back with the goat, but Tamar was nowhere to be found. Still unaware that the prostitute was Tamar in disguise, Judah decided it was best to let her keep his seal and staff, and hoped the matter would die. The Bible goes on to explain: "About three months later, Judah was told, 'Your daughter-in-law Tamar has played the whore; moreover, she is pregnant as a result of whoredom.' And Judah said, 'Bring her out, and let her be burned.' As she was being brought out, she sent word to her father-in-law, 'It was the owner of these who made me pregnant.' And she said, 'Take note, please, whose these are, the signet and the cord and the staff.' Judah, astonished and humbled, acknowledged that he owned the items. He said, "She is more right than I, since I did not give her to my son Shelah.'" (NRSV, Genesis 38:24–26)

What was the name of Tamar's baby?

She had twin boys, Perez and Zerah. In another delivery switcheroo, while Tamar was in labor, "one put out a hand; and the midwife took and bound on his hand a crimson thread, saying, 'This one came out first.' But just then, he drew back his hand, and out came his brother; and she said, 'What a breach you have made for yourself!' Therefore he was named Perez. Afterward his brother came out with the crimson thread on his hand; and he was named Zerah." (NRSV, Genesis 38:28–30)

Did Joseph move back to Canaan to be with father?

No. Jacob moved to Goshen, an area near Egypt, to be with Joseph. One night while he traveled, Jacob had a dream. "God spoke to Israel in visions of the night, and said, 'Jacob, Jacob.' And he said, 'Here I am.' Then he said, 'I am God, the God of your father; do not be afraid to go down to Egypt, for I will make of you a great nation there. I myself will go down with you to Egypt, and I will also bring you up again; and Joseph's own hand shall close your eyes.'" (NRSV, Genesis 45:2–4)

Did Joseph adopt Egyptian ways completely?

On the surface, it seemed so. However, as the famine continued, Joseph told the Egyptians to trade their livestock in exchange for food from the stockpile. When their livestock was gone, Joseph told them to trade in their land, and then he leased it back to them. Then, accepting the people's desperate bargain, Joseph "made slaves of them from one end of Egypt to the other." (NRSV, Genesis 47:21)

Did Joseph have any children?

Yes. He had two sons. Mindful of God's guidance and protection, Joseph named his sons with names that honored God. The first born was name Manasseh, whose name means "God has made me forget all my hardship and all my father's house." The second son was named Ephraim, whose name means "God has made me fruitful in the land of my misfortunes." On his deathbed, Jacob adopted Manasseh and Ephraim as his own children.

What happened to Jacob's family tree right before he died?

He pruned some here and grafted some there. On his deathbed, Jacob bucked tradition by shaking up the order in which he blessed his sons. Tradition held that the oldest son be blessed first, and be given the lion's share of the inheritance. However, Jacob blessed Joseph, his penultimate son, first. Then, Jacob adopted Joseph's sons, Manasseh and Ephraim, as his own.

Jacob died. The Egyptians embalmed him. Then, according to Jacob's wishes, he was buried with his ancestors in Canaan.

EXODUS

What is the book of Exodus about?

The word exodus means "a going out" or "departure," usually of a large number of people. In the Bible, the Exodus refers to the departure of Jacob's descendants, the Israelites—600,000 men, plus women and children—from their adopted home of Egypt to a land that God promised to them since the time of Abraham.

When did the Exodus occur?

The book opens around four hundred years after the death of Joseph. While Joseph was alive, the Israelites were treated hospitably. At some point during those four hundred years, however, his family and their descendants were forced into slavery. The book of Exodus concerns God calling Moses to save his people and lead them to the Promised Land.

In I Kings 6:1 there is a description of the building of the Lord's temple: "in the four hundred eightieth year after the Israelites came out of the land of Egypt, in the fourth year of Solomon's reign over Israel." Solomon began to rule in 970 B.C.E. So the fourth year of his reign was 966 B.C.E. Some scholars place the events of Exodus around 1446 B.C.E. Proponents of a later year point to Exodus 1:11: "Therefore they set taskmasters over them to oppress them with forced labor. They built supply cities, Pithom and Ramses, for Pharaoh." Ramses, it is argued, must be named for one of the Ramses pharaohs, probably Ramses II. That places the year of the Exodus around 1290 B.C.E.

A DEATH SENTENCE

Why was Pharaoh mad at the Israelites?

Pharaoh said to the Egyptians, "Behold, the people of the children of Israel are more and mightier than we." (KJV, Exodus 1:9) Pharaoh was afraid the Israelites would overpower the Egyptians. Still, he did not want the Israelites to move away, because he could use them as his slaves.

What was Pharaoh's plan?

When working them hard did not diminish their numbers, Pharaoh commanded the Israelite midwives to kill all the baby boys as they were born. This did not work either, because "the midwives feared God; they did not do as the king of Egypt commanded them, but they let the boys live." (NRSV, Exodus 1:17) Still, the Israelites' numbers increased. Then Pharaoh commanded: "Every boy that is born to the Hebrews you shall throw into the Nile, but you shall let every girl live." (NRSV, Exodus 1:22)

Did the Egyptians obey Pharaoh and throw the Israelite baby boys into the river?

The Bible does not say what most Egyptians did. The Bible describes the actions of one Egyptian who did not. That was Pharaoh's daughter.

How did Pharaoh's daughter disobey the edict?

She found an Israelite baby in a papyrus basket plastered with bitumen and pitch. The basket was placed among the reeds in the river. If she had obeyed her father, she would have drowned the baby.

What is papyrus? What is bitumen?

Papyrus is a plant that grows in marshy areas. In ancient Egypt, papyrus was used to make rope, sandals, mats, and paper. The English word "paper" derives from the word "papyrus." Bitumen is a black, solid, lumpy mineral deposit. In ancient Egypt, it was used for waterproofing and for mortar.

Which Pharaoh was in power at this time?

The Bible does not say. However, based on what is known about Egyptian history, many scholars believe the pharaoh most likely identified with the Exodus was Thutmose III, who ruled 1500–1450 B.C.E. If correct, then it might have been his half-sister, Hatshepsut, who was the Pharaoh's daughter that drew baby Moses out of the Nile.

What happened when Pharaoh's daughter found the baby?

"She saw the child. He was crying, and she took pity on him. 'This must be one of the Hebrews' children,' she said." The baby's older sister was standing nearby, and asked

A stained glass window in a Brussels cathedral depicts the baby Moses being rescued from the Nile River.

Pharaoh's daughter, "Shall I go and get you a nurse from the Hebrew women to nurse the child for you?" (NRSV, Exodus 2:6–7) The sister went and called her mother. In that way, the baby's mother nursed the baby she thought she had to give him up. The baby stayed with his mother until he was weaned. At that time, she took him to Pharaoh's daughter.

What was the baby's name?

Pharaoh's daughter named the baby Moses because she said, "I drew him out of the water." (NRSV, Exodus 2:10)

MOSES

What was Moses like as a child?

The Bible does not address his childhood. If Moses was treated like other children growing up in Pharaoh's court, he was educated. The Bible says he had the appearance of an Egyptian. (Exodus 2:19) Well-to-do Egyptian men during that time wore light linen tunics, and kept their facial hair shaved. Some Egyptian men shaved their heads as well. Elaborate wigs were popular.

The Bible picks up the thread of Moses' life when he was grown. The first recorded action of his adulthood is murder. Whether Moses was aware of his Israelite lineage growing up or he became aware of it as an adult is unclear. One day, he went out to the

Israelites, and saw how they were enslaved. He saw an Egyptian beating an Israelite. Then "he looked this way and that way, and when he saw that there was no man, he slew the Egyptian, and hid him in the sand." (KJV, Exodus 2:12)

What did Moses do then?

The next day, he saw two Israelites fighting. He broke up the fight, and said to the one who was wrong, "Why do you strike your fellow Hebrew?" The man answered, "Who made you a ruler and judge over us? Do you mean to kill me as you killed the Egyptian?" (NRSV, Exodus 2:13–14) With this, Moses knew his crime was known. Certainly Pharaoh knew, and because of it, he sought to kill Moses. So Moses ran away to the land of Midian. In Midian, Moses became a shepherd, got married, and had a son.

How far was Midian from Egypt?

The exact location of Midian is not known, because it does not exist any longer. When Moses got to Midian, he sat by a well. The seven daughters of the priest of Midian went out to water their flock at the well. Some other shepherds tried to run them off, but Moses interceded on their behalf, and watered the daughters' flock for them.

What did Moses do after that?

The priest of Midian invited Moses to eat dinner with them. In addition, the priest of Midian gave Moses his daughter, Zipporah, to be his wife.

Did Moses and Zipporah have any children?

Yes. They had a son, Gershom. "Ger" is Hebrew for alien. Moses said, "I have been an alien residing in a foreign land." (NRSV, Exodus 2:22)

What was Moses' occupation in Midian?

Moses was a shepherd.

As a shepherd, what were Moses' responsibilities?

The Bible does not address Moses' situation specifically. Generally, flock animals were kept for their meat, milk, and skin/wool. So these animals were a precious commodity. The responsibility of the shepherd was great. It was his job to usher the flock intact from one pasture to another while protecting it from predators. In addition, the shepherd had to make sure the flock got to market in time for shearing.

MOSES AND THE BURNING BUSH

What was the burning bush?

The incident with the burning bush marked God's call to Moses. One day while Moses was out tending his flock, he came to Horeb, the mountain of God. An angel of the LORD appeared to him in a bush that was on fire but not consumed by the flames. Today, some people claim that the bush must have been a fraxinella, or gas plant. Gas plants emit a highly flammable scent that combusts under the intense heat of the sun.

Whether or not the biblical burning bush was a fraxinella, Moses went to look at the bush more closely. "When the LORD saw that he had turned aside to see, God called to him out of the bush, 'Moses, Moses!'" (NRSV, Exodus 3:1) Moses' response to this call had ramifications that continue to this day.

What did Moses say to God?

Moses said, "Here I am." (NRSV, Exodus 3:4) With that, Moses chose to acknowledge God's mighty presence, and listen to what God had to say.

What did God tell Moses?

In a statement that shaped the rest of Moses' life and the faith of people from then to now, God said, "I have surely seen the affliction of my people which are in Egypt, and have heard their cry by reason of their taskmasters; for I know their sorrows; And I am come down to deliver them out of the hand of the Egyptians, and to bring them up out of that land unto a good land and a large, unto a land flowing with milk and honey; unto the place of the Canaanites, and the Hittites, and the Amorites, and the Perizzites, and the Hivites, and the Jebusites. Now therefore, behold, the cry of the children of Israel is

A Victorian-era stained glass window showing Moses prostrating himself before the burning bush from which God's voice commands him.

come unto me: and I have also seen the oppression wherewith the Egyptians oppress them. Come now therefore, and I will send thee unto Pharaoh, that thou mayest bring forth the children of Israel out of Egypt." (KJV, Exodus 3:7–10)

Was Moses excited about this turn of events?

Excited? The Bible does not say. Stunned and reluctant? Yes. Moses rattled off excuses. Who was he, Moses, that he could go before Pharaoh requesting the freedom of slaves? What if the Israelites did not believe him? How could he speak for hundreds of thousands of people when he was "slow of speech and of a slow tongue?" (KJV, Exodus 4:10) Each of Moses' objections was met by God with reassurance and proof of his presence. God empowered Moses with awesome proofs of divine power. Moses had to convince not only Pharaoh, but the Israelites as well. Once again, God showed an inclination for calling an unlikely person to do something marvelous.

BRIDEGROOM OF BLOOD

Why did God try to kill Moses?

When Moses packed up his family and headed back to Egypt, they stopped one night to camp. There, "the Lord met him and tried to kill him". In reaction, Zipporah, Moses' wife, took a flint and circumcised their son. She touched Moses' feet with the foreskin and cried, "Truly you are a bridegroom of blood to me!" (NRSV, Exodus 4:25) After that, God let Moses alone. What went on here? There is only speculation. One interpretation is that God was going to prevent Moses from carrying out a divine mission while his household was still uncircumcised. Zipporah's cry might have been the result of exasperation she felt at not understanding fully this new phase in her life.

What else happened while they traveled?

Aaron, Moses' brother, came to meet them. After Moses complained about being slow of tongue, God decided that Aaron would go with Moses and be his spokesperson.

What happened when Moses and Aaron related their news of God's deliverance to Pharaoh?

He was not impressed. He was angered. Pharaoh attributed the Israelites' desire to go meet God in the wilderness as laziness. The Israelites were doing the arduous work of brickmaking. Pharaoh increased their daily quota, and made it so that they had to gather their own straw for the bricks as well. The demands were impossible. Some of the Israelites got mad at Moses and Aaron, and accused them of being troublemakers. Probably, Moses felt very guilty and confused. He prayed, "Oh Lord, why have you brought trouble upon this people? Is this why you sent me? Ever since I went to Pharaoh to speak in your name, he has brought trouble upon this people, and you have not rescued your people at all." (NIV, Exodus 5:22–23)

Why was brickmaking such a dangerous job?

When Pharaoh told the Israelites to make more bricks, for all intents and purposes it was a death sentence. Brickmaking was outside work. The Israelites worked all day in blistering heat. They had no hats and no sunblock. It is unlikely that their taskmasters allowed them to stop every ten minutes for a water break. It is likely that untold numbers of Israelites died of dehydration and heatstroke.

What happened when Moses and Aaron related their news of God's deliverance to the Israelites?

The people bowed down and worshiped.

What happened after Moses prayed?

Moses repeated to the Israelites what God told him. Again, God reminded Moses of his covenant with the Israelites: "I will take you as my own people, and I will be your God. Then you will know that I am the LORD your God, who brought you out from under the yoke of the Egyptians. And I will bring you to the land I swore with uplifted hand to give to Abraham, to Isaac and to Jacob. I will give it you as a possession. I am the LORD." (NIV, Exodus 6:7–9) The Israelites were broken in spirit and body. They did not believe Moses.

How did Moses respond to the Israelites' disbelief?

He listened to God. God told him to approach Pharaoh again, and demand the Israelites' permanent release. God had only just begun to unleash his power.

PLAGUED WITH PLAGUES

What kind of power did God show?

Through Moses and Aaron, God inflicted a series of plagues on Egypt. Each plague was met with Pharaoh's anger and refusal to release the Israelites.

What kind of plagues were there?

1. Blood. Aaron struck the Nile with Moses' staff, and the water was turned to blood immediately. The river smelled horrible. People could not drink from it. All the fish died.
2. Frogs. The frogs were not just outside. They were inside Pharaoh's palace and in his bed. They were in the houses of all the Egyptians, and in their ovens and kneading bowls.
3. Gnats. All the dust of the earth turned to gnats. They swarmed around people and animals.

4. Flies. Flies flooded every Egyptian household. The Bible says, "In all the land of Egypt, the land was ruined because of the flies." (NRSV, Exodus 8:24)

5. Diseased livestock. The donkeys, camels, and other herds and flocks belonging to the Egyptians were slain by sickness. The animals belonging to the Israelites remained well.

6. Boils. At God's direction, Moses took soot from the kiln and tossed it into the air in the sight of Pharaoh. The soot became fine dust all over the land, and it caused festering boils on all Egyptian people and animals.

7. Hail. God was getting fed up with Pharaoh by this point. God told Moses to tell Pharaoh that he could have killed Pharaoh by now if he wanted. God did not kill Pharaoh because he wanted Pharaoh to see his power and repent. God's display of power was terrifying. "There was hail with fire flashing continually in the midst of it, such heavy hail as had never fallen in all the land of Egypt since it became a nation. The hail struck down everything that was in the open field throughout all the land of Egypt, both human and animal." (NRSV, Exodus 9:24–25) There was no hail where the Israelites were.

8. Locusts. An east wind blew all day and all night, and then ushered in a dense swarm of locusts. The locusts ruined what few crops remained after the hailstorm.

9. Three days of darkness. This was no ordinary darkness. It was a darkness that could be felt. Only the Egyptians were affected. The Israelites were not.

10. Death of the firstborn son. In the most tragic and dramatic of plagues, all of the firstborn children and animals belonging to the Egyptians were killed. There was a loud cry through all of Egypt as their firstborn were killed. No harm came to the firstborn of the Israelites, because God wanted to emphasize the distinction between the Israelites and the Egyptians.

Were the plagues really out of the ordinary? Could they have been naturally occurring events?

Some scholars of the Bible argue that the plagues were part of natural ecological cycles. For example, they say that the diseased livestock might have died of anthrax. The boils might have been caused by the disease-carrying stable fly. Others argue that even if the theories turned out to be true, God's role in all of it would not be minimized. After all, who made anthrax? Who made the stable fly?

How were Pharaoh's magicians able to reproduce some of the same plagues?

The Bible says the magicians duplicated the first two plagues with "secret arts."

What was the significance of the plagues God sent?

The Bible does not address this issue, but some scholars say that God picked these plagues specifically because each plague represented one or more of the many Egyptian gods. There were hundreds of gods in the pantheon of ancient Egypt, so there are many possibilities for linking them to the plagues God sent. By using those ten specific plagues to demolish the physical landscape of Egypt, God demolished the spiritual landscape as well. Some possibilities are as follows:

The final plague that God sends down to Egypt is the death of the first born child of each Egyptian family.

1. The plague of blood was aimed at the Egyptians' belief in Khnum, the guardian of the Nile; Hapi, the spirit of the Nile; Osiris, the giver of life (whose very blood was the water of the Nile); or Nephthis, the river goddess.

2. The plague of frogs was aimed at the Egyptians' belief in Heqt, the goddess of resurrection. She had the body of a human and the head of a frog.

3. The plague of gnats came up from the dust of the earth. So this plague was aimed at Geb, god of the earth. Another possibility is Kephri, whose head was that of the sacred scarab beetle.

4. The plague of flies was aimed at Kephri, whose head was that of the sacred scarab beetle, or Shu, the god of air.

5. The plague of livestock was aimed at Hathor, the mother goddess who had cow horns, or Apis, the bull god.

6. The plague of boils was aimed at Isis, the goddess of healing, or Imhotep, the god of medicine.

7. The plague of hail was aimed at Nut, the goddess of the sky, or Seth, the protector of crops and god of storms.

8. The plague of locusts, likewise, was aimed at Nut or Seth.

9. The plague of darkness was aimed at Ra, the most powerful god in the Egyptian pantheon, god of the sun.

10. The death of the firstborn was aimed at Bes, the god of mothers and children; Osiris, the giver of life; or Tawaret, the goddess of childbirth and fertility. More pointedly, another possibility is that the death of the firstborn was aimed at Pharaoh. Pharaoh was considered to be the son of Ra. As the most powerful person in all of Egypt, even Pharaoh was not immune to the powers of the one true God.

The Israelites did not have to follow any instructions to be protected from the first nine plagues. What made the tenth plague different?

The tenth plague was a grand finale. It was the most heart wrenching and tragic of all the plagues because it involved the death of the young. The tenth plague was the plague that got the Israelites out of Egypt. Accordingly, God told Moses and Aaron to mark the event as the beginning of the Israelite year. This feast would be known as the Passover.

During the first five plagues, Pharaoh hardened his own heart. During the remaining five plagues, God hardened Pharaoh's heart. Why did God harden Pharaoh's heart? Moses had free will. Why didn't Pharaoh?

The Bible does not address this question. The Bible says simply that was the way of it. For centuries, students of the Bible have puzzled over this. Part of the answer might have to do with Pharaoh's unique role in Egypt. He was considered to be the physical manifestation of the most powerful Egyptian god. In all likelihood, Pharaoh enjoyed a supremely privileged upbringing. Anything he wanted was his by royal command. Pharaoh ate the choicest foods, wore the finest clothes, and enjoyed the most thorough education. He had the best of everything. Add a little more speculation to the picture. Suppose, too, that Pharaoh was never taught (or never accepted) lessons in humility, gratitude, and compassion. Instead, he cultivated a personality of pride, selfishness, and tyranny.

Throughout the first few confrontations between Moses and Pharaoh, God gave Pharaoh several chances to change his mind and repent. Pharaoh didn't, though. That was his choice. Still, God knew Pharaoh's heart, just like he knew Moses'. So during the last five plagues, perhaps God simply expedited what was bound to be Pharaoh's reaction anyway.

THE FIRST PASSOVER

What did God want the Israelites to do to commemorate the event?

First, God gave the Israelites a set of very detailed instructions on selecting and preparing a sacrificial lamb. Then, God told them to mark their doorposts with some of the lamb's blood. By that sign, God would know to pass over their houses when he went around and killed all the firstborn. In addition, God told the Israelites to eat the lamb roasted along with unleavened bread and bitter herbs. Collectively, these observances were (and are) the Passover. Moses said, "You shall observe this rite as a personal ordinance for you and your children. When you come to the land that the LORD will give you, as he has promised, you shall keep this observance. And when your children ask you, 'What do you mean by this observance?' you shall say, 'It is the passover sacrifice to the LORD, for he passed over the houses of the Israelites in Egypt, when he struck down the Egyptians but spared our houses.' And the people bowed down and worshiped."

63

(NRSV, Exodus 12:24–27) After God killed the firstborn, the Egyptians cried out and urged the Israelites to leave. So they did.

THE ISRAELITES LEAVE EGYPT

What is one of the first things the Israelites did when they left Egypt?

They obeyed God by establishing a custom of consecrating the firstborn of man and animal to God. God said, "Dedicate to me all the firstborn sons of Israel and every firstborn male animal. They are mine." (NLT, Exodus 13:1) The Israelites did not have to sacrifice their firstborn children. Instead, God gave them instructions to sacrifice animals. God told the Israelites to keep this observance every year, and tell their children the significance of it.

What route did the Israelites take to get to the Promised Land?

Tracing the route on a map, it is apparent that the Israelites took a roundabout way to get there. God could have led them through the land of the Philistines. However, God said to himself, "If the people are faced with a battle, they might change their minds and return to Egypt." (NLT, Exodus 13:17) So God led them along the scenic route, through the wilderness.

What promise did Moses keep as he left Egypt?

He remembered the promise his ancestors gave to Joseph. Joseph made his sons promise to take his bones out of Egypt when it came time to go to the Promised Land. In the last chapter of Genesis, Joseph was embalmed and placed in a coffin. So presumably, Moses packed up a mummy—and maybe a sarcophagus—and took it with him.

God promised to lead the Israelites as they traveled. How did he do it?

During the day, God appeared to the Israelites as a pillar of cloud. At night, God appeared to them as a pillar of fire. "Neither the pillar of cloud by day nor the pillar of fire by night left its place in front of the people." (NRSV, Genesis 13:22)

What is mummification?

Mummification was the process of embalming dead people in ancient Egypt. Jacob and Joseph were both mummified. The process involved removing the stomach, intestines, liver, and lungs, and storing them in jars. The brain was removed by sliding a small hook up into the nose and scraping the brain out bit by bit. The body cavity was stuffed with natron, a type of salt. Oils and spices were spread over the body, and then the body was wrapped in linen strips. Voila! Mummy!

FICKLE PHARAOH

What happened to the Israelites before they had gone very far?

Pharaoh changed his mind about letting them go. Pharaoh, along with his chariots and soldiers, pursued the Israelites. Upon seeing the Egyptians' rapid approach, the Israelites cried to Moses, "Was it because there were no graves in Egypt that you have taken us away to die in the wilderness? What have you done to us, bringing us out of Egypt? Is this not the very thing we told you in Egypt, 'Let us alone and let us serve the Egyptians?' For it would have been better to serve the Egyptians than to die in the wilderness." (NRSV, Exodus 14:11–12) It was going to take some convincing to assure the Israelites that God would keep his promise of being with them always and leading them to the Promised Land.

Did the Egyptians recapture the Israelites?

No. According to God's instructions, Moses stretched out his hand over the sea. God drove the sea back using a strong east wind. A dry path formed between two great walls of water. The Israelites and all of their livestock passed through on dry ground. When the Egyptians started on the dry path, God collapsed the two walls of water, drowning the Egyptians in the re-formed sea. "And Israel saw that great work which the LORD did upon the Egyptians: and the people feared the LORD, and believed the LORD, and his servant

In this work by Luca Giordana displayed in Bergamo, Italy, Moses is seen parting the Red Sea during the Israelites' escape from Egypt.

Moses," (KJV, Exodus 14:31) The promise God made to Abraham centuries ago started to come to visible fruition. The covenant between God and his people grew stronger.

What did the Israelites do after they escaped the Egyptians?

They celebrated! Moses and the others sang a song praising God in what is thought to be one of the oldest compositions in the Bible. In the song, the Israelites praised God for being their strength and salvation. They acknowledged God as their only God and the God of their fathers, and they recounted God's triumphs over the Egyptians (Exodus 15:1–18). Then Moses and Aaron's sister, Miriam, made her first biblical appearance since she watched over baby Moses in the reeds. She played her tambourine. She and the other women danced and sang, "Sing ye to the LORD, for he hath triumphed gloriously: the horse and his rider hath he thrown into the sea." (KJV, Exodus 15:21)

ARE WE THERE YET? ARE WE THERE YET? ARE WE THERE YET?

Did the Israelites maintain their upbeat attitude?

No. They had not learned to trust Moses, much less God. They were used to staying in one place. Now they were caught up in a cycle of traveling and camping. They feared the unknown. They doubted. They complained. They rebelled.

How did Moses deal with all of that complaining?

God helped him. When the Israelites complained about the scarcity of bread and meat, God sent them manna from heaven, and quail for meat. When the Israelites complained about lack of water, God made it so that when Moses struck a rock with his staff, water gushed from the rock.

What was manna like?

The word "manna" means "what is it"? The Israelites did not know what it was. The Bible says it was "a fine, flaky substance, as fine as frost on the ground" (NRSV, Exodus 16:14) and "like coriander seed, white and the taste of it was like wafers made with honey." (Exodus 16:31) Some scholars theorize that manna was the secretion left by certain insects feeding on tamarisk trees.

Was the manna and quail more than just a way for the Israelites to fill their bellies?

Yes. The manna and quail were proof of God's care. The Israelites did not have to do anything for those things to appear. Significantly, the manna and quail came with instructions. Giving the Israelites small, manageable steps, God used the manna and quail as a way to teach the Israelites about the Sabbath. The instructions specified that the Israelites should gather just as much manna as each person needed for the day. They were not to save any for the next day. On the sixth day of the week, they were to gather twice as much as they did for the

A 1620 oil painting by Hendrick de Clerck shows the Israelites gathering the manna sent by God.

other days. That way, they could eat the next day without gathering it. The seventh day of the week was a day of rest, a day of Sabbath to the LORD.

Manna was such an important part of the Israelite experience that God commanded the Israelites to save a little of it in a jar to show future generations.

Did the Israelites meet any other people on their journey?

Yes. The first people they met were the warmongering Amalekites. The Israelites fought the Amalekites and won, but it was not easy. As the fighting went on, whenever Moses held up his hand, the Israelites prevailed. When Moses lowered his hand, the Amalekites prevailed. Moses got tired of holding up his hand but could not stop lest the Israelites lose. So Aaron, helpful brother as always, gave Moses a rock to sit on and he and Hur held Moses' hands up.

Evidently, at some earlier, unspecified point in the Moses narrative, Moses' wife Zipporah and their two sons were sent back to Midian to live again, because the next people the Israelites meet are those very people, newly arrived from Midian.

What was life like for Israelites now?

They were semi-nomadic, meaning that they camped for a while, then moved on. As they grew accustomed to their new lifestyle, disagreements between people popped up here and there. At first, Moses mediated the disagreements himself, but thanks to a suggestion from his father-in-law, he appointed able men from among the Israelites to act as judges. There were two major benefits of this plan. First, Moses did not have to assume the tremendous, tiring responsibility of mediating disagreements for all of those people. Second, by teaching the Israelites God's statutes and instructions and by giving them say-so in their daily affairs, Moses helped the Israelites develop a personal, vested interest in the welfare of the community.

NEW LAWS FOR THE ISRAELITES

What laws did the Israelites have?

The laws of the Israelites revolved around God's promise to Abraham, Isaac, Jacob, and their ancestors. God reminded the Israelites of the covenant promise: "Now therefore, if ye will obey my voice indeed, and keep my covenant, then ye shall be a peculiar treasure unto me above all people; for all the earth is mine. And ye shall be unto me a kingdom of priests, and a holy nation." (KJV, Exodus 19:5–6) The people agreed.

The first laws they had were the Decalogue, or Ten Commandments. The Ten Commandments regulate people's behavior and attitude to God and other people. Showing majesty and power, God appeared on Mount Sinai in the form of a dense cloud. The mountain trembled and smoked and the voice of God was heard. The Israelites, circled at the base of the mountain, were in such awe of God's presence that they asked Moses to act as mediator between them and God. Moses agreed. The Ten Commandments were written down at this point.

What are the Ten Commandments?

1. You shall have no other gods before me.
2. You shall not make for yourself an idol.
3. You shall not make wrongful use of the name of the LORD your God.
4. Remember the Sabbath day and keep it holy.
5. Honor your father and mother.
6. You shall not commit murder.
7. You shall not commit adultery.
8. You shall not steal.
9. You shall not bear false witness against your neighbor.
10. You shall not covet your neighbor's property. (NRSV, Exodus 20:3–17)

Did God give the Israelites any other laws?

Yes, many! After God gave the Israelites the Ten Commandments, he gave Moses more laws to give to them. Chapters 21–23 of Exodus details God's laws for the Israelites regarding the rights of slaves, laws regarding accidental and intentional killing, laws regarding harming a pregnant woman, and laws regarding personal property and negligence. Moses told the people the laws (Exodus 24:3), and they agreed to follow the laws. Then Moses wrote the laws down in "the book of the covenant." (Exodus 24:4) At this point, Moses read the laws to the Israelites (Exodus 24:7), and again, they agreed to follow the laws.

What was the law of retaliation?

This refers to Exodus 21:23–24 (NLT). Regarding personal injury, "the offender must be punished according to the injury. If the result is death, the offender must be executed. If an eye is injured, injure the eye of the person who did it. If a tooth gets knocked out, knock out the tooth of the person who did it. Similarly, the payment must be hand for hand, foot for foot, burn for burn, wound for wound, bruise for bruise." Historically, this law has fostered the belief among some people that unrestrained vengeance is biblical. However, many Bible scholars say that the opposite is true. They say that the law of retaliation places limitations on revenge. Only the equivalent of the damage may be taken. More on laws is covered in the chapter on Leviticus.

The Ten Commandments form the core of Judeo-Christian morality.

Why were the laws so detailed?

As a new community, the Israelites had no established code of laws. They started from square one. As God's chosen people, they could not just adopt Egyptian laws or laws from neighboring peoples. The people acting as judges needed high level of detail to make correct, godly decisions.

When were the Ten Commandments written down?

After Moses read the book of the covenant to the Israelites, God again called Moses to the top of Mount Sinai. Moses was there forty days and forty nights. During that time, God gave him the Ten Commandments on tablets of stone. (Exodus 24:12)

Did Moses receive anything else from God while on this trip to the top of Mount Sinai?

Yes. God gave Moses instructions for making the Tabernacle and its furnishings.

FICKLE FAITH

What did the Israelites do while Moses was on Mount Sinai communicating with God?

They lost their patience and their faith. The Israelites said to Aaron, "Come, make us gods who go before us. As for this fellow Moses who brought us up out of Egypt, we don't know what has happened to him." (NIV, Exodus 32:1) So the Israelites wanted to believe in the God who rescued them from Egypt, but they grew tired waiting to hear from him again. Aaron took jewelry from the Israelites and fashioned a gold calf out of it. Aaron proclaimed, "These are your gods, O Israel, who brought you up out of Egypt." (NIV, Exodus 32:4) The next day, the Israelites had a party.

What did God do when he discovered what the Israelites did?

He got so angry that he threatened to destroy the Israelites. Moses demonstrated his great belief in God's goodness and asked God not to do so.

What did Moses do when he came down from Mount Sinai?

Moses intended to lay down the law, but he broke it instead—Moses intended to give the Israelites the tablets, but he broke them. He carried with him the two tablets of the covenant. God's writing was on the front and back of the tablets, and conveyed all that God told Moses while he was on Mount Sinai. Moses saw the Israelites partying, and was furious.

He threw the tablets to the ground, breaking them. Moses' action and its result were not only expressions of anger, but symbols of God's anger and the now broken covenant between the Israelites and God. Moses burned the gold calf, and ground it into powder. He scattered the powder in water, and made the Israelites drink it.

Did Moses get angry at Aaron for his role in the scandal of the golden calf?

Moses got angry at his brother, Aaron. However, Aaron deflected blame to the people: "You know how prone these people are to evil." He continued, "So I said to them, 'Whoever has gold jewelry, take it off'; Then they gave me the gold, and I threw it into the fire, and out came this calf!" (NIV, Exodus 32:22, 24)

Did God punish the Israelites?

Yes. The author of Exodus squeezes a tragic, puzzling account into a few verses near the end of Exodus 33. Moses told the Levites that God ordered them to take their swords and go throughout the camp and kill their brother, friend, and neighbor. That day, the Levites killed about three thousand of the Israelites. In addition, God sent a plague on the people. Though the Bible does not say so directly, generally the plague is associated with some of the Israelites getting sick from the water tainted with burnt, pulverized gold.

After the punishment, God told Moses to continue leading the Israelites to the Promised Land, the land he promised to Abraham, Isaac, and Jacob. Moses had misgivings, though. He wanted to know for sure that God would be with them. He asked to see God. God obliged. Moses stood in the cleft of a big rock. God covered Moses' face with God's hand while he passed. Once God passed, God took God's hand away so Moses could see his back. To see God's face would overwhelm Moses and kill him.

Now that the tablets of the Covenant were broken, how did Moses communicate God's law to the Israelites?

At God's direction, Moses went back up on Mount Sinai. God instructed Moses, "'Write these words; in accordance with these words, I have made a covenant with you and Israel.' He was there with the LORD forty days and forty nights; he neither ate bread nor drank water. And he wrote on the tablets the words of the covenant, the Ten Commandments." (NRSV, Exodus 34:27–28) The covenant between God and the Israelites was reestablished.

When Moses came down from Mount Sinai this time, his face shone because he had talked with God. This foreshadowed the Transfiguration of Jesus many years later.

TRAVEL–SITE WORSHIP

Did the Israelites have a place to worship?

Because they traveled so much, the Israelites did not build a place of worship on a specific piece of ground. Instead, they built a transportable place of worship, the Tabernacle, or Tent of Meeting. It served as the earthly dwelling place of God until Solomon built another temple around 1000 B.C.E. God gave Moses instructions for it when he was on Mount Sinai for forty days and forty nights. The time Moses spent on the mountain foreshadowed the time Jesus, many years later, spent in the wilderness being tempted.

What did the Tabernacle look like?

Basically, the Tabernacle was a tent. God gave Moses very detailed directions about the Tabernacle's construction right down to the material the Israelites should use for the pegs (bronze), and how many coverings the Ark of the Covenant should have (four). God gave Moses instructions on how to build the tabernacle and its furnishings, and the types of materials to use in Exodus 25–31. In Exodus 36–39, the Israelites carried out God's instructions.

Ten linen curtains were made. They were interwoven with blue, purple, and red yarns. Images of cherubim were worked into each curtain. Each curtain was about forty-two feet long and five feet wide. Each curtain was edged with loops of yarn. Using gold clasps, the loops from one curtain were linked to the loops of another curtain. In this way, ten big curtains made two really big curtains. Curtains of goat hair were linked together in a similar way. The goat hair curtains covered the linen curtains. Curtains of ram skins covered the goat hair curtains. Fine leather curtains covered the goat hair curtains. The layers of curtains were the only kind of roof over the Tabernacle.

The curtains were held up by frames made of acacia wood overlaid in gold. Each frame was held up by two silver bases. Bars of acacia wood overlaid with gold ran through the frames. Rings of gold held the bars in place.

Based on biblical descriptions, this is a recreation of what the Ark of the Covenant might look like.

The curtain that divided the Tabernacle in two was made of fine linen interwoven with blue, purple, and red yarns. Cherubim were woven into the fabric. The curtain hung from gold hooks between four pillars of acacia wood overlaid with gold. The pillars stood in bases of silver. The curtain was to separate the holy place from the most holy place.

A linen screen embroidered in blue, purple, and red was made for the entrance to the Tabernacle.

The Ark of the Covenant

What was the Ark of the Covenant?

The Ark of the Covenant was one of the items God told the Israelites to make. It was a box. The dimensions were about 44" × 26" × 26". It was made of acacia wood, and overlaid with gold inside and out. Four rings of gold were attached to each bottom corner. Poles made of acacia wood and overlaid in gold were slid through the rings. The poles were used as handles. In this way, the Ark of the Covenant was carried from place to place. God told the Israelites to put the covenant, or tablets of the law, in the ark for safe keeping. The saved bottle of manna and Aaron's staff were put in the ark as well.

The mercy seat, or atonement cover, was a lid for the ark. It was made of pure gold. Two cherubim were made of pure gold. One cherub sat on each side of the mercy seat. The cherubim faced the mercy seat, and spread their wings over it.

Other Items in the Tabernacle

What were some of the other items in the Tabernacle?

In the Tabernacle there was a table on which to put sacred vessels. This table was slightly smaller than the Ark of the Covenant. It was made of acacia wood and overlaid with gold. The table had a rim and molding of gold as well. Four rings of gold were attached to the legs of the table, close to the rim. Poles made of acacia wood and overlaid with gold were slid through the rings. In this way, the table was carried from place to place.

Plates, bowls, and cups used in worship were made of pure gold, and were to be used only at the table. Every Sabbath, twelve loaves of bread, or the Bread of Presence, were placed on the table. Only the priests were allowed to eat this bread.

A lampstand of pure gold was made to stand directly across from the table. Branches extended from the side of the lampstand. Ornate hammered work in the shape of almond blossoms ran the length of each branch. The entire lamp was made from one piece of gold. It is guessed that the lampstand was about five feet tall and weighed about one hundred pounds. The snuffers and trays for the lamp were made of pure gold as well. This lamp was the first menorah. God commanded the Israelites to keep the priests supplied with olive oil for lamp fuel. The priests were to keep the lamp burning always. (Exodus 27:21)

What was the Court of the Tabernacle?

This was a courtyard that surrounded the Tabernacle. The courtyard was about 150 feet long and 75 feet wide. The perimeters of the courtyard were established by a rectangular arrangement of bronze pillars. Each bronze pillar was wrapped with bands of silver. Linen curtains hung from the pillars. The gate of the court was a screen made of blue, purple, and red embroidered linen. The screen hung from four bronze pillars.

What was the altar?

This was a platform where the priests sacrificed animals to God. The altar was outside the Tabernacle. It stood in the courtyard. The altar was made of (surprise!) acacia wood overlaid with—gotcha!—bronze. The use of a less valuable metal symbolized the less holy aspect of the area outside the Tabernacle. The altar measured about 7' × 7' × 4'. Four animal horns pointing up, one for each of the four corners of the altar, were made as one piece with the altar. Four bronze rings were formed at each corner, too. Four poles overlaid with bronze slid through the rings. In that way, the altar was carried from place to place. The pots, pans, and other utensils that went along with the altar were made of bronze as well. Specific animal sacrifices prepared in a specific way were burned on the altar every day.

What was the incense altar?

The incense altar was made of acacia wood overlaid with pure gold. It measured about 17.5" × 17.5" × 35". Horns and two gold rings were made in one piece with it. Poles of acacia wood overlaid with gold slid through the rings. In this way the incense altar was carried from place to place. Aaron offered incense on it every morning. The incense was made of stacte and galbanum (both aromatic resins), onycha (a perfume from a mollusk found in the Red Sea), other spices, and myrrh. This recipe was holy. The incense was not to be used anywhere except in the Court of the Tabernacle.

What was the Basin?

Basically, it was a big sink. The basin and its stand were made of bronze. It stood between the Tabernacle and the altar. Water was poured into it. Aaron and his sons washed their hands and feet with the water before they made an offering.

What was the anointing oil?

The priests used this oil to anoint the Tabernacle, the Ark of the Covenant, the utensils, the basin, and the stand. The anointing oil was made of liquid myrrh, cinnamon, cane, cassia, and olive oil. This recipe was holy. The oil was not to be used in any other way.

What did the priests wear?

As in other areas of temple design, God was quite specific about what he wanted the priests to wear. Aaron and his sons—and their sons in perpetuity—were designated as priests. Aaron, as the high priest, wore the most elaborate vestments. His vestments consisted of a breastpiece, an ephod (an apron-like garment worn to secure the breastpiece), a robe, a tunic, a turban, and a sash. All of the garments were made using gold, blue, purple, and red yarn, and fine linen. Aaron's sons' vestments consisted of tunics, sashes, and headdresses.

This stained-glass window in the Saint Nicholas Church in Nérac, Lot-et-Garonne, France, depicts the high priest Aaron.

The breastpiece, called the breastpiece of judgment, was made of linen. Gold, blue, purple, and red yarns were woven into it. On the front of the breastpiece were four rows of precious stones. Three stones were in each row, for a total of twelve stones altogether. The stones were carnelian, chrysolite, emerald, turquoise, sapphire, moonstone, jacinth, agate, amethyst, beryl, onyx, and jasper. Each stone was set in gold filigree. Each stone was engraved with a name of a tribe of Israel. God specified which stone represented which tribe. Symbolically, Aaron bore the names of the sons of Israel on his heart when he ministered to God. The breastplate was said to hold objects called Urim and Thummim. Some scholars believe they were similar to dice. Urim and Thummim were used by the priest on occasion to determine God's will, hence the name given to it, "breastpiece of judgment."

Each ephod, or shoulder cover, was made of gold. Blue, purple, and red yarns were woven into it. Two onyx stones were engraved as a memorial with the names of the sons of Israel, six names on each stone. The names were written in order of their birth. The onyx stones were put in settings of gold filigree and attached to the shoulders of the ephod, one stone on each shoulder.

The robe was made of all blue fabric. The hem had a woven binding on it so it would not fray. (God thought of everything!) Also around the hem were embroidered pomegranates of blue, purple, and red. Between each pomegranate were gold bells. The bells were there so that the priest would be heard as he entered and exited the Tabernacle, and would not die.

The turban was made of fine linen. On the front of the turban was a rosette of pure gold. The words "Holy to the Lord" were engraved on it. It was fastened to the turban with a blue cord.

The tunic was made of fine linen. The sash was embroidered. Underneath the tunics, both Aaron and his sons wore linen undergarments.

Were Aaron and his sons consecrated as priests?

Yes. In an elaborate ritual involving animal sacrifice, Aaron and his sons were consecrated. Moses acted as priest during this ceremony.

What happened during the ceremony?

The ceremony involved many steps. First, Aaron and his sons were anointed. This was accomplished when Aaron and his sons lay their hands on a bull's head and slaughtered it at the entrance to the Tabernacle. Aaron and his sons took some of the bull's blood and put it on the horns of the altar. The rest of the blood they poured out at the base of the altar. They burned the fat that covered the bull's entrails, and the bull's liver and kidneys on the altar. They burned the bull's flesh, skin, and dung outside the camp as a sin offering.

Then, Aaron and his sons slaughtered a ram and took its blood and dashed it against all sides of the altar. They cut the ram into pieces, washed the pieces, then burned them on the altar as a burnt offering.

After that, Aaron and his sons slaughtered another ram, and took some of the blood and put it on the lobe of Aaron's right ear and the right ears of his sons. Also, they took some of the blood and put it on Aaron's right big toe and the right big toes of his sons. They dashed the rest of the blood against all sides of the altar. Once Aaron and his sons were anointed by some of the blood on the altar and some oil, they and their vestments were holy.

Finally, Moses took the fat that covered the ram's entrails, the ram's liver and kidneys, and the ram's right thigh, along with pieces of bread, and put them in the palms of Aaron and his sons. Aaron and his sons raised their palms as an elevation offering.

Then they put the offering on the altar and burned it. Moses took the breast of this ram and raised it as an elevation offering to God. Also, the flesh of this ram was boiled. Aaron and his sons ate it, along with some of the apportioned bread.

Where did the Israelites get all these materials?

God told Moses to ask the Israelites to give of their personal possessions as their hearts prompted. (Exodus 25:2) The Israelites gave so generously that Moses asked them to stop because more than enough had been given to build the Tabernacle and all that went with it. Also, God picked people of intelligence and ability in every kind of craft to make the Tabernacle and everything that went with it. (Exodus 31:3)

When did the Israelites first worship using the laws God gave to Moses on Mount Sinai?

It was nine months after they arrived at Mount Sinai. Moses set up the Tabernacle and all its implements himself. He did everything just as God commanded him. When everything was set up, the glory of the God filled the Tabernacle. The pillar of cloud that God used to guide the Israelites covered the Tabernacle. When God wanted the Israelites to pick up and move, the cloud moved from above the Tabernacle. In that way, the Israelites began to worship God as they travelled to the Promised Land.

Are any parts of the Tabernacle around today?

No. People have been searching for years for the Ark of the Covenant. No one knows for sure at what point it disappeared or was destroyed, but the Bible provides a couple of hints. In I Kings 14:25 (NRSV), "King Shishak of Egypt came up against Jerusalem; he took away the treasures of the king's house." This may or may not have included the Ark of the Covenant. Even if it did include the Ark, there is the possibility that at some later point it was restored. Another possibility is seen in the deuterocanonical book II Maccabees 2:4–8: "It was also in the same document that the prophet, having received an oracle, ordered that the tent and the ark should follow with him, and that he went out to the mountain where Moses had gone up and had seen the inheritance of God. Jeremiah came and found a cave dwelling, and he brought there the tent and the ark and the altar

---

Where is Mount Sinai located?

The exact location of the biblical Mount Sinai is a matter of dispute. The location most widely accepted as Mount Sinai is Jebel Musa, which is Arabic for "mountain of Moses." Located on the Sinai Peninsula, Jebel Musa rises more than 7,000 feet above sea level. At the foot of Jebel Musa sits the 1,500-year-old Monastery of Saint Catherine. Home to monks of the Greek Orthodox Church, the monastery is believed by many to be on the site of the burning bush.

of incense, then he sealed up the entrance. Some of those who followed him came up intending to mark the way, but could not find it."

LEVITICUS

What is the book of Leviticus about?

Leviticus is a book of laws. Many of the laws were established especially for the priests. These laws defined their role in worship and in the community. Other laws in the book were for all of the Israelites. These laws defined proper attitudes and behaviors. The name Leviticus derives from the Greek word "Leuitikon," which is the adjective form of "Levitical." The word "Levitical" harkens back to when Jacob's son, Levi, and all of his descendants were set apart by God as priests. This segregation applied more specifically to Levi's descendant, Aaron, and Aaron's descendants. Traditionally, Moses is considered the author of Leviticus.

Why did the Israelites make so many animal sacrifices?

This practice came about because of what happened when the Israelites left Egypt. One of the first things the Israelites did to commemorate this first step to the Promised Land was to sacrifice an animal. God told the people: "Dedicate to me all the firstborn sons of Israel and every firstborn male animal. They are mine." (NLT, Exodus 13:1) The Israelites did not have to sacrifice their firstborn children. Instead, the children were redeemed. Redemption was accomplished when the child's parents paid a price to the priest.

What kinds of sacrifices, or offerings, were there?

1. Burnt offerings involved the sacrifice of animals. This kind of sacrifice purified the worshiper of sin. Burnt offerings were more common than the other offerings. In addition to the offerings made for individuals, burnt offerings were made twice a day for the whole community.

2. Grain offerings involved the sacrifice of grain from the harvest as a way of saying thanks to God.

3. Peace offerings involved the sacrifice of animal parts to express thanks to

Burnt sacrifices of animals were a common form of offering made by the Jews to God. Such offerings were to atone both for individuals and for the community.

God. The worshiper could eat the sacrifice. In some Bible translations this is referred to as the well-being offering, or fellowship offering.

4. Sin offerings were of two kinds. There were offerings for intentional sinning, and offerings for unintentional sinning.

5. Guilt offerings. This overlapped somewhat with sin offerings, but the distinctive quality of guilt offerings was that they had to do with restitution or repayment.

No matter what kind of offering the Israelite gave, it could not have any bruises or blemishes. It had to be the best of what the Israelite had. The priests were the only ones allowed to perform the sacrifice. In addition, the priests were allowed to keep portions of offerings as food for themselves and their families.

Did Aaron's sons perform well as priests?

Being a priest was a huge responsibility. There was a lot to remember. Accordingly, God gave the priests extremely detailed instructions on how to carry out their duties, right down to how to dispose of unneeded animal parts. Soon after Aaron and his sons were ordained (Leviticus 9), two of Aaron's sons, Nadab and Abihu, misused their priestly position by using coals from a banned, unspecified source. When they did that, "fire came out from the presence of the LORD and consumed them, and they died before the LORD." (NRSV, Leviticus 9:2)

CLEAN AND UNCLEAN, HOLY AND COMMON, LEVITICUS 11–15

Besides offerings, did the Israelites have other ways to worship?

God wanted a relationship with the Israelites. As a way of building and maintaining that relationship, God told Aaron to teach the Israelites the difference between clean and unclean, holy and common. These regulations had to do with acceptable and unacceptable foods, protocol for circumcisions, how to diagnose and treat skin diseases, and how to treat household mold. Other regulations had to do with regular and irregular discharges from both men and women. In all cases, the perimeters for uncleanness were defined clearly, as were the procedures for making the person or thing clean.

DAY OF ATONEMENT

What was the Day of Atonement?

The Day of Atonement was instituted after Aaron's sons, Nadab and Abihu, were killed in the sanctuary of God. The Day of Atonement occurred once a year. On this day—and only on this day—the high priest entered the inner part of the Tabernacle where the Ark of the Covenant sat to make atoning sacrifices for the sins of all the Israelites. It was a solemn occasion for all Israelites, marked by rest and fasting. Today, this commemoration is known as Yom Kippur.

Why did the priest need two goats on this day?

The priest cast lots over two goats. One goat was burned as a sacrifice. The other goat was presented alive to God. Atonement was made over it. Then the goat was sent off into the wilderness, bearing all the sin of the people. This is the origin of the term "scapegoat."

THE HOLINESS CODE

What is the Holiness Code?

Scholars use the name Holiness Code for the group of laws in Leviticus, Chapters 17–26, because God says this many times throughout this section (NRSV): "You shall be holy, for I, the LORD your God, am holy."

If God expected the Israelites to be holy, does that mean God expected them to be perfect?

God is perfect. The Israelites, like all humans, were not. God knew that and still does. Scholars point out that the word "holy" has a few shades of meaning. God's holiness separates God from the world. In the Levitical sense, God separates those God wishes to devote to himself. Most scholars agree that God was telling the Israelites to separate themselves from the world by their distinct devotion to his laws.

Were the laws in the Holiness Code more important than the other laws?

No. All the laws were of the same importance to the Israelites.

What kinds of laws are in the Holiness Code?

The laws cover a range of issues. One law made it a sin to eat or drink blood. God said, "For the life of a creature is in the blood, and I have given it to you to make atonement for yourselves on the altar; it is the blood, and I have given it to you to make atonement for yourselves on the altar; it is the blood that makes atonement for one's life." (NIV, Leviticus 17:11) Other laws made it a sin to sacrifice children or to prostitute daughters. Some laws pertained to sexual relations, idolatry, honesty, and keeping the Sabbath, while other laws pertained to handling corpses, and being generous to those less fortunate.

Why were there so many laws?

There were laws regarding white, eruptive places on the skin, laws dealing with rashes on the skin. There were laws on dealing with menstruation and baldness. To modern-day readers, some of the laws might seem nitpicky. However, at the time, all of the laws were necessary to ensure the sustained physical and spiritual welfare of the Israelites. God was in the process of taking an uneducated, irreligious people, and making a new, godly nation out of them.

Why is leprosy mentioned so many times in the laws?

The modern definition of leprosy is more specific than it was in biblical times. Today leprosy refers to a chronic bacterial disease with outward symptoms of severe skin lesions. In biblical times, leprosy referred to a host of skin disorders, including psoriasis, boils, and burns.

Besides the Day of Atonement, did God command the Israelites to observe any other special days?

Yes. In addition, God gave the Israelites a ritual calendar. The calendar was based on the agricultural year. Determining the correct day to observe some of the special days required them to count off days, weeks, months, and years in various combinations of seven. For example, the Sabbath day was observed on the seventh day of the week. Some of these special days and events are observed still.

Sabbath Day. God gave this directive in Genesis, but he reiterated it many times throughout the Bible, including in Leviticus.

Sabbath Year. God told the Israelites that when they arrived in the Promised Land, they were to work the land for six years, but in the seventh year, they were to let the land rest.

Year of Jubilee. God told the Israelites to count off forty-nine years. The fiftieth year was the Year of Jubilee. In this year, all debts were forgiven and all slaves were freed. If during the previous forty-nine years someone sold land due to financial difficulty, the land was restored to that person.

Passover. God gave this directive in Exodus when the Israelites left Egypt, but he reiterated it in Leviticus to underscore its importance in the life of the Israelites. Passover was also known as the Festival of Unleavened Bread. It commemorated when God passed over the homes of the Israelites and did not kill their firstborn, but did kill the firstborn of the Egyptians. The first fruits of the harvest were offered during this time as well.

The Festival of Weeks (now known as Pentecost). Observed annually, the Festival of Weeks was celebrated seven weeks after Passover. It was a joyous time, and a time for the Israelites to offer thanks for the harvest. The word "pentecost" comes from the Greek for "count fifty."

Festival of Trumpets (now known as Rosh Hashanah). Observed annually, the Festival of Trumpets marked the new year for the Israelites. It was (and is) marked by the celebratory blowing of trumpets.

The Festival of Booths (also known as the Festival of Tabernacles). Observed annually, this seven-day festival celebrated the harvest. Once the Israelites were established in the Promised Land, the Israelites marked the occasion by living in tents for a week. This reminded them of God's provision for them while they were in the desert.

Sabbath Month. The Day of Atonement is on the tenth day of this month. Festival of Booths is on the fifteenth day of this month. Israelites lived in booths (tents) for seven days to commemorate their time in the wilderness.

NUMBERS

What is the book of Numbers about?

It concerns the Israelites' travels in the wilderness. During this time, God gave the Israelites instructions for camp arrangement, conducting a census, and the arrangement of the group while traveling. Traditionally, Moses is considered to the author of Numbers. The English name of the book, Numbers, refers to all of the numbers taken during the census. The Hebrew title for the book, Ba-Mid-bar, means "in the wilderness."

THE CENSUS

In the book of Numbers, what is the first thing Moses and Aaron do?

At God's direction, they conducted a census of eleven of the tribes. Primarily, the census was a way to gauge how many soldiers were among the Israelites. Accordingly, only men twenty years old or older were counted. The members of the tribes of Levi were not counted because they were dedicated to being priests—never soldiers.

How many men fit the description of being twenty years old or older?

The numberof men in this age group totaled 603,550.

Were any other groups counted?

Yes. All of the firstborn males from one month old to age twenty were counted. They numbered 22,273. Levites were excluded from this count.

CAMP LIFE

How was the Israelite camp arranged?

Keeping so many people organized was no easy task. Numbers provides detailed logistics for that purpose. The Tabernacle was the center of the camp. Three tribes camped on each of the four sides of the Tabernacle. Each tribe faced the Tabernacle. The Tabernacle faced east. The camp was arranged this way each time the Israelites camped in a new place.

What were the responsibilities of the Levites when the Israelites traveled?

The Levites were responsible for the care and keeping of the Tabernacle, and all that went with it. Moses and Aaron divided the Levites into their smaller clans, and assigned each clan a specific task. For example, the Kohathites prepared the Ark of the Covenant for travel and carried it to the next location, using the acacia wood poles overlaid with gold. The Gershonites carried the curtains of the Tabernacle, the curtains for the courtyard, and the coverings for the Tabernacle.

Did God give the Israelites more laws than the ones found in Leviticus?

Yes. One law in Numbers concerning adultery went into vivid detail. The law applied to women only. If a woman was suspected of being an adulteress, her husband brought her before the priests. The priests, in turn, performed an elaborate ritual where he prepared the woman a drink containing water, dust from the floor of the Tabernacle, and ink from where the priest recorded the curses spoken to the woman. Then the priest spoke to the woman, "The LORD make you an execration and an oath among your people, when the LORD makes your uterus drop, your womb discharge; now may this water that brings the curse enter your bowels and make your womb discharge, your uterus drop!" (NRSV, Numbers 5:21–22) The woman was instructed to say, "Amen, Amen," and she drank the liquid. The idea behind this ritual was that God would cause a miscarriage if the woman was pregnant due to infidelity, but that he would bless her with fertility if she was innocent. Rituals for determining blame were common in other societies at this time. This law differs from Leviticus 20:10 in which both the adulterous man and adulterous woman are put to death.

What was the Nazirite vow?

This vow was made by men and women who wished to set themselves apart for God's service for a prescribed time, or for life. As a rite of consecration, the Nazirite was not allowed to drink vinegar or eat anything produced on the grapevine. He was not allowed to cut his hair or go near a corpse, even if the deceased was a parent or sibling. The Nazirite made special offerings to God. Once the time of his consecration ended, he shaved his head and put the hair on the fire along with a sacrifice of well-being.

What was the Aaronic blessing?

Also known as the priestly blessing, this prayer was prescribed by God to Aaron and his sons as a way to bless the Israelites. The blessing is, "The LORD bless you and keep you;

Mount Sinai, located in Egypt, is where Moses received God's laws.

the LORD make his face to shine upon you, and be gracious to you; the LORD lift up his countenance upon you, and give you peace." (NRSV, Numbers 6:24–26) Churches all over the world use the Aaronic blessing to this day.

How long did the Israelites stay at the camp near Mount Sinai?

The Israelites camped there for about a year. They knew it was time to decamp when they saw the cloud representing God lift from over the Tabernacle. It took the Israelites about two months to get from Egypt to Mount Sinai. So in all, the Israelites had been gone from Egypt for just over a year at this point.

TROUBLEMAKERS

Why did the Israelites complain this time?

Not all of the Israelites complained—just "the rabble." (Numbers 11:4) As troublemakers are wont to do, these troublemakers complained because they had no meat. Sure, they had manna—but they were tired of manna. They wept, "We remember the fish, which we did eat in Egypt freely; the cucumbers, and the melons, and the leeks, and the onions, and the garlic: But now our soul is dried away: there is nothing at all, besides this manna, before our eyes" (KJV, Numbers 11:5–6)

83

Why did God strike Miriam with leprosy?

She complained against Moses. Aaron complained against Moses, too, but nothing happened to him. Miriam was shut out of camp for seven days while her leprosy cleared up.

How did God respond to this complaint?

God got angry. Moses got angry because God got angry. Moses said to God, "Wherefore hast thou afflicted thy servant? And wherefore have I not found favor in thy sight, that thou layest the burden of all this people upon me? Have I conceived all this people? Have I begotten them, that thou shouldest say unto me, Carry them in thy bosom, as a nursing father beareth the sucking child, unto the land which thou swarest unto their fathers?" (KJV, Numbers 11:11–12)

To the rabble among the Israelites, God responded about the lack of meat: "Sanctify yourself against tomorrow, and ye shall eat flesh: for ye have wept in the ears of the LORD, saying, Who shall give us flesh to eat? For it was well with us in Egypt: therefore the LORD will give you flesh and ye shall eat. Ye shall not eat one day, nor two days nor five days, neither ten days, nor twenty days; But even a whole month, until it come out at your nostrils, and it be loathsome unto you: because that ye have despised the LORD which is among you, and have wept before him, saying, Why came we forth out of Egypt?" (KJV, Numbers 11:18–20) Indeed, that was an understatement. God sent tons of quail their way, so much so that the quail piled up three feet deep. While the rabble was eating, God struck them with a terrible plague, and many died.

SO CLOSE, YET SO FAR

The Israelites left Egypt just over a year ago. Now they were about to enter Canaan, the Promised Land. What did God want them to do before they entered?

God wanted them to send a small group of Israelites on a reconnaissance mission to Canaan. Moses picked one man from each of the twelve tribes. So there were twelve spies in all.

What was the purpose of the mission?

Moses told the spies to find out what the land was like, whether the people were strong or weak, whether they were many or few, whether the towns were walled or not, and what types of trees and fruit were there.

How long were the spies in Canaan?

Forty days and forty nights.

What did the spies report to Moses?

The spies gave Moses some grapes, pomegranates, and figs they found in Canaan. So far, so good. Also, the spies told Moses that, indeed, the land flowed with milk and honey, but that the people who lived there were strong, and the towns were fortified. In addition to several other peoples, the spies said they saw Amalekites, a race of warrior giants, while they were there. Not so good.

Caleb, one of the twelve spies, told Moses, "Let us go up at once, and possess it: for we are well able to overcome it." The other spies disagreed. "We be not able to go up against the people; for they are stronger than we." (KJV, Numbers 13:30, 31) Caleb was outnumbered. The spies gave the Israelites a discouraging report of what they saw in Canaan.

What did the Israelites say?

"Let us make a captain, and let us return into Egypt." (KJV, Numbers 14:4) Despite God's continuous guidance and plentiful provisions, the Israelites doubted he would deliver on his promise.

What did Moses say to that?

Moses and Aaron fell on their faces before the Israelites. At that moment, Moses had God on his side. From among the people, however, Moses had only Aaron, Joshua, and Caleb on his side. Joshua and Caleb pleaded with the people, "The land, which we passed through to search it, is an exceeding good land." They continued, "Only rebel not ye against the LORD, neither fear ye the people of the land; for they are bread for us: their defense is departed from them, and the LORD is with us: fear them not." (KJV, Numbers 14:7, 9) At that, the Israelites threatened to stone Joshua and Caleb.

Did the Israelites enter Canaan then?

No. God told them there was no way he would let them into Canaan now. God told them that all the Israelites would have to keep traveling in the wilderness until all those who insulted

God forced the Israelites to wander the desert for forty years until all those who had insulted him had died, never to see the land of Canaan.

him died. God did not want the ones who insulted him to see Canaan. It took forty years for them to die off. Thus, the Israelites wandered in the wilderness for forty more years.

WILDERNESS TRAVELS, CONTINUED

What was one of the results of continued travel?

The Israelites warred with other peoples, and fought among themselves as well.

What happened when a priest named Korah and a few other priests rebelled against Moses and Aaron?

"The earth opened its mouth and swallowed them up, along with their households—everyone who belonged to Korah and all their goods. So they with all that belonged to them went down alive into Sheol; the earth closed over them, and they perished from the midst of the assembly." (NRSV, Numbers 16:32–33)

Did the rest of the Israelites fall in line after that?

No! They, too, rebelled against Moses and Aaron. As a result, God sent a plague, but allowed Aaron to stop it with an offering of incense. Aaron "stood between the dead and the living; and the plague was stopped." (NRSV, Numbers 16:48) As a result of the plague, 14,700 people died.

What did God do so that the Israelites would not doubt Aaron's priestly status anymore?

Among the staffs belonging to the various tribes, God caused Aaron's staff to put forth buds, blossoms, and then almonds. It was at this point that Aaron's staff was stored in the Ark of the Covenant as a reminder to future generations that Aaron's priesthood was legitimate.

FORTY YEARS LATER

As the Israelites approached Canaan this time, what sad event happened?

First, Miriam died and was buried. Second, the Israelites complained.

What did the Israelites complain about this time?

They complained about the scarcity of water. They still doubted God's ability—and his promise!—to provide for them. This time, Moses and Aaron doubted, too, because God delivered this fateful line: "Because you did not trust in me, to show my holiness before the eyes of the Israelites, therefore you shall not bring this assembly into the land that I have given them." (NRSV, Numbers 20:12)

What happened when the Israelites started to cross over into Canaan?

Aaron died. The people mourned his death for thirty days.

What happened the next time the Israelites complained?

God sent poisonous snakes among the people. Many people died of snake bites. To stop the plague of snakes, God instructed Moses to fashion a snake of bronze and mount it on a pole. Everyone who was bitten looked at it and lived. Some scholars say this event foreshadowed Jesus' crucifixion.

THE TALKING DONKEY

Who was Balaam?

Balaam was a seer sought by Balak, king of Moab, to curse the Israelites. By this point, the Israelites had fought and won many battles with peoples in the area. Balak heard these reports and was afraid. God came to Balaam in a dream, and told him not to curse the Israelites. Balak asked again. Balaam refused again. Balak asked again. This time, God told Balaam he could go meet with Balak. So Balaam mounted his donkey and went. For an unexplained reason, God gave Balaam permission to go, but then made his journey unusually difficult.

How did God make Balaam's journey difficult?

It started with the talking donkey. While Balaam rode his donkey on the road, the donkey saw the angel of the LORD, sword drawn, standing in the middle of the road. So the donkey turned off the road and went into a field. Balaam whipped the donkey to get it back on the road. Then the angel of the LORD stood in a narrow, walled path. When the donkey saw the angel of the LORD, it brushed against the wall and caused Balaam to scrape his foot. Balaam struck the donkey again. A third time, the angel of the LORD appeared. The donkey could not turn to the right or the left, so it lay down under Balaam. By this time, Balaam was angry. He struck the donkey again. This time, "the LORD opened the mouth of the donkey, and it said to Balaam, 'What have I done to you, that you have struck me these three times?' Balaam said to the donkey, 'Because you have made a fool of me! I wish I had a sword in my hand! I would kill you right now!'

"But the donkey said to Balaam, 'Am I not your donkey, which you have ridden all your life to this day? Have I been in the habit of treating you this way?' And he said, 'No.'" (NRSV, Numbers 22:28–30)

After this unusual exchange, God opened the eyes of Balaam so he, too, could see the angel standing there. The angel told Balaam that he could continue on his journey, but that he should only speak to Balak what God told him to speak.

What did Balaam tell Balak?

Three times Balaam told Balak that he could not and would not curse the Israelites.

Final Stages of the Wilderness Journey

Since God told Moses he could not go to the Promised Land, who does God choose to lead the people there?

Joshua, Moses' faithful assistant all this time.

The Gadites and the Reubenites came up with a plan. What was it?

The Gadites and Reubenites (descendants of Jacob's sons, Gad and Reuben) had a lot of cattle. Respectfully, they asked Moses and the other leaders if they could claim their portion of land right where they were because it was good land for cattle. At first, Moses was angry because he thought all of the tribes should go into Canaan together. However, the Gadites and Reubenites promised to not claim their portion of land until they had gone with the rest of the Israelites to claim theirs, and would fight with them if need be. Moses was fine with this plan.

How many stops did the Israelites make in the wilderness?

They stopped and set up camp forty-two times of the forty years they spent in the wilderness. Because God told Moses to write down the stages of the journey, there is a record of all the stops the Israelites made. (Numbers 33) However, because place names have changed many times over the years, the exact route cannot be determined.

What was the last stop in the wilderness for the Israelites?

A place called Shittim. Its modern-day location is unknown. While the Israelites were in Shittim, some of the Israelite men engaged in illicit activities with the local, idol-worshiping women. Another plague put an end to that trend.

What important information did God give the Israelites before they entered Canaan?

God told them the exact boundaries for each tribe. Also, God told them about the cities of refuge.

What unusual real estate transaction took place during this last stop?

Three women inherit land. In a patriarchal society such as the Israelites had, this was worth noting. The women—Mahlah, Noah, and Hoglah—were daughters of Zelophehad. Zelophehad died in the wilderness, but not because he was one of the ones who mocked God. He died without sons, so God told Moses it was acceptable for the inheritance to go to his daughters.

What were the cities of refuge?

Because the Levites did not have land for themselves, they were given forty-eight cities throughout the land. Six of those cities were cities of refuge. These cities were places where someone who killed another person by accident could take refuge until a trial could take place before the congregation. By taking refuge in a city of refuge, the person who killed was assured he would not be sought out and killed in revenge.

DEUTERONOMY

What is Deuteronomy about?

This book opens where Numbers left off. The Israelites are about to enter the Promised Land. The word "deuteronomy" comes from two Greek words meaning "second law."

ALMOST THERE

What happened as the Israelites waited to enter the Promised Land?

Moses spoke to them. He summarized events that had happened to them in the wilderness. Moses confirmed that God kept his promise—the Israelites were indeed more numerous than the stars in the sky. Moses reminded them of their complaints, of God's patience and impatience, of God's wrath and God's provision. Moses reminded them of battles in which they had been engaged, and of the laws which God gave them.

What major command did Moses give the people?

After recapping God's laws for the Israelites, Moses said, "Hear, O Israel: The LORD our God is one LORD: And thou shalt love the LORD thy God with all thine heart, and with all thy soul, and with all thy might. And these words, which I command thee this day, shall be in thine heart: And thou shalt teach them diligently unto thy children, and shalt talk of them when thou sittest in thine house, and when thou walkest by the way, when thou liest down, and when thou risest up. And thou shalt bind them for a sign upon thine hand and they shall be as frontlets between thine eyes. And thou shalt write them upon the posts of thy house, and on thy gates." (KJV, Deuteronomy 6:4–9) Through the ages, this has come to be known as the Great Commandment.

What did God want the Israelites to do when they met the people who lived in the land where they were going?

God warned the Israelites about being friends with the people they met. God told the Israelites not to make treaties with them or intermarry with them, lest the Israelites succumb to the other people's idolatrous lifestyles. Instead, God told the Israelites that—with God's help—they would destroy the other people completely.

How did God say the Israelites should treat each other?

Moses reminded the Israelites of all God had told them earlier regarding caring for the less fortunate among them. God said, "If there be among you a poor man of one of thy brethren within any of thy gates in the land which the LORD thy God giveth thee, thou shalt not harden thine heart, nor shut thine hand from thy poor brother: But thou shalt open thine hand wide unto him, and shalt surely lend him sufficient for his need, in that which he wanteth." (KJV, Deuteronomy 15:7–8)

What did God tell the Israelites would happen to them if they did not obey his laws?

God told the Israelites that they would meet with every kind of disaster ranging from infertility to military defeat, from madness and scurvy to bad crops.

What is the last thing Moses did before he died?

He blessed the Israelites, giving a specialized blessing to each of the twelve tribes.

Where was Moses buried?

No one knows for sure. The Bible says, "And he [God] buried him in a valley in the land of Moab, over against Bethpeor: but no man knoweth of his sepulcher unto this day." (KJV, Deuteronomy 34:6)

Why did God keep Moses' burial place a secret?

The Bible does not say why for sure, but many people think it was to prevent Moses' grave from being a source of idolatry.

How old was Moses when he died?

He was 120 years old. He did not have the ailments associated with a long, hard life. Rather, "his eye was not dim, nor his natural force abated." (KJV, Deuteronomy 34:7)

Who was Moses' successor?

Joshua, the son of Nun. Joshua was Moses' assistant for a long time. He was one of the spies who reported back truthfully about the land of Canaan. God believed Joshua was now ready to lead.

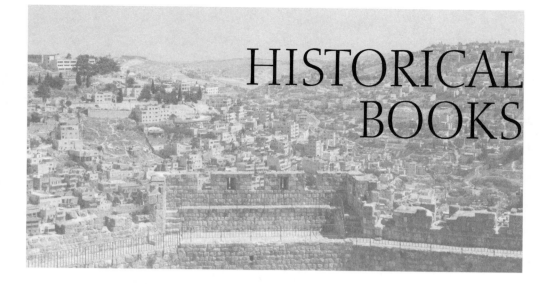

HISTORICAL BOOKS

JOSHUA

What is the book of Joshua about?

The book of Joshua relates the conquest of Canaan and the allotment of the land to the Israelite tribes. It is widely believed that the events in Joshua took place between 1400 B.C.E. and 1200 B.C.E.. While the book gets its name from Joshua, it is not known who wrote the book.

What was God's first command to Joshua as leader of the Israelites?

God told Joshua, "Now that my servant Moses is dead, you must lead my people across the Jordan River into the land I am giving them." (NLT, Joshua 1:2)

What did Joshua need to do to accomplish this?

God told Joshua to be strong and courageous, and to think about and act in accordance with God's laws. If Joshua did that, God told Joshua that he would be with him wherever he went.

RAHAB AND THE SPIES

How did Joshua go about claiming Canaan for the Israelites?

The first thing Joshua did was to send spies into Canaan.

What did the spies do?

Joshua asked the spies to check out the land, especially the city of Jericho. Sneaking into the city, the spies entered the house of a prostitute, Rahab. Presumably, the spies wanted to go somewhere where they would blend in.

Did the spies blend in?

No. Word of their presence got to the king of Jericho. The king commanded Rahab to turn in the spies.

Did Rahab obey the king?

Rahab had heard all the stories about the parting of the Red Sea and the battles won by the Israelites, so she knew their God had meant for them to inherit Canaan.

Why did Rahab help the spies?

Rahab told the spies, "I know the LORD has given you this land…. We are all afraid of you. Everyone is living in terror." (LT, Joshua 1:9)

How did Rahab know that God had given the land to the Israelites?

Rahab had heard all the stories about the parting of the Red Sea and the battles won by the Israelites, so she knew their God had meant for them to inherit Canaan.

Did Rahab ask anything in return for helping the spies?

Yes. She asked the spies to spare her and her family when the Israelites came to conquer. The spies agreed. Rahab and the spies agreed that she would tie a red cord in the window of her house so the Israelites would know which house to spare.

JOSHUA THE LEADER

Did the Israelites accept Joshua's leadership?

Yes. God took steps to make sure they had faith in Joshua. The first amazing thing God allowed Joshua to do was to hold back the waters of the Jordan so the Israelites could cross over.

How did Joshua accomplish this?

Joshua had some of the priests stand in the middle of the Jordan holding the Ark of the Covenant. As they stood, the waters were held back on both sides. The Israelites crossed right over into Canaan.

What special steps did the Israelites take in order to memorialize the event?

The Israelites took twelve stones from the middle of the Jordan, one stone for each of the twelve tribes of Israel. At their next camp, they set up the stones as a memorial to God's miraculous help as they crossed the Jordan.

> ## Why did the Israelites name a place the Hill of the Foreskins?
>
> **N**o Israelite men were circumcised in the wilderness. At God's command, Joshua had the Israelites renew their covenant with God by having the men circumcised at Gibeath-haaraloth. "Gibeath-haaraloth" means "Hill of the Foreskins."

What was the first festival the Israelites celebrated in Canaan?

They celebrated Passover. The next day, the Israelites ate the food of the land. God did not send anymore manna.

THE WALLS OF JERICHO

What was the Israelites' plan for conquering Jericho?

By the time the Israelites arrived in Jericho, the city was around seven thousand years old. It was an impressive, wealthy city on a hill. It had strong fortifications. To this day, Jericho is the oldest settlement known.

God gave them the idea of marching around the city once a day for six days in a row. On the seventh day, the Israelites marched around the city seven times. Israelite musicians blew trumpets, but the rest of the people did not say a word. On the seventh day after the seventh lap, the Israelites shouted, and the protective wall around the city crumbled to the ground.

Who came unexpectedly and helped the Israelites conquer Jericho?

God appeared to Joshua and told him the ground was sacred. (Joshua 5:14)

Did anyone try to rebuild Jericho?

When Jericho fell, Joshua pronounced a curse on it: "Cursed before the LORD is the man who undertakes to rebuild this city, Jericho: 'At the cost of his firstborn son will he lay its foundations, at the cost of his youngest will he set up its gates.'" (NIV, Joshua 6:26)

In I Kings 16:34 (NIV), a man named Hiel mocked Joshua's prophecy when he rebuilt Jericho. The curse was fulfilled, however, when Hiel "laid its foundation at the cost of Abiram his firstborn, and set up its gates at the cost of his youngest son Segub, according to the word of the LORD, which he spoke by Joshua.

Did the Israelites honor their promise to spare Rahab and her family?

Yes, they did. After that, "the LORD was with Joshua, and his fame spread throughout the land." (NIV, Joshua 6:27) A woman by the name of Rahab is listed in the genealogy of Jesus in the first chapter of Matthew. It is not known for a certainty, but is widely accepted that the Rahab in the genealogy is the same one who was the prostitute in Jericho. One indication that the Rahabs are one and the same is that in the genealogy Rahab married an Israelite named Salmon. Caleb, a contemporary of Joshua and Moses, had a son name Salmon. (I Chronicles 2:51)

MILITARY SUCCESSES AND FAILURES

Did the Israelites continue to have success?

No. They were supposed to turn the booty over to the priests, but not everyone did. Achan of the tribe of Judah kept some things out for himself. God got mad and left the Israelites to their own devices in the next confrontation with enemies. During the next spy mission, some of the Israelites were killed. Achan was found out, and was stoned to death.

What were some the military expeditions of the Israelites?

They conquered a kingdom, Ai, by luring its soldiers into the open, and then ambushing them. Another kingdom, Gibeon, decided to trick the Israelites. They pretended to be poor by making their clothes ragged, and by carrying dry and moldy food. They lied, telling the Israelites that they were from far away. They asked to make a treaty with the Israelites because they were afraid of being ransacked by the Israelites. The Israelites agreed, even though God had warned them many times not to make treaties with other peoples.

Did the Israelites ever find out they were tricked?

Yes. They found out that the Gibeonites were from the area, but a treaty was a treaty. They could not ransack Gibeon. So Joshua made the Gibeonites serve as hewers of wood and drawers of water for the altar of God.

Jerusalem is an ancient city that was originally under the power of the Amorites. When the Israelites defeated King Adoni-zedek, they took the city over and it has served as their traditional political and spritual center.

What was Shiloh?

Shiloh was the city the Israelites used as headquarters before Jerusalem became their capital. The name Shiloh means "place of peace."

How did God show the enemies of the Israelites that he was the one in control?

When the five kings of the Amorites banded together to conquer the Gibeonites, Joshua came to the aid of the Gibeonites. God threw the Amorites into a panic. Then God pummeled them with hailstones. "There were more which died with hailstones than they whom the children of Israel slew with the sword." (KJV, Joshua 10:11) Also on that day, God made the sun and moon stand still until the Amorites were subdued. One of the Amorite kings, King Adoni-zedek, ruled an impressive city that, once conquered, would prove vital to the development of the Israelite nation. The city was Jerusalem.

The author of Joshua refers to the Book of Jasher. What is that?

The passage reads, "Is not this written in the book of Jasher? So the sun stood still in the midst of heaven, and hasted not to go down about a whole day." (KJV, Joshua 10:13) The Book of Jasher was a collection of poetry honoring Israel's military prowess. The book no longer exists.

How long did the Israelites fight the peoples of Canaan?

The Bible does not say exactly, only that "Joshua made war a long time with all those kings." (KJV, Joshua 11:18) Joshua and the Israelites ransacked cities, killed all the people, and collected booty. The Israelites did as God commanded.

What happened when the Israelites took all the land?

They divided it into tribal allotments. The tribes of Gad and Reuben, and half the tribe of Manasseh, kept their end of the deal they made with Moses. Even though these two-and-a-half tribes found land they wanted before crossing the Jordan, they promised Moses they would go on ahead with the rest of the tribes and help them fight. Now that much of the fighting was done, the two-and-a-half tribes crossed back over the Jordan to begin their settlements there.

What did Joshua do right before he died?

He reminded the Israelites of all that God had done for them: "I handed you a land for which you did not work, town you did not build. And here you are now living in them and eating from vineyards and olive groves you did not plant." (The Message, Joshua 24:13) Joshua gave the Israelites a choice. He said, "If you decide that it's a bad thing to worship GOD, then choose a god you'd rather serve—and do it today. Choose one of the gods your ancestors worshiped from the country beyond the River, or one of the gods

95

of the Amorites, on whose land you're now living. As for me and my family, we'll worship God." (The Message, Joshua 24:15) The people recognized the wisdom of Joshua's words, and reaffirmed their commitment to God.

How old was Joshua when he died?

Joshua died at 110 years old. The Israelites served God all the days of Joshua's life, and all the days of the elders who outlived Joshua.

JUDGES

What is the book of Judges about?

The book of Judges describes the formative years of Israel as a nation. Before Israel had kings, it had judges who acted as military and social leaders. Presumably, Israel did not need a human king because God was their king. Generally, it is believed that the judges ruled between 1200 B.C.E. and 1025 B.C.E. The Israelites had entered into a covenant with God, but they did not keep their end of the deal.

THE DOWNWARD SPIRAL OF THE ISRAELITES

What did the Israelites do after Joshua died?

After Joshua and all the other elders of that generation died, the Israelites lost sight of their purpose. They began to follow the practices of their idolatrous neighbors. They worshiped the gods Baal, Astarte, and Asherah.

What were Baal, Astarte, and Asherah?

Baal was the Canaanite god of storms. Astarte was the goddess of fertility, and the consort of Baal. Asherah was the goddess of heaven.

What happened to the Israelites at the beginning of Judges?

The Israelites fought some of the remaining peoples in Canaan. According to their promise to God, they were supposed to kill all the people. However, they did not. When God saw that the Israelites did not do as they were supposed to do, he sent an angel to admonish them.

> Now the angel of the LORD went up from Gilgal to Bochim, and said, "I brought you into the land that I had promised to your ancestors. I said, 'I will never break my covenant with you. For your part, do not make a covenant with the inhabitants of this land; tear down their altars.' But you have not obeyed my command. See what you have done! So now I say, I will not drive them out before you; but they shall become adversaries to you, and their gods shall be a snare to you." (NRSV, Judges 2:1–5)

How did the Israelites react to this visit?

They wept and were sorry. They made sacrifices to God, but they continued to follow the evil practices of their neighbors. Consequently, God made them lose many battles.

THE JUDGES AND THEIR STORIES

What did God do to try to get the Israelites back on the right path?

God did not drive out the rest of the peoples of Canaan. Instead, God used them to test the Israelites and try to bring them back to God's holy ways. God raised up judges who brought the Israelites out of the hands of their enemies. However, a pattern developed. While the judge was alive and helping the Israelites, the people obeyed God. When the judge died, there was a period of time during which the people disobeyed God. This happened time and time again. Thus began a downward spiral for Israel.

How many judges are described in the Bible?

Thirteen.

Who were the judges?

Othniel, Ehud, Shamgar, Deborah, Gideon, Abimelech, Tola, Jair, Jephthah, Ibzan, Elon, Abdon, and Samson.

What did Othniel do?

Othniel was Caleb's younger brother. The spirit of God was in him. He won many military victories.

What did Ehud do?

The Bible points out that Ehud, a Benjaminite, was left-handed. This proved to be important. The Israelites had to pay tribute to King Eglon of Moab. Ehud went to deliver it. After he delivered the tribute, Ehud said, "I have a secret message for you, O king." The king sent his attendants away so he could hear Ehud's message. With the element of surprise on his side, Ehud pulled his sword from its scabbard using his left hand. Most soldiers were right-handed. Presumably, the king was not alarmed when he saw Ehud reach into his cloak with his left hand. In a scene of graphic detail, Ehud killed the king of Moab: "Ehud took the sword from his right thigh, and thrust it into Eglon's belly; the hilt also went in after the blade, for he did not draw the sword out of his belly; and the dirt came out. Then Ehud went out into the vestibule, and closed the doors of the roof chamber on him, and locked them." (NRSV, Judges 3:21–23) When the king's servants saw that the doors were locked, they assumed the king was using the bathroom, so they waited. And they waited. They waited until they were embarrassed. They unlocked the doors, and there was the king, dead on the floor. Because the servants hemmed and hawed, Ehud was able to escape. After that, the Moabites were not a threat to the Israelites.

Because he was left-handed Ehud was able to surprise and kill the Moab King Eglon.

What did Shamgar do?

After Ehud judged, God raised up Shamgar to be judge. Shamgar killed six hundred Philistes with an oxgoad, or cattle prod, thus delivering the Israelites from their enemies.

What did Deborah, the only female judge, do?

During Deborah's time as judge, the Israelites won a major battle that began a forty-year time of peace. Before this battle, the Israelites were subject to King Jabin of Canaan. Sisera was the commander of King Jabin's army. Deborah summoned the warrior Barak, and told him God would give him success if he drew out Sisera. Barak said he would do it if Deborah went with him. So Barak and Deborah drew out Sisera and his army. God caused Sisera's army to panic. The Israelites killed every single man in Sisera's army. Sisera, however, fled on foot to the tent of Jael, the wife of Heber the Kenite. There was peace between the Kenites and the Canaanites, so Sisera thought his escape plan was good. If ever a man was wrong, it was Sisera. Jael fed Sisera and gave him a place to rest. While Sisera slept, Jael "picked up a tent peg and a hammer, and went quietly to him while he lay fast asleep, exhausted. She drove the peg through his temple into the ground, and he died." (NIV, Judges 4:21) Jael was not an Israelite. The Bible does not say why she acted on behalf of the Israelites. Perhaps, like Rahab, Jael knew the wonders God had worked through the Israelites, and recognized him as the one true God.

What is the Song of Deborah?

After Sisera and his men were killed, Deborah and Barak celebrated with a song. This song is recorded in the fifth chapter of Judges. In the song, Deborah and Barak recounted the battle and praised God.

What person was introduced in the song but was not mentioned in the battle scene?

Sisera's mother. In a song of celebration and praise, the stanzas about Sisera's mother added a shade of pity, not just for Sisera's mother, but for mothers everywhere who wait for their beloved sons to come home from war. Sisera's mother was described as peering out of a latticed window waiting for her son to come back from battle. " 'Why is his chariot so long in coming? Why is the clatter of his chariots delayed?' The wisest of her ladies answer her; indeed, she keeps saying to herself, 'Are they not finding and diving the spoils: a girl or two for each man, colorful garments as plunder for Sisera, colorful garments embroidered, highly embroidered garments for my neck—all this as plunder?'" (NIV, Judges 5:28–30)

What did Gideon do?

The judge after Deborah was Gideon. An angel of God went to speak to Gideon, who was grinding grain in a winepress in order to hide it from the Midianites. The angel told Gideon that God wanted him to deliver the Israelites from the oppression of the Midianites.

What kind of character did Gideon have?

Gideon's personality was one entrenched in fear and doubt. He feared the enemies of the Israelites. He doubted his own abilities—and God's. After all, he was the youngest son of a family who was part of the smallest tribe. He asked for and received proof that it was really an angel who talked to him. He asked for repeatedly—and received—proof from God that God really and truly wanted him, Gideon, to go up and fight for the Israelites. Once again, God showed his penchant for picking unlikely people to carry out his purpose.

How did Gideon obey God's call?

Under the cover of night (he's doubtful still), Gideon broke down his father's altar to Baal and the Asherah pole beside it. He replaced those with an altar to God.

How did God finally convince Gideon that God would deliver on his promise to be with him if he went up against the Midianites?

God winnowed out Gideon's troops and sent many of them home. Gideon was left with three hundred men. They were chosen on the basis that they lapped water like a dog. The Midianite troops outnumbered Gideon's army greatly. So when Gideon and his troops won, it was clear that the victory was due to God's intervention, not human skill.

Did Gideon stay faithful to God?

At first, it seemed as if he would. After the victory over the Midianites, the Israelites wanted to make Gideon and his ancestors rulers over them in perpetuity. Gideon recognized the idolatrous bent of this request, and declined. Sometime later, however, Gideon made an idol of gold to commemorate his victory, and stood it in the old places of the Baal and Asherah altars. The Bible says, "All Israel prostituted themselves by worshiping it there, and it became a snare to Gideon and his family." (NIV, Judges 8:27) Still, the Israelites enjoyed peace for forty years after Gideon's victory.

What did Abimelech do

Abimelech was the only self-appointed judge. He was one of Gideon's more than seventy sons. He seized leadership over the Israelites by killing all of his brothers except for Jotham, who hid from Abimelech and his murderous cronies. Abimelech made himself king. He ruled Israel for three years.

What happened that ended Abimelech's reign?

He and his soldiers went to conquer the city of Arumah. Abimelech and his men killed townspeople as they fled the city. He razed the city, and sowed it with salt. What parts Abimelech did not raze, he torched. Then, a woman threw an upper millstone on Abimelech's head, crushing his skull. Abimelech, fearful lest he be remembered for dying at the hand of a woman, commanded his armor bearer to finish him off with his sword.

Who were Tola and Jair?

Tola was a judge for twenty-three years; after that, Jair led Israel for twenty-two years.

Who was Jephthah?

The next judge, Jephthah, was the son of a Gileadite and a prostitute. He was a skilled warrior and an outlaw. He delivered the Israelites from their enemies.

What kind of character did Jephthah have?

He was courageous, but like all humans, he was flawed. He let his emotions get the better of his intellect. Jephthah made a vow to God, "If you will give the Ammonites into my hand, then whoever comes out of the doors of my house to meet me, when I return victorious from

The tragic story of Jephthah and his daughter has been commemorated in paintings and statues like this one by sculptor Emil Wolff in Reingau, Germany.

the Ammonites, shall be the LORD's, to be offered up by me as a burnt offering." (NRSV, Judges 11:31) Jephthah was so enamored with the idea of military conquest that he did not consider the ramifications of such a rash, unholy vow.

Why did Jephthah vow to sacrifice a person? After all, the sacrifice of people was banned by the laws handed down by Moses.

It is possible that the "whoever" is a mistranslation. The intended word might be "whatever," in which case, Jephthah referred to an animal, not a person. Indeed, the word "whatever" is used in the New International Version and in The Message; "thing" is used in the New Living Translation, and "whatsoever" in the King James Version.

Who was the first person to come out of Jephthah's house after he returned victorious from fighting with the Ammonites?

The person was Jephthah's only child, a daughter. She came out of the house playing timbrels and dancing.

Did Jephthah sacrifice her?

Yes, he did. Before that, however, he honored his daughter's request to roam the mountains with her friends for two months mourning her virginity. Ironically, Jephthah delivered the Israelites from the Ammonites, a group known for sacrificing their children. In the end, Jephthah sacrificed his child, too.

Did Jephthah say "Po-tay-to" or "Po-tah-to"?

The Bible does not address Jephthah's pronunciation of "potato." However, the Bible does say how Jephthah pronounced another word—"shibboleth." The pronunciation debacle came about when Jephthah and his men quarreled with a neighboring tribe, the Ephraimites. When the Ephraimites tried to get back across the river to their land, Jephthah and his men devised a test. Jephthah and his men stopped each Ephraimite as he came across, and asked him if he was an Ephraimite. Each Ephraimite wanted to save his hide, so he said "no." Then Jephthah and his men asked each Ephraimite to pronounce "shibboleth". If the Ephraimite said "sibboleth," he was killed promptly. Evidently, leaving out the "h" sound was a dead (ooh, bad pun) giveaway that the Ephraimite was indeed an enemy. Leaving out the "h" sound was common—42,000 Ephraimites died as a result of failing Jephthah's test. (Judges 12)

What did Ibzan do?

Ibzan of Bethlehem judged after Jephthah. He disobeyed God's laws by allowing his children to intermarry with people who were not Israelites. He judged Israel for seven years.

What did Elon do?

Elon was of the tribe of Zebulon. He judged Israel for ten years.

What did Abdon do?

Abdon, son of Hillel, the Pirathonite, judged after Elon. He judged Israel for eight years.

What did Samson do?

Before Samson was even conceived, an angel of God visited his mother. The angel said to her, "Behold now, thou art barren, and bearest not: but thou shalt conceive, and bear a son. Now therefore beware, I pray thee, and drink not wine nor strong drink, and not any unclean thing: For lo, thou shalt conceive, and bear a son; and no razor shall come on his head: for the child shall be a Nazirite unto God from the womb: he shall begin to deliver Israel out of the hand of the Philistines." (KJV, Judges 13:3–5) Here is another example of God using an unlikely person in unfavorable circumstances to carry out his will.

Why didn't Samson's parents want him to marry a Philistine?

Samson's parents tried to dissuade him from seeking a wife among the Philistines because the Law of Moses forbade marrying with other peoples. However, God used Samson's desire for good. Living with the Philistines later gave Samson the opportunity to act against them.

What happened when Samson came across a lion?

The spirit of God entered him, and he tore the lion to pieces. Then Samson made a couple of selfish, unholy decisions. First, he did not tell his mother and father what happened. Since he was a Nazirite, his parents would make him observe the eight-day purification ritual. Presumably, Samson did not want to participate in that. Second, when Samson found bees and a honeycomb in the lion carcass, he ate of the honey and took some to his parents as well. Samson did not care that eating something from a dead animal made him and his parents ritually unclean.

What happened when Samson told riddles?

Nothing good came out of Samson's riddles. At his wedding feast, Samson promised his companions fancy clothes if they solved his riddle, "Out of the eater came forth meat, and out of the strong came forth sweetness" (KJV, Judges 14:14) Samson did not think his companions would be able to figure the riddle out. However, his new wife coaxed the answer out of him. Then his wife told her people the answer to the riddle. Samson got mad and killed thirty men of the town. He took their clothes and settled his bet. After that, he gave his wife to his best man.

Why did Samson light the tails of three hundred foxes?

Samson attempted reconciliation with his wife by offering her family a goat. The wife's father would not let Samson see her. In a fit of prideful anger, Samson caught three hundred foxes, bound them in pairs by the tails, and set fire to the tails. The foxes went berserk in their agony and confusion, spreading fire to the Philistine crops.

What did Samson's relatives think of all this?

They got mad at Samson because he provoked the Philistines to anger. Three thousand Israelites captured Samson and bound his arms so they could turn him in to the Philistines. When the Philistines approached, the spirit of God entered Samson, and he broke the cords as if they were made of paper.

What use did Samson find for the jawbone of a donkey?

Samson killed one thousand Philistines with a donkey jawbone.

What happened when Samson fell in love with Delilah?

Delilah stole Samson's strength by cutting his hair, as shown here in a 1495 artwork by Andrea Mantegna.

The Philistines told Delilah to persuade Samson to tell her what the source of his strength was. She tried to get the answer from Samson. At first, Samson teased her with false answers. Eventually, though, he told her the truth: "There hath not come a razor upon mine head; for I have for I have been a Nazirite unto God from my mother's womb: If I be shaven, then my strength will go from me, and I shall become weak, and be like other men." (KJV, Judges 16:17)

Did Delilah give this information to the Philistines?

Yes. She did so quickly, and accepted their money in return. While Samson was asleep, she called in a barber to shave his head. Then Delilah cried, "The Philistines be upon thee, Samson!" (KJV, Judges 16:20) Samson woke up expecting to best the Philistines as he had done before. Because his hair was gone, however, he could not. The power of God was gone from him.

What did the Philistines do to Samson?

They gouged out his eyes, bound him with bronze shackles, and set him to grinding grain, a task usually done by women.

How did Samson use a natural occurrence to get revenge on the Philistines?

Samson's hair grew back. So did his strength. When the Philistines brought Samson out to show him off at a party, he prayed to God and used the last of his strength to push down the pillars that supported the house. Everyone, including Samson, was killed.

Samson helped the Israelites by killing some of their enemies, but he could have done so much more if he had lived according to God's laws.

TRIBE AGAINST TRIBE

What horrific event was the precursor for conflict between the twelve tribes?

It all started with a Levite, a member of the priestly tribe. This certain Levite had a concubine who was of the tribe of Judah. After traveling all day, they sought shelter in Gibeah, a town belonging to the Benjaminites. None of the Benjaminites offered them hospitality. A man from the tribe of Ephraim, however, happened to be staying in Gibeah because of his work. He offered the Levite and his concubine shelter for the night. At some point during the night, some wicked men from Gibeah started pounding on the Ephraimite's door, and demanded that he send the Levite out to him so they could rape him.

Did the Ephraimite obey the men?

The Ephraimite tried to distract the wicked men by offering them his own daughter and the Levite's concubine instead. The Ephraimite pleaded, "Ravish them and do whatever you want to them; but against this man do not do such a vile thing." (NRSV, Judges 19:24) The wicked men were not appeased, so the Levite threw his concubine out to the wicked men. The men raped and abused the concubine until dawn, at which point the woman crawled to the door of the Ephraimite and collapsed.

At full light, the concubine's "master got up, opened the doors of the house, and when he went out to go his way, there was his concubine lying at the door of the house, with her hands on the threshold. 'Get up,' he said to her, 'we are going.' But there was no answer. Then he put her on the donkey; and the man set out for his home." (NRSV, Judges 19:27–28)

Was the woman alive or dead?

The Bible does not say whether the woman died of the brutal attack, or whether she died on the journey home. Maybe she was dead then; maybe not. What the Bible does say is that when the Levite got home with his concubine, he took a knife and cut her into twelve pieces. He sent one piece to each of the twelve tribes with this message, "Has such a thing ever happened since the day that the Israelites came up from the land of Egypt until this day? Consider it, take counsel, and speak out." (NRSV, Judges 19:30) As far as the other tribes knew, the Levite was blameless in the whole affair. So the Levite was willing to pit the majority of the tribes against the Benjaminites, just so he could have revenge.

What did the Benjaminites say to all of this?

The other tribes gave them a chance to send out the wicked men for punishment and spare the rest of the Benjaminites. The Benjaminites refused this offer, and civil war ensued.

What happened to the Benjaminites?

The other tribes defeated them. The Benjaminite population was decimated. Their cities were razed and burned. After the battle, the other tribes swore not to give any of their children in marriage to the Benjaminites who were left.

Did the Benjaminite tribe die out then?

No. In a tragic move of irony, the elders of the tribes gave the remaining Benjaminites the authorization to kidnap virgins from Shiloh and take them as wives. The practice of rape continued. Thus, the book of Judges ends with tribes acting without consulting God, and in direct defiance of his laws.

RUTH

What is the book of Ruth about?

The events in Ruth took place during the time of the judges. However, Ruth and Judges differ greatly in terms of themes and overall tone. Judges is weighted with details of battles, pillaging, and conquests. Ruth, on the other hand, is a warm, earthy account of rural living, family, and love. Ruth relates how a Moabite woman named Ruth met and married Boaz. Today, Ruth continues to be held up as a model of faith and loyalty.

Who was Naomi?

Naomi was the wife of Abimelech of the tribe of Judah. They had two sons, Mahlon and Chilion.

Whom did the sons marry?

Both sons married Moabite women. One was named Orpah, the other was named Ruth.

How did Ruth and Naomi end up alone?

The book of Ruth does not begin happily. Abimelech died. Mahlon and Chilion died. Orpah went back to her family. It was just Ruth and Naomi. They were poor, and they were women. Being a poor widow in ancient times was a scary proposition. Women could not earn a respectable living without the help of a man. Just about the only course open to a widow was to go back to her family. Orpah saw the wisdom in this option, and

---

What modern-day television mogul is named after Orpah?

Oprah Winfrey was named after Orpah. Oprah was born Orpah Gail Winfrey, but her family took to calling her "Oprah," and the name stuck.

returned to her family. Ruth, however, refused to go back to her family. She pleaded with Naomi, "Don't force me to leave you; don't make me go home. Where you go, I go: and where you live, I'll live. Your people are my people, your God is my god; where you die, I'll die, and that's where I'll be buried, so help me GOD—not even death itself is going to come between us!" (The Message, Ruth 1:16)

Ruth's statement is not an idle promise made to pacify her worried mother-in-law. Ruth's statement is a vow before God, a vow made from the outpouring of her sincere love and generosity.

Where did Ruth and Naomi go?

They went to Bethlehem, Naomi's hometown, arriving at the time of the barley harvest. There, the women of the town wondered at Naomi's reduced state in life. So Naomi said she wanted to change her name to Mara, which means "bitter."

Is Ruth's Moabite heritage important in the story?

Yes. The Moabites were the ancestors of Lot's incestuous relationship with his oldest daughter. Because Lot was Abraham's nephew, the Moabites were related distantly to the Israelites. The Moabites, like many of their Canaanite neighbors, worshiped many

After the death of her husband and sons, Naomi decided to move back with her family. Her daughter-in-law Ruth made a vow before God to stay by her side, while the other daughter-in-law, Orpah, went back to her own family.

gods and engaged in human sacrifice. Thus, the Moabites were seen as a snare to the Israelites. So when Ruth arrived in Bethlehem, she was viewed as an outsider.

Who was Boaz?

Boaz was a distant relative of Naomi's husband.

What is *hesed*, and why is it important in the book of Ruth?

Hesed is a Hebrew word that does not have a precise equivalent in English. In his 1535 translation of the Bible, Miles Coverdale translated hesed as "loving-kindness," a term that is used to this day. *Hesed* encompasses the covenant love between God and his people. It is merciful and compassionate. The concept is important throughout Ruth, manifesting itself in how the people treat each other.

How did Boaz and Ruth meet?

As a poor, foreign widow, Ruth was entitled to glean the fields. Evidently she knew the Israelite law handed down from Moses: "When you harvest your grain and forget a sheaf back in the field, don't go back and get it; leave it for the foreigner, the orphan, and the widow so that GOD, your God, will bless you in all your work." (The Message, Deuteronomy 24:19) So she went out to Boaz's fields and worked behind his workers, picking up what they left behind. Boaz saw Ruth, and invited her to work in his fields throughout the harvest. In that way, Ruth's safety was assured.

How did Ruth respond to Boaz's generosity?

She fell down at his feet and cried, "Why have I found such favor in your eyes, that you me, a foreigner?" Boaz replied, "I've been told all about what you have done for our mother-in-law since the death of your husband—how you left your father and mother and your homeland and came to live with a people you did not know before. May the LORD repay you for what you have done. May you be richly rewarded by the LORD, the God of Israel, under whose wings you have come to take refuge" (NIV, Ruth 2:11–12)

BRINGING IN THE SHEAVES

What work was required to harvest barley?

Just before the barley was ripe, workers went through the fields reaping, or cutting down, the stalks of barley with a sickle. Then workers went through the fields and gathered up the stalks into bundles called sheaves. The sheaves were stacked upright in groups, or shocks, of fifteen to twenty. The sheaves leaned against each other, making a pyramid shape. Standing the sheaves, as opposed to leaving them on the ground, allowed air to circulate through them, thereby preventing mold or rot.

After a few days, the shocks were taken to the threshing floor, a circular, paved area outdoors. The shocks were loosened and scattered over the threshing floor. Then the valuable grain was loosened, or threshed, from the husks in one of two ways. One option was when a pair of oxen, cattle, donkeys, or horses dragged a heavy, serrated board over the stalks. Another option was when workers used paddles to beat the stalks until the grain was loosened. At this point, workers separated the grain from the chaff, or unusable portion of the stalk, using a pitchfork-type device called a winnowing fork. Using the winnowing forks, workers tossed the broken-down stalks and grain into the air and allowed the wind to carry away the lightweight chaff while the heavier grain fell to the ground. The grain was gathered, then roasted as is, or ground into flour.

Ruth worked hard during the harvest. She gleaned in the field, beat out what she gleaned, and split it with Naomi.

What did Naomi tell Ruth to do in order to ensure a secure future for herself?

Naomi told Ruth to wash up, put on perfume, and go to where Boaz was winnowing barley. Naomi told Ruth that once Boaz laid down to rest, she should lie down and uncover his feet. Naomi assured Ruth that once she did all of this, Boaz would tell her what to do next.

Since Naomi was a widow like Ruth, why didn't she seek out Boaz as a husband?

Naomi was "too old to have a husband." (KJV, Ruth 1:12) Most likely, this meant she was menopausal, and thus unable to bear children. The family line could not continue through Naomi. It had to be done through Ruth.

Is there a double meaning in Naomi's instructions to Ruth?

Maybe. In Hebrew, the word "feet" can be used as a euphemism for genitals. It is not known for sure whether Ruth uncovered Boaz's feet or his "feet." Still, considering Ruth's earlier shows of integrity, it seems most likely that Ruth acted with modesty.

What happened when Ruth did as Naomi instructed?

Boaz awoke and saw Ruth at his feet. Ruth said, "I am Ruth, your servant; spread your cloak over your servant, for you are next of kin." (NRSV, Ruth 3:9) In some translations, "next of kin" is translated as "kinsman redeemer." The concept of kinsman redeemer implies something more than just being a relative. A kinsman redeemer had the privilege and responsibility of acting on behalf of female relatives if the female relatives had no father, brother, or husband.

Boaz informed Ruth that there was a kinsman who was a closer relative than he, so they had to consult him first.

What did covering her with his cloak have to do with anything?

There are two possibilities. Ruth might be asking Boaz to marry her, or she might just be asking for his ongoing protection.

Boaz, a distant relative of Ruth's late husband, saw how hard she worked in the fields and would agree to take care of her.

What did the other kinsman say about protecting or marrying Ruth?

When Boaz approached the other kinsman, Boaz began by saying that he was acting on Naomi's behalf in selling a piece of land that had belonged to her husband. The kinsman, because he was the next relative, had "dibs" on purchasing the property first. Boaz added that Ruth was part of the purchase, so that the dead man's name would continue. The kinsman refused.

What did Boaz do when the kinsman refused the land—and Ruth?

Boaz claimed the right of next of kin. He bought the land and married Ruth. Boaz was a distant relative, not a brother of Naomi's husband. Boaz went beyond the letter of the law to provide protection for his relatives.

Did Boaz and Ruth have any children?

Yes. They had a son, Obed. Obed was like a son to Naomi, too.

Why is the story of Ruth important?

It is a story about love, generosity, and selflessness. It is about people sticking together during rough times, and celebrating together in times of joy. Also, the story provides ad-

109

ditional framework for Jesus' lineage. Ruth, a Moabite, was an unlikely wife for Boaz, an Israelite. Again, God worked through unusual circumstances using humble people to work his will. Ruth and Boaz's son, Obed, was the father of Jesse. Jesse was the father of David. David was an ancestor of Jesus.

I AND II SAMUEL

What are I and II Samuel about?

Though the author or authors of I and II Samuel are unknown, it is likely that the books were written in the years immediately following the Babylonian Captivity.

That being the case, the content of I and II Samuel serves as a refresher history course for the exiles. The two books recount the establishment of the united monarchy, the time when all of the tribes were ruled by one king. First, there was Saul, then David, and then Solomon. Along with I and II Kings, I and II Samuel tell the entire history of the kingdom of Israel. Also, the books remind the exiles why their kingdom crumbled, and why the captivity happened. They and their ancestors broke covenant with God.

Why are there two books of Samuel?

In the Hebrew Bible, Samuel is one book, as is Kings and Chronicles. It was when the Greek translation, the Septuagint, was written that the books were divided in two.

SAMUEL, PRIEST AND LAST JUDGE

Who is Hannah and why did the priest at the temple think she was drunk?

Hannah was to be Samuel's mother. She went to the temple to pray, but because she moved her mouth, yet prayed silently, the priest who saw her thought she was drunk.

What was Hannah's prayer concern?

Hannah was barren for a long time. Her husband's second wife, Peninnah, teased her about it mercilessly. Hannah prayed, "O LORD of hosts, if thou wilt in deed look on the affliction of thine handmaid, and remember me, and not forget thine handmaid, but wilt give unto thine handmaid a man child then I will give him unto the LORD all the days of his life, and there shall no razor come upon his head" (KJV, I Samuel 1:11)

Was Hannah's prayer answered?

Yes. She had a son named Samuel.

What is the Song of Hannah?

That is the name given to Hannah's heartfelt prayer of thanksgiving to God. The song recounts God's greatness and his attention to the poor and sad. One of the most memorable lines of the song is, "For the pillars of the earth are the LORD's, and he hath set the world upon them." (KJV, I Samuel 2:8)

Did Hannah keep her promise to make him a Nazirite?

Yes. When she weaned Samuel, she took him to the temple and left him in the care of the priest, Eli. Most likely, Samuel was two or three years old at the time.

How was Eli the priest tipped off about his sons' imminent death?

Eli's sons were scoundrels. They treated their priestly duties with contempt. So, "a man of God" visited Eli, and told him that God would raise up another priest who would do right by God. Also, the man of God told Eli that his no-account sons would die soon, and both on the same day.

How did Samuel come to be favored by God?

One night, Samuel was lying down in the temple when he heard someone call, "Samuel! Samuel!" He thought it was Eli calling him, so he went to find Eli. Eli assured Samuel that he had not called, so Samuel went back to bed. Again, Samuel heard someone call his name, "Samuel! Samuel!" Again, he thought it was Eli calling him, so he went to find Eli. Eli realized, then, that Samuel heard God calling him. Eli told Samuel to go back to bed, and if he heard the call again to answer, "Speak, LORD, for thy servant heareth." (KJV, I Samuel 3:9) So Samuel did as Eli said. God told Samuel that he would bring down Eli's family.

Did Samuel tell Eli what God said?

At first, Samuel was afraid, but Eli reassured him. So Samuel told Eli what God

At first, Samuel thought it was Eli who had called him, but Eli made him understand that it was God talking to him.

said. After that, God stayed with Samuel as he grew up, and he became a respected prophet and judge in Israel. He was a devout man who cared about the Israelites and their role as God's people.

RAIDERS OF THE ARK

Who stole the Ark of the Covenant?

The Philistines. The Israelites lost to them in battle, and the Philistines captured the Ark. It was at this point that Eli's sons were killed. When Eli heard that the Ark was captured and that his sons were killed, he fell over and died.

Who was born the same day that the Ark was captured?

Ichabod, Eli's grandson. Ichabod's mother died giving birth to him. His name means "the glory has departed from Israel." (KJV, I Samuel 4:21)

What did the Philistines do with the Ark?

They put it in their temple for Dagon, the Philistine god of grain. The next day, the Philistines discovered that the statue of Dagon had fallen down before the Ark, so they stood it back up. The next day, the Philistines discovered that the statue of Dagon had fallen down before the ark again. This time, Dagon's head and hands lay dismembered on the threshold.

Were the Philistines scared by this?

Yes, but there was more to come. In I Samuel 5:6 (NIV), it reads, "The LORD's hand was heavy upon the people of Ashdod and its vicinity; he brought devastation upon them and afflicted them with tumors." The Philistines passed the Ark from city to city, but everywhere it rested, people were afraid. The Ark was with the Philistines for seven months. Then they returned it to the Israelites. They did not return it empty, either. They sent with it five gold tumors and five gold mice as a guilt offering. The gold tumors represented the real tumors, and the mice represented the leaders of the Philistine territories.

Did Samuel have children?

Yes. He had two sons, Joel and Abijah. They were judges, too, but they did not follow in the righteous ways of Samuel. According to the Bible, "They turned aside after dishonest gain and accepted bribes and perverted justice." (NIV, I Samuel 8:3)

Who became judge after Samuel?

No one did. Samuel was the last judge. The Israelites demanded a king. Samuel pointed out reasons having a king was not a good idea: kings demand soldiers, servants, taxes, and gifts. The Israelites argued that they wanted a king because other nations had kings.

SAUL, ISRAEL'S FIRST KING

Who was Israel's first king?

Saul, a Benjaminite. God picked him, and told Samuel to anoint him. Saul reigned from around 1050 B.C.E. to around 1010 B.C.E.

What was Saul's first major undertaking as king?

He recruited three thousand Israelites (See! Samuel said that would happen!), and fought the Philistines.

Was Saul a good king?

Saul started out as king with God's favor upon him. However, Saul began to doubt God, and trust in his own abilities more. Once, while the Philistines pressed in on Saul and his troops, Saul panicked when Samuel did not arrive at the agreed-upon time. So Saul performed the priestly duty of making a burnt offering instead of waiting a little longer for Samuel. On another occasion, Saul made a rash oath by calling down a curse on any of his troops who ate before evening, and before he was avenged of his enemies. Jonathan, Saul's son, was a capable warrior. He did not hear his father make the oath. He ate some honey. When Saul found out, he threatened to kill Jonathan, but the Israelites persuaded him not to do it.

As far as Saul's shortcomings, what was the straw that broke the camel's back?

God told Saul to destroy the Amalekites completely—buildings, people, animals—everything. Saul did not obey, but he told Samuel he did: "May you be blessed by the LORD; I have carried out the command of the LORD." Samuel was no dummy: "What then is this bleating of sheep in my ears, and the lowing of cattle that I hear?" Saul said, 'They have brought them from the Amalekites; for the people spared the best of the sheep and the cattle, to sacrifice to the LORD your God; but the rest we have utterly destroyed.'" (NRSV, I Samuel 15:13–15) Of note, Saul said, "your God", not "our God." This suggests that Saul no longer saw the importance of faithful worship in God. Not only did Saul not obey God's instructions in this battle, he set up a monument to himself afterwards.

Samuel, the last judge of the Israelites, followed God's command and annointed Saul the first king.

Saul asked for forgiveness. Was it lip service? Was it heartfelt? The Bible does not say. What the Bible does say is laced

113

with tragic poignancy: "Samuel said to Saul, 'I will not return with you; for you have rejected the word of the LORD, and the LORD has rejected you from being king over Israel.' As Samuel turned to go away, Saul caught hold of the hem of his robe, and it tore. And Samuel said to him, 'The LORD has torn the kingdom of Israel from you this very day, and has given it to a neighbor of yours, who is better than you.'" (NRSV, I Samuel 15:26–28)

Who was the neighbor?

David, the son of Jesse, a Benjaminite. David reigned as king from around 1010 B.C.E. to around 970 B.C.E.

Why was David an unlikely candidate for the kingship?

He was a shepherd. He was the youngest son in his family. And his family was from the smallest tribe.

Why was David anointed before Saul died?

David needed to know he would be king years before he actually became king. The intervening years gave David the time he needed to study and train for military and political leadership. Once David became Saul's armor bearer, David was in the ideal position to do that. At first, Saul did not know that David was to be king after him. If he had known, he would have tried to kill David immediately. As it was, Saul grew to hate David anyway. Actually, Saul grew to hate a lot of people.

Why was Saul so full of hatred?

The Bible says, "Now the spirit of the LORD departed from Saul, and an evil spirit from the LORD tormented him." (NRSV, I Samuel 16:14)

If God is supremely good, how did an evil spirit come from him?

Scholars continue to debate this. One possibility has to do with shades of meaning. In English, the word "evil" means spiritual wickedness. In Hebrew, "evil" carries with it connotations of dysfunction and suffering, not only in a person but in the physical world as well. So in Saul's case, the evil spirit might refer to, say, mental illness. Many scholars think Saul suffered from clinical depression.

What kind of man was David?

When David was introduced, he was "ruddy, and withal of a beautiful countenance, and goodly to look to." (KJV, I Samuel 16:12) He was religious, musically inclined, shrewd in military matters, and just an all-around smart man. He had flaws, but those became manifest later.

Who was Goliath?

Goliath was a champion warrior of the Philistines.

What circumstances brought David and Goliath face to face?

The Philistine army and the Israelite army were positioned for battle. One army camped on one mountain. The other army camped on the opposite mountain. A valley was between the two armies. Goliath challenged the Israelites to send forth their best man to fight him. Saul and the other Israelites were afraid of Goliath. After all, Goliath was an intimidating figure. He was about nine-and-a-half feet tall. He wore a helmet and armor of bronze. His spear was enormous.

David arrived on the scene, and was incensed that Goliath insulted the Israelites. David volunteered to fight Goliath. David tried on Saul's armor, but it was too big and heavy. David could not move in it, much less fight. So David picked up a few stones and prepared his slingshot.

A classic tale of the little guy beating the odds is David versus Goliath. David's success in war would inspire Saul's hatred.

David called out to Goliath, "Thou comest to me with sword, and a spear, and with a shield: but I come to thee in the name of the LORD of hosts, the God of the armies of Israel, whom thou has defied. This day will the LORD deliver thee into mine hand, and I will smite thee, and take thy head from thee; and I will give the carcasses of the host of the Philistines this day unto the fowls of the air and to the wild beasts of the earth, that all the earth may know that there is a God in Israel. And all this assembly shall know that the LORD saveth not with sword and spear; for the battle is the LORD's and he will give you into our hands." (KJV, I Samuel 17:45–47)

Under the protection of God, David slew Goliath and created one of the most famous and beloved stories in the entire Bible. After David killed Goliath, he went on to become amazingly successful in other military campaigns. He became so successful that people came up with a song, "Saul has killed his thousands, and David his ten thousands." That song added fuel to Saul's dislike of David.

Who was Jonathan?

Jonathan was one of Saul's sons and David's best friend.

Who was Michal?

Michal was one of Saul's daughters and David's first wife.

What did Saul require from David as a marriage present?

Saul required that David bring him one hundred Philistine foreskins. Saul knew the Philistines would not give up their foreskins without a fight. He hoped David would be killed in the fight. David was not killed, and he gave the foreskins to Saul. After that, Saul saw that God was with David. Accordingly, Saul became relentless in his drive to have David killed. As a result, David ran off into the wilderness with some men who were loyal to him.

DAVID THE INSANE

Why did David pretend to be insane?

David was not safe in Israel since Saul sought to kill him. He thought he would be safer with the enemies, the Philistines. The Bible does not say why David thought he would be safer with the Philistines. Perhaps he thought they would not recognize him as the one who killed Goliath, and that they would welcome him as a wayfaring stranger. The Bible does say that when David arrived in the Philistine town, people recognized him right away. After all, in addition to killing Goliath, David had a reputation for exceptional military prowess.

David became afraid when the Philistines recognized him. Would they imprison him? Kill him? So David pretended to be insane: "pounding his head on the city gate and foaming at the mouth, spit dripping from his beard." (The Message, I Samuel 21:13) The Philistines wanted nothing to do with him. Achish the king said, "Can't you see he's crazy? Why did you let him in here? Don't you think I have enough crazy people to put up with as it is without adding another? Get him out of here!" (The Message, I Samuel 21:15) And so, David managed to escape.

Who was Nabal?

He was a "brutish and mean" Calebite. (The Message, I Samuel 25:3) He was wealthy. David and his men provided protection at some point for Nabal's shepherds. David sent some of his men to Nabal to ask him for food or wine as a gift of appreciation. Nabal refused. David readied his men to kill Nabal and Nabal's family, but Abigail intervened.

Who was Abigail?

Abigail was Nabal's wife. She was "intelligent and good-looking." (The Message, I Samuel 25:3) She brought David and his men many gifts, and persuaded David not to kill anyone that day. David was touched by Abigail's gifts and words, and did as she requested. When Nabal found out what she did, " he had a heart attack and fell into a coma." (The Message, I Samuel 25:37) Ten days later, Nabal died. David did not forget Abigail. After Nabal died, David wooed her and married her.

So David was married to Michal and Abigail?

Yes. And Ahinoam of Jezreel. Even though David was married to Michal, Saul gave Michal to another man, Palti of Gallim.

Why did David go back to the Philistines?

David was pursued by Saul. David spent some time in the wilderness, but eventually he sought out the Philistines, hoping to live among them. Achish made David his body-guard, and expected him to participate in raids against the Israelites.

THE WOMAN OF SPIRITS AT ENDOR

Why did Saul seek out a medium?

Mediums were forbidden by Israelite law. Saul, earlier in his reign, rid the land of mediums. However, when the Philistines closed in on the Israelites again, Saul became afraid, and wanted some help. Saul prayed to God, but saw no help in that. So, he wore a disguise and went to see a medium, or woman of spirits, at Endor. There, Saul asked the medium to summon Samuel from the dead. Samuel came, and asked, "Why have you disturbed me by bringing me up?" After hearing Saul's plea of distress, Samuel replied, "Because you did not obey the voice of the LORD, and did not carry out his fierce wrath against Amalek, therefore the LORD has done this thing to you today. Moreover the LORD will give Israel along with you into the hands of the Philistines; and tomorrow you and your sons shall be with me; the LORD will also give the army of Israel into the hands of the Philistines." (NRSV, I Samuel 28:18–19)

The next day, it happened just as Samuel said. Saul was wounded severely. He begged his armor bearer to kill him, but the armor bearer was afraid to do that. So Saul took his own sword and fell upon it. In addition, three of Saul's sons, including Jonathan, were killed that day. The Philistines occupied the Israelite towns.

What is the book of II Samuel about?

This book mainly concerns the rise of David from shepherd to king of all of Israel. The book describes many of David's triumphs, and many of David's sins.

After Saul died, who ruled the Israelite tribes?

This was where the kingships among the tribes got complicated. Ishbaal, one of Saul's sons, became king of most of Israel. David became king of Judah. A lengthy war ensued between the two kingdoms.

Who was Abner?

Abner was the commander of Saul's army. Abner was responsible for installing Ishbaal on the throne. Also, in a show of power, Abner slept with Rizpah, one of Saul's concubines.

Who was Joab?

Joab was the commander of David's army. Abner killed Joab's brother. Joab got mad and killed Abner in return.

Who was Mephibosheth?

Mephibosheth was Saul's youngest son. He was five years old when his father died. When news of Saul's death reached his family, they were afraid they would be killed, too. Mephibosheth's nurse scooped him up and fled. In her haste, the nurse dropped the boy, who became lame in both feet.

What was one of the first things David did that showed his darker side?

David demanded the return of his wife Michal. Michal, Saul's daughter, was married to David, but then given to Paltiel. David did not seem to miss Michal until it became politically expedient for him to have her with him. With Saul's daughter by his side, David had an "in" with Saul's kingdom. Michal had no say in the matter. "Ishbaal sent and took her from her husband Paltiel the son of Laish. But her husband went with her, weeping as he walked behind her all the way to Bahurim. Then Abner said to him, 'Go back home!' So he went." (NIV, II Samuel 3:16). Michal hated David for it.

Who were Baannah and Rechab?

They killed Ishbaal and took his head to David, expecting a reward for killing David's enemy. However, David was angered by their actions, and killed them in turn.

Who ruled Saul's kingdom after Ishbaal was killed?

David became king over all of Israel at this point. The Bible says, "So David reigned over all Israel, doing what was just and right for all his people." (NIV, II Samuel 8:15) Most likely, Michal and Paltiel did not agree with this assessment.

JERUSALEM, CITY OF DAVID, ZION

What is the difference between Jerusalem, City of David, and Zion?

There is no difference. All three names refer to the same place. All three names are used in II Samuel 5 when David conquers the city of Jerusalem and makes it his capital.

A statue of King David at the Borghese Chapel of the Basilica di Santa Maria Maggiore in Rome, Italy.

What happened to the Ark of the Covenant when David became king over all of Israel?

David retrieved the Ark from Kiriath-jearim, where it was left according to I Samuel 7.1. David and thousands of Israelites formed a caravan to transport the ark back to Jerusalem. However, tragedy struck before they arrived at their destination.

What tragedy occurred during the transporting of the ark from Kiriath-jearim to Jerusalem?

At first, the mood was happy. The Bible says, "David and all the people of Israel were celebrating before the LORD with all their might, singing songs and playing all kinds of musical instruments—lyres, harps, tambourines, castanets and cymbals." (NLT, II Samuel 6:5) They transported the ark using a team of oxen. At one point, the oxen stumbled. Uzzah, son of Abinidab the priest, reached out his hand to steady the ark. The Bible says, "The LORD's anger blazed out against Uzzah for doing this, and God struck him dead beside the Ark of God." (NLT, II Samuel 6:7)

Uzzah was just trying to help. Why did God kill him?

For centuries, people have struggled with this scripture. The most prevalent theory is not that God is mean or unfair, but that his actions are sometimes not easy to understand. For example, humans tend to view death as punishment, but maybe for Uzzah it was not.

Was David alarmed by this turn of events?

Yes. "David was afraid of the LORD that day; he said, 'How can I ever bring the Ark of the LORD back into my care?'" (NLT, II Samuel 6:9) So David left the ark at the house of Obed-edom for three months. During that time, God blessed the house of Obed-edom. After that, David took courage and began to transport the ark again.

Who hated the sight of David dancing?

Michal, his wife. She was the one who was Saul's daughter, and was used as a pawn by both her father and husband in political maneuverings. When she saw David come dancing into Jerusalem with the ark, "she was filled with contempt for him." (NLT, II Samuel 6:16)

Once the ark was established in Jerusalem, what was David's next big plan?

He wanted to build a permanent temple for God, but God said no, not yet. God said he wanted to save that for David's heirs.

BATHSHEBA

Who was Bathsheba?

She was the wife of Uriah the Hittite. Uriah was in David's army. Bathsheba was beautiful.   119

How did David and Bathsheba meet?

David was on the roof of his palace when he saw Bathsheba across the way on the roof of her house. She was bathing after her period, as prescribed by Leviticus. David sent a messenger to find out who she was. The messenger came back and reported that the woman was Bathsheba, wife of Uriah the Hittite. Then "David sent messengers to get her, and she came to him, and he lay with her." (NRSV, II Samuel 11:4) Later, Bathsheba realized she was pregnant, and told David. The Bible does not say what Bathsheba thought about all of this. Did she have sex with David willingly, or did he force her?

What did David do when he found out Bathsheba was pregnant?

There was no way the baby could be Uriah's. Uriah was off fighting in David's army. So David arranged for Uriah to come home for a break. David assumed that Uriah would sleep with his wife, but Uriah did not. Instead, Uriah slept on David's doorstep. Uriah explained that he could not in good conscience go sleep in his comfortable home with his beautiful wife when the rest of the army was camping in the open fields.

So did Uriah find out that his wife, Bathsheba, was pregnant with David's child?

No. After David failed to trick Uriah, he plotted to have him killed. David sent word to Joab, the commander of his army, and told him to place Uriah in the most dangerous part of the battle and leave him exposed to the enemy. Joab did as David commanded. Uriah the Hittite was killed.

What happened to Bathsheba after Uriah was killed?

She mourned her husband. Then David sent for her. She lived in the palace, and bore David's son.

Did David's sins get found out?

Yes. God was mad. God told Nathan the priest to tell David that he was in major trouble. Nathan told David that the Lord said, "'Now therefore the sword shall never depart from your house for you have despised me, and have taken the wife of Uriah

King David's lust for the married Bathsheba contributed greatly to his moral downfall in the eyes of God.

the Hittite to be your wife.' Thus says the LORD: 'I will raise up trouble against you from within your own house; and I will take your wives before your eyes and give them to your neighbor, and he shall lie with your wives in the sight of this very sun. For you did it secretly; but I will do this thing before all Israel, and before the sun'." (II Samuel 12:11–12)

In addition, Bathsheba and David's baby became ill and died.

Did David and Bathsheba have other children?

Yes. They had another son, Solomon. Solomon means "his replacement."

GOD MEANT WHAT HE SAID

Who was Amnon?

Amnon was David's firstborn son and his favorite.

Who was Absalom?

Absalom was another of David's sons.

Who was Tamar?

Tamar was one of David's daughters. Tamar and Absalom had the same mother. Amnon had a different mother.

What did Amnon do that began the punishment ordained by God against David?

Amnon was infatuated with his beautiful half-sister, Tamar. He pretended to be ill so that she would come to his house and make him food. When Tamar got to Amnon's house, he began to force himself on her. She protested and pleaded, "No, my brother, do not force me; for such a thing is not done in Israel; do not do anything so vile! As for me, where could I carry my shame?" (NRSV, II Samuel 13:12) Amnon paid no attention to Tamar's words. He raped her. After that, he hated her and sent her away. So "Tamar put ashes on her head, and tore the long robe that she was wearing; she put her hand on her head, and went away, crying aloud as she went." (NRSV, II Samuel 13:19)

Did David find out what Amnon did?

Yes, he found out. He did not do anything about it, though, because Amnon was his firstborn and favorite.

Did Absalom find out what Amnon did?

Yes, Tamar told him. Absalom hated Amnon for what he did, but kept quiet about it for a couple of years.

121

What did Absalom do finally?

During the season of sheepshearing, a time of celebration, Absalom had Amnon killed. After that, Absalom fled to a neighboring kingdom where he stayed for about three years. David missed Absalom, and longed for him to come back. After a few years, Absalom went back to Jerusalem, and was welcomed by David.

Did Absalom and David forge a strong father/son relationship after the tragedies?

No. Absalom had other things on his mind. He went to Hebron, the same place where David was made king of Israel and Judah years before. Many Israelites loved Absalom. He planned to use that to his advantage. He planned to take the throne from David.

Was David concerned at this turn of events?

Yes. David was afraid of Absalom's popularity and increasing power, so he and most of his household fled to the Mount of Olives. David left behind ten concubines to tend his house.

Did Absalom become king?

No. It was not for lack of trying, though. Absalom went to David's palace and slept with the ten concubines who were there looking after things. This showed the Israelites that Absalom was in power. It was just as God said. David took one man's wife and tried to keep it secret. David's son, Absalom, took ten of his father's concubines, and made it so that all of Israel knew about it.

Ultimately, David's men won the battle against Absalom's men. Absalom was killed in a most inglorious manner. As he rode his mule through the battlefield, he passed under a tree. His head got stuck in the branches. While he hung suspended from the tree, one of David's men came and killed him.

Did God's punishment end there?

No. There was another failed insurrection, more battles, and famine.

ON TO THE NEXT BAD THING THAT DAVID DID

What was the next really bad thing David did?

He conducted a census. The Bible does not say why this was bad, but one theory is that David wanting a census meant that he trusted in numbers, and not in God.

Did God have anything to say about the census?

Yes. He was mad. God gave David three options: three years of famine for David and his people, three months of David being pursued by enemies, or three days of pestilence in the land. David said, "I am in deep distress. Let us fall into the hands of the LORD, for his mercy is very great; but do not let me fall into the hands of men." (NIV, II Samuel 24:14) So a pestilence fell on the land. Seventy thousand people died from Dan to Beer-sheba, but God kept the pestilence from spreading to Jerusalem. David was sorry and repented.

I KINGS

What are I and II Kings about?

The authors of these books are unknown. These books describe how the Israelites tried—and, in many cases, failed—to live according to God's laws in the Promised Land. The books describe in methodical detail the reign of each king, and whether or not he obeyed God's laws. Highlights and lowlights of various reigns are included.

Who was next in line to be king after David?

David's son, Adonijah. He was the next son born after Absalom. He was handsome, and David had never been displeased with him. Adonijah "exalted himself, saying, 'I will be king'; he prepared for himself chariots and horsemen, and fifty men to run before him." (NRSV, I Kings 1:5) Adonijah had influential backers, but it was not enough to secure his seat on the throne.

Who became king after David?

Solomon, David's son by Bathsheba. Just before he died, David advised Solomon, "I go the way of the all the earth: be thou strong therefore, and show thyself a man; and keep the charge of the LORD thy God, to walk in his ways, to keep his statutes, and his commandments, and his judgments, and his testimonies, as it is written in the law of Moses, that thou mayest prosper in all that thou doest, and withersoever thou turnest thyself." (KJV, I Kings 2:2–3) Solomon reigned from around 970 B.C.E. to around 931 B.C.E..

Did Solomon do as his father advised?

Solomon loved God and obeyed him—most of the time.

What happened when God appeared to Solomon in a dream?

God asked Solomon, "Ask what I shall give thee." (KJV, I Kings 3:5) Solomon replied, "Give therefore thy servant an understanding heart to judge thy people, that I may discern between good and bad: for who is able to judge this thy so great a people?" (KJV, I Kings 3:9) God was pleased with Solomon's answer. In addition to wisdom, God gave him riches and honor as well.

123

What was the first duty Solomon had after this dream?

Two prostitutes appeared before Solomon requesting his help. One of them told King Solomon,

> Please, my lord, this woman and I live in the same house; and I gave birth while she was in the house. Then on the third day after I gave birth, this woman also gave birth. We were together; there was no one else with us in the house, only the two of us were in the house. Then the woman's son died in the night, because she lay on him. She got up in the middle of the night and took my son from beside me while your servant slept. She laid him at her breast, laid her dead son at my breast. When I rose in the morning to nurse my son, I saw that he was dead; but when I looked at him closely in the morning, clearly it was not the son I had borne. (NRSV, I Kings 3:17–21)

King Solomon, shown here in a Greek Catholic icon created in the eighteenth century, became David's successor.

The women argued before Solomon about who was the rightful mother.

What did Solomon decide?

Solomon told a servant to divide the baby in two with a sword. That way, each woman would have half of the child. The woman who brought the case before Solomon offered to give the baby to the other woman rather than see the baby cut in two. The other woman said it was fine with her if the baby was cut in two—if she could not have the baby, no one would. Solomon believed the first woman, and gave her son back to her.

What were some of the other good things Solomon did in his reign?

He dispensed wisdom to the far ends of the kingdom. Also, "he composed three thousand proverbs, and his songs numbered a thousand and five. He would speak of trees, from the cedar that is in Lebanon to the hyssop that grows in the wall; he would speak of animals, and birds, and reptiles, and fish." (NRSV, I Kings 4:32–33) People from many nations came to hear him speak.

SOLOMON, THE MASTER BUILDER

What was Solomon's biggest building project?

He constructed the temple. Construction on the temple began nearly five hundred years after the Israelites left Egypt. Thousands of men were forced to work on the temple. Solomon spared no expense. The temple took seven years to build.

What did the temple look like?

It was a larger, more substantive version of the Tabernacle used in the wilderness travels. By today's standards, the new temple was small. It measured thirty yards long, ten yards wide, and fifteen yards high. For the time, though, the temple was enormous. It towered over any other structure around.

The temple was built with stone. Elaborate wood carvings of lilies and pomegranates were everywhere. The interior walls were overlaid with gold. The furnishings inside and out were made of bronze, silver, and gold. The temple consisted of a porch, sanctuary, and inner sanctuary.

Aside from being larger and made from more expensive materials, the so-called "molten sea," the large basin where priests bathed before entering the temple, was very innovative in design. It was a large bronze basin measuring fifteen feet across. It was nearly eight feet high. The basin sat on twelve bronze statues of oxen. Three oxen faced west, three faced east, three faced north, and three faced south.

The temple stood for four hundred years until Babylonian invaders ransacked it in 586 B.C.E.

What else did Solomon build?

He built a palace for himself. Again, he spared no expense. The palace was more than twice the size of the temple, and was not just one building, but a series of buildings. Just one part of the palace, the House of the Forest, was bigger than the entire temple. Also, there was the Hall of Pillars, the Hall of the Throne, and homes for his wives. It took nearly twice as long to build the palace as it did to build the temple.

In addition to the temple and the palace, Solomon built many cities. Some of the cities had specific functions. There were cities for his cavalry, cities for his chariots, and cities for storage.

Why did Solomon need cities with such specific functions?

He had a lot of stuff. All that stuff had to be kept and tended to somewhere. For example, Solomon collected horses—12,000 of them. The horses, along with 1400 chariots, were kept and tended in the chariot cities.

Who did Solomon get to build all of this?

He used slave labor. The slaves were the people of countries the Israelites conquered.

125

WHO DO YOU THINK YOU ARE? THE QUEEN OF SHEBA?

Who was the Queen of Sheba?

The Queen of Sheba was—well, the Queen of Sheba. Sheba was located in what is now Yemen. According to the Bible, the queen visited Solomon because she wanted to see whether Solomon was really as wise as his reputation suggested. The queen came to Jerusalem "with a large group of attendants and a great caravan of camels loaded with spices, huge quantities of gold and precious jewels. When she met with Solomon, they talked about everything she had on her mind." (NLT, I Kings 10:2) Solomon answered all of the queen's questions. She was impressed greatly with his wisdom and wealth.

In a lot of classical artworks, such as this circa 1620s piece by Frans Francken, the Queen of Sheba is inaccurately portrayed as white.

Why did the Queen of Sheba go all that way just to hear Solomon talk?

Sure, Solomon was wise, but going on that kind of journey was no small undertaking. Sheba was at the southern tip of the Arabian Peninsula. Jerusalem was 1200 miles to the north. Though the Bible does not say so, it is possible that the queen had other reasons for visiting Solomon. The land of Sheba was a major power in sea trade. It is possible that the Queen of Sheba felt threatened by Solomon's increasing seafaring power. So her trip to Jerusalem could be construed as a treaty-making mission.

What other forms of wealth did Solomon have?

People brought him presents from all over the world. He had "gifts of silver and gold, clothing, weapons, spices, horses, and mules." In addition, Solomon "made silver as plentiful in Jerusalem as stones." (NLT, I Kings 10:25, 27)

SOLOMON'S WEAKNESS FOR WOMEN

How many wives did Solomon have?

He had 700 princess wives, and 300 concubines.

Why did Solomon have so many wives?

There are a few reasons. Solomon loved women. Having so many wives was a sign of his wealth. Also, marrying foreign women helped when it came to forming peaceful or reciprocal alliances with other nations.

How did the presence of so many wives affect Solomon's faith in God?

In laws passed down by Moses, God warned the Israelites about marrying foreign women. God did not want the Israelites to follow the gods of other nations. That is just what happened with Solomon. The Bible says, "In Solomon's old age, they [his foreign wives] turned his heart to worship their gods instead of trusting only in the LORD his God, as his father, David, had done." (NLT, I Kings 11:4)

What did God do after Solomon acquired all of these wives?

God got mad. He swore to Solomon that he would tear all but one tribe away from the house of David, and give the tribes to one of Solomon's servants. God said he would not do this in Solomon's lifetime, but in the reign of his son.

A HOUSE DIVIDED

Who became king after Solomon's death?

One of his many sons, Rehoboam.

Was Rehoboam a good king?

No. He relied on the advice of his buddies instead of the advice of the elders. He insulted the Israelites when they complained of their heavy workload by saying, "My father made your yoke heavy; I will make it even heavier. My father scourged you with whips; I will scourge you with scorpions" (NIV, I Kings 12:11)

Who was the servant that God appointed as the next king?

Jeroboam, an Ephraimite. When Rehoboam insulted the Israelites, all but the tribe of Judah broke off and made Jeroboam their king. Rehoboam remained king of the tribe of Judah.

So there were two kingdoms then?

Yes. The southern kingdom was Judah. It consisted of the tribes of Judah and Benjamin. The capital was Jerusalem. Rehoboam was the king. The northern kingdom was Israel. It consisted of the remaining ten tribes. The capital was Samaria. Jeroboam was king, as God commanded.

Kings of Judah	Kings of Israel
Rehoboam (922–915 B.C.E.)	Jeroboam (922–901 B.C.E.)
Abijah (915–913 B.C.E.)	Nadab (901–900 B.C.E.)
Asa (913–873 B.C.E.)	Baasha (900–877 B.C.E.)
	Elah (877–876 B.C.E.)
	Zimri (876 B.C.E.)
Jehoshaphat (873–849 B.C.E.)	Omri (876–869 B.C.E.)
	Ahab (869—850 B.C.E.)
Jehoram (849–842 B.C.E.)	Ahaziah (850–849 B.C.E.)
Ahaziah (842 B.C.E.)	Jehoram (849–842 B.C.E.)
Athaliah (Queen 842–837 B.C.E.)	Jehu (842–815 B.C.E.)
Joash (837–800 B.C.E.)	Jehoahaz (815–801 B.C.E.)
Amaziah (800–783 B.C.E.)	Joash (801–786 B.C.E.)
Uzziah (783–742 B.C.E.)	Jeroboam II (786–746 B.C.E.)
	Zechariah (746–745 B.C.E.)
	Shallum (745 B.C.E.)
	Menahem (745–738 B.C.E.)
Jotham (742–735 B.C.E.)	Pekakiah (738–737 B.C.E.)
	Pekah (737–732 B.C.E.)
Ahaz (735–715 B.C.E.)	Hoshea (732–724 B.C.E.)
	Fall of Samaria to the Assyrians (722 B.C.E.)
Hezekiah (715–687 B.C.E.)	
Manasseh (687–642 B.C.E.)	
Amon (642–640 B.C.E.)	
Josiah (640–609 B.C.E.)	
Jehoahaz (609 B.C.E.)	
Jehoiakim (609–598 B.C.E.)	
Jehoiachin (598–597 B.C.E.)	
Zedekiah (597–587 B.C.E.)	
Fall of Jerusalem to the Babylonians (587 B.C.E.)	

What was one of the first things that Jeroboam did as king of the northern kingdom?

He disobeyed God's commandments by taking part in idolatry. He was fearful that if his subjects went to Jerusalem to worship as they were accustomed to doing, then their hearts would soften towards Rehoboam. If that happened, Jeroboam was afraid he would be killed. So, Jeroboam made two calves of gold, and told the Israelites that they were the gods who brought them out of Egypt.

Did the Israelites go for that?

Yes, they did. In addition, they embraced the new festivals and new worship places, and they did not mind that Jeroboam made priests out of men who were not Levites.

What major event happened in Jerusalem during Rehoboam's reign?

The Egyptians came and took away the gold treasures in the temple. Rehoboam replaced them with bronze copies.

When Jeroboam and Rehoboam died, did the kingdoms unite?

No. The kingdoms remained split.

THE KINGS OF ISRAEL AND JUDAH

Who became the kings after Jeroboam and Rehoboam died?

For the next 450 years, a variety of kings ruled both Israel and Judah. All of the kings of Judah were descendants of David. Throughout the 450 years, fighting and sinister intrigue between Israel, Judah, and other nations never ceased.

Who were some of the worst kings?

King Ahab was one of the worst. He and his consort, Jezebel, ruled Israel for about twenty years in the mid-800s B.C.E. The Bible says, "Ahab, pushed by his wife Jezebel and in open defiance of GOD, set an all-time record in making big business of evil. He indulged in outrageous obscenities in the world of idols, copying the Amorites whom GOD had earlier kicked out of Israelite territory." (The Message, I Kings 21:26) Jezebel, in fact, was so wicked that her name became a label for any shameless, scheming woman.

King Manasseh was horrible as well. He was the son of a good king, Hezekiah. Manasseh sacrificed his own son in the fire, and practiced all kinds of divination and witchcraft.

One of the worst kings was actually a queen. Her name was Athaliah. The only woman to reign, she brought the worship of Baal to Judah. She was the mother of King Ahaziah, and during his rule she served as his counselor. When he died in battle, she had the male heirs to the throne killed. She sat on the throne for six years and then was replaced by Joash, Ahaziah's son who had managed to escape execution.

Who were some of the best kings?

King Hezekiah brought about extensive religious change in Judah. He commanded that the temple be refurbished, and the idols be removed from all over the land. Also, Hezekiah reinstituted the tithe and religious services. Hezekiah also made sure that in case of siege, Jerusalem would have enough water. He accomplished this by expanding the perimeter of the city walls so that the city's main source of water, the Gihon Spring, was included in

Queen Athaliah was the only woman to reign over Judah. She did so by killing all possible successors to King Ahaziah, but one, Joash, survived. A rebellion brought an end to her six-year reign.

129

the city's defenses. In addition, Hezekiah built an underground tunnel six hundred yards in length through solid rock so that the water could flow freely into the city without the enemy knowing. The tunnel exists today, and is visited frequently by tourists.

King Josiah was a good king, too. After Hezekiah, there were a couple of bad kings, so many of Hezekiah's reforms were abandoned. When Josiah became king, he set about to set things right. He commanded that the temple be refurbished. During the renovations, the high priest found the book of law. When the laws were read to him, Josiah mourned, because he realized Israel had not done as God commanded. After that, Josiah made many positive reforms in Israel by getting rid of idolatrous temples, and reinstituting the worship of God.

Why did the kingships end?

The rule of kings ended at separate times for Israel and Judah. The Israel kingship ended around 722 B.C.E., when the Assyrians destroyed their capital city, Samaria, and captured the Israelites. The Judah kingship ended around 586 B.C.E., when the Babylonians destroyed Jerusalem and captured the Israelites there. Some of the reigns of the kings are chronicled in II Kings.

ELIJAH

Who was Elijah?

Elijah was one of God's prophets. He lived in Israel during the reign of Ahab. Ahab did not like Elijah because he said Elijah always prophesied bad things about him.

What is Elijah known for?

Elijah is known for speaking according to God's word. He warned the Israelites time and time again not to follow other gods and the practices of other religions. By and large, the people ignored him. God gave Elijah the authority to stop it from raining, with the idea that drought would make the Israelites turn back to God. The drought did not have its intended effect. The people continued in their idolatrous ways.

How did God provide for Elijah?

God sent ravens to feed Elijah. (I Kings 17:4) The ravens brought Elijah food in the morning and in the evening. Elijah drank water from a wadi, a stream bed that is filled only during the rainy season.

Later, God sent Elijah to a poor widow's house. The widow was almost out of food for herself and her son, but while Elijah stayed with them, there was enough food for all three of them. At one point, the widow's son got sick and died. Elijah prayed to God, and the son came back to life.

What was the significance of these miraculous events?

These events were testaments of God's power over life and death. The events served to highlight God's power, and to highlight that what Elijah said was the word of God and always true.

How did Elijah shame the prophets revered by Ahab and Jezebel?

Elijah challenged the prophets of Asherah to a kind of duel. The 450 prophets of Baal received a bull. Elijah received a bull. If God set Elijah's bull aflame, then God won. If Baal set the prophets' bull aflame, then Baal won.

Who won?

God, of course. The prophets made a big production of crying and wailing to petition Baal, but they got no response. Elijah taunted the prophets, "Shout louder!… Surely he is a god! Perhaps he is deep in thought, or busy, or traveling. Maybe he is sleeping and must be awakened" (NIV, I Kings 18:27) Elijah encouraged bystanders to soak his bull with water. That way, he could not be accused of trickery. He prayed to God, and God caused the bull to go up in flame. After that, Elijah ran into the wilderness because King Ahab wanted to kill him.

ELIJAH, THE FUGITIVE

Was Elijah happy with this success?

Presumably he was. Still, he became discouraged with life on the run. He begged God to let him die. In despair, Elijah fell asleep under a broom tree. He awoke when an angel touched him on the shoulder and said, "Get up and eat." (NIV, I Kings 19:5) Elijah ate the bread and drank the water that was set before him. He slept again, and was awakened in the same manner again. This time the angel said, "Get up and eat, for the journey is too much for you." (NIV, I Kings 19:7) Elijah received enough strength from that meal to sustain him for forty days and forty nights.

What amazing thing happened to Elijah at Mount Horeb?

Elijah was discouraged and afraid. God came to him with the ultimate encouragement. Elijah saw the presence of God. "Then a great and powerful wind tore the mountains apart and shattered the rocks before the LORD, but the LORD was not in the wind. After the wind there was an earthquake, but the LORD was not in the earthquake. After the earthquake came fire, but the LORD was not in the fire. And after the fire came a gentle whisper." (NIV, I Kings 1911–12)

At this, Elijah wrapped his face in his mantle, and God spoke to him out of the silence.

What did God say?

God told Elijah to go and anoint Hazael as king over Aram, Jehu as king over Israel, and anoint Elisha as his own successor.

King Ahab's wife Jezebel was a villainess in the Bible, persecuting the prophets of God, spreading the worship of false gods such as Baal, and using false evidence to have Naboth put to death. She was later killed by her own retinue.

ELIJAH MEETS HIS NEMESIS AGAIN

Did Elijah ever meet King Ahab again?

King Ahab wanted Naboth's fine vineyard. Naboth would not hand it over because the vineyard was on his ancestral land. King Ahab pouted. He went to bed. He refused to eat. Queen Jezebel came up with a plan to make King Ahab feel better.

What was Jezebel's plan?

She had Naboth framed for treason. He was stoned to death. King Ahab got his vineyard.

What was Elijah's role in all of this?

After Naboth was stoned to death, Elijah obeyed God's command, and went to King Ahab. Elijah said to the king, "Thus says the LORD: In the place where dogs licked up the blood of Naboth, dogs will also lick up your blood." (NRSV, I Kings 21:19) Concerning Jezebel, Elijah said, "The dogs shall eat Jezebel within the bounds of Jezreel." (NRSV, I Kings 21:23) Jezreel was the town where King Ahab and Queen Jezebel lived. It happened just as God said it would.

II KINGS

How does II Kings begin?

King Ahaziah of Israel fell through a lattice in his upper chamber. He sent messengers to the prophets of Baal to ask if he would recover from his injuries. God sent Elijah to intervene. Elijah said to the messengers, "Is it because there is no God in Israel that you are going to inquire of Baal-zebub, the god of Ekron?" (NRSV, II Kings 1:3) Ahaziah died as a result of his injuries.

Who was Elisha?

Elisha was the man God told Elijah to recruit as his successor. Elisha and Elijah traveled together for a while before God took Elijah. Elisha was devoted to God and Elijah.

How did God take Elijah?

As Elijah and Elisha were talking, a chariot of fire and horses separated the two of them, and Elijah was taken up into heaven in a whirlwind. Elisha received a double portion of Elijah's spirit.

What did Elisha look like?

The only thing the Bible says about his physical description is that he was bald. Baldness was looked upon with suspicion in Elisha's day. It was a sign of mourning, or a sign of sickness. Bald men were not allowed to serve as Levitical priests.

In what ways did God show his power through Elisha?

Through God, Elisha saved a widow from being forced to sell her children as slaves to satisfy her deceased husband's creditors. Elisha accomplished this by increasing the amount of lamp oil that the woman owned so much that she was able to sell the oil, pay her husband's debts, and live off of the proceeds.

Another miraculous event occurred when Elisha promised a kind but barren woman that she would have a son. The woman did have a son. A few years later, when the son became ill and died, Elisha prayed to God in distress, and the boy was brought back to life.

How did Elisha feel about his baldness?

It mattered to him. One day as Elisha walked along, some boys came up to him and taunted him, "Go away, you baldhead.... Go away, you baldhead!" (NLT, II Kings 2:23) Elisha got mad and cursed them in God's name. Two bears came out of the woods and mauled some of the boys.

133

On another occasion, God gave Elisha the power to cure a commander of the army, Naaman, of leprosy. Elisha did not meet Naaman, but sent a messenger, saying, "Go and wash yourself seven times in the Jordan River. Then your skin will be restored, and you will be healed of leprosy." Naaman felt slighted. "I expected him to wave his hand over the leprosy and call on the name of the LORD his God and heal me! Aren't the Abana River and Pharpar River of Damascus, better than all the rivers of Israel put together? Why shouldn't I wash in them and be healed?" Naaman's servants counseled him, "Sir, if the prophet had told you to do some great thing, wouldn't you have done it? So you should certainly obey him when he says simply to go and wash and be cured!" So Naaman went and did as Elisha instructed and he was cured of the leprosy. (NLT, II Kings 5:10–13) Elisha's actions foreshadow those of Jesus many years later.

THE ASSYRIAN CAPTIVITY

What major event happened shortly after Elisha's death?

During King Hezekiah's reign, the Israelites feared the imminent threat of the Assyrians. Hezekiah prayed to God, and God promised that the Assyrians would not enter their gates. The Assyrians camped outside of the city gates fully prepared to conquer Jerusalem the next day. That night, however, God struck the Assyrian camp. When dawn came, 185,000 Assyrians were dead.

Was that the end of the Assyrians?

No. There continued to be antagonism between them and the Israelites. Around 722 B.C.E., when Hoshea was king of the northern kingdom of Israel, King Shalmaneser of Assyria conquered Israel. He scattered the Israelites throughout his empire. This policy for handling prisoners of war shattered the captives' sense of national unity, thereby decreasing the likelihood they would rebel. This became known as the Assyrian Captivity, the less well known, but no less significant, counterpart of the Babylonian Captivity.

Who were the Assyrians?

Assyria was a major player in the ancient Near East. Between 875 B.C.E. and 627 B.C.E., it nearly tripled in size. It formed in what is now part of Turkey, part of Syria, and part of Iraq. It grew to include more portions of what is now Turkey, Syria, and Iraq, plus portions of modern-day Iran and Egypt.

The Assyrian army had a reputation for fierce fighting and the use of brutality on opposing armies and prisoners of war. The Assyrians worshiped thousands of gods. The Assyrian Empire came to an end in 605 B.C.E. when the Babylonians conquered it.

What happened to the captive Israelites after the Assyrian Empire ended?

The Babylonians had the same practice of scattering conquered peoples. The Israelites were scattered already, so they stayed that way.

THE BABYLONIAN CAPTIVITY

What is the last event recorded in II Kings?

The Babylonian Captivity. King Nebuchadnezzar II of Babylon (reigned 605–562 B.C.E.) came to Judah in 588 B.C.E. and seized Jerusalem. He destroyed Solomon's temple, and had the gold vessels in the temple cut into small pieces and carried back to Babylon. Worse still, he captured tens of thousands of the people of Judah and took them to Babylon. This marked the end of the four-hundred-year rule of the house of David.

Under King Nebuchadnezzar II, the Babylonians invaded Judah in 588 B.C.E., destroying the temple and Jerusalem.

Who were the Babylonians?

Babylon started out as a small province in what is now part of Iraq. As the Assyrian Empire declined, the Babylonians seized the moment to conquer it and take its land. Also, the Babylonian Empire included a large portion of what is now Saudi Arabia. The Babylonians worshiped hundreds—maybe thousands—of gods, many of which were introduced to the empire by conquered peoples.

Why was Babylon so important in the ancient Near East?

Babylon emerged as a state around 2000 B.C.E., roughly the same time of the Hebrew patriarchs. The Babylonians conquered many peoples and took their lands, thereby turning Babylon into an empire. The Babylonian Empire flourished under the rule of King Nebuchadnezzar. It was a model of opulent city life. It was during his reign that the famous Hanging Gardens of Babylon were built. Nebuchadnezzar built the lush gardens with imported plants to please his wife. The Gardens are known as one of the Seven Wonders of the Ancient World. The Babylonian Empire ended in 539 B.C.E. when Cyrus the Great of Persia conquered it.

What was life like for the people of Judah during the captivity, or exile?

Essentially, they were slaves because they were taken forcibly from their homes. However, once they got to Babylon and to the other cities where they were placed, they were allowed to own homes and businesses there.

What happened to the captives when the Babylonian Empire ended?

They were encouraged by the new king to go back to Judah. Some returned, but some stayed in Babylon or went to Egypt, Syria, or Asia Minor. In all of those places, Jewish communities began to flourish. Those who went back to Judah settled into towns and set about to rebuild the temple.

I AND II CHRONICLES

What are I and II Chronicles about?

Essentially, I and II Chronicles recap the events of I and II Samuel and I and II Kings. Some of the negative stuff is left out.

Why is some of the negative stuff left out?

Events like David's affair with Bathsheba were omitted not as a public relations move, but because the Israelites knew all the bad stuff already. The purpose of I and II Chronicles is to remind the Israelites—who are in exile at this time—of God's promises, and how God has protected them through the years and will continue to do so.

I and II Chronicles cover about five hundred years of Jewish history, beginning with King Saul and ending with the Persian Empire releasing the Jewish exiles. The history of the northern kingdom, Israel, is left out entirely because the writer viewed the northern kingdom as an affront to God.

Who was the writer of I and II Chronicles?

Tradition holds that it was Ezra the priest, but that is not definite. Since the author's identity is not certain, the author has come to be known as the Chronicler.

How does I Chronicles begin?

It begins with a genealogy that lists Adam first, and goes up to the time of the last kings of Judah.

Who is the main character in I Chronicles?

David. His military campaigns are listed, as are his efforts to bring the Ark to Jerusalem. One tragedy that is included is David's taking of a census, which God punished by killing thousands of Israelites with a plague.

What other actions of David are recorded in I Chronicles?

David's administrative moves are described. He assigned staff for the temple—the musicians, the gatekeepers, the treasurers, officers, judges, and so on.

How does I Chronicles end?

It ends with the crowning of King Solomon.

How does II Chronicles begin?

It begins with Solomon asking God for wisdom and knowledge.

Who is the main character in II Chronicles?

Solomon. His accomplishments are described, including the building of the new temple, his palace, and cities.

What other actions of Solomon are recorded in II Chronicles?

Solomon's meeting with the Queen of Sheba is described, as is the great wealth attributed to Solomon.

Does II Chronicles describe what happened after Solomon died?

Yes. Rehoboam's ascension to the throne and his reign are described in much more detail than in I Kings. The Chronicler describes Rehoboam's dependence on the bad advice of his pals, but goes on to say that Rehoboam heeded God's word in other matters.

Are the reigns of other kings described?

Yes. The reigns of the other Judean kings are described much in the same way they are described in I and II Kings. At least one account is described in painful detail: the story of Jehoram. Jehoram did not do as God commanded. When he became king, he killed all of his brothers. He made altars to other gods, and led the inhabitants of Judah into idolatry. Jehoram met a terrible end when "the LORD struck him in his bowels with an incurable disease. In the course of time, at the end of two years, his bowels came out because of the disease, and he died in great agony." As if that was not bad enough, no one missed him. The Bible says, "he departed with no one's regret. They buried him in the city of David, but not in the tombs of the kings." (NRSV, II Chronicles 21:18, 20) Jehoram was forty years old when he died.

How does II Chronicles end?

II Chronicles ends with the people of Judah being released from captivity in Babylon by King Cyrus of Persia.

Why did King Cyrus have any say in the matter?

Because King Cyrus of Persia conquered the Babylonians in 539 B.C.E.

How long did the Babylonian Captivity, or Babylonian Exile last?

It lasted for nearly fifty years, from the end of Zedekiah's reign in 586 B.C.E. to the Persian conquest of Babylonia in 539 B.C.E. When King Cyrus took over, he proclaimed, "Thus says King Cyrus of Persia: 'The LORD, the God of heaven, has given me all the kingdoms of the earth, and he has charged me to build him a house at Jerusalem, which is in Judah. Whoever is among you of all his people, may the LORD his God be with him! Let him go up.'" (NRSV, II Chronicles 36:23)

EZRA

Who was Ezra?

Ezra was a descendant of Aaron, Moses' brother. He lived in exile in Babylon. Along with other Jews, he returned to Judah after King Cyrus' edict at the end of II Chronicles. He was a scribe "a ready scribe in the law of Moses, which the LORD God of Israel had given: and the king granted him all his request, according to the hand of the LORD his God upon him." (KJV, Ezra 7:6)

What is the book of Ezra about?

In the Hebrew Bible, Ezra and Nehemiah are one book. In the Protestant Bible, Ezra and Nehemiah are separate books. The book of Ezra, composed around 400 B.C.E., deals with the exiles' return from Babylon, and the completion and the dedication of the new temple.

What did the exiles plan to do when they returned to Judah?

They planned to rebuild the temple. King Cyrus gave back all the treasures King Nebuchadnezzar stole. When the Jews laid the foundation in 537 or 536 B.C.E., they celebrated and praised God.

How many exiles returned to Judah?

Including servants and livestock, 42,360. Evidently, some of the Jews became well-to-do in Babylon.

Was the rebuilding project successful?

Ultimately, yes, but it got off to a rough start. Non-Jews who lived in Judah because of the Assyrian prisoner-of-war relocation policy tried to stop the building by bribing officials, and by spreading rumors about the nature of the Jewish religion. King Artaxerxes of Persia believed the rumors, and had the rebuilding stopped. Building did not resume until around 520 B.C.E., when Darius became king of Persia. Building was completed around 515 B.C.E.

The prophet Ezra was a descendant of Aaron, Moses' brother.

How did the Jewish people celebrate the rebuilding of the temple?

They observed the Passover.

What did Ezra plan to do when he, too, left Babylon and returned to Judah?

He planned to study God's laws, and teach the ordinances and statutes to the people.

Did Ezra have any help?

Yes. King Artaxerxes gave Ezra his full support. The king gave Ezra silver, gold, and animals to take back with him, and the king authorized Ezra to take with him any willing Israelite in Persia back to Judah. Also, the king believed in the importance of the law of Moses, and told Ezra he could reinstitute those laws in Judah.

What happened when Ezra and the others arrived in Jerusalem?

Some of the newly appointed Levitical priests pointed out to Ezra that many of the returned exiles had taken on the worship practices of their foreign neighbors. They worshiped God, but they worshiped many other gods as well.

What did Ezra do when he heard this?

Ezra wrote, "And when I heard this thing, I rent my garment and my mantle, and plucked off the hair of my head and of my beard and sat down astonished." (KJV, Ezra 9:3) These actions were indications of deep grieving. Then Ezra prayed to God, and confessed the collective sin of the people.

How did the people react when they saw Ezra's grief?

The people supported Ezra, and wanted to please him and God. At the suggestion of one of the leaders, the men who had married foreign women while in exile sent their wives away. Any children they had with their foreign wives were sent away as well. The people wanted to be rid of anyone who might tempt them to turn after other gods. Of note, Ezra 10:44 in the Christian Bible says the wives and children were turned away. Ezra 10:44 in the Hebrew Bible does not say that. In the Hebrew Bible, their fate is left unknown.

Where did the foreign wives and children go?

Ezra does not say specifically.

NEHEMIAH

Who was Nehemiah?

Nehemiah, whose name means "Yahweh comforts," was a cupbearer to King Artaxerxes.

What is the book of Nehemiah about?

It is about the rebuilding of the city wall in the mid-fifth century B.C.E. after some of the exiles returned to Jerusalem. Also, it is about the rebirth of communal worship in Judah. Most likely, the book was written shortly after the events described.

What was a cupbearer's job?

It was the cupbearer's responsibility to serve the king his wine. In a time when plots to murder royalty were commonplace, the cupbearer had to be someone whom the king trusted very much. After all, the king did not want his wine to be poisoned.

Nehemiah returned to Jerusalem to repair the destroyed city wall.

Why did Nehemiah want a leave of absence from his job in Persia?

He wanted to go to Judah to repair the city wall of Jerusalem, Judah's capital.

Did King Artaxerxes approve of Nehemiah's leaving?

Yes. He gave Nehemiah letters of introduction so that any authority figure who stopped him would know he had the king's blessing.

What happened when Nehemiah arrived in Jerusalem?

The people of Judah approved of his plan, but there was resistance from instigators among the Samaritans, the Ammonites, the Ashdodites, and others. These troublemakers used insults and lies and threats of violence. As a result, all of the Jewish men carried weapons as they worked on the wall.

Despite these difficulties, the wall went up piece by piece until, fifty-two days later, all the gaps were filled in, and the gates were erected.

What were other obstacles the Jewish people encountered?

In addition to the obstacles brought about by people outside their faith, the Jewish people dealt with infighting as well. Some of the wealthier Jewish people took pledges on loans. Mosaic Law forbids this. When Nehemiah found out, he was angry. He said to the ones in the wrong, "Let us stop this taking of interest. Restore to them, this very day, their fields, their vineyards, their olive orchards, and their houses, and the interest on money, grain, wine, and oil that you have been exacting from them." (NRSV, Nehemiah 5:11) The people saw the error of their ways, and did as Nehemiah said.

What did Judah's neighbors think when the wall was finished?

They were afraid. The wall was a major step in Judah's ascension to nationhood. Other nations saw that as a threat. Also, the neighbors saw the great accomplishment done in so short a time, and "perceived that this work was wrought of our God." (KJV, Nehemiah 6:16) That being said, the Jewish people were considered still to be vassals of Persia. They were expected to give taxes and tribute to the king of Persia.

What significant event took place when the building of the wall was complete?

Ezra the scribe read the Law of Moses to all the people. This prompted the rebirth of community worship among the people.

What are some of the definitive verses from the book of Nehemiah?

"Then I said to them, 'You see the trouble we are in, how Jerusalem lies in ruins with its gates burned. Come, let us rebuild the wall of Jerusalem, so that we may no longer suffer disgrace.'" (NRSV, Nehemiah 2:17)

"All the people gathered together into the square before the Water Gate. They told the scribe Ezra to bring the book of the law of Moses, which the LORD had given to Israel. Accordingly, the priest Ezra brought the law before the assembly, both men and women and all who could hear with understanding." (NRSV, Nehemiah 8:1–2)

ESTHER

What is the book of Esther about?

It is about how a young Jewish woman, Esther, saved her people from being annihilated.

When was Esther written?

The events in Esther took place between 486–465 B.C.E., in Susa, the Persian capital. The king of Persia at the time was Xerxes I, also known as Ahasuerus. The book was written shortly after the events it describes.

How does the book of Esther begin?

It begins with a party. The king had a party that lasted seven days. It was a party for the ages:

> The party was in the garden courtyard of the king's summer house. The courtyard was elaborately decorated with white and blue cotton curtains tied with linen and purple cords to silver rings on marble columns. Silver and gold couches were arranged on a mosaic pavement of porphyry, marble, mother-of-pearl, and colored stones. Drinks were served in gold chalices, each chalice one-of-a-kind. The royal wine flowed freely—a generous king! (The Message, Esther 1:6–7)

What was Esther's Jewish name?

Esther's Jewish name was Hadassah, which means "myrtle." Esther was her Babylonian name.

What happened when the king got drunk?

He told his wife, Queen Vashti, to appear before him and his guests. She was beautiful, and he wanted to show her off. She refused him.

Why did Queen Vashti refuse?

The Bible does not say specifically, but it is possible that she simply did not want to be ogled by men who had been drinking for seven days straight.

What did the king do when Queen Vashti refused?

He got mad. Because he feared her insolence might incite other women to do the same to their husbands, he banished her from his presence forever.

Who became queen after Ahasuerus dethroned Vashti?

There was no one there to take her place. At the advice of servants, the king sponsored what amounted to a mandatory beauty contest. All of the beautiful young virgins from across the land were gathered and brought to the palace, where for one year they were massaged with oil, perfumed, and given special foods and fine clothing. The idea was that by year's end, the king would have a harem full of gorgeous women from whom he could pick his new queen.

Who was Mordecai?

Mordecai was a Jewish man who worked in the king's palace. Mordecai's family was from Jerusalem, but they were taken to Babylonia (now Persia) a hundred years before.

Who was Esther?

Esther was Mordecai's cousin. Because Esther's parents died when she was young, Mordecai raised her as if she was his daughter. Esther was selected to go to the king's palace as one of the beautiful young virgins who would vie for the queen's seat.

Who did the king select to be his queen?

He selected Esther. She pleased him more than any other woman. At Mordecai's command, she did not tell the king about her Jewish ancestry—yet.

How did Esther use her influence with the king?

When Mordecai overheard a plan being made to kill the king, he told Esther about it. Esther told the king, and the people who were plotting to kill the king were discovered and hanged on the gallows.

Who was Haman?

Haman was the king's right-hand man. Haman did not like Mordecai because Mordecai did not bow down to him. Mordecai was a Jew, so Haman persuaded the king to issue an edict that all the Jews in the land be killed. They cast a lot—or *Pur*—to determine the day of execution.

What did Mordecai do about this?

He was distressed. He sent a message to Esther asking her to try to change the king's mind.

After King Xerxes I dismissed his wife, dethroning her, he selected the Jewish woman Esther to be the new queen of Persia.

Did Esther do as Mordecai requested?

Yes, but she had misgivings. It was the custom in the palace that no one enter the king's presence unless summoned. If someone entered the king's presence without being summoned, that person was put to death. Esther had not been summoned in a month. So she was nervous. Mordecai told her, "Don't think that just because you live in the king's house you're the one Jew who will get out of this alive. If you persist in staying silent at a time like this, help and deliverance will arrive for the Jews from someplace else; but you and your family will be wiped out. Who knows? Maybe you were made queen for just such a time as this." (The Message, Esther 4:14) To prepare herself, she fasted for three days, and asked Mordecai to have the other Jews in Susa do the same.

What happened when Esther entered the king's presence?

The king was pleased that she came. He said to her, "And what's your desire, Queen Esther? What do you want? Ask and it's yours—even if it's half my kingdom." (The Message, Esther 5:3)

How did Esther reply?

She did not come right out and tell the king her concern. First, she offered to have two banquets for the king and Haman. The king accepted her offer. Esther provided one banquet right then, and promised to have the second banquet the following day.

What did Haman think about being included?

He was delighted because he thought that was a sure sign that he was esteemed by the queen and king. The only thing that stood in the way of his complete satisfaction was the situation with Mordecai. At his family's encouragement, Haman had a gallows built, intending to have Mordecai hanged there.

What happened when the king could not sleep on the night before the second banquet?

He decided to read over old court records. In his reading, he discovered that Mordecai had not been rewarded for thwarting the plot to kill the king. The king wanted to reward Mordecai for his faithful service.

What happened on the morning of the day of the second banquet?

The king asked Haman for his advice: "What shall be done for the man whom the king wishes to honor?" Haman thought the king meant to honor him, so he replied, "For the man whom the king wishes to honor, let royal robes be brought, which the king has worn, and a horse that the king has ridden, with a royal crown on his head. Let the robes and the horse be handed over to one of the king's most noble officials; let him robe the man whom the king wishes to honor, and let him conduct the man on horseback through the open square of the city, proclaiming before him, 'Thus shall it be done for the man whom the king wishes to honor.'" (NRSV, Esther 6:6, 7–9)

Did the king take Haman's advice?

Yes. However, the man the king wanted to honor was not Haman, but Mordecai.

What did Haman do when he found out?

Haman did as the king commanded. He robed Mordecai in the king's clothes, set him on a horse, and led him around the city square, proclaiming, "Thus shall it be done for the man whom the king wishes to honor." (Esther 6:11)

What happened when the time came for the banquet?

As the king, Haman, and Esther dined together, the king asked Esther again what was her wish. She told the king, "If I have won your favor, O king, and if it pleases the king, let my life be given me—that is my petition—and the lives of my people—that is my request. For we have been sold, I and my people, to be destroyed, to be killed, and to be annihilated." (NRSV, Esther 7:3–4) At this point, Esther explained the whole of Haman's wicked plan to the king.

What was the king's response?

He was angry, and had Haman hanged on the very gallows he built for Mordecai. After that, the king sent out another edict. This one said that the Jews could defend themselves when they were attacked.

How did the Jews respond?

When they were attacked, they fought back. They were strong, and killed many who sought to destroy them.

What was the final result of the conflict with Haman?

Jews wanted to remember always that an enemy tried to determine their fate by casting a lot called *Pur*. They wanted to remember always that they were delivered from that fate. Accordingly, they established a two-day festival to be marked every year. The festival was named Purim, which is the plural form of *Pur*.

WISDOM AND POETICAL BOOKS

JOB

What is the book of Job about?

It is about a devout man, Job, who has it all—good health, sound finances, and a large, loving family. The issue is whether Job remains devout when he loses everything.

Who wrote the book of Job?

The book is anonymous. Scholars think it was written between the seventh and fourth centuries B.C.E. The events recorded might go back as far as the time of Abraham.

How does the book of Job begin?

It begins with heavenly beings presenting themselves before God.

FROM BAD TO WORSE, THEN MORE WORSE

How did Job's change in circumstances begin?

The Bible reads, "One day the heavenly beings came to present themselves before the LORD, and Satan also came among them. The LORD said to Satan, 'Where have you come from?' Satan answered the LORD, 'From going to and fro on the earth, and from walking up and down on it.' The LORD said to Satan, 'Have you considered my servant Job? There is no one like him on the earth, a blameless and upright man who fears God and turns away from evil.' Then Satan answered the LORD, 'Does Job fear God for nothing? Have you not put a fence around him and his house and all that he has, on every side?'" (NRSV, Job 1:6–10)

Why was Satan at a meeting in heaven?

Many scholars believe that in the Old Testament, Satan is not the personal name of the devil as it is in the New Testament. The Hebrew term for Satan is ha-Satan, which means the Accuser or the Adversary. So in the book of Job, Satan is seen as a heavenly prosecutor who goes among men to tempt them, and then reports back to God.

What was Satan's role in Job's tragedies?

First, God allowed Satan to take Job's possessions and kill members of his family. Second, God allowed Satan to afflict Job's body. Satan was convinced Job would end up cursing God.

What were the first tragedies to befall Job?

Job's livestock was killed in a series of horrific events—slaughtered by marauders, burned up by fire from heaven, and stolen by raiders. Then a house collapsed on his children and killed them.

What was Job's reaction to these calamities?

He expressed his grief as was customary: He tore his robe and shaved his head. Also, he worshiped God and said, "Naked I came out of my mother's womb, and naked shall I return thither; the LORD gave, and the LORD hath taken away; blessed be the name of the LORD." (KJV, Job 1:21)

What were the second set of tragedies to befall Job?

God allowed Satan to afflict Job with "loathsome sores" from the soles of his feet to the top of his head. Still, Job did not curse God.

JOB DIDN'T NEED ENEMIES—HE HAD FRIENDS LIKE THESE

Did Job have any friends or family left?

Yes. He had a wife. She was not much help. When Job became covered in sores, his wife said to him, "Doest thou still retain thine integrity? Curse God, and die." (KJV, Job 2:9)

Also, he had three friends who came to visit him. The friends' names were Eliphaz, Bildad, and Zophar. Traditionally, the friends are known as "Job's comforters," because their intent in visiting Job was to offer him sympathy and companionship.

What did Job tell his friends?

Job and his friends had a lengthy discussion about the probable causes of Job's suffering and Job's attitude towards his suffering. Job cursed the day he was born. He cried, "Why did I not die at birth, come forth from the womb and expire? Why were there knees to receive me, or breasts for me to suck?" (NRSV, Job 3:11–12) Job complained that God focused too much of his time on him. In Psalm 5, the psalmist admired God's attention to the minutiae of his life. Here, Job asked for some space: "What are human beings, that you make so much of them, that you set your mind on them, visit them every morning, test them every moment? Will you not look away from me for a while, let me alone until I swallow my spittle?" (Job 7:17–19) Also, Job expressed desire to speak to God one on one: "But I would speak to the Almighty, and I desire to argue my case with God." (NRSV, Job 13:3)

Job talked to his friends about his miseries, and they tried to advise him, but Job felt they were unfairly judging him.

What did Job's friends tell him?

The friends offered lengthy theories on why Job suffered. Eliphaz said that trouble comes to all men, and that it is the duty of men to accept what God sends: "For misery does not come from the earth, nor does trouble sprout from the ground; but human beings are born to trouble just as sparks fly upward." (NRSV, Job 5:6–7) So, Eliphaz reasoned, "How happy is the one whom God reproves; therefore do not despise the discipline of the Almighty. For he wounds, but he binds up; he strikes, but his hands heal. He will deliver you from six troubles; in seven no harm shall touch you." (NRSV, Job 5:17–19)

Bildad added to Eliphaz's reasoning: "Does God pervert justice? Or does the Almighty pervert the right? If your children sinned against him, he delivered them into the power of their transgression." (NRSV, Job 3–4). By this, Bildad suggested that Job must have sinned horribly for God to treat him so.

Zophar accused Job of inflating his own worth at the expense of God. Zophar said, "Should a multitude of words go unanswered, and should one full of talk be vindicated? Should your babble put others to silence, and when you mock, shall no one shame you?" (NRSV, Job 11:2–3) Zophar continued, "Know then that God exacts of you less than your guilt deserves." (NRSV, Job 11:6)

What did Job think of his friends' attempts at comfort?

Job thought their comfort amounted to unfair judgment. He exclaimed, "How long will you torture me? How long will you try to break me with your words? Ten times you have meant to insult me. You should be ashamed of dealing with me so harshly." (NLT, Job 19:2–3) Still, Job did not curse God. Instead, he cried, "But as for me, I know that my Redeemer lives, and that he will stand upon the earth at last. And after my body has

149

decayed, yet in my body I will see God! I will see him for myself. Yes, I will see him with my own eyes. I am overwhelmed at the thought!" (NLT, Job 19:25–27)

Who was Elihu?

Elihu was a fourth friend. Though not mentioned at the beginning, he listened to the conversation between Job, Eliphaz, Bildad, and Zophar, and he criticized all they had to say. The gist of Elihu's argument was that God's actions and reasons are unknowable, and to try to figure them out is not only useless, but arrogant. Elihu said of God and his actions, "He causes things to happen on earth, either as a punishment or as a sign of his unfailing love." (NLT, Job 37:13) "Therefore," Elihu warned, "mortals fear him; he does not regard any who are wise in their own conceit." (NLT, Job 37:24)

THE GRAND FINALE OF THE BOOK OF JOB: GOD

Who besides Job's friends spoke to Job?

After Job's friends finished talking, God spoke to Job out of the whirlwind. God did not give the answers Job or his friends expected. God began by questioning Job: "Where were you when I laid the foundation of the earth? Tell me, if you have understanding. Who determined its measurements—surely you know!" (NRSV, Job 38:4–5)

What else did God say to Job?

God went on to describe the many wonders he created, such as night and day, clouds, seas, stars, rain, and lightning. It is only by God's wisdom that the hawk soars in the sky, and that the eagle makes its nest way up high. All of these things God created and put in their places.

What was Job's response?

Job was awed by God's response, and said, "See, I am of small account, what shall I answer you? I lay my hand on my mouth." (NRSV, Job 40:4) When God finished speaking to him, Job replied, " ... I despise myself and repent in dust and ashes." (NRSV, Job 42:6)

What are the behemoth and the leviathan?

Two mystery animals are mentioned in Job. Job 40:15 (NRSV) reads, "Look at Behemoth, which I made just as I made you; it eats grass like an ox. Its strength is in its loins, and its power in the muscles of its belly." Job 41:1 (NRSV) reads, "Can you draw Leviathan with a fishhook, or press down its tongue with a cord? Can you put a rope in its nose, or pierce its jaw with a hook? Will it make supplications to you? Will it speak soft words to you?" Many scholars think the behemoth is the hippopotamus, and the leviathan is the crocodile.

How does the book of Job end?

God chastised Job's friends for not speaking correctly of God. Job prayed for his friends, and God forgave them. In addition, God restored Job's fortune, "and the LORD gave Job twice as much as he had before." (NRSV, Job 42:10) Job's brothers and sisters came to him and comforted him, and gave him money. In addition, Job had seven more sons and three daughters. Job lived to see his great-great-grandchildren.

PSALMS

What is the book of Psalms about?

The book of Psalms is a collection of sung poetic prayers. The psalms deal with a range of issues. Psalms describes praising, petitioning, following, and falling away from God. Psalms express hope, despair, love, fear, and thanksgiving. The full range of human emotions are expressed in the psalms.

Why were the psalms written?

They were written to be used in the temple. They are still used in Jewish and Christian worship today.

Who wrote the Psalms?

King David wrote many of the psalms. However, some of the psalms reference life in exile, so that means the authorship of the whole collection spans at least five hundred years.

If the psalms are poems, why don't they rhyme?

Hebrew poetry does not rhyme. There is structure, though. Some psalms are acrostic. In other words, some psalms are structured so that the first letters of the stanzas are the Hebrew alphabet in order.

Another common literary device in the psalms is parallelism. This means that the first line in a stanza expresses the same or opposite of what is expressed in the second line of a stanza. One example is found in Psalm 38:11 (KJV). It reads, "My lovers and

What is the longest chapter in the Bible?

The longest chapter of the Bible is in the book of Psalms. Chapter 119 has 176 verses. Chapter 119 is notable, too, because it is an acrostic poem that uses the entire Hebrew alphabet from *aleph* to *tav*. The shortest chapter of the Bible is in the book of Psalms as well. Chapter 117 has two verses.

friends stand aloof from my sore, and my kinsmen stand afar off." The same idea is expressed twice.

In Psalms 37:21 (NRSV), the second idea contrasts with the first idea: "The wicked borroweth, and payeth not again: but the righteous showeth mercy, and giveth." Parallelism is common in the book of Proverbs.

Where does the saying "out of the mouth of babes" originate?

The saying, "out of the mouth of babes" comes from Psalms 8:2 (NRSV). It reads, "Out of the mouth of babes and infants, you have founded a bulwark because of your foes, to silence the enemy and the avenger."

What does "selah" mean?

This word appears at the end of many psalms. No one knows for sure what it means. It might be a musical term instructing the musicians to pause, or sing louder, or sing quieter. It might be a term used to introduce the cymbals. It might mean something else altogether.

What does "miktam" mean?

This word appears in the title of some psalms. No one knows for sure what it means. Some scholars think it might be a musical notation of some sort.

What does "maskil" mean?

This word appears in the title of some psalms. No one knows for sure what it means. Some scholars think it might denote a psalm of instruction.

How are the psalms organized?

The psalms are organized into five books. A short hymn concludes each book. Each short hymn begins with the lyrical formula, "Praise the Lord."

What are the Hallel psalms?

The Hallel psalms are Psalms 113–118. *Hallel* means "praise." Since ancient times, these psalms have been sung by Jews as part of the Passover observation.

What are the Songs of Ascents?

The Songs of Ascents are psalms 120–134. These psalms were designed to be sung without instrumental accompaniment. There are two possible reasons why the word "ascents" is used. "Ascents" might refer to the uphill walk of all pilgrims visiting Jerusalem, or it might refer to climbing the steps of the temple.

PROVERBS

What is the book of Proverbs about?

The book of Proverbs consists of wise sayings designed to provide advice on nearly every kind of human activity. Most of the proverbs are short, snappy sayings that can be committed to memory.

Who wrote the book of Proverbs?

King Solomon is considered to be the author of most of the proverbs. That means the book was written between 970 and 931 B.C.E., the years of King Solomon's reign.

Is gender an issue in the book of Proverbs?

Yes. The proverbs were written by old men for the edification of young men. The proverbial view of women is split. Part of the time women are seen as a snare: "Do not desire her beauty in your heart, and do not let her capture you with her eyelashes; for a prostitute's fee is only a loaf of bread, but the wife of another stalks a man's very life." (NRSV, Proverbs 6:25–26) And: "It is better to live in a corner of the housetop than in a house shared with a contentious wife." (NRSV, Proverbs 21:9)

The rest of the time, women are lauded for their wifely virtues: "Who can find a virtuous and capable wife? She is worth more than precious rubies. Her husband can trust her, and she will greatly enrich his life." (NLT, Proverbs 31:10–11) And: "The man who finds a wife finds a treasure and receives favor from the LORD." (NLT, Proverbs 18:22)

The female gender has another role in Proverbs as well. Wisdom is personified as a woman: "Happy is the person who finds wisdom and gains understanding. For the profit of wisdom is better than silver, and her wages are better than gold." (NLT, Proverbs

---

Did William Shakespeare help translate the King James version of the Bible?

Is it possible that William Shakespeare was one of the translators for the King James Bible? No one knows for sure if this is true, but Psalm 46 provides a tantalizing clue. The forty-sixth word from the beginning of Psalm 46 is "shake". The forty-sixth word from the end of Psalm 46 is "speare". Shakespeare turned 46 in 1610. The King James Bible was written between 1604 and 1611. Either Shakespeare was a translator, or he had an admirer who was.

3:13–14) Another proverb reads, "Does not wisdom call, and does not understanding raise her voice? On the heights, beside the way, at the crossroads she takes her stand; beside the gates in front of the town, at the entrance of the portals she cries out: 'To you, O people, I call, and my cry is to all that live. O simple ones, learn prudence; acquire intelligence, you who lack it.'" (NLT, Proverbs 8:1–5)

Are there themes in the book of Proverbs?

Yes. Some of the recurring ideas are listed here.

- Having a strong work ethic:
  - —"Yet a little sleep, a little slumber, a little folding of the hands to sleep: so shall thy poverty come as one that traveleth; and thy want as an armed man." (KJV, Proverbs 24:33–34)
  - —"As the door turneth upon its hinges, so doth the slothful upon his bed." (KJV, Proverbs 26:14)
- Not being sexually immoral:
  - —"The lips of an immoral woman are as sweet as honey, and her mouth is smoother than oil. But the result is as bitter as poison, sharp as a double-edged sword." (NLT, Proverbs 5:3–4)
  - —"Can a man scoop fire into his lap and not be burned? Can he walk on hot coals and not blister his feet? So it is with the man who sleeps with another man's wife. He who embraces her will not go unpunished." (NLT, Proverbs 6:27–29)
- Not overindulging in food and drink:
  - —"Who has woe? Who has sorrow? Who has strife? Who has complaints? Who has needless bruises? Who has bloodshot eyes? Those who linger over wine, who go to sample bowls of mixed wine." (NIV, Proverbs 23:29–30)
  - —"If you find honey, eat just enough—too much of it, and you will vomit." (NIV, Proverbs 25:16)
- Making sound financial decisions:
  - —"It is senseless to give a pledge, to become surety for a neighbor." (NRSV, Proverbs 17:18)
- Not being a blabbermouth:
  - —"A fool's mouth is his destruction, and his lips are the snare of his soul." (KJV, Proverbs 18:7)
  - "Whoso keepeth his mouth and his tongue keepeth his soul from troubles." (KJV, Proverbs 21:23)
- Forming healthy, lasting friendships:
  - —"One who forgives an affront fosters friendship, but one who dwells on disputes will alienate a friend." (NRSV, Proverbs 17:9)

"Make no friends with those given to anger, and do not associate with hotheads, or you may learn their ways and entangle yourself in a snare." (NRSV, Proverbs 22:24–25)

• Being a generous, just person:

—"Withhold not good from them to whom it is due, when it is in the power of thine hand to do it." (KJV, Proverbs 3:27)

"He that hath a bountiful eye shall be blessed; for he giveth of his bread to the poor." (KJV, Proverbs 22:9)

• Trusting God:

—"Trust in the LORD with all thine heart; and lean not unto thine own understanding." (KJV, Proverbs 3:5)

—"The name of the LORD is a strong tower; the righteous runneth into it, and is safe." (KJV, Proverbs 18:10)

How does the book of Proverbs end?

The book of Proverbs ends with Chapter 31. It is an acrostic poem, alike in structure to some of the poems in the book of Psalms. In this poem, a good wife is praised for her fine qualities. A good wife works hard making food and clothes for her family, she is a smart shopper, and she is generous to the poor.

ECCLESIASTES

What is Ecclesiastes about?

The name Ecclesiastes is from the Hebrew name Qohelet, which means "teacher" or "preacher." Dating the book is difficult. Some scholars point to the use of certain words in the text that suggest a time in the 600s or 500s B.C.E. However, most scholars consider King Solomon to be the author of the book, which dates the book to between 970 and 931 B.C.E.

In the book, the teacher grapples with some tough questions. Why are we here? What's the point of being here?

How does Ecclesiastes begin?

It begins with this introduction: "The words of the Teacher, the son of David, King in Jerusalem. Vanity of vanities, says the Teacher, vanity of vanities! All is vanity!" (NRSV, Ecclesiastes 1:1-2) Vanity in this sense means "meaningless," not "being conceited."

In what ways did the Teacher try to find meaning in life?

He acquired wisdom; he tried to cheer up by drinking; he built buildings and planted vineyards; he acquired many possessions. Still, he concluded, "And I hated everything

I'd accomplished and accumulated on this earth. I can't take it with me—no, I have to leave it to whoever comes after me. Whether they're worthy or worthless and who's to tell? They'll take over the earthly results of my intense thinking and hard work." (The Message, Ecclesiastes 2:18–19)

What are some of the Preacher's thoughts on various matters?

- "There is no new thing under the sun." (KJV, Ecclesiastes 1:9)
- "For in much wisdom is much vexation, and those who increase knowledge increase sorrow." (NRSV, Ecclesiastes 1:18)
- "Two are better than one, because they have a good return for their work: If one falls down, his friend can help him up." (NIV, Ecclesiastes 4:9–10)
- "So I recommend having fun, because there is nothing better for people to do in this world than to eat, drink, and enjoy life. That way they will experience some happiness along with all the hard work God gives them." (NLT, Ecclesiastes 8:15)
- "I returned and saw under the sun, that the race is not to the swift, nor the battle to the strong, neither yet bread to the wise, nor yet riches to men of understanding, nor yet favor to men of skill; but time and chance happeneth to them all." (KJV, Ecclesiastes 9:11)

How does Ecclesiastes end?

It ends in Chapter 12: "Let us hear the conclusion of the whole matter: Fear God, and keep his commandments; for this is the whole duty of man. For God shall bring every work into judgment, with every secret thing, whether it be good, or whether it be evil." (KJV, Ecclesiastes 12:13–14)

THE SONG OF SOLOMON

What is the Song of Solomon about?

The Song of Solomon is a collection of poems celebrating love. Scholars continue to debate the type of love described in the book. Some say the love is that between a man and a woman. Some say the love imagery is symbolic of God's love for his people. The book might have been written in the tenth century B.C.E., or as many as five or six hundred years later. The language in the book is noted for its sensuousness and its vivid imagery.

Are there other names for the Song of Solomon?

Yes. The book is known also as Song of Songs, and the Canticles.

Who are the people in the Song of Solomon?

There are two people, figuratively or literally. One is a man. One is a woman. They take turns speaking.

How does the Song of Solomon begin?

The first line introduces the work as Solomon's. The next line is, "Let him kiss me with the kisses of his mouth: for thy love is better than wine." (KJV, Song of Solomon 1:2)

What is "nard"?

Song of Solomon 1:12 (NRSV) reads, "While the king was on his couch, my nard gave forth its fragrance." Nard is an aromatic ointment derived from the spikenard plant.

What is a "palanquin"?

Song of Solomon 3:9 (NRSV) reads, "King Solomon made himself a palanquin from the wood of Lebanon. He made its posts of silver, its back of gold, its seat of purple; its interior was inlaid with love." A palanquin is a form of transport, usually for one person. It is box-shaped, and is carried on the shoulders of two or more people by the use of poles.

ISAIAH

Who was Isaiah?

Isaiah, whose name means "salvation of the lord," was a prophet active during the reigns of Uzziah, Jotham, Ahaz, and Hezekiah, all kings of the southern kingdom of Judah. The years of Isaiah's work spanned about 740–700 B.C.E. He was passionately committed to spreading the word of God.

What was the role of the prophet in the Bible?

The prophet's role was to give the people messages from God about the present. Another role of the prophet was to advise the king in matters of religion, wars, and social issues. Sometimes prophets spoke of the distant future, but not always.

What is the book of Isaiah about?

The book of Isaiah concerns God's anger at the people of Judah for falling away from God's word. Also, the book is filled with allusions to the birth and ministry of Jesus, some 700 years after Isaiah's lifetime. At God's instruction, Isaiah spoke to the people about his visions. Isaiah wrote with power, persuasion, and elegance. The book is full of vivid imagery and symbolism, making it nearly impossible for scholars to agree on the precise meaning of some of the passages.

ISAIAH, CAN YOU SEE?

How does the book of Isaiah begin?

It begins with Isaiah having a vision.

What did Isaiah see in the vision?

He said he heard God speak to him about the sinful inclination of the people of Judah. God told Isaiah that he was tired of the people's idolatry, arrogance, and selfishness. God wanted the people to return to his laws. When talking to the people, Isaiah pulled no punches: "How is the faithful city become an harlot! It was full of judgment; righteousness lodged in it; but now murderers." (KJV, Isaiah 1:21)

Isaiah told the people that God would punish them, but then redeem them: "Therefore saith the Lord.... 'And I will turn my hand upon thee, and purely purge away thy dross, and take away all thy tin: And I will restore thy judges as at the first, and thy counsellors as at the beginning: afterward thou shalt be called, The city of righteousness, the faithful city.'" (KJV, Isaiah 1:25–26)

What is a seraph?

An angel.

What did Isaiah think about seeing God?

He was awed and afraid. He said, "Woe is me! I am lost, for I am a man of unclean lips, and I live among a people of unclean lips; yet my eyes have seen the King, the LORD of hosts!" (NRSV, Isaiah 6:5)

What was one of Isaiah's most famous visions?

Yes. In Chapter 6, Isaiah described a vision he had in which God sat on his throne: "In the year that King Uzziah died, I saw the LORD sitting on a throne, high and lofty; and the hem of his robe filled the temple. Seraphs were in attendance above him; each had six wings: with two they covered their faces, and with two they covered their feet, and with two they flew. And they called to one another and said: 'Holy, holy, holy is the LORD of hosts; the whole earth is full of his glory.'" (NRSV, Isaiah 6:1–3)

Isaiah went on to describe in vivid detail how the threshold shook and the room filled with smoke.

What happened to Isaiah after he confessed his sin and expressed his awe?

One of the seraphs flew to him and placed a burning coal from the altar on Isaiah's lips and said, "Lo, this hath touched thy lips; and thine iniquity is taken away, and thy sin purged" (KJV, Isaiah 6:7)

Did God speak to Isaiah in the vision?

Yes. God said to him, "Whom shall I send, and who will go for us?" Isaiah replied, "Here am I; send me!" (KJV, Isaiah 6:8)

THE WILLING PROPHET

What did God want Isaiah to do?

First, God wanted Isaiah to give the people bad news. The bad news was that invaders were going to overrun the northern and southern kingdom, and that the northern kingdom, Israel, would be no more. Also, God wanted Isaiah to warn the people that many of them would be taken away as captives.

Second, God wanted Isaiah to give people good news. God told Isaiah to remind the people of God's mercy and love. God told Isaiah that he would bring the people back for a fresh start. One example of this is, "Therefore with joy shall ye draw water out of the wells of salvation. And in that day shall ye say, 'Praise the LORD, call upon his name, declare his doings among the people, make mention that his name is exalted'." (KJV, Isaiah 12:3–4)

Third, God wanted Isaiah to speak oracles against idolatrous foreign nations. One example is an oracle about Babylon: "Even the strongest hearts melt and are afraid. Fear grips them with terrible pangs, like those of a woman about to give birth. They look helplessly at one another as the flames of the burning city reflect on their faces." (NLT, Isaiah 13:8)

What else did God tell Isaiah?

God told Isaiah that he would send a messiah from King David's family to set up a kingdom more wonderful than anything ever seen.

Are there predictions about Jesus in the book of Isaiah?

There are several takes on this. The New Testament cites passages in Isaiah as being predictions of Jesus' birth, ministry, and death. For many Christians, this belief carries on to this day. However, some modern-day Christians believe that Isaiah's prophecies dealt with Isaiah's time only. Then there is the possibility that one theory does not negate the validity of the other. One prediction can apply to more than one event.

For instance, Isaiah 7:14 (NRSV) reads, "Therefore the LORD himself will give you a sign. Look, the young woman is with child and shall bear a son, and shall name him Immanuel." The identity of the young woman could be Mary, the mother of Jesus. If this was the case, Isaiah was speaking of something that will happen some seven hundred years in the future. Or the woman could be Hezekiah's mother or Isaiah's wife. That interpretation means Isaiah was speaking to the people about the impending Assyrian captivity of Israel, and the impending Babylonian Captivity of Judah.

Perhaps the most striking example of how one prophecy can be read more than one way is found in Chapter 53. In this chapter, Isaiah describes the suffering servant: "Surely he has borne our infirmities and carried our diseases; yet we accounted him stricken, struck down by God and afflicted. But he was wounded for our transgressions, crushed for our iniquities; upon him was the punishment that made us whole, and by his bruises we are healed." (NRSV, Isaiah 53:4–5) Many scholars say this is a plain and unveiled prediction of Jesus and his death on the cross, while others say this is a reference to Israel.

Which prophet is quoted more in the New Testament than any other prophet?
Isaiah.

ISAIAH'S APOCALYPSE

What was Isaiah's description of the apocalypse?

In the Bible, an apocalypse is an uncovering or revelation, especially about end times. Isaiah Chapters 24 and 25 uses striking imagery to paint a picture of future calamity. He spoke of the earth's form being twisted (24:1), and of people being caught in snares and pits (24:18).

Is Isaiah's depiction of the apocalypse all doom and destruction?
No. Isaiah spoke of hopeful things, too. He foretold a time when God "will swallow up death in victory; and the Lord GOD will wipe away tears from off all faces." (KJV, Isaiah 25:8)

ISAIAH'S GHOSTWRITER

Is there more than one book of Isaiah?

Some scholars think so. Chapters 40–66 shifts from Isaiah's day to 150 years in the future during the time of the Babylonian captivity. This shift could indicate a different, later authorship, or it could simply indicate a change of topic in Isaiah's prophecy.

Why did Isaiah say that Cyrus was God's anointed?

Chapter 45:1 (NLT) reads, "This is what the LORD says to Cyrus, his anointed one, whose right hand he will empower. Before him, mighty kings will be paralyzed with fear." The Cyrus in this case is Cyrus II, founder of the Persian Empire. He ruled from about

558–530 B.C.E. Isaiah was referring to the as-yet distant event of Cyrus freeing the Jewish exiles and sending them back to their homeland, Judah.

JEREMIAH

Who was Jeremiah?

Jeremiah lived in the kingdom of Judah, and was a prophet during the reigns of King Josiah, King Jehoiakim, and King Zedekiah, until the Babylonian captivity in 587 B.C.E.

What is the book of Jeremiah about?

It is about Jeremiah telling the people of Judah about God's anger with them. God was angry because of their idolatry, social injustice, greed, and all-around wickedness. God was not angry with only the people of Judah. He was angry with the nations surrounding Judah as well.

How does the book of Jeremiah begin?

The book of Jeremiah begins with God commissioning Jeremiah: "Before I formed thee in the belly, I knew thee; and before thou camest forth out of the womb I sanctified thee, and I ordained thee a prophet unto the nations." (KJV, Jeremiah 1:5)

THE RELUCTANT PROPHET

Was Jeremiah willing to be a prophet?

No. When God commissioned him, Jeremiah said, "Ah, Lord GOD! Behold, I cannot speak: for I am a child." (KJV, Jeremiah 1:6) Jeremiah's reluctance, hesitation, and self-doubt continued throughout his career.

What did God want Jeremiah to tell the people?

God told Jeremiah to remind the people how he, God, had led the people through the wilderness, and had never forsaken them. In addition, God told Jeremiah to chastise the people for their idolatrous ways. God said, "Thine own wickedness shall correct thee, and thy backslidings shall reprove thee." (KJV, Jeremiah 2:19)

Jeremiah was a reluctant prophet who was trusted with God's message even though God himself said no one would listen.

161

What was God's warning to Jeremiah?

God told Jeremiah to go about his business of being a prophet but that no one would pay attention to what he said. In addition, God told Jeremiah not to pray for the people, and to be on the lookout because people were plotting to murder him.

What were some of God's specific complaints against the people?

"They know no limits in deeds of wickedness; they do not judge with justice the cause of the orphan, to make it prosper, and they do not defend the rights of the needy." (NRSV, Jeremiah 5:28)

"For their tongues aim lies like poisoned arrows" (NLT, Jeremiah 9:8)

"Like a scarecrow in a melon patch, their idols cannot speak; they must be carried because they cannot walk." (NIV, Jeremiah 10:5).

"The bones of the kings of Judah, the bones of its officials, the bones of its priests, the bones of the inhabitants of Jerusalem shall be brought out of their tombs; and they shall be spread before the sun and the moon and all the host of heaven, which they have loved and served, which they have followed, and which they have inquired of and worshipped; and they shall not be gathered or buried." (NRSV, Jeremiah 8:1–2)

"Therefore I will give their wives unto others, and their fields to them that shall inherit them: for every one [sic] from the least even unto the greatest is given to covetousness, from the prophet even unto the priest every one dealeth falsely." (KJV, Jeremiah 8:10)

A MAN OF VISION

What was one of Jeremiah's first visions?

He saw a boiling pot tilted away from the north. God said to Jeremiah, "Out of the north disaster shall break out on all the inhabitants of the land. For now I am calling all the tribes of the kingdoms of the north, says the LORD; and they shall come and all of them shall set their thrones at the entrance of the gates of Jerusalem, against all its surrounding walls and against all the cities of Judah." (NRSV, Jeremiah 1:14–15)

God did not speak to Jeremiah of only generalities. God said, "I am going to send for all the tribes of the north, says the LORD, even for King Nebuchadnezzar of Babylon, my servant, and I will bring them against this land and its inhabitants, and against all these nations around; I will utterly destroy them, and make them an object of horror and of hissing, and an everlasting disgrace." God continued, "And these nations shall serve the king of Babylon seventy years." (NRSV, Jeremiah 25:8–9, 11) This referred to the impending Babylonian captivity. It happened just as God said it would.

What were some of Jeremiah's other visions?

He saw the results of God's judgment on the people and the planet: "I beheld the earth and, lo, it was without form, and void; and the heavens, and they had no light. I be-

What is a "jeremiad"?

Jeremiah complained so much, he had noun named after him: jeremiad. A jeremiad is a long, mournful complaint.

held the mountains, and, lo, they trembled, and all the hills moved lightly." (KJV, Jeremiah 4:23–24)

Also, Jeremiah saw two baskets of figs placed before the temple. One basket had good figs. The other basket had bad, inedible figs. God told Jeremiah that the basket of good figs represented the remnant of people God planned to bring back from captivity. The basket of bad figs represented those, especially King Zedekiah, who consistently disobeyed God. (Jeremiah: 24:3–10)

God told Jeremiah to go to the potter's house. Once there, Jeremiah saw the potter at work on his wheel. The piece he worked on became misshapen, so he reworked it into another piece. God told Jeremiah, "Behold, as the clay is in the potter's hand, so are ye in mine hand, O house of Israel." (KJV, Jeremiah 18:1–6)

What other things did God tell Jeremiah to do?

God gave Jeremiah several symbolic acts to perform. God told Jeremiah to buy a new loincloth, wear it for a while, and then bury it by the Euphrates. Sometime later, God told Jeremiah to dig it up. The loincloth "was ruined and completely useless." (NIV, Jeremiah 13:7) This symbolized the ruin of Israel and Judah.

God told Jeremiah not to marry or have children while in Judah. If Jeremiah did, they would suffer the same fate as everyone else. Furthermore, Jeremiah was not allowed to mourn the death of anyone. (Jeremiah 16:2–4)

God told Jeremiah to buy a plot of land in Judah as a symbolic gesture of confidence in the future of the people after the Babylonian captivity: "For this is what the LORD Almighty the God of Israel, says: Houses, fields and vineyards will again be bought in this land." (NIV, Jeremiah 32:15)

What were some of Jeremiah's complaints to God about being a moral person and prophet?

"Why does the way of the wicked prosper? Why do all the faithless live at ease?" (NIV, Jeremiah 12:1)

"What sadness is mine, my mother, Oh, that I had died at birth! I am hated everywhere I go." (NLT, Jeremiah 15:10)

"For whenever I speak, I must cry out, I must shout, 'Violence and destruction!' For the word of the LORD has become for me a reproach and a derision all day long. If I say, 'I will not mention him, or speak any more in his name,' then within me there is something like a burning fire shut up in my bones; I am weary with holding it in, and I cannot." (NRSV, Jeremiah 20:9)

"Why was I ever born? My entire life has been filled with trouble, sorrow, and shame?" (NLT, Jeremiah 20:18)

WHAT THE NEIGHBORS THOUGHT

What did the people think about Jeremiah?

Not much. At various times, he was threatened, arrested, thrown into a well, and imprisoned. Some people went so far as to plot his murder.

When the Babylonians came, what happened to Jeremiah?

The Babylonians offered Jeremiah a choice. He could go to Babylonia, where the captain of the guard promised to take good care of him, or he could stay in Judah. Jeremiah chose to stay in Judah.

Did Jeremiah have any good news for the people?

Yes. God told Jeremiah to tell the people that hope was not lost. If the people confessed their guilt, then God would not be angry any longer. The people did not confess their guilt.

Did God plan to desert the people forever?

No. After the conquerors came and took everyone away, God said, "Then I myself will gather the remnant of my flock out of all the lands where I have driven them, and I will bring them back to the fold, and they shall be fruitful and multiply." (NRSV, Jeremiah 23:3)

What are some of the famous verses from Jeremiah?

"Is there no balm in Gilead?" (NRSV, Jeremiah 8:22)

"'For I know the plans I have for you,' declares the LORD, 'plans to prosper you and not to harm you, plans to give you hope and a future. Then you will call upon me and come and pray to me, and I will listen to you. You will seek me and find me when you seek me with all your heart'." (NIV, Jeremiah 29:11–13).

"Yea, I have loved thee with an everlasting love." (KJV, Jeremiah 31:3).

"The days are surely coming, says the LORD, when I will fulfill the promise I made to the house of Judah. In those days and at that time I will cause a righteous Branch to spring up for David; and he shall execute justice and righteousness in the land. In those days Judah will be saved and Jerusalem will live in safety. And this is the name by which it will be called: 'The LORD is our righteousness.'" (NRSV, Jeremiah 33:14–16).

LAMENTATIONS

What is the book of Lamentations about?

The book is a series of five poems that mourn the destruction of Jerusalem by the Babylonians in 586 B.C.E. Most scholars believe Jeremiah wrote Lamentations.

How does the book of Lamentations begin?

It begins with Jerusalem's reaction to the destruction. Jerusalem is likened to a widow: "She sobs through the night; tears stream down her cheeks." (NLT, Lamentations 1:2)

How is the destruction described?

The language is startling in its vivid portrayal of violence and ruin. Murder, cannibalism, rape, torture, and starvation are described:

- "Should mothers eat their little children, those they once bounced on their knees? Should priests and prophets die within the Lord's temple?" (NLT, Lamentations 2:20)
- "Because of thirst the infant's tongue sticks to the roof of its mouth; the children beg for bread, but no one gives it to them." (NIV, Lamentations 4:4)
- "Women are raped in Zion, virgins in the towns of Judah." (NRSV, Lamentations 5:11)

How does the book of Lamentations end?

It ends on a note of tentative hope: "Restore us to yourself, O LORD, that we may return; renew our days as of old unless you have utterly rejected us and are angry with us beyond measure." (NIV, Lamentations 5:21–22)

What are some of the definitive verses from the book of Lamentations?

"Judah has been led away into captivity, afflicted and enslaved. She lives among foreign nations and has no place of rest. Her enemies have chased her down, and she has nowhere to turn." (NLT, Lamentations 1:3).

"The LORD is in the right, for I have rebelled against his word; but hear all you peoples, and behold my suffering; my young women and young men have gone into captivity." (NRSV, Lamentations 1:18).

What does the word "lamentation" mean?

It means an expression of grief or sorrow.

165

"For the LORD will not reject forever. Although he causes grief, he will have compassion according to the abundance of his steadfast love; for he does not willingly afflict or grieve anyone." (NRSV, Lamentations 3:31–33).

EZEKIEL

Who was Ezekiel?

Ezekiel was a prophet who was among those of Judah who were exiled into Babylon in 598 B.C.E. It was in the fifth year of his exile that Ezekiel was called by God to be a prophet.

What is the book of Ezekiel about?

It is about Ezekiel's prophecies against the people of Judah, both those in exile and those still in Judah. The book of Ezekiel is one of the most puzzling books in the Bible. It is filled with surreal imagery and enigmatic symbolism, so much so that it is difficult—if not impossible—to differentiate between Ezekiel's physical experiences and his mental experiences.

How does the book of Ezekiel begin?

It begins with Ezekiel having a vision. As Ezekiel walked along the river Chebar in Babylon, he watched as "an immense dust storm come from the north, an immense cloud with lightning flashing from it, a huge ball of fire glowing like bronze." (The Message, Ezekiel 1:4)

What was in the cloud?

There were four living creatures. Each had the form of a human, but each one had four wings. The sound of the wings was "like the roar of a great waterfall, like the voice of The Strong God, like the noise of a battlefield."(The Message, Ezekiel 1:24) Each figure had four faces. The faces were those of a human, a lion, an ox, and an eagle. The creatures gleamed like polished bronze.

Underneath each creature was a wheel. Each wheel had another wheel inside it. The wheels moved back and forth and to the sides. The creatures moved along with the wheels. This was a chariot. Later, in Chapter 10, the wheels of the chariot are described as being full of eyes.

Above the heads of the creatures was a throne. The creatures guarded the throne. Seated on the throne was a figure shaped like a human. Fiery light surrounded the throne in splendid, beautiful brightness. "This," Ezekiel writes, "was the appearance of the likeness of the glory of the LORD." (NRSV, Ezekiel 1:28)

Was there anything else to the vision?

Yes. God spoke to Ezekiel from the throne. God said, "Mortal, I am sending you to the people of Israel, to a nation of rebels who have rebelled against me.... I am sending you to them, and you shall say to them, 'Thus says the Lord GOD.'" (NRSV, Ezekiel 2:3–4) Ezekiel knew what to tell the people because God had him eat a scroll containing God's message.

What happened to Ezekiel once he received his commission from God?

God swept him up and bore him away, and placed him among the exiles. Ezekiel was in shock from the experience. Stunned, he sat among the people for seven days. Also, God rendered Ezekiel mute unless he was prophesying. Later, when Jerusalem was invaded by the Babylonians, Ezekiel regained his power of speech.

When Ezekiel first received his commission from God, he could only speak in prophecies.

EZEKIEL'S MISSION

What was Ezekiel's first assignment?

Ezekiel drew a picture of Jerusalem on the face of a brick, complete with the conqueror's battering rams and other weapons of siege. Then Ezekiel placed an iron plate between him and the picture. Ezekiel lay down on his left side and stayed like that for 390 days, a symbolic representation of Israel's time in exile. After that, Ezekiel lay down on his right side and stayed like that for forty days, a symbolic representation of Judah's time in exile.

What else did Ezekiel have to do?

He ate coarse bread cooked over animal dung. This foretold the time when the people of Judah would be degraded and impoverished by invaders.

He cut his hair and beard, and threw some of the strands into the fire, struck some of the strands with a sword, and scattered some of the hair in the wind. These three actions represented different ways Jerusalem was going to be destroyed.

VALLEY OF DRY BONES

What was the valley of dry bones?

It was something Ezekiel saw in a vision. In the vision, God took Ezekiel and set him down in the middle of a valley. The valley was full of old, dry bones. God said to Ezekiel, "'Mor-

167

tal, can these bones live?' Ezekiel replied, 'O Lord GOD, you know.' Then God commanded Ezekiel: 'Prophesy to these bones, and say to them; O dry bones, hear the word of the LORD.' As Ezekiel prophesied, 'suddenly there was a noise, a rattling, and the bones came together, bone to its bone.' Also, 'there were sinews on them, and flesh had come upon them, and skin covered them; but there was no breath in them.'" (NRSV, Ezekiel 37:1–8)

Did the bodies receive breath?

Yes. God told Ezekiel to summon the wind. When Ezekiel did, the wind entered the bodies and "they all came to life and stood up on their feet—a great army of them." (NLT, Ezekiel 37:11)

What did the bodies represent?

The bodies represented the decimation and ultimate rejuvenation of the house of Israel.

A LIGHT AT THE END OF THE TUNNEL

Did God give Ezekiel anything hopeful to say?

Yes. God said that the good things would not happen until the time of the exile was finished. After the exile, God promised all kinds of good for the people of Judah:

- "I myself will search for my sheep, and will seek them out." There was more: "I will rescue them from all the places to which they have been scattered on a day of clouds and thick darkness." (NRSV, Ezekiel 34:11, 12)
- "See, I am concerned for you, and I will come to help you. Your ground will be tilled and your crops planted." (NLT, Ezekiel 36:9–11)
- "A new heart also will I give you, and a new spirit will I put within you: and I will take away the stony heart out of your flesh and I will give you an heart of flesh." (KJV, Ezekiel 36:26)

Did God have other plans for the people?

Yes. He gave Ezekiel the blueprints for the restored temple. God gave Ezekiel all the information the people would need to build the temple, including the specifications about sacrifices and priestly duties. In addition, God gave Ezekiel the land assignments for the tribes.

What is hepatoscopy?

The Babylonians practiced hepatoscopy, or fortunetelling by analyzing markings on an animal liver. Ezekiel referenced this: "For the king of Babylon stands at the parting of the way, at the fork in the two roads, to use divination; he shakes the arrows, he consults the teraphim (religious images), he inspects the liver." (NRSV, Ezekiel 21:21)

DANIEL

Who was Daniel?

Daniel was a young man of Jerusalem when he was among those marched into exile in Babylon in 605 B.C.E. He was a man of high standing in Jerusalem, and his intelligence put him in good standing in Babylon. Daniel could interpret dreams and visions. He served as an adviser to kings in Babylon, then in Persia.

What is the book of Daniel about?

The book of Daniel is made up of two parts. The first part, Chapters 1–6, consists of biographical material concerning David and his friends. Daniel and his friends survived under harsh, deadly conditions because they kept the tenets of their faith. They remembered the Hebrews' covenant with God. The second part, Chapters 7–12, consists of Daniel's dreams. The theme of the dreams is that God's people will suffer, but afterwards, they will be restored to him forever.

How does the book of Daniel begin?

It begins with Daniel and his friends being selected to receive special training to serve in the Babylonian court.

"THANKS, BUT I'LL JUST HAVE A SALAD": DANIEL IN THE KING'S COURT

What were Daniel's friends' names?

Their names were Hananiah, Mishael, and Azariah. In Babylon, their names were changed to Shadrach, Meshach, and Abednego. Daniel's name was changed to Belteshazzar.

God gave Daniel the ability to interpret dreams of the king of Babylon.

169

Why were their names changed?

It was common for conquerors to change the names of people they conquered. The idea was that changing names lessened the conquered people's individual and national identity.

Why were Daniel and his friends chosen?

They were chosen because of their noble ranking in Jerusalem, their good looks, and their intelligence.

What was the special training?

It consisted of a thorough three-year education in the literature and language of the Babylonians. The trainees were required to eat food and wine from the royal supplies.

What did Daniel and his friends think of the special training?

They did not mind learning the literature and language as long as they could remain faithful to God. They did not like being forced to partake of the king's food because it went against the strict dietary laws set forth by Moses.

What did Daniel do about the food issue?

Daniel requested that he and his friends be allowed to eat only vegetables and drink water. At first, the king's steward was reluctant to agree to Daniel's proposal, because he was afraid that Daniel and his friends would suffer physically and he, the steward, would get in trouble. After a trial run, however, it was determined that Daniel and his friends thrived under their kosher diet.

NEBUCHADNEZZAR'S FIRST DREAM

What was it like working for Nebuchadnezzar?

Nebuchadnezzar was a loose cannon. He was willful, unreasonable, and quick-tempered. Early in Daniel's career in Babylon, Nebuchadnezzar had a troubling dream. Not only did he want his advisers to tell him the meaning of the dream, he wanted them to describe the dream to him, or else be torn limb from limb.

Was anyone able to do what Nebuchadnezzar commanded in regard to his troubling dream?

Yes. After Daniel and his friends prayed to God, God gave Daniel the insight to reveal the dream and its meaning to the king.

What was the dream?

In the dream, Nebuchadnezzar saw a huge statue in the shape of a man. The head was gold, the chest and arms were silver, the middle and thighs were bronze, the legs were iron, and the feet were part iron and part clay. As the king watched, a rock crushed the feet of the statue. The statue shattered and all of its pieces were scattered by the wind. The rock itself became a mountain that filled the earth.

What was the meaning of the dream?

According to the interpretation God gave to Daniel, the gold head of the statue represented Nebuchadnezzar's kingdom. The other parts of the statue, in order of decreasing monetary value, represented kingdoms to come after the fall of Babylon. The feet of iron and clay represented a split kingdom. The mountain represented God's coming kingdom that would surpass them all.

What kingdoms were represented by the different parts of the statue?

In the Bible, the kingdoms are not named. However, it is common belief that gold represented Babylon, silver represented Media, bronze represented Persia, and iron and clay represented Greece after it was divided following Alexander the Great's death in 323 B.C.E.

Was Nebuchadnezzar impressed with Daniel's interpretation?

Yes, he was impressed. Daniel gave credit to God, but that did not stop the king from acting against God.

FROM THE FRYING PAN INTO THE FIRE

What did the king do that was against God?

The king made a large gold statue and forced everyone in Babylon to worship it, or else be thrown into the fire.

Did everyone follow the king's order?

No. Shadrach, Meshach, and Abednego ignored the king's command, and continued to worship God. They said, "O Nebuchadnezzar, we have no need to present a defense to you in this matter. If our God whom we serve is able to deliver us from the furnace of blazing fire and out of your hand, O king, let him deliver us. But if not, be it known to you, O king, that we will not serve your god, and we will not worship the golden statue that you have set up." (NRSV, Daniel 3:17–18) Shadrach, Meshach, and Abednego were confident that God could rescue them, not that he would rescue them.

What did Nebuchadnezzar do in response to Shadrach, Meshach, and Abednego's rebellion?

He had the furnace heated to seven times its usual intensity. Then he had the trio bound and thrown into the fire. The fire was so hot that the soldier escorting the trio was killed just by standing near the door of the furnace.

171

What happened to Shadrach, Meshach, and Abednego?

They were thrown into the furnace, but they did not die. In fact, when Nebuchadnezzar looked at them, he saw four figures instead of three. The fourth was an angel of God. Nebuchadnezzar called Shadrach, Meshach, and Abednego out from the furnace. Nebuchadnezzar praised the men for their bravery, and acknowledged that God was the one who helped them.

NEBUCHADNEZZAR'S SECOND DREAM

What was Nebuchadnezzar's second dream?

He dreamed of a large, healthy tree standing at the center of the earth. In the dream, a messenger came down from heaven, commanding the tree be cut down, and the stump bound in a band of iron and bronze. In what reads as a mixed metaphor, the messenger said the tree would no longer have the mind of a human, but that of a wild animal. A period of time specified as "seven times" would pass before the tree regained its rightful mind. Scholars continue to debate how long "seven times" was.

Did Daniel interpret this dream?

Yes. He said the tree represented Nebuchadnezzar, a king who provided sustenance for his people like a tree provides fruit and shade for animal and man. As for the rest of the dream, Daniel interpreted it this way: "You will be driven from human society, and you will live in the fields with the wild animals. You will eat grass like a cow, and you will be drenched with the dew of heaven." (NLT, Daniel 4:25) Nebuchadnezzar would stay in this state until he recognized fully God's authority.

Did Nebuchadnezzar's dream come true?

Yes. The Bible says that one day while Nebuchadnezzar was out on the roof of his house, "he was driven from human society. He ate grass like a cow, and he was drenched with the dew of heaven. He lived this way until his hair was as long as eagles' feathers and his nails were like birds' claws." (NLT, Daniel 4:33) When that period was over, Nebuchadnezzar lifted his eyes to heaven. His reason was restored, and he praised God as being ruler of all.

From what mental disease did Nebuchadnezzar suffer?

There are several theories on what specific mental illness afflicted Nebuchadnezzar. One theory is that Nebuchadnezzar suffered from clinical lycanthropy, a condition in which a person believes he is an animal, maybe even a werewolf. Another theory is that Nebuchadnezzar suffered from paralytic dementia as a result of an advanced case of syphilis.

THE WRITING ON THE WALL

Who was King Belshazzar?

The Bible says that Belshazzar was the son and successor of Nebuchadnezzar. Many scholars, however, think that Nabodinus was Belshazzar's father, and that Nebuchadnezzar was more of a mentor to Belshazzar. At any rate, Belshazzar was king or at least co-regent of Babylon for several years.

What events in Belshazzar's life are recorded in the book of Daniel?

A festival he sponsored, and his death.

What did Belshazzar do at the festival?

The Bible says that Belshazzar sponsored a festival for a thousand of his lords. They drank a lot of wine, and worshiped their gods of metal and stone. In addition, Belshazzar and his cohorts drank wine from vessels of gold and silver that Nebuchadnezzar stole from the temple in Jerusalem.

What happened when Belshazzar and the others drank from the vessels from the temple in Jerusalem?

Suddenly, the fingers of a human hand appeared in the air, and began writing on the wall of the palace.

What was Belshazzar's response?

Seeing the hand write under the illumination of a nearby lampstand, Belshazzar grew pale, and so afraid that "that his knees knocked together and his legs gave way." (NIV, Daniel 5:6) He called his magicians, diviners, and wise men to see if they could tell him the meaning of the writing. None of them could interpret the writing.

Did Belshazzar find anyone who could interpret the writing?

Yes. The queen suggested that Belshazzar call Daniel. When Belshazzar summoned Daniel, he promised him wealth and rank. Daniel replied, "You may keep your gifts for yourself and give your rewards to someone else. Nevertheless, I will read the writing for the king and tell him what it means." (NIV, Daniel 5:17)

Daniel interpreted the mysterious writing on the wall for Belshazzar as bad news for the king.

173

What was the meaning of the writing?

The words were "Mene, Mene, Tekel, Parsin." Each of the words has to do with measurement or weight. The word "Mene" meant that God had numbered the days of Belshazzar's kingdom. The word "Tekel" meant that God had weighed Belshazzar as a human being, and found him lacking. The word "Parsin" meant that Belshazzar's kingdom would be divided, and given to the Medes and Persians. That night, Belshazzar was killed, and Darius the Mede took over the kingdom.

A MAN AMONG LIONS

Did Daniel serve Darius as he had Nebuchadnezzar and Belshazzar?

At first, yes. However, some of Darius' officials grew jealous of Daniel, and conspired against him. At his officials' suggestion, King Darius established an edict whereby anyone who prayed to anyone or anything except for the king during the next thirty days would be thrown into the lions' den. This became an irrevocable law.

What was Daniel's reaction to the edict?

He knew about it, but he continued to pray to God every day. Expecting Daniel to react this way, the king's officials were quick to spy on Daniel, and reported back to the king that Daniel broke the law.

What did Darius do when he discovered Daniel broke the law?

He liked Daniel, and did not want harm to come to him. Still, he made the law, and had to see it through. So Darius put Daniel in the den of lions. The Bible says, "A stone was brought and laid on the mouth of the den, and the king sealed it with his own signet and with the signet of his lords, so that nothing might be changed concerning Daniel." (NRSV, Daniel 6:17) Then Darius went to his palace and fasted all night. The next morning, Darius hurried to the lions' den and cried out, "O Daniel, servant of the living God, has your God whom you faithfully serve been able to deliver you from the lions?" (NRSV, Daniel 6:20) Daniel replied, "O king, live forever! My God sent his angel and shut the lions' mouths so that they would not hurt me,

Though Daniel was thrown into the lion pit by Darius, he emerged unharmed because he was guiltless of any wrong doing and God saved him from the lions' teeth.

> ## What was one form of capital punishment in biblical times?
>
> **"D**amnatio ad bestia" is Latin for condemnation to beasts. It refers to the ancient form of capital punishment in which prisoners were put in pens with wild animals until the animals killed them.

because I was found blameless before him; and also before you, O king, I have done no wrong." (NRSV, Daniel 6:22)

DANIEL THE DREAMER

What do Daniel's dreams mean?

For centuries, people have debated this. There are a wide variety of interpretations.

What was Daniel's first recorded dream?

The dream happened during Belshazzar's reign. In the dream, Daniel saw the four winds stirring up the ocean. Four beasts came out of the sea. By and large, it is believed that the beasts refer to specific kingdoms:

1. The first beast was a lion with eagle's wings. As Daniel watched, the beast's wings were plucked off, and the beast was made to stand on two feet like a man. It was given the mind of a human. This beast is thought to represent Babylon.

2. The second beast was a bear, and had three tusks in its mouth. It was told to devour many bodies. This beast is thought to represent the Medo-Persian empire, or Media.

3. The third beast was a leopard with four heads and four wings. Dominion was given to it. This beast is thought to represent Greece or Persia. If it is Greece, the leopard might represent Alexander the Great. The four heads might represent his four generals who, upon Alexander's death, divided the kingdom into four smaller, weaker kingdoms.

4. The fourth beast was stranger and more frightening than the rest. It devoured and tore everything with its strong iron teeth. The beast had ten horns. As Daniel watched, three of the horns fell away to make room for one little horn that had eyes and a mouth that spoke arrogantly. This beast is thought to represent Rome or Greece. If it is Rome, the little horn that spoke arrogantly might represent Nero, the final Roman emperor who was noted for tyranny, murder, and extravagance. If it is Greece, the little horn might represent Antiochus IV Epiphanes, the Seleucid ruler who committed outrageous crimes against the Jews.

5. The ten horns might refer to any number of destructive rulers throughout history—Attila the Hun, Napoleon, or Hitler, for example.

As Daniel watched all of this, thrones were set in place, and the Ancient One took his throne. His "clothing was white as snow, and the hair of his head was white like wool. His throne was flaming with fire, and its wheels were all ablaze." (NIV, Daniel 7:9) Tens of thousands served on God's court. They took their seats and opened their books. The books are thought to hold the recorded deeds of the nations in question.

By and large, this dream is thought to be alike in meaning to the dream Nebuchadnezzar had about the statue made of different kinds of materials in that four kingdoms would arise but ultimately come to ruin by God's hand.

What was Daniel's second recorded dream?

In this dream, Daniel saw a ram standing beside a river. The ram had two long horns of uneven length. The ram charged west, then north, and then south. The ram was stronger than any other creature. As Daniel watched, a male goat appeared from the west. The goat had a horn between its eyes. It attacked the ram, and caused the ram's horns to fall off. The goat trampled the ram. At the height of its power, the goat's horn broke. Four smaller horns took the big horn's place. Out of one of these horns, another horn grew. This horn grew to be very big and powerful. It grew so big that it reached the heavens and threw down some of the heavenly host and stars and trampled on them.

Daniel tried to understand the vision, but could not. Suddenly, a human-like figure appeared beside him. A voice called, "Gabriel, tell this man the meaning of the vision." (NIV, Daniel 8:16) So Gabriel, an archangel and God's messenger, got nearer to Daniel and said, "Understand, O mortal, that the vision is for the time of the end." (NRSV, Daniel 8:17) Gabriel said that the ram with two horns represented the two kings of Media and Persia. The male goat represented the king of Greece. The first horn represented one very powerful Greek king, while the four smaller horns represent four weaker Greek kings. After the Greek kings have their reigns, a bold king will rise up. According to Gabriel, this king would be cunning. He would cause great destruction. Ultimately, this king would be broken by divine power. As in the earlier dream, the powerful Greek king might refer to Alexander the Great, and the four smaller horns might refer to Alexander's four weaker successors.

Was Daniel supposed to reveal this dream to anyone?

No. Gabriel told him, "But seal up the vision, for it concerns the distant future." (NIV, Daniel 8:26)

> ## What is the significance of the number seven?
>
> In the Bible, the number seven represents wholeness and completeness.

What do references to time mean in the book of Daniel?

Daniel uses puzzling phrases when talking about time. Scholars continue to debate the meaning of the phrases. For instance, Daniel says several times that something will happen in "a time, two times, and half a time." No one knows for sure what this phrase means, but there are a couple of prevalent theories. One theory is that "a time" is one year. So the phrase might mean three-and-a-half years. Another theory is that the phrase means a really long time of unspecified duration.

Other time-related terms appear in Daniel 9 when Gabriel speaks to Daniel. Gabriel says, "Seventy weeks are decreed for your people and your holy city; to finish the transgression, to put an end to sin, and to atone for iniquity, to bring in everlasting righteousness...." (NRSV, Daniel 9:24) Again, no one knows for sure what the times mean, but there are theories. Some think that the seventy weeks are interpreted to mean seventy times seven (or 490) years. Others think the seventy weeks are interpreted to mean seventy weeks literally. Still others think the number seventy is symbolic of a time known only to God.

Also, debate continues as to whether Daniel's dreams addressed events in Daniel's time (or soon after his time), or events that have yet to take place.

HOSEA

Who was Hosea?

Hosea, whose name means salvation, was a prophet active from around 750 to around 720 B.C.E., the last thirty years the Northern Kingdom of Israel existed as an independent country.

What is the book of Hosea about?

In the book, Hosea criticizes the social and religious wrongs that were rampant in the Northern Kingdom of Israel before the Assyrians conquered it in 722 B.C.E. Though Hosea began by focusing on Israel, by Chapter 5, he included the Southern Kingdom of Judah as well.

What was the first recorded command God gave to Hosea?

God told Hosea to marry a whore. More precisely, God said, "Find a whore and marry her. Make this whore the mother of your children. And here's why: this whole country has become a whorehouse, unfaithful to me, GOD." (The Message, Hosea 1:2)

Why did God tell Hosea to do that?

God wanted to use Hosea's family life as an illustration of God's relationship with the people of Israel. God loved and protected the people of Israel like a good husband.

Did Hosea do as God commanded?

Yes. Hosea married a woman named Gomer. While they were married, Gomer had three children. Because God told Hosea to have "children of whoredom," presumably the children were not Hosea's. At God's direction, Hosea gave the three children names that symbolized the sorrowful turn the relationship between God and the Israelites took.

Jezreel means "God sows." Lo-ruhamah means "not loved" or "not pitied." Lo-ammi means "no kin of mine."

An eighteenth-century Russian icon shows the prophet Hosea.

Did Hosea prophesy in words as well as actions?

Yes. Hosea pointed out to the people of Israel the many ways they trespassed against God's laws. They stole, swore, lied, and committed adultery. They worshiped idols of gold and silver. The priests sought dishonest gain.

What did Hosea say would happen if the people of Israel did not amend their ways?

Hosea said, "They shall soon writhe under the burden of kings and princes." (NRSV, Hosea 8:10)

Did the people amend their ways?

They did not. By 722 B.C.E., they writhed under the burden of their Assyrian conquerors.

How does the book of Hosea end?

It ends with reassurance from God: "GOD's paths get you where you want to go. Right-living people walk them easily; wrong-living people are always tripping and stumbling." (The Message, Hosea 14:9)

What is another meaning for the word "gomer"?

In addition to being Hosea's wife's name, the word gomer is used to refer to an undesirable hospital patient. In this sense of the word, gomer is an acronym for Get that per-

> ### What sort of imagery did Hosea favor in his prophecies?
>
> He used many images that evoked scenes of family life. Hosea referred to God as a faithful husband and a loving parent. God said, "I led them with cords of human kindness, with bands of love. I was to them like those who lift infants to their cheeks. I bent down and fed them." (NRSV, Hosea 11:4) Also, Hosea used agricultural imagery. God said, "For they sow the wind, and they shall reap the whirlwind." (NRSV, Hosea 8:7)

son *Out of My Emergency Room*. The word *gomer* is used also to describe an oafish, social misfit. Think Gomer Pyle from the 1960s television series *The Andy Griffith Show*.

JOEL

Who was Joel?

Joel, whose name means "Yahweh is God," was a prophet in Judah. The precise dates about Joel's life and career are unknown. Guesses range from 800 B.C.E. to 300 B.C.E.

What is the book of Joel about?

Joel criticized the people for turning away from God. Joel compared an attack of locusts to the wrath of God. Though God punishes, he saves as well.

How did Joel describe the plague of locusts?

It was an event to be remembered throughout all generations: "What the locust swarm has left the great locusts have eaten; what the great locusts have left the young locusts have eaten; what the young locusts have left other locusts have eaten." (NIV, Joel 1:4)

What were the effects of the plague of locusts?

The locusts decimated crops. Without crops, the people faced starvation. Joel used vivid imagery to paint a picture of privation and barrenness: "The seeds are shriveled beneath the clods. The storehouses are in ruins, the granaries have been broken down, for the grain has dried up. How the cattle moan! The herds mill about because they have no pasture; even the flocks of sheep are suffering." (NIV, Joel 1:17–18)

What is the day of the Lord?

The concept of the day of the Lord appears in both the Old and New Testaments. It refers to a day or days when God will intervene in human history to bring about a specific outcome. Some people view the day of the Lord as something that will happen only at the end of time, while others view it as a collection of events, some of which have happened already, others of which have yet to happen or will happen at the end of time.

What happens on the Day of the Lord in the book of Joel?

Most people agree that the first chapter in Joel is about an attack of locusts. The attack was a manifestation of God's wrath: "Alas for that day! For the day of the LORD is near, and it will come like destruction from the Almighty. Has not the food been cut off before our very eyes—joy and gladness from the house of our God?" (NIV, Joel 1:15–16)

Opinions differ as to what happened on the Day of the Lord in Chapter 2. Joel filled the chapter with images of a military campaign: "Let all the inhabitants of the land tremble, for the day of the LORD is coming, it is near—a day of darkness and gloom, a day of clouds and thick darkness! Like blackness spread upon the mountains a great and powerful army comes; their like has never been from of old, nor will be again after them in ages to come." (NRSV, Joel 2:1–2) Some people view this as a continuation of the first chapter. The great and powerful army refers to the locusts. Some people see the event as the coming of God, in which case the great and powerful army refers to the army of God.

AMOS

Who was Amos?

Amos, whose name means encumbered or burdened, was a shepherd and farmer from the southern kingdom of Judah. He was a prophet during the reign of Judah's King Uzziah (783–742 B.C.E.) and Israel's King Jeroboam II (786–746 B.C.E.).

What was King Uzziah's reign like?

For the most part, King Uzziah was a capable, fair ruler. One of his accomplishments was that on the city wall he set up "machines, invented by skilled workers, on the towers and the corners for shooting arrows and large stones" at approaching enemies. Uzziah grew prideful with his many successes. He tried to take on the duties of a temple priest by making a sacrifice on the altar of incense. For this sacrilegious action, Uzziah was stricken immediately with leprosy. He spent the rest of his life in a house separate from the palace. (NRSV, II Chronicles 26)

What is the book of Amos about?

Though Amos was from Judah, God sent him north to Israel to prophesy to the people about their sinful behavior.

How does the book of Amos begin?

It begins with a diatribe against the neighboring nations of Damascus, Gaza, Tyre, Edom, Ammon, and Moab. These countries were guilty of a variety of wrongs, including engaging in slave trade, desecrating the corpses of people they conquered, and tearing open the bellies of pregnant women who were prisoners of war. The last two nations to be criticized were Judah and Israel.

What were God's specific complaints against Israel?

Amos told the people of Israel that God was angry because they lounged about on "beds of ivory" and sang "idle songs to the sound of the harp" while they "turned justice into poison." (NRSV, Amos 6:4, 5, 12)

How did Amos envision the day of the Lord?

Originally, the Israelites looked forward to the day of the Lord as a time when God would rescue them from their enemies. However, Amos warned the Israelites not to be smug: "Why do you want the day of the LORD? It is darkness and not light; as

Amos was a prophet during times of prosperity in the kingdoms of Judah and Israel, and God charged him to remind the people not to become idle or forget the law and justice.

if someone fled from a lion, and was met by a bear; or went into the house and rested a hand against the wall, and was bitten by a snake." (NRSV, Amos 5:18–19)

What bold move did Amos take to emphasize Israel's demise?

He wrote a funeral lament years before the "death" occurred. It begins in Chapter 5: "The virgin Israel has fallen, never to rise again! She lies forsaken on the ground, with none to raise her up." (NLT, Amos 5:2)

Did Amos have visions?

Yes. In one he saw God preparing to send a plague of locusts on Israel. In another he saw God preparing to send a rain of fire on Israel. When Amos interceded on Israel's behalf, God relented temporarily.

Did Amos have other visions?

Yes. Amos saw God standing by a wall built with a plumb line, a device used to determine the correct verticality of buildings. God held a plumb line in his hand. The significance of this was that Israel did not measure up to God's standards. As a result, God planned to destroy Israel. Amos did not intercede.

In another vision, Amos saw a basket of ripe summer fruit. Israel, like the fruit, would not be around for much longer. The nation of Israel succumbed to the Assyrians in 722 B.C.E.

OBADIAH

Who was Obadiah?

Little is known about this prophet whose name means "servant of God."

What is the book of Obadiah about?

In it, Obadiah prophesied against Edom, Judah and Israel's neighbor. Judah and Israel had a long history of discord with Edom. Centuries earlier, the Edomites refused to allow Moses and the Israelites to pass through Edom on their way to the Promised Land. As a result, the Israelites had to take a long detour.

This time, however, Edom went too far. The Edomites helped the Babylonians capture Judah. "You shouldn't have plundered the land of Israel when they were suffering such calamity. You shouldn't have gloated over the destruction of your relatives, looting their homes and making yourselves rich at their expense. You shouldn't have stood at the crossroads, killing those who tried to escape. You shouldn't have captured the survivors, handing them over to their enemies in that terrible time of trouble." (NLT, Obadiah 1:13–14)

At twenty-one verses, Obadiah is the shortest book in the Bible.

What was God's message to Edom?

God told Obadiah to tell the Edomites that they should not be prideful because their day of ruination was coming. God said, "You are proud because you live in a rock fortress and make your home high in the mountains. 'Who can ever reach us way up here?' you ask boastfully. Don't fool yourselves! Though you soar as high as eagles and build your nest among the stars, I will bring you crashing down. I, the LORD, have spoken!" (NLT, Obadiah 1:2–3)

If it was the Babylonians whom the Edomites helped, then Obadiah's prophecy came true quickly. In 553 B.C.E., thirty-three years after Jerusalem was conquered by the Babylonians, the Babylonians conquered Edom.

> ## Where was Edom located?
>
> Edom was located southeast of Judah, in what is now the country of Jordan.

Why were the Edomites prideful?

Part of what made the Edomites proud was their geographic advantage over their enemies. Part of Edom was situated on rocky cliffs, which formed a natural barrier against invaders. The cliffs, most scholars contend, were none other than Petra, whose stately red rock carvings continue to attract visitors today.

JONAH

Who was Jonah?

Jonah, whose name means "dove," was a prophet in the northern kingdom of Israel during the reign of Jeroboam II (786–746 B.C.E.) Jonah is mentioned in II Kings 14:25 as being someone through whom God spoke.

What is the book of Jonah about?

It details Jonah's reluctance to deliver God's word to the people of Nineveh. In the process, God's extravagant mercy and forgiveness are displayed.

Where was Nineveh?

Nineveh was the capital city of Assyria, the nation that conquered Israel in 722 B.C.E. Assyria was an enormous empire known for its cruel war practices. At the height of its power, its territory included much of modern-day Turkey, Syria, and Iraq. Nineveh was in the center of the empire.

What was God's first recorded instruction to Jonah?

God said, "Arise, go to Nineveh, that great city, and cry against it; for their wickedness is come up before me." (KJV, Jonah 1:2)

Did Jonah do what God commanded him to do?

No. Jonah hightailed out of Judah. First, he went to Joppa, a port on the coast of Judah. From there, he took a ship that was headed to Tarshish.

Where was Tarshish?

The exact location is unknown, but the best guess is that it was on the southern tip of the Iberian Peninsula, which is modern-day Spain. To people of the ancient Near East,

183

Tarshish was as far west as west could be. Jonah thought by traveling so far, he could get away from God.

The Great Fish

Did Jonah make it to Tarshish?

No. On his way there, a great storm threatened to tear the boat into pieces. While the storm raged, Jonah slept. While Jonah slept, the sailors cast lots to determine who was to blame for the storm. The lot fell to Jonah.

What happened when the sailors found out that the storm was brought about on account of Jonah?

Jonah acknowledged his culpability. Wanting to spare the sailors any more danger, Jonah told them to throw him overboard. At first they refused, but when the storm showed no sign of letting up, the sailors relented, and threw Jonah overboard.

What happened to Jonah when he was thrown overboard?

The Bible says, "Now the LORD had prepared a great fish to swallow up Jonah. And Jonah was in the belly of the fish three days and three nights." (KJV, Jonah 1:17)

What did Jonah do while he was in the fish?

He prayed. Jonah's prayer was one of thanksgiving that God had preserved his life. When Jonah finished praying, "the LORD spake unto the fish, and it vomited out Jonah upon the dry land." (KJV, Jonah 2:10)

What happened to Jonah then?

God told Jonah to go to Nineveh. This time Jonah went.

The Pouting Prophet

What did Jonah tell the people of Nineveh?

In what is the only explicit prophecy in the book, Jonah walked around Nineveh proclaiming, "Forty more days and Nineveh will be overturned." (NIV, Jonah 3:4)

Did the prophecy come true?

No. Oftentimes when prophets spoke to people, the prophets spoke of what would

The Bible does not state that Jonah was swallowed by a whale, just a "great fish."

184

Did Jesus believe the story of Jonah and the fish?

Many people view the events in Jonah as myth. However, Jesus referred to the book of Jonah and he said it was a fact: "For just as Jonah was three days and three nights in the belly of the sea monster, so for three days and three nights the Son of Man will be in the heart of the earth" (NRSV, Matthew 12:40).

happen if the people did not change their ways. In this case, the people changed their ways: "The Ninevites believed God. They declared a fast, and all of them, from the greatest to the least, put on sackcloth." (NIV, Jonah 3:5) Their repentance was sincere, so God refrained from sending ruin upon them.

What did Jonah think about his prophecy not coming true?

Instead of being happy that the people of Nineveh repented, he was bitter that he did not get to deliver a prophecy that came true. He complained to God, "O LORD! Is not this what I said while I was still in my own country? That is why I fled to Tarshish from the beginning; for I knew that you were a gracious God and merciful, slow to anger, and abounding in steadfast love, and ready to relent from punishing. And now, O LORD, please take my life from me, for it is better for me to die than to live." (NRSV, Jonah 4:2–3) Then Jonah pouted. He walked to the outskirts of the city and waited and watched, thinking the city might be destroyed still. While he waited, he sat under a makeshift shelter.

How did God respond to Jonah's less than admirable attitude?

God asked, "Have you any right to be angry?" (NIV, Jonah 4:4) Still, God watched over Jonah. God made a bush grow right by Jonah to provide shade for him.

How did Jonah respond to God's kind gesture?

He was not impressed, especially when a worm came and ate the bush. A hot wind blew, and that just made the situation worse. God asked, "Is it right for you to be angry about the bush?" Jonah, still sulking, replied, "Yes, angry enough to die." (NRSV, Jonah 4:9)

How does the book of Jonah end?

It ends with God giving Jonah a firm talking-to. God said, "But Nineveh has more than a hundred and twenty thousand people who cannot tell their right hand from their left, and many cattle as well. Should I not be concerned about that great city?" (NIV, Jonah 4:11)

MICAH

Who was Micah?

Micah (whose name means "who is like God?") was a Judean prophet active during the reigns of Jotham, Ahaz, and Hezekiah. That means Micah prophesied sometime between the years 742–687 B.C.E.

What is the book of Micah about?

Micah prophesied about the downfall of his brothers to the north in Israel. However, he said the people of Judah were just as guilty as those in Israel.

How does the book of Micah begin?

It begins with Micah receiving word from God to condemn Samaria and Jerusalem, the capitals of Israel and Judah. Micah delivered the same message as many of the other prophets. That is, Israel and Judah were flagrant in their sins and angered God.

Why was God mad at Samaria and Jerusalem?

As capital cities, Samaria and Jerusalem were centers of business and industry. Also, they were hives of idolatry, deceit, arrogance, and jealousy. In particular, Micah criticized the wealthy for cheating poor people of the land that was their birthright: "When you want a certain piece of land, you find a way to seize it. When you want someone's house you take it by fraud and violence. No one's family or inheritance is safe with you around!" (NLT, Micah 2:2)

Did the people believe Micah's prophecies?

No. "'Don't say such things,' the people respond. 'Don't prophesy like that. Such disasters will never come our way!'" (NLT, Micah 2:6) Micah responded by saying that the kind of preacher that would satisfy them was one who would go around "uttering empty falsehoods, saying, 'I will preach to you of wine and strong drink.' Such a man would be the preacher for this people!" (NRSV, Micah 2:11)

Did Micah prophesy anything encouraging or hopeful?

Yes. He foresaw a time when Jerusalem would be restored: "In the days to come the mountain of the LORD's house shall be established as the highest of the mountains, and shall be raised up above the hills. Peoples shall stream to it, and many nations shall come and say: 'Come, let us go up to the mountain of the LORD, to the house of the God of Jacob; that he may teach us his ways and that we may walk in his paths." (NRSV, Micah 4:1–2)

Did Micah prophesy about anything else besides downfall and redemption?

Yes. He prophesied about a ruler who would come from Bethlehem in Israel. According to God's instructions, Micah promised wonderful things about this ruler: "And he shall

God told Micah to spread his message to Samaria and Jerusalem that they were straying from the righteous path.

stand to lead his flock with the LORD's strength, in the majesty of the name of the LORD his God. Then his people will live there undisturbed, for he will be highly honored around the world. And he will be the source of peace." (NLT, Micah 5:4–5)

Who was this person?

Micah does not say who the person is. Some people think the person was a king who was supposed to rescue the Israelites from the Assyrians. Others say the person is an as yet unidentified king who will bring about the restoration of the Hebrew people in Jerusalem at an unspecified future time. To others, the person referenced was Jesus.

NAHUM

Who was Nahum?

Nahum, whose name means "comforter," was a prophet from the southern kingdom of Judah. He was active during the reign of King Josiah (640–609 B.C.E.)

What is the book of Nahum about?

In the book, the fall of the Assyrian capital, Nineveh (612 B.C.E.), is imminent or just happened. Either way, Nahum was delighted, and assured his listeners that God was behind the downfall for good reason.

How does the book of Nahum begin?

It begins with a reminder of God's intolerance against those who disobey him persistently: "The LORD is a jealous God, filled with vengeance and wrath. He takes revenge on all who oppose him and furiously destroys his enemies!" (NLT, Nahum 1:2)

What specific message did Nahum have for the king of Nineveh?

"And this is what the LORD says concerning the Assyrian in Nineveh: 'You will have no more children to carry on your name. I will destroy all the idols in the temples of your gods. I am preparing a grave for you because you are despicable and don't deserve to live.'" (NLT, Nahum 1:14)

Who was the "shatterer?"

Nahum said, "A shatterer has come up against you. Guard the ramparts; watch the road; gird your loins; collect all your strength." (NRSV, Nahum 2:1) This prophecy refers to the Medians and the Babylonians, those who conquered Nineveh.

To whom did Nahum compare Nineveh?

Nahum compared Nineveh to a prostitute: "Fatally seductive, you're the Witch of Seduction, luring nations to their ruin with your evil spells. 'I'm your enemy, Whore Nineveh—I, GOD-of-the-Angel-Armies! I'll strip you of your seductive silk robes and expose you on the world stage.'" (The Message, Nahum 3:4–5)

How does the book of Nahum end?

It ends with a promise to Nineveh that no one will miss it: "When the story of your fate gets out, the whole world will applaud and cry 'Encore!' Your cruel evil has seeped into every nook and cranny of the world. Everyone has felt it and suffered." (The Message, Nahum 3:19)

HABAKKUK

Who was Habakkuk?

Habakkuk, whose name means "embracer" or "wrestler," was a prophet who lived in the northern kingdom of Judah around 600 B.C.E., just before the Babylonian invasion in 597 B.C.E. Most likely, he was active during the reigns of Jehoiakim and Jehoiachin.

What is the book of Habakkuk about?

In it, Habakkuk saw visions of the coming invasion and was terrified by what he saw. Habakkuk wondered why God allowed the innocent to suffer along with the guilty.

How does the book of Habakkuk begin?

It begins with a complaint from Habakkuk to God: "O LORD, how long shall I cry for help, and you will not listen? Or cry to you 'Violence!' and you will not save?" (NRSV, Habakkuk 1:2) Habakkuk was unhappy with the status quo in Judah.

How did God respond to Habakkuk's complaint?

God assured Habakkuk that he was working on a plan in which the Babylonians, as bad as they were, would be the tool of ridding Judah of injustice—by getting rid of Judah.

What did Habakkuk think about God's plan to use the Babylonians to rid Judah of injustice?

He was not pleased with the idea. He questioned God: "Why then do you tolerate the treacherous? Why are you silent while the wicked swallow up those more righteous than themselves?" (NIV, Habakkuk 1:13)

How does the book of Habakkuk end?

It ends with a song of praise. In the song, Habakkuk exclaimed, "Though the fig tree does not bud and there no grapes on the vines, though the olive crop fails and the fields produce no food, though there are no sheep in the pen and no cattle in the stall, yet I will rejoice in the LORD, I will be joyful in God my Savior." (NIV, Habakkuk 3:17)

ZEPHANIAH

Who was Zephaniah?

Zephaniah, whose name means "hidden or protected by God," was a prophet in the southern kingdom of Judah during the reign of King Josiah (640–609 B.C.E.)

What is the book of Zephaniah about?

Zephaniah prophesied about the day of the Lord, a day seen by Zephaniah as a day of global catastrophe brought on by idolatry and other forms of breaking the Law of Moses.

How does the book of Zephaniah begin?

It begins with a solemn promise from God: "I will sweep away everything from the face of the earth.... I will sweep away both men and animals; I will sweep away the birds of the air and the fish of the sea. The wicked will have only heaps of rubble when I cut off man from the face of the earth." (NIV, Zephaniah 1:2–3)

A frescoe by nineteenth-century artist Carl Mayer depicts the prophet Zephaniah in the Altlerchenfelder church in Vienna, Austria.

Why was God mad?

He was mad at Judah and other countries for their idolatry, cruelty, and arrogance.

How did Zephaniah describe the day of the Lord?

He described it in terms of an inescapable military siege: "The great day of the LORD is near—near and coming quickly. Listen! The cry on the day of the LORD will be bitter, the shouting of the warrior there. That day will be a day of wrath, a day of distress and anguish, a day of trouble and ruin, a day of darkness and gloom, a day of clouds and blackness, a day of trumpet and battle cry against the fortified cities and against the corner towers." (NIV, Zephaniah 1:14–16)

What did Zephaniah foresee that would undo one of God's earlier actions?

Zephaniah foresaw a time when everyone would speak the same language so they could serve God "with one accord." (NRSV, Zephaniah, 3:9) This would undo God's confusing the people's language at the tower of Babel. (NRSV, Genesis 11:9)

Was everyone included in the destruction?

No. Zephaniah said there was a faithful group of people who were not included in the destruction: "But I will leave within you the meek and humble, who trust in the name of the LORD. The remnant of Israel will do no wrong; they will speak no lies, nor will deceit be found in the mouths. They will eat and lie down and no one will make them afraid." (NIV, Zephaniah 3:12–13)

How does the book of Zephaniah end?

It ends with a solemn promise from God. This time the promise was one of hope and re-assurance: "At that time I will bring you home, at the time when I gather you; for I will make you renowned and praised among all the peoples of the earth, when I restore your fortunes before your eyes, says the LORD." (NRSV, Zephaniah 3:20)

HAGGAI

Who was Haggai?

Haggai, whose name means "festive," prophesied to the exiles after they returned to Is-rael. When Cyrus, the king of Persia, conquered Babylon, he issued a decree saying that the Israelites could return to their homeland. Haggai's book dates from about 520 B.C.E.

What is the book of Haggai about?

In it, Haggai encouraged the returning exiles to rebuild the temple.

How does the book of Haggai begin?

It begins with Haggai delivering a message to Zerubbabel, the governor of Judah, and Joshua, the high priest. The message encouraged them to rebuild the temple.

Why hadn't the people rebuilt the temple already?

They built their own houses and planted crops first. Those were necessary things, but God said attention should have been paid to the temple as well: "You've had great am-bition for yourselves, but nothing has come of it. The little you have brought to my tem-ple I've blown away—there was nothing to it. And why?" (This is a Message from GOD-of-the-Angel-Armies, remember.) "Because while you've run around, caught up with tak-ing care of your own houses, my Home is in ruins. That's why. Because of your stingi-ness." (The Message, Haggai 1:8–9)

Did Zerubabbel, Joshua, and the others pay attention to Haggai?

Yes. They began to rebuild the temple.

Was the new temple like the old one?

No. Haggai asked the people, "Who is left among you that saw this house in its former glory? How does it look to you now? Is it not in your sight as nothing?" (NRSV, Haggai 2:3) However, Haggai assured the people that God would bless the temple. God told Haggai to tell the people: "My spirit abides among you; do no fear. For thus says the LORD of hosts: Once again, in a little while, I will shake the heavens and the earth and the sea and the dry land; and I will shake all the nations, so that the treasure of all nations shall come, and I will fill this house with splendor, says the LORD of hosts." (NRSV, Haggai 2:5–7)

How does the book of Haggai end?

It ends with God approving Zerubbabel as ruler of the people.

ZECHARIAH

Who was Zechariah?

Zechariah, whose name means "the Lord remembers," was a prophet active around 520 B.C.E.. This was during the early years of the exiles returning to their homeland and rebuilding the temple.

What is the book of Zechariah about?

In it, Zechariah encouraged the returned exiles as they rebuilt the temple. Also, he described visions of the coming of the Messiah, whom many believe was Jesus.

How does the book of Zechariah begin?

It begins with Zechariah telling the people to return to God's ways. God promised, "I will return to Jerusalem with mercy, and there my house will be rebuilt. And the measuring line will be stretched out over Jerusalem." (NIV, Zechariah 1:16)

What was Zechariah's first recorded vision?

Zechariah saw divine watchmen on horses. The horsemen patrolled the earth, and reported back that the "whole earth remains at peace." (NRSV, Zechariah 1:11) Most scholars take this to mean that the region was relatively peaceful under the rule of the Persian Empire. The Persian king, Darius, showed tolerance to people of religions other than his own, including the Hebrews. It was Darius, after all, who decreed that the Hebrews should rebuild their temple for worship when they returned to their homeland.

Did Zechariah have other visions?

The first several visions conveyed messages about the rebuilding of the temple and the safe, prosperous future of the Hebrews under the protection of God. In one vision, Zechariah saw four horns. An angel told him the horns represented the nations that destroyed Judah and Israel and scattered the people to sundry places. In addition, Zechariah saw four blacksmiths who represented agents of God who would strike down the horns.

In another vision, Zechariah saw a man with a measuring line in his hand. The man said he was going to "to measure Jerusalem, to find out how wide and how long it is.'"

The tomb where the prophet Zechariah is buried is located in an ancient cemetery in Jerusalem.

(NIV, Zechariah 2:2) Then another angel told Zechariah that Jerusalem would be a city without brick walls because the Lord would build a wall of fire around it and under God's protection, the city would prosper.

Then Zechariah had a vision in which he saw the high priest Joshua clothed in dirty clothes. Most scholars say this represents the sinfulness of the people. Joshua's dirty clothes were taken from him and he was clothed in fine, priestly clothes. Most scholars say this represented God removing the people's sins from them.

Later, Zechariah saw a lampstand with seven lamps on it. The word "lampstand" in Hebrew is "menorah." The menorah represents the eternal light of God's word. By the lampstand were two olive trees. Most scholars think that the two olive trees represent Joshua, high priest and Zerubbabel, the governor God put in charge of rebuilding the temple after the exiles returned. In essence, God's word was present and his temple was being rebuilt.

In another vision, Zechariah saw a woman crammed into a basket. The woman represented wickedness. After that, Zechariah saw two women flying towards him. The women lifted the basket and flew off with it. When Zechariah asked an angel where they were going, the angel replied, "To the country of Babylonia to build a house for it. When it is ready, the basket will be set there in its place." (NIV, Zechariah 5:11).

Zechariah was not through with visions yet. He had one more. In this vision, he saw four chariots. The four chariots, each led by powerful horses, flew off into the four directions of the world to patrol for God. Also as part of this vision, God told Zechariah to col-

193

lect gold and silver from the exiles and make a crown for Joshua the high priest. God told Zechariah to tell Joshua: "Here is the man called the Branch. He will branch out where he is and build the temple of the LORD. He will build the LORD's temple, and he will receive royal honor and will rule as king from his throne. He will also serve as priest from his throne, and there will be perfect harmony between the two." (NLT, Zechariah 6:12–13)

What other subjects are covered in Zechariah?

The book brims with inexplicable images that continue to baffle readers. In Chapter 11, Zechariah described a shepherd who was paid thirty pieces of silver for his work. Some scholars interpret this to mean that Zechariah, as a prophet, was the shepherd. Some scholars interpret this to mean that Judas Iscariot was a shepherd who was paid thirty pieces of silver for his work of betraying Jesus. Another puzzling image shows up in Chapter 12. Zechariah described a time when the people of Jerusalem looked "on me whom they have pierced and mourn for him as for an only son. They will grieve bitterly for him as for a firstborn son who has died." (NLT, Zechariah 12:10) Some scholars say the pierced one is an unidentifiable historic member of David's family. Other scholars say the pierced one is an allusion to the crucifixion of Jesus.

How does the book of Zechariah end?

Zechariah ends this way: "And there shall no longer be traders in the house of the LORD of hosts on that day." (NRSV, Zechariah 14:21) This suggests that Zechariah looked forward to a day when God's earthly temple would be free from the sullying effects of commerce.

MALACHI

Who was Malachi?

Malachi, whose name means "my messenger," was a prophet who was active in the fifth century B.C.E. His book presumes the completion of the temple reconstruction. That happened in 515 B.C.E.

What is the book of Malachi about?

It is about how most of the priests did not obey the laws as set forth by God. Over and over, they offered sick or maimed animals as sacrifices, and saved the best for themselves. With their disloyalty to God, they led people astray. All of this was insulting to God. Also, Malachi talked about divine justice.

What did Malachi say were the responsibilities of the priests?

A priest should "teach the truth. teach the truth. People are supposed to look to them for guidance. The priest is the messenger of GOD-of-the-Angel-Armies." (The Message, Malachi 2:7)

What did Malachi have to say about divine justice?

The temple was rebuilt, but the people were discouraged because the messiah referred to by earlier prophets had not come yet. The people felt God was being unjust to them. Malachi said, "See I am sending my messenger to prepare the way before me, and the LORD whom you seek will suddenly come to his temple. The messenger of the covenant in whom you delight— indeed, he is coming, says the LORD of hosts." (NRSV, Malachi 3:1)

Who was the messenger?

Many people think the messenger was Jesus. Some say the messenger has yet to come. Based on Malachi 4:5, some people think the messenger refers to Elijah: "Behold, I will send you Elijah the prophet before the coming of the great and dreadful day of the LORD." (KJV, Malachi 4:5)

A frescoe of the prophet Malachi, who was sent by God to tell the priests that God was not pleased with their disloyalty.

How does the book of Malachi end?

Chapter 4 deals with the day when God will demolish all evil people. For the people faithful to God's word, however, God made a promise: "But unto you that fear my name shall the Sun of righteousness arise with healing in his wings; and ye shall go forth, and grow up as calves of the stall. And ye shall tread down the wicked; for they shall be ashes under the soles of your feet in the day that I shall do this." (KJV, Malachi 4:3)

New Testament

GOSPELS AND ACTS OF THE APOSTLES

INTRODUCTION TO THE GOSPELS

What does the word gospel mean?

It means "good news."

What is the good news, according to the New Testament?

Jesus is the Messiah, the one foretold in the Old Testament whose coming brought about the beginning of God's kingdom on earth.

What are the Four Gospels?

Matthew, Mark, Luke, and John.

What are the Synoptic Gospels?

Matthew, Mark, and Luke. The word "synoptic" comes from the Greek word "synoptikos" which means "view together." Essentially, the authors of Matthew, Mark, and Luke wrote during the same time about the same people and events.

Are there discrepancies between the Gospels?

Yes. The accounts differ in some ways. While critics point to the differences as proof that the writers of the books made up some of the stories and details, adherents say that the differences are proof that the writers were human. The situation can be likened to that of three people witnessing a car wreck. Three people see the same car wreck. Different details stand out to different witnesses. The witnesses even disagree on some points. So it is with the events described in the Gospels. Some scholars think the Gospels derived from the Q document.

Why isn't the book of John a Synoptic Gospel?

The book of John differs from the others in that its chronology of events is different, as are details concerning events in Jesus' life.

What is the difference between an apostle and a disciple?

The word "apostle" is from the Greek word "apóstolos," which means "to send out." In biblical studies, an apostle is someone Jesus sent out into the world to spread the gospel. The word "disciple" comes from the Latin "discipulus," which means "to learn." In biblical studies, a disciple is someone who learns or follows the teachings of Jesus. Tradi-

This fresco on the wall of a Greek Orthodox church in Capernaum, Israel, depicts Jesus with his twelve apostles.

tionally, the word apostle is used to designate any of the original twelve disciples called by Jesus to preach the gospel.

Who are the apostles?

Simon (also known as Peter), the brothers James and John, Andrew, Philip, Bartholomew (also known as Nathanael), Matthew (also known as Levi), Thomas, James (the son of Alpheus), Thaddaeus, Simon the Zealot, and Judas. So, all of the apostles were disciples, but not all of the disciples were apostles.

Why aren't Mark and Luke listed as apostles?

Mark and Luke were not in the inner circle of the Apostles. Mark became friends with Peter, and then became a follower of Jesus. Luke became friends with Paul, and then became a follower of Jesus after Jesus' death and resurrection.

GEOGRAPHY

How had the geographic boundaries changed in Judah from the end of the Old Testament to the beginning of the New Testament?

Roughly four hundred years passed between the end of the Old Testament and the beginning of the New Testament. The northern kingdom of Israel was demolished during the Assyrian Captivity of 733 B.C.E. Then there was only the southern kingdom of Judah. Judah, too, was demolished during the Babylonian Captivity of 583 B.C.E.

After the Babylonian Captivity, the regions of Israel and Judah experienced political and military turmoil that resulted in a centuries-long ebb and flow of geographical boundaries and changes in place names. For instance, after the Maccabean revolt ended in 145 B.C.E., the area became a relatively independent state known as the Hasmonean kingdom. This dynasty lasted until 63 B.C.E., at which time the area came under the control of the Roman Empire.

How big was the Roman Empire?

At its height, the Roman Empire encompassed all the countries in the Mediterranean, Spain, Portugal, France, portions of Great Britain, portions of North Africa, and portions of the Near East and Middle East.

Why are there so many letters in the New Testament?

These letters, sometimes called epistles, were written by church leaders to other individuals and groups. The authors of the epistles wrote to teach, encourage, reprimand, and warn individuals and groups. Letter writing was the only way to communicate with people far away.

THE GOSPEL OF MATTHEW

Who was Matthew?

The Matthew mentioned in the book of Matthew was a tax collector. Later, he became one of Jesus' apostles. Nothing is known about Matthew the apostle's life, other than that he obeyed Jesus' call to follow him.

When was the book of Matthew written?

Most scholars date the book to around 200 C.E.

What is the book of Matthew about?

In the book, Jesus' life and ministry are described against the backdrop of the politics and social mores of first-century Palestine. There is much discussion about Jewish law, and how Old Testament prophecy was fulfilled by Jesus.

How does the book of Matthew begin?

It begins with a genealogy of Jesus' family, beginning with Abraham and going on up to Jesus. This genealogy is the ideal segue from the end of the Old Testament to the new era ushered in by Jesus in the New Testament.

MARY AND JOSEPH

Who was Mary?

Mary was the mother of Jesus. In first-century Palestine, it was common for girls to marry early, even as young as twelve years old. Though the Bible does not say how old Mary was when Jesus was born, it stands to reason that she was a teenager. The name Mary is derived from the Hebrew name Mara, which means "bitter."

Who was Joseph?

Joseph was Mary's fiancé, and later her husband. Also, he was Jesus' earthly father. The name Joseph is derived from the Hebrew name Yosef, which means "he will add."

When did Mary find out she was pregnant?

She found out she was pregnant before she began to live with Joseph. The Bible reads,

A statue of Matthew looks over the gate to the Christ the Savior Temple in Moscow, Russia.

"Joseph discovered she was pregnant. (It was the Holy Spirit, but he didn't know that)." (The Message, Matthew 1:18)

What did Joseph think about her pregnancy?

Joseph did not want to disgrace Mary, but he did not want to marry her, either. At that time, an engagement was as legally binding as marriage. The Law of Moses was not on Mary's side. One law stated, "If there is a young woman, a virgin already engaged to be married, and a man meets her in town and lies with her, you shall bring both of them to the gate of that town and stone them to death." (NRSV, Deuteronomy 22:23–24). So if Mary was raped, then she (along with the baby) would be stoned.

Many artists have depicted the Annunciation, including Fra Angelico, whose fresco can be found in the friary of San Marco in Florence, Italy.

Another law stated, "If the man meets the engaged woman in the open country, and the man seizes her and lies with her, then only the man who lies with her shall die. You shall do nothing to the young woman; the young woman has not committed an offense punishable by death, because this is like that of someone who attacks and murders a neighbor." (NRSV, Deuteronomy 22:25–26) So if Mary had been raped, she would not be stoned, but would face shame as an unwed mother, and possibly be banished.

For these reasons, Joseph planned to divorce Mary discreetly.

Whatt happened that changed Joseph's mind?

An angel of God appeared to Joseph in a dream, and said, "Joseph, son of David, don't hesitate to get married. Mary's pregnancy is Spirit-conceived. God's Holy Spirit has made her pregnant." (The Message, Matthew 1:20–21) So Joseph married Mary, but did not have marital relations with her until after Jesus was born. For a long time, people just assumed the baby was Joseph's, and Mary's reputation was protected.

What is the Feast of the Annunciation?

In the Western liturgical year, the Feast of the Annunciation is celebrated on March 25. Also called Lady Day, the day marked the beginning of the New Year in England until 1752.

When was Jesus born?

In dating events in history, B.C.E. stands for Before the Common Era. C.E. stands for Common Era. These secular labels have become more common than B.C. (Before Christ) and A.D. (Anno Domino, or In the Year of Our Lord). Still, the B.C.E. and C.E. system uses the birth of Jesus as its starting point. So, the year 30 B.C.E., for instance, is the same as 30 B.C.. The year 20 C.E. is the same as 20 A.D.

So it seems like 1 C.E. or 1 A.D. would be the logical answer to the question of when Jesus was born. However, most scholars agree that Jesus was born between 6 and 4 B.C.E. This analysis is based on clues within the Bible, and on what is known about history outside of the Bible. For instance, Matthew reads, "In the time of King Herod, after Jesus was born in Bethlehem of Judea...." (NRSV, Matthew 2:1) The argument is that since Herod died in 4 B.C.E., Jesus could not have been born any later than that year.

A nativity scene painting from 1567 created by the artist Bernardinus Indisur and displayed at the San Bernardino church in Verona, Italy.

Was Jesus really born on December 25?

Most scholars say no. The custom of celebrating Jesus' birth was not common until at least the third century C.E., maybe even later. Some scholars think that December 25 was chosen because it was nine months from the time when Mary is believed to have conceived Jesus. The celebration for that event was already being celebrated on March 25. Other scholars think that the December 25 date was selected because it coincided with certain pagan festivals.

KING HEROD AND THE WISE MEN

Who was King Herod?

There were several Herods. The one Matthew refers to when laying the groundwork for Jesus' birth is Herod the Great, who reigned in Judea from 37 B.C.E. to 4 B.C.E. Because Herod the Great had to answer to the rulers of the Roman Empire, he was more of a governor than king. Herod was noted for his harsh policies and political scheming. Herod appears in all four Gospels.

What was the role of wise men?

In the ancient Near East, wise men, or magi (which comes from the Greek word "magoi"), were royal advisors and ambassadors schooled in astrology and alchemy. Part of their job was to carry diplomatic messages, including gifts, to neighboring nations.

Were the wise men who visited Jesus really named Balthazar, Melchior, and Caspar?

Matthew is the only book in the Bible in which the wise men's visit to Jesus is described, and in Matthew's account, they are not named. The names are from non-canonical accounts of Jesus' birth.

How many wise men visited Jesus?

Because the wise men are described as having brought three types of gifts to Jesus, posterity has it that there were three wise men, one for each gift offered. However, the account in Matthew reads simply, "Then Herod sent a private message to the wise men, asking them to come see him." (NLT, Matthew 2:7) There could have been any number of them.

Why did the wise men go to Bethlehem?

King Herod summoned the wise men to find out from them the exact time of the star's appearance. Then King Herod ordered the wise men to go to Bethlehem. He said, "Go to Bethlehem and search carefully for the child. And when you find him, come back and tell me so that I can go and worship him, too!" (NLT, Matthew 2:8) Really, King Herod wanted to know where Jesus was so he could kill him. When the wise men left King Herod to start for Bethlehem, "the star appeared to them, guiding them to Bethlehem." (NLT, Matthew 2:9)

Tradition has it that the wise men, or magi, who came to see the baby Jesus were named Balthazar, Melchior, and Caspar, but this is never mentioned in the Bible.

How did the wise men know to follow the star?

Scholars continue to debate this. The most widely accepted theory is that, like the Jewish people, the wise men were familiar with prophecy concerning the arrival of a messiah. As astrologers, the wise men looked to the stars for information, and information they found.

What happened when the wise men reached Bethlehem?

They followed the star until it stopped over Joseph and Mary's house. The wise men were "filled with joy" (NLT, Matthew 2:10), and they entered the house and paid Jesus homage.

What gifts did the wise men offer Jesus?

They offered gold, frankincense, and myrrh. Gold is a long-lasting and beautiful metal. Frankincense is a resin found in certain balsam trees. It is used widely to make perfumes and incense. Frankincense was used as an ingredient in the incense used in the temple. Myrrh is a resin found in the gum myrrh tree. It is used widely to make perfumes, incense, and anointing oil. All of these items are rare and expensive. The items were not typical gifts to give a child, but they were typical gifts to give a king.

The magi presented the baby Jesus with gold, frankincense, and myrrh.

Where did the wise men go once they left Bethlehem?

They were supposed to report back to Herod, but "being warned of God in a dream that they should not return to Herod, they departed into their own country another way." (KJV, Matthew 2:12)

What did Herod do when he found out that the wise men did not obey him?

"Then Herod, when he saw that he was mocked of the wise men, was exceeding wroth, and sent forth, and slew all the children that were in Bethlehem, and in all the coasts thereof, from two years old and under, according to the time which he had diligently inquired of the wise men." (KJV, Matthew 2:16) This verse provides a key to understanding the chronology of events surrounding Jesus' birth. Because King Herod commanded that all male children two and under be killed, the wise men might have seen the star rise two years prior to actually meeting King Herod and then Jesus. When the wise men met Jesus, he might have been a toddler. Accordingly, despite all of the artistic depictions of the wise men and shepherds being present right after Jesus' birth, most scholars believe the wise men did not meet Jesus until later. The book of Matthew does not describe the role of the shepherds at all.

What good things did King Herod do for Jerusalem?

Herod was brutal when it came to people. When it came to property development, though, he was a visionary. Under Herod's rule, Jerusalem underwent major renovations. One of Herod's great achievements was renovating the temple.

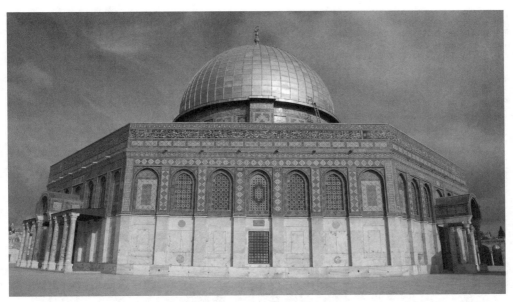

The Dome of the Rock was constructed in the seventh century as a holy site for Muslims where the Prophet Muhammud is said to have been taken into heaven by the angel Gabriel. But it is also a holy site for Jews and Christians and is supposedly where the second temple once stood.

207

When the Jewish exiles returned to Jerusalem from Babylon a few hundred years prior to Herod's rule, they rebuilt Solomon's temple. This second temple did not match Solomon's temple in beauty or grandeur. Herod changed that. He expanded the platform on which the temple sat. On the extended platform he built courts, terraces, and arched doorways. Elaborate carvings and statues were placed throughout. The various rooms served as offices for state business.

The Western Wall, or the Wailing Wall, is the only supporting wall of the temple that remains today. The wall is a place of prayer for Jews and Christians.

THE SLAUGHTER OF INNOCENTS

How did Jesus escape being killed under King Herod's edict?

An angel of God appeared to Joseph in a dream, who said, "Arise, and take the young child and his mother, and flee into Egypt, and be thou there until I bring thee word: for Herod will seek the young child to destroy him." (KJV, Matthew 2:13) Joseph did as the angel commanded.

Did Herod kill all of the children two and under?

Scholars continue to debate this. Those who believe the event happened refer to it as the Slaughter of Innocents, or the Massacre of Innocents. The event has been memorialized by countless artists throughout the centuries.

The Milk Grotto in Bethlehem, Israel, is the shrine where Jesus' family hid themselves from the murderous designs of King Herod.

When did Joseph return with his family to Israel?

Matthew reads, "When Herod died, an angel of the LORD suddenly appeared in a dream to Joseph in Egypt and said, 'Get up, take the child and his mother, and go to the land of Israel, for those who were seeking the child's life are dead.'" (NRSV, Matthew 2:19–20) Herod died in 4 B.C.E., so presumably Joseph and his family were in Egypt at least for a few months, but perhaps for as long as a couple of years.

PROPHECIES FULFILLED

According to the book of Matthew, what were some of the Old Testament prophecies that were fulfilled through Jesus' birth, life, ministry, death, and resurrection?

- Jesus himself said, "Do not think that I have come to abolish the law or the prophets; I have come not to abolish but to fulfill." (NRSV, Matthew 5:17)
- "But you, O Bethlehem Ephrathah, are only a small village in Judah. Yet a ruler of Israel will come from you, one whose origins are from the distant past." (NLT, Micah 5:2)
- "I shall see him, but not now: I shall behold him, but not nigh: there shall come a Star out of Jacob, and a Scepter shall rise out of Israel." (KJV, Numbers 24:17)
- "Rejoice greatly, O Daughter of Zion! Shout, Daughter of Jerusalem! See, your king comes to you, righteous and having salvation, gentle and riding on a donkey, on a colt, the foal of a donkey." (NIV, Zechariah 9:9)
- "Surely he has borne our infirmities and carried our diseases; yet we accounted him stricken, struck down by God, and afflicted. But he was wounded for our transgressions, crushed for our iniquities; upon him was the punishment that made us whole, and by his bruises we are healed." (NRSV, Isaiah 53:4–6)

JOHN THE BAPTIST

Who was John the Baptist?

The book of Matthew does not describe the events surrounding the birth of John the Baptist. Matthew picks up the thread of John's life when John has already started his career as a prophet: "His message was simple and austere, like his desert surroundings: 'Change your life. God's kingdom is here.'" (The Message, Matthew 3:1)

Was the life and ministry of John the Baptist foretold in the Old Testament?

According to Christian tradition, yes. Malachi 4:5 (The Message) reads, "But also look ahead: I'm sending Elijah the prophet to clear the way for the Big Day of God—the decisive Judgment Day!"

Many people of John's day believed he was Elijah come back to earth.

What were some of John's personality traits?

He wore clothing made of camel hair, and ate locusts and wild honey. Ascetic lifestyle choices were common among prophets.

Why was John called "the Baptist"?

As part of his ministry, John baptized people with water after they confessed their sins. People from all over the region came to John for baptism.

Why did John baptize people?

John and the people who came to him were Jews. The concept of being baptized in the name of the Father, the Son, and the Holy Spirit was unknown to them. So what was the significance of baptism to

John the Baptist was an important prophet who foretold the coming of Judgment Day.

them? It had to do with "mikveh," or traditional Jewish ritual cleansing. Becoming spiritually clean by water dated back to the time of Moses, and was a common practice among Jews. Mosaic Law specified that certain life events such as menstruation, childbirth, having sex, and touching a dead person required cleansing with pure water. John took it a step further. His baptism expressed repentance in the face of imminent judgment.

Who were the Pharisees and Sadducees, and why didn't John like them?

Pharisees were a large group of community leaders who had great influence in political and religious matters. Sadducees were another group of leaders made up of the rich descendants of priests. Both groups had merits, but John the Baptist—and later, Jesus—criticized them for keeping the letter of the law, but ignoring the spirit of it. Jesus criticized these religious leaders at length in Matthew 23.

How did John the Baptist die?

King Herod put John in prison because John chastised him for deserting his wife in order to marry Herodias, his brother's wife. At the wish of Herodias, Herod had John beheaded.

Are there any relics to be found today that involve John the Baptist?

Several purported relics related to John the Baptist exist to this day. Some people believe that the head enshrined in a clear case at the church of San Silvestro in Capite in Rome, Italy, is that of John the Baptist. Others believe that John the Baptist's head is enshrined at the Great Mosque of Damascus in Syria.

The Baptism of Jesus

What did John say about Jesus?

John predicted, "I baptize you with water for repentance. But after me will come one who is more powerful than I, whose sandals I am not fit to carry. He will baptize you with the Holy Spirit and with fire." (NIV, Matthew 3:11)

What is the Holy Spirit?

The Holy Spirit is the powerful third person of the Trinity, through whom God communicates with people to empower them and reveal his will. The Holy Spirit is mighty and mysterious. It is both distant and deeply involved in the lives of individuals.

Why did Jesus get baptized?

John knew he was inferior to Jesus, and was reluctant to baptize him. However, Jesus said to John, "Let it be so now: it is proper for us to do this to fulfill all righteousness." (NIV, Matthew 3:15) So, by being baptized, Jesus was doing God's will.

What happened when Jesus was baptized?

As Jesus came out of the water, "and lo, the heavens were opened unto him, and he saw the Spirit of God descending like a dove, and lighting upon him: And lo a voice from heaven saying, 'This my beloved Son, in whom I am well-pleased.'" (KJV, Matthew 3:6–7)

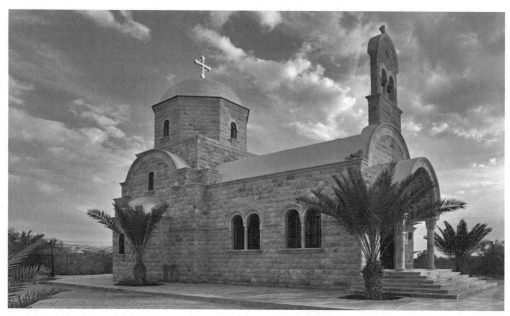

Located by the Jordan River, the Orthodox Church of St. John the Baptist was built near the place where John baptised Jesus.

What did Jesus say about John the Baptist?

Jesus said, "This is the one about whom it is written, 'See, I am sending my messenger ahead of you, who will prepare your way before you.'" (NRSV, Matthew 11:10) Also, Jesus pointed out the hypocrisy of some of the church leaders because they disapproved of John and Jesus: "For John came neither eating nor drinking, and they say, 'He has a demon;' the Son of Man came eating and drinking, and they say, 'Look, a glutton and a drunkard, a friend of tax collectors and sinners!'" (NRSV, Matthew 11:18–19)

FORTY DAYS IN THE WILDERNESS

What happened to Jesus in the wilderness?

After he was baptized, Jesus was swept by the Holy Spirit into the wilderness, where he fasted for forty days. At the end of the forty days, Jesus was famished. The devil tempted Jesus when he was weak.

What temptations did Jesus face?

The devil told Jesus, "If you are the Son of God, command these stones to become loaves of bread." (NRSV, Matthew 4:3) Jesus set the example for generations of believers by re-calling scripture when tempted. Jesus quoted Deuteronomy 8:3 (NRSV) when he replied, "One does not live by bread alone but by every word that comes from the mouth of God."

Then the devil took Jesus to Jerusalem, and they stood on top of the temple. The devil twisted scripture from Psalm 91 to fit his argument: "If you are the Son of God, throw yourself down, for it is written, 'He will command the angels concerning you,' and 'On their hands they will bear you up, so that you will not dash your foot against a stone.'" (NRSV, Matthew 4:6) To this, Jesus replied with Deuteronomy 6:16: "Again it is written, 'Do not put the Lord your God to the test.'" (NRSV, Matthew 4:7)

A third time the devil tempted Jesus. The devil took Jesus to the top of a mountain. They looked down on all the kingdoms and wonders of the world. The devil said, "All these I will give you, if you will fall down and worship me." Jesus rebuked the devil, and said, "Away with you, Satan!" Then Jesus quoted Deuteronomy 6:13 (NRSV): "Worship the Lord your God and serve only him." (NRSV, Matthew 4:10) At

Jesus went into the wilderness, where he was tempted by Satan with great riches and power if Jesus would serve him.

this, the devil fled from Jesus, and the angels came to attend to Jesus. Afterwards, Jesus began his career in public ministry.

Does the modern church honor Jesus' time in the wilderness?

Many Christian denominations honor Jesus' time in the wilderness by observing Lent. The length of Lent varies from church to church, but for the most part, it is the six weeks prior to Easter. It is a solemn season marked by fasting, prayer, penitence, and contemplation of Jesus' life. Sometimes, believers fast by giving up a favorite food or beverage for the duration of Lent.

JESUS' MINISTRY

What was Jesus' mission about?

Jesus wanted to bring people to God: "Repent, for the kingdom of heaven is at hand." (KJV, Matthew 4:17) Jesus understood the struggles of being human: "When he saw the crowds, he had compassion for them because they were harassed and helpless, like sheep without a shepherd." (NRSV, Matthew 9:36) Jesus summed up his mission this way: "Those who are well have no need of a physician, but those who are sick. Go and learn what this means, 'I desire mercy, not sacrifice.' For I have come to call not the righteous but sinners." (NRSV, Matthew 9:12–13) Also, Jesus taught his followers the importance of loving each other, and treating each other with fairness, compassion, and understanding.

How did Jesus' disciples interpret Jesus' ministry?

Knowing Old Testament scripture, Jesus' followers expected a messiah. They believed Jesus was the messiah. However, they thought Jesus meant to establish a kingdom on earth, a powerful kingdom in the style of King David. They did not understand until after his resurrection that Jesus' kingdom was a spiritual one in heaven. The book of John describes it this way: "When the people saw the sign that he had done [feeding the five thousand with five loaves of bread and two fish], they began to say, 'This is indeed the prophet who is come into the world.' When Jesus realized that they were about to come and take him by force to make him king, he withdrew again to the mountain by himself." (NRSV, John 6:14–15)

If Jesus was concerned about love, why did he say, "Do not think I have come to bring peace on earth; I have not come to bring peace but a sword. For I have come to set a man against his father, and a daughter against her mother, and a daughter-in-law against her mother-in-law; and one's foes will be members of one's own household" (NRSV, Matthew 10:34–36)?

Some people chose to follow Jesus, and other people chose not to follow Jesus. Rifts were inevitable. Jesus did not advocate violence. But he recognized that it was an outcome of people's selfish, wicked choices.

213

Pilgrims visit ruins in the ancient town of Capernaum. This was a fishing village and Peter's home when Jesus recruited him.

Who were the first apostles to be recruited by Jesus?

Two brothers, Simon (also known as Peter) and Andrew. The brothers made their living fishing. Jesus called to them, "Come with me. I'll make a new kind of fisherman out of you. I'll show you how to catch men and women instead of perch and bass." (The Message; Matthew 4:19) Immediately, the brothers stopped their work and followed Jesus.

As Jesus, Simon Peter, and Andrew walked, they came across two more brothers, James and John. Like Simon Peter and Andrew, James and John were fishermen, and like Simon Peter and Andrew, they stopped what they were doing and followed Jesus.

Where did Jesus go?

He walked all over Galilee, and taught in the synagogues. He proclaimed the good news about the kingdom of God being near. In addition, Jesus cured many people of their sicknesses and disabilities. He attracted crowds and followers everywhere he went.

What is the Sermon on the Mount?

This is the name given to the sermon in which Jesus described the Beatitudes. These Beatitudes, or Blessings, describe the characteristics Jesus wants in his followers:

"Blessed are the poor in spirit, for theirs is the kingdom of God."

"Blessed are those who mourn, for they will be comforted."

"Blessed are the meek, for they will inherit the earth."

"Blessed are those who hunger and thirst for righteousness, for they will be filled."

"Blessed are the pure in heart, for they will see God."

"Blessed are the peacemakers, for they will be called children of God."

"Blessed are those who are persecuted for righteousness' sake, for theirs is the kingdom of heaven."

"Blessed are you when people revile you, and persecute you, and utter all kinds of evil against you falsely on my account. Rejoice and be glad, for your reward is great in heaven, for in the same way they persecuted the prophets who were before you." (NRSV, Matthew 5:3–12)

One of the high points of Jesus' ministry was his Sermon on the Mount.

Oftentimes, the Beatitudes are viewed through the distorted lens of worldly standards. Accordingly, some people read the Beatitudes and think that Jesus expected his followers—then and now—to live their lives as weak, passive victims in order to receive their eternal reward in Heaven. Most Bible scholars, however, point out that the opposite is true. Jesus never promised that his followers would live trouble-free lives, but he did promise that if followers lived by his words that he would fill their hearts and minds with new understanding. This new understanding inspired followers—then and now—to allow their worldly, selfish attitudes to be kneaded into Christ-like attitudes of humility, generosity, gentleness, and strength.

In what ways did Jesus change his followers' understanding of the Law of Moses?

Jesus elaborated on the Jewish law by explaining that the spirit in which the law was obeyed was just as important as the act of obeying. Getting through the day without murdering someone is obeying the letter of the law. However, what about gossiping about someone? Getting through the day without having sex with the neighbor's spouse is obeying the letter of the law. What about fantasizing about the neighbor's spouse?

Jesus said, " This is how I want you to conduct yourself in these matters. If you enter your place of worship and, about to make an offering, you suddenly remember a grudge a friend has against you, abandon your offering, leave immediately, go to this friend and make things right. Then and only then, come back and work things out with God." (The Message; Matthew 5:23–24)

"You have heard that it was said, 'Do not commit adultery.' But I tell you that anyone who looks at a woman lustfully has already committed adultery with her in his heart." (NIV, Matthew 5:27–28)

The Mount of Beatitudes Catholic chapel is constructed near the Mount of Beatitudes near Lake Kinneret, Israel, where Jesus is said to have delivered his Sermon on the Mount.

"You have heard that it was said, 'An eye for an eye and a tooth for a tooth.' But I say to you, do not resist an evildoer. But if anyone strikes you on the right cheek, turn the other also … " (NRSV, Matthew 5:38–39)

"You're familiar with the old written law, 'Love your friend,' and its unwritten companion, 'Hate you're your enemy.' I'm challenging that. I'm telling you to love your enemies. Let them bring out the best in you, not the worst. When someone gives you a hard time, respond with the energies of prayer, for then you are working out of your true selves, your God-created selves. This is what God does—he give his best—the sun to warm and the rain to nourish—to everyone, regardless: the good and bad, the nice and nasty. If all you do is love the lovable do you expect a bonus? Anybody can do that. If you simply say hello to those who greet you, do you expect a medal? Any run-of-the-mill sinner does that." (Matthew 5:43–48)

Most scholars contend that Jesus did not expect his followers to be doormats, nor did he set them up for failure by exacting upon them unattainable standards of conduct. Rather, Jesus' intention was to challenge his followers' view of the law. Jesus wanted his followers to align not only their actions, but their attitudes as well, with the law. In doing so, they would be whole and complete.

THE LORD'S PRAYER

What is the Lord's Prayer?

Jesus encouraged his followers to pray with simple sincerity, and refrain from using trite, overwrought phrases. Jesus offered this as a model for prayer: "Our Father which art in heaven, hallowed by thy name. Thy kingdom come, thy will be done in earth as it is in heaven. Give us this day our daily bread. And forgive us our debts, as we forgive our debtors. And lead us not into temptation but deliver us from evil: For thine is the power and the glory for ever. Amen." (KJV, Matthew 6:9–13)

In The Message, a modern take on the Bible, the passage reads this way: "Our Father in heaven, reveal who you are. Set the world right; Do what's best—as above, so below. Keep us alive with three square meals. Keep us forgiven with you and forgiving others. Keep us safe from ourselves and the Devil. You're in charge! You can do anything you want! You're ablaze in beauty! Yes. Yes. Yes."

JESUS' INSTRUCTIONS FOR RIGHT LIVING

What was Jesus' attitude about personal possessions?

Jesus was fine with personal possessions—as long they did not usurp a person's faith. Jesus said, "Lay not up for yourselves treasures upon earth, where moth and rust doth corrupt, and where thieves break through and steal: But lay up for yourselves treasures in heaven, where neither moth nor rust doth corrupt, and where thieves do not break through nor steal: For where your treasure is, there will your heart be also." (KJV, Matthew 6:19–21)

What was Jesus' attitude about worry?

He said, "Do not worry about your life, what you will eat or what you will drink, or about your body, what you will wear. Is not life more than food, and the body more than clothing? Look at the birds of the air; they neither sow nor reap nor gather into barns, and yet your heavenly Father feeds them. Are you not of more value than they?" Jesus continued, "Therefore do not worry, saying, 'What will we eat?' or 'What will we drink?' or 'What will we wear?' For it is the Gentiles who strive for all these things; and indeed your heavenly Father knows that you need all these things. But strive first for the kingdom of God and his righteousness, and these things will be given to you as well." (NRSV, Matthew 6:25–26, 31–33)

What did Jesus say about judging other people?

He said, "Do not judge, or you too will be judged. For in the same way you judge others, you will be judged, and with the measure you use, it will be measured to you. Why do you look at the speck of sawdust in your brother's eye and pay no attention to the plank in your own eye?" (NIV, Matthew 7:1, 3)

Jesus did not expect his followers to rely solely on their own skills to accomplish these radical lifestyle changes. He encouraged followers to seek God's help through prayer: "Keep on asking, and you will be given what you ask for. Keep on looking, and you will find. Keep on knocking, and the door will be opened. For everyone who asks, receives. Everyone who seeks finds. And the door is open to everyone who knocks." (NLT, Matthew 7:7–8)

What did Jesus say about forgiveness?

Peter asked Jesus, "Lord, if another member of the church sins against me, how often should I forgive? As many as seven times?" Jesus replied, "Not seven times, but, I tell you, seventy-seven times." (NRSV, Matthew 18:21, 22)

According to Jesus, what was the greatest commandment?

"You shall love the Lord your God with all your heart, and with all your soul, and with all your mind." The next greatest commandment was, "You shall love your neighbor as yourself." (NRSV, Matthew 22:37, 38)

THE MIRACLES OF JESUS

What kinds of miracles did Jesus perform?

Jesus healed diseases and infirmities of all kinds. He healed people who suffered from leprosy, demon possession, blindness, muteness, paralysis, chronic bleeding, and epilepsy. Also, he raised people from the dead.

Why did Jesus spend so much time healing sick people?

Jesus loved people, and he cared about their lives. In Jesus' time, something easily treated today, such as a urinary tract infection, might lead to death. The average lifespan in the first century C.E. was age fifty. So Jesus ministered in a way that was not only helpful, but dramatic.

Did Jesus perform other miracles besides healing people?

Yes. He did a lot more!

Jesus calmed a storm that threatened to overturn his boat. (Matthew 8:23–26)

Jesus fed a crowd of people with very little food. (Matthew 14:13–21), (Matthew 15:32–38) The first passage, in which Jesus feeds five thousand people, is the only one of his miracles recorded in all four Gospels.

Jesus walked on water. (Matthew 14:25–27)

Jesus healed the lame and the sick, including those with epilepsy and chronic bleeding.

Why did Jesus appear to be reluctant to heal the Canaanite woman's daughter?

A Canaanite woman saw Jesus and cried to him, "Have mercy on me, Lord, Son of David; my daughter is tormented by a demon." At first Jesus did not respond to her. He said to his disciples, "I was sent only to the lost sheep of Israel." Jesus finally spoke to the woman, and said, "It is not fair to take the children's food and throw it to the dogs," to which the woman replied, "Yes, Lord, yet even the dogs eat the crumbs that fall from their masters' table." At this, Jesus remarked, "Woman, great is your faith! Let it be done for you as you wish." (NRSV, Matthew 15:21–28) The woman's daughter was healed at that instant.

Jesus traveled to many places, including Gennesaret, where he spread the word of his Father and healed the sick.

At a glance, it seems that Jesus was being callous. However, most scholars say there is a lot going on between the lines. First, Jesus had been preaching to Jews, and despite the healings and miracles, many rejected him. Here, then, was a woman who was not a Jew. Still, she embraced Jesus' message, and believed in his power to heal. Jesus' initial words to the woman were a test. The results of the test were twofold. They proved the enormous faith of this non-Jewish woman. Her faith, in turn, brought about the healing of her daughter, but highlighted also the stubbornness of so many of the Jews to whom Jesus spoke.

What did Jesus' critics say about his ministry?

Jesus' opponents were jealous of him, and afraid of him. To bring him down, they accused him of blasphemy when he healed someone (Matthew 9:3), when he picked grain on the Sabbath (Matthew 12:2), when he ate with sinners (Matthew 9:11), and when they thought he used the power of the devil to cast out demons. (Matthew 9:34)

People in Jesus' hometown of Nazareth were suspicious of him. They said, "Is not this the carpenter's son? Is not his mother called Mary? And are not his brothers James and Joseph and Simon and Judas? And are not all his sisters with us? Where then did this man get all this?" (NRSV, Matthew 13:55–56) The critics in Nazareth did not think the Messiah and their next-door neighbor could be one and the same.

JESUS RECRUITS HIS NEXT APOSTLE

Who was Jesus' next apostle?

Matthew. Jesus came across Matthew as Matthew was working at a tax booth. Jesus commanded Matthew, "Follow me," and he did. In Jesus' day, tax collectors were disliked by most people. Tax collectors had the reputation for extortion, so Matthew seemed an unlikely choice for an apostle.

What was the role of the apostles?

Jesus gave all the apostles the authority to cure every disease and sickness. Jesus' instructions to them were this: "As you go, preach this message, 'The kingdom of heaven is near.' Heal the sick, raise the dead, cleanse those who have leprosy, drive out demons." (NIV, Matthew 10:7–8) This is recounted in Luke 10 as well.

What did Jesus tell the apostles to do if they got in trouble?

Jesus told them, "Do not worry about how you are to speak or what you are to say; for what you are to say will be given to you at that time: for it is not you who speak, but the Spirit of your Father speaking through you." (NRSV, Matthew 10:19–20)

THE PARABLES OF JESUS

What is a parable?

A parable is a short story with a lesson in it. Jesus used parables to teach about the nature of the kingdom of God.

What is the kingdom of God?

There are a variety of closely related meanings. The Jewish people expected a new political kingdom. Jesus had something else in mind. Jesus wanted his followers to realize that part of the kingdom was knowable to them right then when they demonstrated love, joy, and peace in Jesus' name. Also, Jesus wanted his followers to realize that the kingdom will be revealed fully when God returns to earth.

Why did Jesus use parables?

Jesus used parables to create lasting images in the minds of his listeners. He used ordinary events to illustrate extraordinary truths. For listeners to understand the parables, they had to listen with open hearts, not just logical minds.

What were some of the parables Jesus told?

The parable of the sower (Matthew 13:18-23). The lives of most of Jesus' listeners were linked closely to farming. Accordingly, Jesus used imagery about seeds and ground to illustrate the various responses of people when they heard Jesus' message about the kingdom of God. Jesus' words were the seeds. Some people had minds and hearts like rocky ground. They received Jesus' message just fine, but did not allow the message to take root. When persecution or trouble came their way, the message withered.

The parable of the weeds (Matthew 13:24-30). In this parable, a farmer sowed good seed in his field. At night, while everyone was asleep, an enemy came and sowed weeds among the good seed. The good seed grew alongside the weeds until the time of harvest. At that time, the farmer separated the healthy, useful crop from the weeds. He gathered the healthy crop into the barn, and burned the weeds. This parable illustrated to Jesus' listeners that wicked people will exist alongside good people until the end of the world, at which time they will be separated for their final destinies.

The parable of the mustard seed (Matthew 13:31–32). In this parable, Jesus compared his message to a tiny mustard seed. Like the mustard seed, when Jesus' message took root, it grew into a thriving tree.

The parable of the leavened bread (Matthew 13:33). In this parable, Jesus likened his message to yeast. His message is a powerful element that is life-giving just as yeast makes plain flour into fortifying bread. When Jesus' message is taken into the hearts of his listeners, lives were transformed, and the message spread.

The parable of the king and his slave (Matthew 18:23–35). In this parable, Jesus likened his kingdom to a king who wished to settle accounts with his slaves. One slave owed the king an immense sum he could not pay. The king ordered that the slave and his family be sold to make good on the debt. The slave fell to his knees and begged the king to forgive him the debt. Pitying the slave, the king agreed. As the slave went home, he came across a fellow slave who owed him a small sum. The first slave seized the other one by the throat and ordered him to pay up. The slave who owed the small sum begged to be forgiven, but the first slave refused and threw him into debtor's prison. Some other slaves saw the injustice of what happened and told the king. The king ordered the slave who owed an immense sum to appear before him again. He scolded the slave: "You wicked slave! I forgave you all that debt because you pleaded with me. Should you not have had mercy on your fellow slave, as I had mercy on you?" (NRSV, Matthew 18:33) The king had the slave tortured until he paid the entire debt.

The parable of the landowner (Matthew 20:1–16). This parable is unique to the book of Matthew. In this parable, Jesus likened the kingdom of heaven to a landowner who promised laborers a certain amount of payment for working in the vineyard. The landowner promised the laborers who had been working all day long a fair day's wage. The landowner promised latecomers the same wage. Here Jesus made the point that a person who decides to follow Jesus late in the game will get the same reward as the person who follows Jesus his whole life.

The parable of the king who gave a banquet (Matthew 22:1–14). In this parable, Jesus compared the kingdom of heaven to a king who gave a wedding banquet for his son. The king sent his slaves to summon the people who were invited to the banquet. The people refused to come. Again, the king sent his slaves to summon the people who were invited to the banquet. Again, the people refused to come. They had various reasons for not coming—one had business to tend to, one had to farm. Still other people went so far as to abuse the king's slaves. This time, the king got mad. He sent soldiers to destroy those people. This time, the king sent his slaves out into the streets "and gathered all whom they found, both good and bad; so the wedding hall was filled with guests." (NRSV, Matthew 22:10) Jesus illustrated how God sent prophets to tell the people about the Messiah. Many of them refused to listen. God opened the discourse to include Gentiles as well.

THE TRANSFIGURATION

What happened when Jesus was transfigured?

Jesus took Peter, James, and John up onto a high mountain. Once there, "Jesus was transfigured before them, and his face shone like the sun, and his clothes became dazzling white. Suddenly there appeared to them Moses and Elijah, talking with him." As Peter and the others looked on, "a bright cloud overshadowed them, and from the cloud a voice said, 'This is my Son, the Beloved; with him I am well pleased; listen to him!'" (NRSV, Matthew 17:2, 5)

With Jesus' Transfiguration, the prophecy of the Old Testament was fulfilled.

What was the significance of the Transfiguration?

The Transfiguration showed the disciples the completion of Old Testament prophecy. The disciples saw Moses the lawgiver, Elijah the prophet who foretold Jesus' coming, and Jesus the fulfillment of the law and prophecy. Also, due to its extraordinary nature, the Transfiguration served as an unforgettable memory that strengthened the disciples' faith in Jesus' divinity.

KINGDOM COME

Did Jesus say anything about end times in Matthew?

Yes. "Beware that no one leads you astray. For many will come in my name, saying, 'I am the Messiah!' and they will lead many astray." (NRSV, Matthew:4–5)

"And wars will break out near and far but don't panic. Yes, these things must come, but the end won't follow immediately. The nations and kingdoms will proclaim war against each other, and there will be famines and earthquakes in many parts of the world. But all this will only the beginning of horrors to come." (NLT, Matthew 24:6–8)

"Then you will be handed over to be persecuted and put to death, and you will be hated by all nations because of me. At that time many will turn away from the faith and will betray and hate each other, and many false prophets will appear and deceive many people. Because of the increase of wickedness, the love of most will grow cold, but he who stands firm to the end will be saved." (NIV, Matthew 24:9–13)

"Then the Son of Man will appear in heaven, and then all the tribes of the earth will mourn, and they will see 'the Son of Man coming on the clouds of heaven' with power and great glory. And he will send out his angels with a loud trumpet call, and they will gather his elect from the four winds, from one end of heaven to the other." (NRSV, Matthew 24:30–31)

"But about that day and hour no one knows, neither the angels of heaven, nor the Son, but only the Father.... Then two will be in the field; one will be taken and one will be left. Two women will be grinding meal together; one will be taken and one will be left. Keep awake therefore, for you do not know on what day your Lord is coming. But understand this; if the owner of the house had known in what part of the night the thief was coming, he would have stayed awake and would not have let his house be broken into. Therefore you must also be ready, for the Son of Man is coming at an unexpected hour." (NRSV, Matthew 24: 36, 41–44)

What did Jesus mean by saying 'Son of Man'?

Jesus referred to himself by this name frequently. Opinions differ as to the phrase's meaning. In the Old Testament, the name is used to refer to the Messiah. So some people believe the phrase is Jesus' confirmation that he is the Messiah. Other people believe the phrase has to do with Jesus' role as God in human form, sharing in the life of humans, with all its imperfections.

THE FINAL WEEK OF JESUS' LIFE ON EARTH

Where did Jesus live during the last week of his life?

He had been traveling around sharing the good news. One week before he was killed, he went back to Jerusalem. He entered the city humbly, riding on a donkey. This was in stark contrast to military leaders of the day who entered cities astride powerful horses.

How did people react to Jesus' entry?

Jesus' followers spread out their cloaks and palm branches ahead of him. They shouted, "Hosanna to the Son of David! Blessed is he who comes in the name of the Lord! Hosanna in the highest!" (NIV, Matthew 21:9) The Bible does not go into detail at this point, but some onlookers were not pleased. In just one week's time, some of the people (some of whom were Jesus' followers) handed Jesus over to the authorities to be killed.

How is this day observed in the church?

In many churches, Jesus' final entry into Jerusalem is observed on Palm Sunday. The event is memorialized with special songs and the waving of palm fronds. Some churches burn the fronds and save the ashes for next year's Ash Wednesday services. On Ash Wednesday, pastors use the ashes to make the mark of the cross on the foreheads of congregants.

Why did Jesus get mad when he was in the temple?

When Jesus entered Jerusalem, he went to the temple. Seeing that the temple had become more of a place for commerce than worship, Jesus drove the merchants out, and exclaimed, "It is written, 'My house shall be called a house of prayer'; but you are making it a den of robbers." (NRSV, Matthew 21:13)

What else did Jesus do while he was at the temple?

He healed the sick people who came to him there, despite the criticism of the temple leaders.

Did Jesus predict his betrayal, death, and resurrection?

Jesus was angered that the temple was being used as a marketplace, and so he drove out the merchants.

Yes. He told his disciples, "We are going up to Jerusalem, and the Son of Man will be betrayed to the chief priests and the teachers of the law. They will condemn him to death and will turn him over to the Gentiles to be mocked and flogged and crucified. On the third day he will be raised to life!" (NIV, Matthew 20:18–19) Later, during the final week of his life on earth, Jesus said to his disciples, "As you know, the Passover is two days away—and the Son of Man will be handed over to be crucified." (NIV, Matthew 26:2)

How did Jesus and the apostles observe the Passover?

They ate the Passover meal at an acquaintance's house. This last meal Jesus had with his apostles became known as the Last Supper.

What happened during this meal?

Jesus gave new meaning to the Passover meal. Jesus took bread, blessed it, divided it among the apostles, and said, "Take, eat; this is my body." Then Jesus took a cup of wine, blessed it, divided it among the apostles, and said, "Drink from it, all of you; for this is my blood of the covenant, which is

An illustration by Gustave Doré of the Last Supper.

poured out for many for the forgiveness of sins." (NRSV, Matthew 26:26, 27) The addition of the word "new" with the word "covenant" in some Bible translations heightens the contrast between the old way of doing these rites under Mosaic law, and the new way of doing things through Jesus. These actions modeled what became a building block for the Christian church—Holy Communion, or Eucharist.

GETHSEMANE

What is Gethsemane?

Since the time of Jesus, Gethsemane has been a public garden located at the foot of the Mount of Olives in Jerusalem. It was on the Mount of Olives that Jesus predicted that the apostles—even Peter—would desert him that very night.

Why did Jesus go to Gethsemane?

After the Last Supper, Jesus and the apostles went to Gethsemane to pray.

What did Jesus ask the apostles to do?

Jesus pleaded with them to stay awake and pray with him. Jesus "began to be filled with anguish and deep distress. He told them, 'My soul is crushed with grief to the point of death. Stay here and watch with me." (NLT, Matthew 26:37–38)

Did the apostles do as Jesus asked?

No. They fell asleep. In anguish, Jesus prayed by himself: "My Father! If this cup cannot be taken away until I drink it, your will be done." (NLT, Matthew 26:42)

If the apostles were not awake to hear Jesus pray, how is it known what words Jesus said when he prayed?

Since Gethsemane is a public place, presumably there were other people there who must have heard Jesus praying.

TWO BETRAYALS

With what crimes was Jesus charged?

Sedition and blasphemy. A false witness twisted what Jesus said about the temple: "Truly I tell you, not one stone will be left

Before he would be betrayed, Jesus went to the public garden of Gethsemane to pray.

225

here upon another; all will be thrown down." (NRSV, Matthew 24:2) The false witness misquoted Jesus thus: "I am able to destroy the temple of God and to build it in three days." (NRSV, Matthew 26:61) Then when a priest questioned Jesus about whether he was the Messiah, Jesus responded, "You have said so. But I tell you, from now on you will see the Son of Man seated at the right hand of Power and coming on the clouds of heaven." (Matthew 26:64–65)

Who betrayed Jesus by handing him over to the authorities?

Judas Iscariot, one of the twelve apostles. On the sly, Judas went to the priests who wanted Jesus arrested, and said, "How much will you pay me to betray Jesus to you?" (NLT, Matthew 26:14–15) The priests paid Judas thirty pieces of silver. From that moment on, Judas looked for an opportunity to betray Jesus.

Did Judas know that Jesus knew of his duplicity?

Yes. Judas knew that Jesus knew, and he did it anyway. During the Last Supper, Jesus said, "Truly I tell you, one of you will betray me." The apostles were upset by this statement and wondered about it. One apostle after another said, "Surely not I, Lord?" Jesus replied, "The one who has dipped his hand into the bowl with me will betray me." Judas,

After betraying Jesus, Judas is said to have hanged himself in the book of Matthew. In Acts, however, Judas trips on rocks and dies when his stomach bursts open.

knowing already that he would betray Jesus, said also, "Surely not I, Rabbi?" Jesus responded, "You have said so." (NRSV, Matthew 26:20–25)

When did Judas betray Jesus?

Judas led the authorities to Gethsemane, where Jesus prayed. Judas greeted Jesus with a kiss, and said, "Greetings, Teacher!" Jesus replied, "My friend, go ahead and do what you have come for." (NLT, Matthew 26:49, 50) After Jesus was arrested, Judas repented, but it was too late. He threw the silver coins down in the temple. He then went and, according to Matthew, hanged himself. In the book of Acts, Luke wrote that Judas died when he tripped over a rock, and his stomach burst open (Acts 1:18).

As Jesus predicted, Peter denied knowing Jesus for fear he would be persecuted as well.

Who betrayed Jesus by denying knowing who he was?

Peter did. Earlier in the evening, Peter promised Jesus, "Even though I must die with you, I will not deny you." Jesus replied, "Truly I tell you, this very night, before the cock crows, you will deny me three times." (NRSV, Matthew 26:34, 35)

When did Peter betray Jesus?

After Jesus was arrested and taken into custody, a servant girl saw Peter standing nearby, and said to him, "You also were with Jesus of Galilee." (NIV, Matthew 26:69) Peter denied it. Another servant girl said the same thing. Peter denied it again. Then some bystanders confirmed what the servant girls said. A third time, Peter denied knowing Jesus. At that moment, a rooster crowed. Peter remembered Jesus' words, and wept bitterly. Later, Peter became a founder of the Christian church.

JESUS AND PILATE

Who was Pilate?

Pilate was the Roman governor of Judea from about 26 C.E. to 37 C.E.

What did Pilate say when Jesus was brought before him?

Pilate asked Jesus about the accusations leveled against him. Pilate believed in Jesus' innocence, but caved under the pressure of Jesus' critics, who cried, "Crucify him!" (NIV, Matthew 27:22). Pilate agreed to the people's demands, but washed his hands ceremoniously in front of the crowd, and said, "I am innocent of this man's blood.... It is your responsibility!" (NIV, Matthew 27:24)

Who was Barabbas?

Barabbas was a notorious insurrectionist and murderer. He was in prison when Jesus was brought before Pilate. According to custom, Pilate offered to free one prisoner of the people's choosing. Would it be Jesus or Barabbas? The people chose Barabbas.

What happened to Jesus after Barabbas was freed?

Jesus was beaten and mocked. Pilate's soldiers stripped Jesus and put a crimson robe on him. They made a crown out of

In this reenactment, an actor portrays Jesus carrying his own cross to his place of execution.

thorns, and pressed it onto Jesus' head. In addition, the soldiers pretended to pay homage to Jesus, and they spat on him. Then the soldiers led Jesus away to be crucified.

Where was Jesus crucified?

On a hill called Golgotha, which means 'place of the skull.' Once there, the soldiers cast lots for Jesus' clothes, and offered him wine mixed with gall. Jesus refused the wine.

What was the official charge against Jesus?

Pilate's soldiers wrote the charge down and nailed it to the top of Jesus' cross for everyone to see. The charge read, "THIS IS JESUS THE KING OF THE JEWS." (KJV, Matthew 27:37) Essentially, the charge was treason.

Who was crucified alongside Jesus?

Two criminals. It is in Luke 23 that more is revealed about the crucifixion of the criminals. One criminal mocked Jesus. The other criminal said to the mocker, "Do you not fear God, since you are under the same sentence of condemnation? And we indeed have been condemned justly, for we are getting what we deserve for our deeds, but this man has done nothing wrong." Then to Jesus the man said, "Jesus, remember me when you come into your kingdom." Jesus replied, "Truly I tell you, today you will be with me in Paradise." (NRSV, Luke 23:40–43) It was a criminal, then, who was the first to understand—not Jesus' apostles—that Jesus' kingdom was in heaven, not on earth.

What were Jesus' last words?

"Eli, Eli, lama sabachthani?" The English translation of this Aramaic phrase is, "My God, My God, why have you forsaken me?" (NIV, Matthew 27:46)

What happened when Jesus died?

When Jesus breathed his last, the curtain of the temple split from top to bottom. Before Jesus died, people could not approach God directly because they were so sinful and he was holy, hence the curtain in the temple. The curtain splitting symbolized people's newfound closeness to God, via Jesus.

In addition, "tombs were opened up, and many bodies of believers asleep in their graves were raised." (The Message, Matthew 27:52) Many believers take this to mean that when Jesus died, he descended into hell, or the place of the dead, and released Old Testament people of faith. In the middle ages, this event became known as the Harrowing of Hell.

Joseph of Arimathea took Jesus' body down from the cross, wrapped the body, and transferred him to a tomb.

Who tended to Jesus after he died?

Joseph of Arimathea, a disciple of Jesus. He wrapped Jesus' body in a clean linen cloth, and laid his body in a new tomb. Then he rolled a big stone in front of the tomb. Mary (the mother of Jesus) and Mary Magdalene watched. Soldiers stood watch by the tomb because they thought Jesus' followers might steal him away in order to make Jesus' prediction about rising after three days look as if it had come true.

What happened on the third day after Jesus' death?

Mary and Mary Magdalene went to the tomb. Suddenly, "the earth reeled and rocked under their feet as God's angel came down from heaven, came right up to where they were standing. He rolled back the stone and then sat on it." (The Message, Matthew 28:2) The soldiers guarding the tomb quivered in fear. The angel said to the women, "Do not be afraid; I know that you are looking for Jesus who was crucified. He is not here; for he has been raised as he said. Come, see the place where he lay. Then go quickly and tell his disciples, 'He has been raised from the dead, and indeed he is going ahead of you to Galilee; there you will see him.'" (Matthew 28:5–6)

How did Mary and Mary Magdalene respond?

Filled with awe and joy, they ran to tell the disciples what the angel said. Suddenly, Jesus appeared to them, and they worshiped him. When the chief priests heard that Jesus arose from the dead, they circulated a rumor that Jesus' disciples simply stole his body during the night while the guards were asleep.

Pilgrims visit the Stone of Anointing at the Church of the Holy Sepulchre in Jerusalem. The stone is where tradition says Jesus' body was prepared for burial.

What were the dates of Jesus' death and resurrection?

No one knows for sure. Today, the celebration of Jesus' resurrection is known as Easter. Easter does not have a fixed date. It is celebrated on the first Sunday after the first full moon after the spring equinox. In the early days of the church, Christian leaders wanted to honor the death and resurrection of Jesus soon after Passover, because the Bible describes how Jesus' death and resurrection took place following Passover. The Jewish calendar is based on lunar cycles, so the date of Passover changes every year. To make sure the date of Jesus' resurrection always came after Passover, the church made that date changeable as well.

Why is the celebration of Jesus' resurrection known as Easter?

The name Easter was derived from the name of a Saxon goddess, Eostre, who was associated with fertility and springtime. As to why the church chose the name Easter, and not, say, Jesus' Resurrection Day, is not clear. Typically, Easter is celebrated with joyous music, prayer, and liturgy.

Besides Easter, are any other events on the church calendar associated with the death and resurrection of Jesus?

Yes. The week prior to Easter Sunday is called Holy Week. Churches around the world commemorate Holy Week in a variety of ways, and to varying degrees.

The Garden Tomb in Jerusalem is where many believe Jesus was buried and from which he arose.

The Sunday before Easter Sunday is Palm Sunday. This commemorates Jesus' final entry into Jerusalem, when people spread palm branches before him. The event is memorialized with special songs and the waving of palm fronds. Some churches burn the fronds and save the ashes for the next year's Ash Wednesday services.

The Thursday of Holy Week is called Maundy Thursday. Most likely, the word "maundy" is derived from the Latin, "mandatum," which is the origin of the word "mandate." A mandate, or command, is what Jesus gave the apostles when he told them at the Last Supper after he washed their feet, "So if I, your Lord and Teacher, have washed your feet you also ought to wash one another's feet. For I have set you an example, that you also should do as I have done to you." (NRSV, John 13:14–15) Usually, the washing of people's feet was the responsibility of a servant, or whoever was of lowest status in the house. So by commanding the apostles to wash each other's feet, Jesus was upending expectations. Jesus wanted the apostles to carry the practice of service and humility into all areas of their lives. Some churches commemorate the day with a solemn service. Some churches commemorate the day by having foot washing ceremonies.

The Friday of Holy Week is called Good Friday. It is called Good, not because of Jesus' ordeal itself, but because of the results of the ordeal—the resurrection of Jesus, which saved all people from their sins. The day is marked with solemn services.

The Saturday before Easter is called Holy Saturday. This day commemorates the time Jesus' body was in the tomb. It is a time for sober reflection, prayer, and contemplation.

Jesus washed the feet of his apostles as a way of symbolically telling them that they should be similarly humble when they go out into the world to serve God.

What was Jesus' final command to his disciples?

"Therefore go and make disciples of all nations, baptizing them in the name of the Father and of the Son and of the Holy Spirit, and teaching them to obey everything I have commanded you. And surely I am with you always, to the very end of the age." (NIV, Matthew 28:19–20)

What do the letters "INRI" mean?

In art, oftentimes the sign on Jesus' cross reads "INRI." This is an acronym for the Latin phrase "Iesus Nazarenus, Rex Iudaeorum." In English, that translates into "Jesus the Nazarene, King of the Jews."

THE GOSPEL OF MARK

Who was Mark?

Mark, whose name means "large hammer," was known also as John. For years, it was widely believed that the book of Mark was written by Mark when he transcribed remi-

---

What Easter tradition comes from the book of Mark?

When the two apostles met Jesus on the road to Emmaus, they did not recognize him as Jesus at first. However, Jesus made himself known. He was their Lord and Savior. This episode inspired a practice that continues to this day. Around Easter time, some church groups organize retreats and other special events to encourage believers to meditate more deeply on their relationship with Jesus. Events include prayer labyrinths and organized hikes. There are companies that specialize in renting and selling labyrinth sets, too.

---

niscenses of Peter. However, most modern-day scholars believe the identity of the author is untraceable at this point.

When was the book of Mark written?

It was written between 70 C.E. and 130 C.E. It is the shortest of the four Gospels.

What is the book of Mark about?

Like the book of Matthew, the book of Mark focuses on Jesus' life and ministry. Mark focuses on what Jesus did, rather what he said.

How does the book of Mark begin?

It begins with John the Baptist's baptism of Jesus.

ONLY IN MARK

What major event appears in Mark but not in the other Gospels?

Jesus' healing of the blind man at Bethsaida.

What did Jesus do to heal the blind man?

Some people brought a blind man to Jesus, and asked Jesus to heal him. Jesus put saliva on the man's eyes, and laid his hands on him. Jesus asked him, "Do you see anything?" The man replied, "I see people; they look like trees walking around." (NIV, Mark 8:22–26) Again, Jesus laid his hands on him. This time, the man's sight was restored.

What other major characteristics set Mark apart from the other Gospels?

There are few events in the book of Mark that are not found in the other Gospels. Many scholars think that the book of Mark was the first Gospel written, and that the other Gospel writers used it as a source to write their own Gospels.

233

What parable appears in the book of Mark but not in the other Gospels?

The parable of the sprouting seed. Jesus said:

"The kingdom of God is as if someone would scatter seed on the ground, and would sleep and rise night and day, and the seed would sprout and grow, he does not know how. The earth produces of itself, first the stalk, then the head, then the full grain in the head. But when the grain is ripe, at once he goes in with his sickle, because the harvest has come." (Mark 4:26–29)

THE GOSPEL OF LUKE

Who was Luke?

Luke, whose name means "light," was a physician, and Paul's steadfast friend and traveling companion. It is commonly believed that Luke is not only the author of the book bearing his name, but the book of Acts as well.

When was the book of Luke written?

It was written sometime between 50 C.E. and 80 C.E.

What is the book of Luke about?

The book of Luke focuses on Jesus' life and ministry in terms of Jesus' holiness. The book is in the form of a letter written to Theophilus.

Who was Theophilus?

No one knows for sure, but there are a couple of theories. Theophilus, which means 'friend of God,' might have been the name of Luke's patron, or the name might be used in a general sense to refer to any Christian reading the book.

How does the book of Luke begin?

It begins with Luke explaining the importance of logic and research in the writing of the book. He explained, "Therefore, since I myself have carefully investigated everything from the beginning, it seemed good also to me to write an orderly account for you, most excellent Theophilus, so that you many know the certainty of the things you been taught." (NIV, Luke 1:3–4)

ONLY IN LUKE

What major events are found in Luke but not in Matthew and Mark?

• The circumstances surrounding the conception of John the Baptist and Jesus.

- The presence of the angels and the shepherds at Jesus' birth.
- The growth and early life of Jesus.
- Jesus' visit with Mary and Martha.
- The Parable of the Good Samaritan.
- Zacchaeus meets Jesus.

MORE ON JOHN THE BAPTIST

Who were Zechariah and Elizabeth?

Zechariah, a priest, was John the Baptist's father. Elizabeth was Zechariah's wife and John the Baptist's mother. Like Abraham and Sarah in the Old Testament, Zechariah and Elizabeth remained childless into their old age.

How did Zechariah and Elizabeth find out that John the Baptist was going to be their son?

The angel Gabriel visited Zechariah as he worked in the temple, and said, "Don't be afraid, Zechariah! For God has heard your prayer, and your wife, Elizabeth, will bear you a son! And you are to name him John. You will have great joy and gladness, and many will rejoice with you at his birth, for he will be great in the eyes of the Lord. He must never touch wine or hard liquor, and he will be filled with the Holy Spirit, even before his birth." (NLT, Luke 1:13)

Did Gabriel say anything else to Zechariah about John's life?

Yes. Gabriel said that John must never drink wine or other strong drink. This characteristic indicated that John the Baptist would—like Samson—be a Nazirite, or one set aside for God. Also, Gabriel said that John the Baptist would be filled with the Holy Spirit even in the womb, and that in life he would have the power of Elijah to "persuade many Israelites to turn to the LORD their God" and the power to "turn the hearts of the fathers to their children, and he will change disobedient minds to accept godly wisdom." (NLT, Luke 1:16, 17)

Did Zechariah believe Gabriel?

Not at first. Because Zechariah doubted, Gabriel struck him with muteness. When Zechariah left the temple, he had to communicate by gesturing, and he remained mute until after John was born.

What did Elizabeth do when she found out she was pregnant?

She went into seclusion for five months.

235

MARY RECEIVED STARTLING NEWS

Who received a similar message from Gabriel several months later?

Mary. In the sixth month of Elizabeth's pregnancy, Gabriel visited Mary, a virgin who was engaged to Joseph. Gabriel had something very important to tell Mary. This announcement to Mary became known as the Annunciation.

What did Gabriel say to Mary?

He began, "Greetings, you who are highly favored! The Lord is with you." (NIV, Luke 1:28) Then he said, "Do not be afraid, Mary, you have found favor with God. You will be with child and give birth to a son, and you are to give him the name of Jesus." (NIV, Luke 1:30–31)

Did Gabriel say anything else to Mary about Jesus' life?

Yes. Gabriel promised, "He will be great, and will be called the Son of the Most High. The Lord God will give him the throne of his father David, and he will reign over the house of Jacob forever, his kingdom will never end." (NIV, Luke 1:32–33)

What was Mary's response?

At first, Mary was puzzled. She said, "How can I have a baby? I am a virgin." (NLT, Luke 1:34) Gabriel assured her, "The Holy Spirit will come upon you, and the power of the

Located in Nazareth, Israel, the Basilica of the Anunciation stands on the spot where the angel Gabriel is said to have told Mary that she would give birth to the savior.

Most High will overshadow you." (NLT, Luke 1:35) Then Mary acquiesced: "I am the Lord's servant, and I am willing to accept whatever he wants. May everything you have said come true." (NLT, Luke 1:38)

Mary Went on a Trip

Where did Mary go on her trip?

Mary went from where she lived in Nazareth to visit her cousin Elizabeth in Jerusalem. At the time of Mary's visit, Elizabeth was in her sixth month of pregnancy with John the Baptist. Mary stayed with Elizabeth for about three months.

What happened when Mary arrived at Elizabeth's house?

When Mary greeted Elizabeth, the baby in Elizabeth's womb leapt. Elizabeth was filled with the Holy Spirit, and exclaimed to Mary, "Blessed art thou among women, and blessed is the fruit of thy womb." (KNJ, Luke 1:42)

What was Mary's response?

She replied with a prayer of praise and thanksgiving to God. The prayer became known as the Magnificat. Oftentimes, the prayer is set to music and sung, especially around Christmastime.

The Birth of Jesus

How does the birth narrative in Luke differ from those in Matthew and Mark?

Mark skips over Jesus' birth entirely. Matthew describes Joseph's early concerns about marrying Mary, and the visit of the Magi. It is in Luke that the praise of the angels and the worshiping shepherds are chronicled.

If Mary and Joseph lived in Nazareth, how was it that Jesus was born in Bethlehem?

Caesar Augustus, who ruled the Roman Empire from 27 B.C.E.–14 C.E., ordered a census. Everyone had to return to his/her hometown to register. Joseph, who was from the family of David, returned to Bethlehem. He took with him his soon-to-be wife, Mary. At the time, Mary was near the end of her pregnancy. While Mary and Joseph were in Bethlehem, Mary had her baby, Jesus.

Where in Bethlehem was Jesus born?

There was no room for Mary and Joseph in the inn. Presumably, there were many travelers on the roads at this time because of the census. The Bible does not say what kind of building Mary and Joseph stayed in, only that Mary laid the baby Jesus in a manger, or trough. It was common for houses of that time to have a room for the animals adjoining the family's living quarters. It might have been in this setting that Jesus was born.

How did the shepherds find out about the birth of Jesus?

An angel told them. The angel said, "Fear not: for, behold, I bring you good tidings of great joy, which shall be to all people." The angel continued, "And this shall be a sign unto you; Ye shall find the babe wrapped in swaddling clothes, lying in a manger." (KJV, Luke 2:10, 12)

What special event accompanied the angel's announcement?

Countless angels appeared by the messenger angel, who sang, "Glory to God in the highest, and on earth peace, good will toward men!" (KJV, Luke 2:14)

What did the shepherds do when they heard the announcement?

They went and looked for Jesus. When the shepherds arrived at the place where Mary, Joseph, and Jesus were, they told Mary and Joseph all that the angel had told them. Then the shepherds returned to their own home, and told everyone what happened.

THE EIGHTH DAY AFTER JESUS' BIRTH

What happened on the eighth day after Jesus was born?

His parents took him to the temple to be circumcised, as was the custom among Jews.

Who did Mary, Joseph, and Jesus meet while they were at the temple?

They met Simeon, a devout man who had been told by the Holy Spirit that "he would not die until he had seen the Lord's Messiah." Simeon cradled the baby Jesus and exclaimed, "Lord, now I can die in peace! As you promised me, I have seen the Savior you have given to all people. He is a light to reveal God to the nations, and he is the glory of your people Israel." (NLT, Luke 2:29–32) Mary and Joseph were amazed by this.

What else did Simeon say to Mary?

Simeon told Mary, "This child will be rejected by many in Israel, and it will be their undoing. But he will be the greatest joy to many others. Thus, the deepest thoughts of many hearts will be revealed. And a sword will pierce your very soul." (NLT, Luke 2:35)

Who was Anna?

Anna was another person Mary, Joseph, and Jesus met while they were at the temple. Anna was an eighty-four-year-old woman who never left the temple. She prayed and fasted all of the time. When she saw Jesus, "she began praising God. She talked about Jesus to everyone who had been waiting for the promised King to come and deliver Jerusalem." (NLT, Luke 2:38)

JESUS AS A BOY

What does the book of Luke say about Jesus' boyhood?

The book of Luke is unique in that it is the only canonical Gospel that describes Jesus' childhood. The account is brief, but describes a time when twelve-year-old Jesus went to Jerusalem with his parents to celebrate the Passover. They traveled with a large group of people, so when they departed Jerusalem to head home, Mary and Joseph did not notice Jesus' absence at first. They found him in the temple, sitting among the religious teachers, "both hearing them, and asking them questions. And all that heard him were astonished at his understanding and answers." (KJV, Luke 2:46–47)

What did Mary and Joseph do when they found Jesus?

They scolded him. They had not been able to find him for three days! Mary said to him, "Son, why hast thou thus dealt with us? Behold, thy father and I have sought thee sorrowing." (KJV, Luke 2:48)

How did Jesus respond to their parental concern and discipline?

He replied, "How is it that ye sought me? wist ye not that I must be about my Father's business?" (KJV, Luke 2:49)

Not much is said about the life of Jesus between his birth and the time he began his ministry, though the Gospel of Luke tells a brief story about Jesus when he was twelve.

239

> ### What does one apocryphal book say about Jesus' life as a young boy?
>
> The Bible says little about Jesus as a boy. A pseudepigraphic gospel called the Infancy Gospel of Thomas recounts stories of Jesus' childhood. As a boy, Jesus tried out his divine powers. In a fit of peevishness, Jesus cursed a neighborhood boy and caused him to wither into a corpse. When the boy's parents complained to Mary and Joseph about Jesus' behavior, Jesus afflicted the boy's parents with blindness. Later, Jesus resurrected the boy, but the boy's parents remained blind.

THE PARABLES OF JESUS

What are some of the parables that appear only in the book of Luke?

The Parable of the Good Samaritan (Luke 10:29–37). When a follower asked for clarification about the term "neighbor," Jesus responded with this parable. In the parable, a man traveled from Jerusalem to Jericho. As he traveled, robbers overtook him and beat him, leaving him nearly dead. A priest happened by and saw the man collapsed on the side of the road. The priest walked right by. A Levite walked right by, too. When a Samaritan man walked by and saw the victim, he took pity on the man. He bandaged his wounds and put him in the care of an innkeeper. He promised to reimburse the innkeeper whatever amount of money he spent to care for the injured man. After he finished telling the parable, Jesus asked the follower who questioned him, "Now which of these three would you say was a neighbor to the man who was attacked by bandits?" The man replied, "The one who showed him mercy." Jesus replied, "Yes, now go and do the same." (NLT, Luke 10:36–37)

Parables of the Lost (Luke 15:8–32). When the Pharisees and scribes criticized Jesus for befriending and eating with sinners, he replied with two parables.

In one, Jesus described a woman who had ten silver coins. She lost one. She lit a lamp and searched every nook and cranny of her house looking for the lost coin. When she found it, she called her friends to rejoice with her.

In another, Jesus described a man who had two sons. The younger son asked his father for his share of the inheritance. When the father gave it to him, the younger son traveled to a distant country and squandered everything he had on dissipated living. When he spent everything he had, it happened also that a severe famine took hold of the land where he resided. He became desperate. He would have eaten pig slop gladly, but no one would give him any. He considered his position, and realized he had been wrong all along. He decided to go back to his father and beg forgiveness. The father saw his son coming down the road, and was filled with compassion. He ran to the younger, prodigal son and embraced him. The son confessed his sin. The father threw an elaborate, impromptu party for his son, and said, "For this son of mine was dead and has now returned to life. He was lost, but now is found." The oldest son got angry because he had towed the line all along and never got a party. His father said to him, "Look, dear son, you and I are very close, and everything I have is yours. We had to celebrate this happy day. For your brother was dead and has come back to life! He was lost, but now he is found." (NLT, Luke 15:24, 31–32)

The Parable of the Rich Man and Lazarus (Luke 16:19–31). Jesus used this parable to illustrate the perils of loving wealth and the importance of repentance before it was too late. Jesus described the relationship between a certain wealthy man and a poor man named Lazarus. The wealthy man dressed in fine clothes and ate the best food, day in and day out. Poor Lazarus, covered in sores, had nothing. Lazarus died and went to enjoy a blessed afterlife. The rich man died, and was tortured in his afterlife. The rich man saw

In Jesus' parable of the good Samaritan, a kind man helps a wounded traveler after a priest and a Levite ignored his plight.

Lazarus and Abraham standing a long way off. The rich man begged Abraham to send Lazarus to him with some water to relieve his thirst. Abraham said, "Son, remember that during your lifetime you had everything you wanted, and Lazarus had nothing. So now he is here being comforted, and you are in anguish." The rich man begged Abraham to send Lazarus to warn his family about the mortal danger of not repenting. Abraham refused this, too, and said, "Moses and the prophets have warned them. Your brothers can read their writings anytime they want to." The rich man persisted, saying that if someone from the dead warned them they would listen. Abraham refused still and said, "If they won't listen to Moses and the prophets, they won't listen even if someone rises from the dead." (NLT, Luke 16:25, 29, 31) Here, Jesus predicted that he, too, would be ignored by some people even after he rose from the dead.

PEOPLE JESUS MET IN LUKE

What happened when Jesus met a widow in the town of Nain?

Jesus and his disciples happened upon the widow as her recently deceased and only son was being carried out of the town on a funeral bier. The widow wept. Jesus had compassion on her, and said to her, "Weep not." Jesus approached the bier and said to the corpse, "Young man, I say unto thee, Arise!" (KJV, Luke 7:13, 14) The young man sat up and was reunited with his mother. The crowd was amazed and joyful. Word spread of Jesus throughout Judea.

What did the woman in the city do to Jesus?

At one point during his ministry, Jesus was invited to eat at a Pharisee's house. Jesus agreed, and took his place at the table. While Jesus was there, "a woman in the city, who was a sinner" went into the Pharisee's house to see Jesus. The woman wept and washed Jesus' feet with her tears and the ointment from an alabaster jar. She dried his feet with her hair, and kissed his feet. The Pharisee said to himself, "If this man were a prophet, he would have known who and what kind of woman this is who is touching him—that she is a sinner." (NRSV, Luke 7:39) Jesus told those present, "Therefore, I tell you, her sins, which were many, have been forgiven; hence she has shown great love. But the one to whom little is forgiven, loves little." (NRSV, Luke 7:47)

Who were Martha and Mary?

Mary and Martha were sisters who were followers of Jesus. In the book of John, readers learn that Mary and Martha lived in the village of Bethany, and were the sisters of a man named Lazarus (not the Lazarus from the rich man/poor Lazarus parable). In John 11:2 and John 12:3, Mary is identified as being the one who washed Jesus' feet and dried his feet with her hair.

What happened when Jesus went to Mary and Martha's house?

Mary sat at Jesus' feet and listened to what he had to say. Martha bustled around, distracted by the duties of playing hostess. Martha complained to Jesus about what she viewed as Mary's laziness. Jesus replied, "My dear Martha, you are upset over all these details! There is really only one thing worth being concerned about. Mary has discovered it—and I won't take it away from her." (NLT, Luke 10:41–42) This brief account reveals a couple of important things about Jesus and his ministry. First, while women were second class citizens in that day and age, Jesus loved and valued them. Second, Jesus pointed out the importance of spending quality time with him. Busyness, even on Jesus' behalf, could take the focus away from what Jesus really wanted from his followers.

Who was Zacchaeus?

Zacchaeus was a wealthy tax collector. When Jesus went to Jericho, Zacchaeus tried to get a glimpse of Jesus. Because it was so crowded—and because Zacchaeus was short—he climbed a tree to get a glimpse of Jesus.

What happened when Jesus saw Zacchaeus perched in a tree?

Jesus said, "Zacchaeus, hurry and come down; for I must stay at your house today." (NRSV, Luke 19:5)

What kind of man did Jesus single out?

The crowd grumbled that Jesus was honoring a sinner by going to Zacchaeus' home. But Zacchaeus replied, "Master, I give away half my income to the poor—and if I'm caught cheating, I pay four times the damages." And Jesus told Zacchaeus that salvation will come to his home today because "the Son of Man came to find and restore the lost." (The Message, Luke 19:8-10)

The story of Jesus' visit to the home of Martha and Mary is an example of Jesus explaining what is really important in life.

THE GOSPEL OF JOHN

Who was John?

John, whose name means "God is gracious," was a fisherman by trade, who became an apostle when Jesus summoned him. John was the brother of James the apostle, and the son of Zebedee.

When was the book of John written?

Probably the late 90s C.E.

What is the book of John about?

John celebrated Jesus' miraculous nature of divinity and humanness.

How does the book of John begin?

John began the book with a spiritual description of Jesus: "The Word was first, the Word present to God, God present to the Word. The Word was God, in readiness from day one.

What did Jesus tell his followers to do to inherit eternal life?

Jesus told them to obey the law, which read, "You shall love the Lord your God with all your heart, and with all your soul, and with all your strength, and with all your mind; and your neighbor as yourself." (NRSV, Luke 10:27)

Everything was created through him: nothing—not one thing!—came into being without him. What came into existence was Life, and the Life was Light to live by. The Life-Light blazed out of the darkness; the darkness couldn't put it out." (The Message, John 1:1–3)

ONLY IN JOHN

How did Jesus describe his relationship to God?

Jesus talked to his followers a lot about his special relationship to God:

- "For God sent not his Son into the world to condemn the world; but that the world through him might be saved." (KJV, John 3:17)
- "But I do nothing without consulting the Father. I judge as I am told. And my judgment is absolutely just, because it is according to the will of God who sent me; it is not merely my own." (NLT, John 5:30)
- "You search the scriptures because you think that in them you have eternal life; and it is they that testify on my behalf. Yet you refuse to come to me to have life. I do not accept glory from human beings. But I know that you do not have the love of God in you. I have come in the Father's name, and you do not accept me." (NRSV, John 5:39–43)
- "No one gets to the Father apart from me. If you really knew me, you would know my Father as well." (The Message, John 14:6)

How did Jesus describe himself?

- "I am the world's light." (The Message, John 8:12).
- "I am the gate for the sheep." (NLT, John 10: 7).
- "I am the good shepherd." (KJV, John 10: 11).
- "I am the resurrection and the life." (NIV, John 11: 25).
- "I am the way, and the truth, and the life." (NRSV, John 14: 6).

Why did some of the synagogue leaders and some of the people criticize Jesus?

They criticized Jesus for several reasons:

- They thought Jesus deceived his followers. (John 7:13).
- Because Jesus said he existed even before Abraham. (John 8:58).
- They thought Jesus was possessed by a demon and insane. (John 10:20).
- They were afraid that everyone would believe in Jesus, and thus alarm the Roman government. They were afraid the Roman government would come and destroy them and the temple. (John 11:47–48).
- Judas, in particular, criticized Jesus for allowing Mary to wash his feet in expensive ointment. Judas said the ointment should have been sold and the money given to the poor. In his account of the footwashing, John pointed out that Judas did not say

this because he really cared about the poor, "but because he was a thief; as keeper of the money bag, he used to help himself to what was put into it." (NIV, John 12:6)

THE WEDDING IN CANA

Why was Jesus at the wedding?

Jesus, his mother, and the apostles were invited to the wedding.

What problem came up during the reception?

The hosts ran out of wine. Mary asked Jesus to help the hosts in some way. At first, Jesus seemed disinclined to help. He said to his mother, "My time has not yet come." (NLT, John 2:4)

What did Jesus mean by that?

The Bible provides no reason for Jesus' mysterious reply. One theory is that Jesus knew that once he performed his first miracle, his private life was over. Every event after that would lead to the cross.

What did Jesus do to help?

Jesus changed the water into wine, and not just any wine, but the best wine.

During the wedding at Cana, Jesus performed his miracle to turning water into wine.

Why did Jesus care enough about refreshments at a wedding to perform a miracle?

The Bible provides no reason as to why turning water into wine was Jesus' first miracle. One theory is that the miracle demonstrated that Jesus cared about every detail of people's lives. He cared about things that worried people, including having enough refreshments at a wedding.

JESUS AND NICODEMUS

Who was Nicodemus?

Nicodemus was a Pharisee, a leader of the Jews.

How did Nicodemus meet Jesus?

Nicodemus waited until it was dark and went to see Jesus secretly.

The Bible does not say why Nicodemus went at night, but presumably it was because he was a respected elder and it would not look right for him to be seeking wisdom from a person some regarded as an upstart.

What did Jesus say to Nicodemus?

Jesus said, "I assure you, unless you are born again, you can never see the Kingdom of God." (NLT, John 3:3)

How did Nicodemus reply to this?

Nicodemus thought about what Jesus said in literal, concrete terms: "How can an old man go back into his mother's womb and be born again?" (NLT, John 3:4) Jesus replied with yet another puzzle: "The truth is, no one can enter the Kingdom of God without being born of water and the Spirit." (NLT, John 3:5) Jesus referred to baptism and accepting the Holy Spirit.

How did Jesus describe his own role to Nicodemus?

Jesus described his role in what became one of the most famous verses in the Bible: "For God so loved the world that he gave his only begotten Son, that whosoever believeth in him should not perish, but have eternal life." (KJV, John 3:16)

JESUS MINISTERS TO WOMEN

Who was the woman at the well?

She was a Samaritan woman. Her name is not given.

How did Jesus meet her?

Jesus approached the woman by the well. He said to her, "Give me to drink." She replied, "How is that thou, being a Jew, askest drink of me, which am a woman of Samaria?" (KJV, John 4:7, 9)

Why was the woman surprised that Jesus spoke to her?

Antagonism between Samaria and Jerusalem went back hundreds of years to the time of the Assyrian Captivity. Samaria was the capital city of the northern kingdom of Israel. When the Assyrians conquered Israel, they sent thousands of Israelites into exile but thousands stayed behind, too. To lessen the likelihood of rebellion and feelings of national pride, the Assyrians re-

Jesus' willingness to speak to a Samaritan woman demonstrated how he held no prejudices and felt that all human beings were important.

placed the exiled people with people they captured from other countries. Many Israelites married into these foreign families. As a result, many Israelites blended Judaism with the worship of the gods of the foreign people. When Ezra, Nehemiah, and other Jews returned to Jerusalem decades later to rebuild the temple and the walls surrounding the city, they refused to let the Samaritans take part. The Jews came to dislike the Samaritans so much that they avoided Samaria even if it meant taking the long way around to get somewhere. Jesus took the long way around to get from Judea back to Galilee. In addition, most people of that era viewed women as second class citizens. So not only did Jesus go out of his way to speak to a Samaritan, but a Samaritan woman at that.

How did Jesus reply to the woman's question?

He said, "If thou knewest the gift of God, and who it is that is saith to thee, 'Give me to drink,' thou wouldst have asked of him, and he would have given thee living water." (KJV, John 4:10) Like Nicodemus, the woman thought about what Jesus said in concrete, literal terms. She said, "Sir, thou hast nothing to draw with, and the well is deep: from whence then hast that living water?" (KJV, John 4:11) Jesus replied, "Whosoever drinketh of this water shall thirst again: But whosoever drinketh of the water that I shall give him shall never thirst; but the water that I shall give him shall be in him a well of water springing up into everlasting life." (KJV, John 4:13–14)

What else did Jesus and the woman talk about?

Jesus knew about the woman's chain of husbands and her current live-in boyfriend, and told the woman so. The woman was amazed, and called Jesus a prophet. Also, the woman

247

told Jesus about her faith: "'I know that Messiah is coming' (who is called Christ). 'When he comes, he will proclaim all things to us.'"(NRSV, John 4:25). Jesus assured her that he was indeed the Messiah for whom she waited. The woman called other Samaritans, and told them about Jesus. The townspeople believed Jesus, too.

Who was the woman caught in adultery?

The Bible does not name her. The scribes and Pharisees took her to the temple where Jesus was teaching. They said, "Teacher, this woman was caught in the very act of committing adultery. Now in the law Moses commanded us to stone such women. Now what do you say?" Jesus knew the scribes and Pharisees were trying to trap him into saying something they could use against him. Jesus bent down and wrote on the ground. Then he straightened up and said, "Let anyone among you who is without sin be the first to throw a stone at her." Again, Jesus bent down and wrote on the ground. One by one the elders went away because they knew in their hearts that they were sinful, too. Jesus stood up and said to the woman, "Go your way, and from now on do not sin again." (NRSV, John 8:4,7,11)

What did Jesus write on the ground?

The Bible does not say.

THE LAME MAN AT THE BETHZATHA POOL

Who was the lame man at the Bethzatha (sometimes spelled as Bethesda) pool?

The Bible does not provide his name, but says that he had been paralyzed for thirty-eight years.

Why was the lame man at the pool?

The pool was reputed to have healing powers. However, there was no one there who would put the man into the pool.

What did Jesus do to help the man?

Jesus asked him if he wanted to be healed. The man said yes. So Jesus said, "Stand up, pick up your sleeping mat and walk." (NLT, John 5:8) Immediately, the man was healed, and stood up and walked.

Why were Jesus and the man criticized?

It was the Sabbath. The man was criticized by others for carrying his mat on the Sabbath. Jesus was criticized for healing on the Sabbath. After this event, the church leaders started persecuting Jesus, and planned to kill him.

JESUS AND LAZARUS

Who was Lazarus?

Lazarus was a close friend of Jesus, and brother to Mary and Martha.

What message did Mary and Martha send to Jesus?

They sent a message that said, "Lord, the one you love is very sick." (NLT, John 11:3).

Did Jesus go to Lazarus right away?

No. He waited two days. Jesus delayed because he knew that Lazarus' sickness and the events that followed would glorify God.

A painting of Jesus resurrecting Lazarus by sixteenth-century artist A. Badile.

What happened when Jesus got to where Lazarus and his sisters lived?

Jesus knew before he got there that Lazarus was dead. So Jesus went to Mary and Martha. He assured them that Lazarus would rise again. They believed Jesus with all their hearts.

What happened when Jesus arrived at Lazarus' tomb?

Jesus wept. Then he prayed. Then he said, "Lazarus, come out!" Lazarus did as Jesus commanded, and he was fine again.

JOHN'S EXTRA DETAILS OF THE LAST SUPPER

What information did John provide about Jesus' last supper with the disciples that Matthew, Mark, and Luke did not?

John described Jesus washing the apostles' feet. (John 13:1–20)

Why did Jesus wash the apostles' feet?

In ancient times, roads were dusty or muddy, depending on the weather. Hosts provided their guests with someone, usually a servant, to wash their feet after their travels. Foot washing was part of daily life. Jesus washed the apostles' feet to set an example for them. Jesus said, "You also should wash one another's feet." (NIV, John 13:14)

Jesus added, "I tell you the truth, no servant is greater than his master, nor is a messenger greater than the one who sent him." (NIV, John 13:16) By washing the apostles' feet, Jesus emphasized the fact that he was taking upon himself the position of a servant. Jesus' role as a servant culminated in his death on the cross.

> ## What is crucifixion like for the unfortunate person who is sentenced to die?
>
> Crucifixion is a slow and painful way to die. Opinions differ as to the lethal component. Common theories are that the victim dies of one or more of the following: asphyxiation, dehydration, blood clots, blood poisoning, or animal predation.

JESUS AND THOMAS

Who was Thomas?

Thomas was one of the twelve apostles.

Why was Thomas nicknamed "Doubting Thomas"?

He was not called Doubting Thomas in the Bible. The nickname came about later. He was called that because of what happened after Jesus was resurrected. After Jesus was resurrected, he went to the house where the apostles were. Thomas was not there. When the others told Thomas that Jesus had appeared to them, Thomas said, "Unless I see the mark of the nails in his hands, and put my finger in the mark of the nails, and my hand in his side, I will not believe." (NRSV, John 20:25)

Did Thomas overcome his doubt?

Jesus appeared to the apostles again. This time Thomas was with them, and he saw Jesus for himself. Jesus said to Thomas, "Put your finger here and see my hands. Reach out your hand and put it in my side. Do not doubt but believe." Thomas exclaimed, "My Lord and my God!" (NRSV, John 20:27–28) So Thomas overcame his doubt, but got the nickname anyway.

JESUS' PROMISES

What did Jesus say to his disciples before he was led away to be crucified?

Jesus gave them words of hope:

- "Do not let your hearts be troubled. Ye believe in God, believe also in me. In my father's house, are many mansions: if it were not so, I would have told you. I go to prepare a place for you." (KJV, John 14:1–2)
- "But the Counsellor, the Holy Spirit, whom the Father will send in my name, will teach you all things, and remind you of everything that I have said to you." (NIV, John 14:26)
- "I am leaving you with a gift—peace of mind and heart. And the peace I give isn't like the peace the world gives. Do don't be troubled or afraid." (NLT, John 14:27)

- "If you keep my commandments, you will abide in my love, just as I have kept my Father's commandments and abide in his love." (NRSV, John 15:10)

THE ACTS OF THE APOSTLES

When was Acts written?

This book, written by Luke, is about the formation and spread of the church after Jesus' death and resurrection.

How does Acts begin?

It begins with an account of Jesus' interaction with his apostles after the resurrection. When Jesus appeared to them, he told them to wait in Jerusalem until it became time for them to be baptized by the Holy Spirit.

JESUS' DISCIPLES AFTER THE RESURRECTION

What happened to all of Jesus' followers after he was resurrected?

The days leading up to Jesus' trial and crucifixion were frightening and chaotic for his followers. Even after he was resurrected, the apostles met in secret to avoid attracting the attention of the Jewish authorities.

After the resurrection, how long did Jesus stay with the apostles?

He stayed for forty days.

What happened after the forty days?

Jesus went to heaven. As the apostles watched, "he was taken up; and a cloud received him out of their sight." (KJV, Acts 1:9)

What were Jesus' final words to the apostles?

"Ye shall be my witnesses unto me both in Jerusalem, and in all Judea and in Samaria, and unto the uttermost part of the earth." (KJV, Acts 1:8)

What did the apostles do after Jesus' ascension?

They went to the upstairs room where they lived. They devoted themselves to prayer.

Who replaced Judas as an apostle?

Matthias.

How many people were followers of Jesus at that point?

About 120.

PENTECOST

What is Pentecost?

It is the birthday of the church. It is when the Holy Spirit came to Jesus' followers. It took place fifty days after Jesus' resurrection.

What happened when the Holy Spirit came?

John said, "And suddenly from heaven there came a sound like the rush of a violent wind, and it filled the entire house where they were sitting. Divided tongues, as of fire, appeared among them, and a tongue rested on each of them. All of them were filled with the Holy Spirit and began to speak in other languages, as the Spirit gave them ability." (NRSV, Acts 2:2–4)

What did people in Jerusalem think when they heard all these different languages being spoken?

Some believed that Jesus' followers were indeed speaking at God's behest. Others believed that Jesus' followers were drunk. Peter told everyone listening that the ability to speak in different languages was in fulfillment of prophecy (Joel 2:28–32).

How many people became followers of Jesus during those first days?

Three thousand. Day by day, that number grew.

TROUBLE

What did Peter advise people to do?

To repent of their sins and turn to God.

What happened when the Sadducees heard Peter and John talking to the people?

The Sadducees arrested Peter and John. They were released the next day. This was the first of many arrests for both of them.

What did Peter say to the high priest and his family when asked by what power he spoke?

He said he spoke in the name of Jesus Christ of Nazareth. The high priest told him not to do that anymore, but Peter said, "Whether it is right in God's eyes to listen to you rather than to God, you decide. As for us, there's no question—we can't keep quiet about what we've seen and heard." (The Message, Acts 4:19) The church continued to grow.

Peter and the other apostles were arrested several times by the jealous Sadduccees who felt threatened by their teachings.

Why did Peter, John, and the other apostles get arrested again later?

The apostles healed people left and right. People came from all over to be healed. This created quite a ruckus in Jerusalem. The Sadducees were jealous, and had the apostles put in prison.

How long were the apostles in prison this time?

Not even for one day. During the night, an angel of God came to them and opened the prison door. The angel commanded them; "Go to the temple and take your stand. Tell the people everything there is to say about this Life." (The Message, Acts 5:20) The next morning, that is just what the apostles did. The church continued to grow.

What did the Sadducees do when they realized the apostles were teaching again?

They had them arrested again. By then, the Sadducees wanted to kill the apostles. However, fearing public reaction, the Sadducees did not kill the apostles, but flogged them and scolded them instead. They warned the apostles to quit preaching about Jesus. As soon as the apostles were released, they started preaching again.

The Church Community

What was the first church community like?

Everyone shared what they had with one another. John wrote, "There was not a needy person among them, for as many as owned land or houses sold them and brought the proceeds of what sold. They laid it at the apostles' feet, and it was distributed to each as any had need." (NRSV, Acts 4:34)

Who were Ananias and Sapphira?

Ananias and Sapphira were husband and wife. They were the first troublemakers in the church community.

What did they do that caused trouble?

Ananias and Sapphira sold a piece of land, but did not give all the money to the apostles. They kept some for themselves.

How was their selfishness discovered?

Peter knew. Maybe he heard about the real estate transaction through the grapevine, or maybe the Holy Spirit gave him the knowledge. The Bible does not say for sure. At any rate, Peter called Ananias on it.

What did Peter say to Ananias?

He gave him a logical, thorough talking-to. He said, "Ananias, how did Satan get you to lie to the Holy Spirit and secretly keep back part of the price of the field? Before you sold it, it was all yours, and after you sold it, the money was yours to do with as you wished. So what got into you to pull a trick like this? You didn't lie to men but to God." (The Message, Acts 5:3–4)

What was Ananias' response to Peter?

Ananias fell over dead.

What happened when Sapphira came in some hours later?

By that time, Ananias had already been taken out and buried. When Sapphira came in, Peter asked her to confirm the price of the land. She told Peter the lesser price that she and her husband had agreed upon.

What was Peter's reaction?

He scolded her like he did her husband.

What was Sapphira's reaction to Peter?

She fell over dead.

THE BUSY APOSTLES

What plan did the apostles come up with to help them manage their growing ministry?

They appointed seven capable, trustworthy men to help out. The men's names were Stephen, Philip, Prochorus, Nicanor, Timon, Parmenas, and Nicolaus.

What were the roles of the seven men?

The Bible is silent on all of the men except for Stephen. He was filled with the Holy Spirit, and preached about Jesus with passion. He got in trouble for it.

What happened to Stephen?

He was arrested and accused of blasphemy by some of the Jewish leaders.

How did Stephen respond to the accusations?

He responded with a lengthy, knowledgeable speech about Moses' life and the Israelites' sojourn in the wilderness. He concluded his speech with this indictment of his accusers: "You deliberately disobeyed God's laws, though you received it from the hands of angels." (NLT, Acts 7:53)

The first Christian martyr was St. Stephen (shown here in a pediment above the front door of Saint Etienne du Mont Church in Paris, France).

> ## Did the word "saint" once have a different meaning?
>
> The word "saint" refers to more than just the most holy of Jesus' followers. In Christianity, the word "saint" refers to all people who believe in Christ.

What did Stephen's accusers say to that?

They became infuriated. As they fumed, Stephen gazed into heaven and saw the glory of God. "Look!" he said, "I see heaven open and the Son of Man standing at the right hand of God!" This made Stephen's accusers even angrier. They rushed at him, dragged him out of the city, and stoned him to death. A man named Saul stood by and approved.

What was the result of Stephen's death?

It spurred persecution against the church. Saul was one of the most vehement persecutors.

Meet Saul

Who was Saul?

Saul was of Jewish descent, and was a Pharisee. Also, he was a Roman citizen.

How did Saul persecute the followers of Jesus?

As in Stephen's case, he approved of killing Jesus' followers. Also, he persecuted them with "murderous threats." (NIV, Acts 9:1) Saul went to Damascus in the hopes of arresting more of Jesus' followers.

Where was Damascus?

Damascus was (and is) in Syria. By the time Saul went to Damascus, the grand city was already thousands of years old, making it the oldest continually inhabited city in the world. Damascus is 135 miles from Jerusalem.

What happened to Saul on the way to Damascus?

As he walked down the road, a light from heaven flashed around him. A voice called to him and said, "Saul, Saul, why do you persecute me?" (NIV, Acts 9:4) The voice was that of Jesus. Jesus told Saul to go on to Damascus, where he would be given instructions on what to do.

Did Saul do as Jesus instructed?

Yes, but Saul needed help. Saul was blinded by the light. The men who traveled with him helped him complete the journey to Damascus.

What happened to Saul once he reached Damascus?

A follower of Jesus, Ananias (not Sapphira's husband), went to Saul. At God's command, Ananias laid his hands on Saul and "immediately something like scales fell from Saul's eyes and he could see again." (NIV, Acts 9:18) Right away, Saul arose and was baptized.

What did Saul do next?

He began preaching the gospel of Jesus in Damascus. He caused such a stir that some of the Jewish leaders plotted to kill him. Saul and some of the other disciples learned of the plot, however, and helped him escape to Jerusalem.

On his travels to Damascus, Saul was blinded by a bright light and Jesus spoke to him so that he became one of Jesus' followers.

What happened to Saul in Jerusalem?

He continued to preach the gospel of Jesus. At first, the other disciples were wary of Saul because he had caused them so much trouble. However, Barnabas convinced them that Saul's conversion was authentic. Saul, Peter, and the others continued to preach the gospel and heal people in God's name. The church continued to grow.

PETER IN JOPPA

Who went to visit Peter in Joppa?

At God's command, a man named Cornelius went to Joppa to seek out Peter.

Where was Joppa?

Joppa (known now as Jaffa) was (and is) located thirty-five miles from Jerusalem.

What kind of man was Cornelius?

He was a centurion who, while not Jewish, was a devout follower of Judaism. He prayed regularly, and gave generously to the poor. He lived in Caesarea.

What happened to Peter just before Cornelius arrived in Joppa?

Peter had a vision from God. He "saw the heaven opened and something like a large sheet being let down to earth by its four corners. It contained all kinds of four-footed animals, as well as reptiles of the earth and birds of the air." Then a voice told him, "Get up, Peter;

kill and eat." Peter replied, "Surely not, Lord! I have never eaten anything impure or unclean." The voice spoke to him a second time, "Do not call anything impure that God has made clean." (NIV, Acts 10:11–15) This exchange was repeated twice more.

What was the significance of the vision?

By the vision, God made all foods clean.

What did Cornelius do when he met Peter?

He asked Peter to go back with him to Caesarea. Peter obliged. Once in Caesarea, he preached about Jesus Christ to Cornelius and his family.

Did Cornelius and his family believe Peter?

Yes. While Peter spoke, the Holy Spirit came upon everyone in attendance. John wrote, "The circumcised believers who had come with Peter were astonished that the gift of the Holy Spirit had been poured out even on the Gentiles." (NIV, Acts 10:45). Cornelius and his family were baptized, and they became the first Gentile converts.

MORE TROUBLE FOR THE FOLLOWERS OF JESUS

Who took advantage of his high position to persecute followers of Jesus?

Herod Agrippa I. Being the grandson of Herod the Great made him a shoo-in for the role of king of Judea. He ruled from 41–44 C.E. Herod Agrippa I "laid violent hands upon some who belonged to the church." (Acts 12:1) He had James killed. He had Peter arrested and put under heavy guard. Herod intended to bring Peter out after Passover. Peter's friends prayed for him while he was in prison.

What happened to Peter in prison?

On the night before Herod was to bring Peter out to the people, Peter slept bound in chains. Two soldiers stood by him. More soldiers guarded the prison door. Suddenly, a visitor came to see Peter.

Who was the visitor?

The visitor was an angel of God. He woke Peter, and told him to get up and leave the prison. The chains fell off Peter's wrists. Peter stood and followed the angel out of the prison. Peter thought he was dreaming. He did not realize his escape was real until he was outside the city gates. Then the angel left.

Where did Peter go?

He went to Mary's house. This Mary was the mother of Mark.

Why was Saul known also as Paul?

Two first names were common then. Just as the apostles had two first names, so did Saul. The name Saul is a Hebrew name. Paul is a Roman name. Saul might have gone by Paul long before he was in Antioch, but it is in this part of the Bible that his use of that name is recorded: "But Saul, also known as Paul, filled with the Holy Spirit, looked intently at him...." (NRSV, Acts 13:9) Because the Bible refers to Saul as Paul after this point, henceforth he will be referred to in this book as Paul as well.

How long did Peter stay there?

He stayed just long enough to tell Mary and the others at the house how the angel released him from prison. Before Peter left the house, he said, "Tell this to James and to the believers." (Acts 12:17)

CHANGES FOR SAUL AND BARNABAS

Where was Antioch?

In Saul's day, Antioch was a popular name for towns. Saul visited at least two cities by that name. Antioch was once the third-largest city in the Roman Empire, after Rome, in Italy, and Alexandria, in Egypt. It was located in Syria. Another Antioch was located in what is modern-day Turkey.

How was Antioch important in spreading the gospel?

It was in Antioch of Syria that preaching the gospel to Gentiles first picked up momentum. Saul and his friend Barnabas spent a year there, teaching many people. The number of Jesus' followers increased greatly. Perhaps it was no surprise then that "the disciples were called Christians first in Antioch." (KJV, Acts 11:26) Christianity was known also as The Way. (Acts 19:23)

Why did Saul and Barnabas leave Antioch?

They left because the Holy Spirit told them to leave. After leaving Antioch, Saul and Barnabas sailed to Cyprus, an island about one hundred miles away in the Mediterranean Sea. From there, they sailed to Pamphylia, which was in the southern part of what is modern-day Turkey, and visited the other Antioch further inland.

PAUL THE TRAVELING MAN

Where did Paul (formerly Saul) go on his journeys?

Throughout his ministry, he traveled thousands of miles by boat and by land to dozens of cities in the Mediterranean. Typically, scholars group Paul's journeys into three categories. He traveled with various disciples over the years. His purpose in traveling was to spread the gospel.

Where did Paul go on his first journey?

In addition to the two Antiochs, Paul and his companions visited other cities and towns throughout modern-day Syria and Turkey, including Selucia, Perga, and Lystra. Most scholars think this journey took place around 47 C.E.

Where did Paul go on his second journey?

During this journey, Paul and his companions traveled further west. They went to Greece and Macedonia (which is now part of Greece), and visited several cities including Thessalonica, Corinth, and Ephesus. Most scholars think this journey took place around 50 C.E.

Where did Paul go on his third journey?

While Paul visited several places while on this journey, including Galatia and Philippi, he spent most of the time in Ephesus. He stayed in Ephesus for nearly three years. There he helped a struggling church become stronger. Most scholars think this journey took place around 53 C.E.

TROUBLE FOR PAUL

Were Paul and his companions successful in spreading the gospel?

Yes. Discipleship grew so much that just 250 years after Paul's journeys, Christianity had spread to more than half the Roman Empire. Still, Paul and his companions met opposition.

In what ways did Paul and his companions meet opposition?

Some people did not agree with their message about the gospel. Some people were open to the message, but twisted it to suit their agenda. For instance, when Paul and Barnabas visited Iconium, a city in what is modern-day Turkey, many people—both Jews and Gentiles—converted to Christianity. Even so, some Jews and Gentiles were hostile to Paul and Barnabas. The oppositionists attempted "to mistreat them and stone them." (NIV, Acts 14:5) Paul was beaten and imprisoned several times throughout his ministry.

At first, the people of Lystra, a city in what is modern-day Turkey, welcomed Paul and Barnabas' message eagerly. The people of Lystra became so excited that they thought because Paul and Barnabas healed a crippled man, they were the gods Zeus and Hermes. Paul and Barnabas set the people straight, but "scarcely restrained the crowds from offering sacrifice to them." (NRSV, Acts 14:18) The people of Lystra proved fickle. When some Jews from Antioch and Iconium came and slandered Paul and Barnabas, the people of Lystra took Paul outside the city and stoned him. They thought they killed him, but he rallied and continued traveling with Barnabas.

Then in Philippi, a city in Greece, Paul and Silas met a girl who had a spirit of divination. She was the slave of people who made money with her fortune-telling. The girl followed Paul and Timothy around, exclaiming: "These men are working for the Most High God. They're laying out the road of salvation for you!" (The Message, Acts 16:17) The girl did this over and over. Paul tried to ignore her but he became annoyed. He turned to her and addressed the spirit in her: "Out! In the name of Jesus Christ, get out of her!" (The Message, Acts 16:18) The spirit went out of the girl right then. When the girl's owners realized that the fortune-telling spirit— and thus their way of making money—was gone from her, they had Paul and Silas brought before the authorities. The crowd and the authorities attacked Paul and Silas, and beat them. Then they had Paul and Silas put in prison.

What happened to Paul and Silas in prison?

One night, Paul and Silas sang hymns and prayed to God. Suddenly, there was an earthquake. The foundations of the prison were shaken. The prison doors flew open, and the chains fell off the prisoners' bodies.

Did Paul and Silas escape?

No. They did not try to escape. The jailer woke up and assumed the prisoners had escaped. He started to kill himself, but Paul shouted at him, "Don't do that! We're all still here! Nobody's run away!" (The Message, Acts 16:28) Amazed and relieved, the jailer exclaimed, "Sirs, what do I have to do to be saved, to really live?" (The Message, Acts 16:30) Paul told the jailer how to believe. Then the jailer called his family to him, and together they were baptized that very night. The next day, the authorities released Paul and Silas.

PAUL'S DEATH

When did Paul die?

The Bible does not say. Paul talked about his death, though. His work was dangerous, and he knew it would be the death of him. He said, "The Holy Spirit testifies to me in every city that imprisonment and persecutions are waiting for me. But I do not count my life of any value to myself, if only I may finish my course and the ministry that I received from the Lord Jesus, to testify to the good news of God's grace." (NRSV, Acts 20:23–24) According to church tradition, Paul was beheaded by Nero around 67 C.E.

What happened to Paul when he visited Jerusalem on his third journey?

He was arrested while he visited the temple. Some of the people tried to kill him, but the Roman officials, "fearing that they would tear Paul in pieces," ordered the soldiers to take Paul to prison." (NRSV, Acts 23:10)

The Bible does not state what happened to Paul, but tradition has it that he was executed by Roman emperor Nero.

What happened to Paul in prison?

On the first night of his imprisonment, "the Lord stood near him and said, "Keep up your courage! For just as you have testified for me in Jerusalem, so you must bear witness in Rome." (NRSV, Acts 23:11)

How long was Paul in prison in Jerusalem?

Not even a day. Originally, the plan was for him to be brought before the Roman authorities the next day. However, that night Paul's nephew overheard the rabble-rousers from earlier in the day plot to ambush Paul while he was on his way from prison to his appearance before the Roman authorities. The nephew told the Roman officials of the plot. So the head Roman official came up with another plan.

What was the official's plan?

He wrote a letter to Felix, the Roman governor of Judea. Guarded heavily for his own protection and so he would not escape, Paul was escorted to Felix.

What happened between Paul and Felix?

Paul spoke freely about his faith. Felix listened attentively, but kept Paul in prison. Two years later, Porcius Festus became governor. He brought Paul before the king, Herod Agrippa II, who ruled Judea from about 53–93 C.E.

What happened between Paul and Agrippa?

Paul spoke to Agrippa about his faith journey. He described how he used to persecute Christians, and how it was that he converted to Christianity. Agrippa saw nothing in Paul that deserved imprisonment or death. However, Paul had said he wanted to take his case to the emperor, and take it he must.

OFF TO SEE THE EMPEROR

Where did the emperor live?

He lived in the capital of the Roman Empire, Rome. So in the company of other prisoners, a centurion, and some soldiers, Paul sailed to Italy. In all, there were 276 people on the ship.

What happened on the journey?

The ship on which Paul sailed lost its way due to storms. The group set sail in autumn, something which usually was not done in that area because of the dangerous weather patterns.

Did the ship reach Italy?

No. The ship became grounded on the main island of Malta off the southwest coast of Italy.

What happened to the people on the ship?

At first, the soldiers planned to kill the prisoners to keep them from escaping. However, the centurion wanted Paul to be safe, so he said that all the prisoners should be spared. So all the men on the ship swam to shore or paddled to shore while holding pieces of wreckage.

What happened to Paul once he got on the island?

Paul and his companions set about to build a fire on the beach. While gathering

On his way to Rome, Paul was shipwrecked on the island of Malta, where he was bitten by a snake but survived. The other passengers thought he must be a god to have lived through both events.

brushwood, Paul was bitten by a deadly viper. When the people of the island saw that Paul survived a shipwreck only to be bitten by a snake, they figured he must be a murderer who was getting his just desserts. When the people saw that Paul did not suffer ill effects from the bite, they decided he must be a god instead.

How long did Paul and the others stay on the island?

They stayed on the island for three months. Then, under military escort, Paul was taken to Rome. He lived there under house arrest for two years, during which time he continued to preach the gospel.

PAUL'S LETTERS

ROMANS

What is the book of Romans?

Written about 57 C.E., Romans is the longest and most theologically dense letter in the New Testament. In it, Paul addressed the specific needs of the church in Rome. In the process, he delivered an eloquent explanation of how Christian beliefs evolved from Jewish beliefs, and he offered advice on how to live accordingly. At this point in his ministry, Paul had not yet been to Rome.

How does Romans begin?

It begins with Paul's greeting to the Roman believers, in which he proclaimed his servitude to Jesus and Jesus' divinity.

What did Paul say about the gospel?

He told them that he was not ashamed of the gospel, and that it was God's method of salvation for everyone who believed.

CONFLICT IN THE ROMAN CHURCH

Why was there conflict among the Christians in Rome?

There was disagreement among some of the Christians in Rome. To some of the Jewish Christians, it did not make sense that just anybody could be a Christian. They thought that only those who had received the Mosaic Law—those who were born Jews—could be Christians, or at the very least, they believed people should convert to Judaism before becoming Christians.

How did Paul respond to that conflict?

Paul wrote: "God will punish the Gentiles when they sin, even though they never had God's written law. And he will punish the Jews when they sin, for they do have the law. For it is not merely knowing the law that brings God's approval. Those who obey the law will be declared right in God's sight." (NLT, Romans 2:12–13) In other words, God would judge all people for their sins, Jew and Gentile alike.

Gentiles did not live by the Mosaic Law. Could they still be made right with God?

Yes. Paul was emphatic about that. He explained, "Even when Gentiles, who do not have God's written law, instinctively follow what the law says, they show that in their hearts they know right from wrong." (NLT, Romans 2:14) He continued, "They show that what the law requires is written on their hearts, to which their own conscience also bears witness; and their conflicting thoughts will accuse or perhaps excuse them on the day when, according to my gospel, God, through Jesus Christ, will judge the secret thoughts of all." (NRSV, Romans 2:15–16)

Besides, as Paul pointed out, there was "no distinction between Jew and Greek; the same Lord is Lord of all and is generous to all who call on him." (NRSV, Romans 10:12)

Was having a Jewish heritage of any importance, then, for Jewish Christians?

Yes. Paul was emphatic about that as well. Paul wrote, "First of all, they have been entrusted with the very words of God." (NIV, Romans 3:2)

What did Paul say about the time-honored Jewish tradition of circumcision?

Conflict arose in the early church as to whether or not Gentiles should be circumcised before they became Christians. Paul said it was not necessary: "Real circumcision is a matter of the heart—it is spiritual and not literal." (NRSV, Romans 2:29) Paul used the example of the patriarch, Abraham. Abraham was made right with God through faith first. His circumcision came later.

Was the Mosaic Law not important any longer?

It was still important. Paul pointed out that it was through the law that people learned what behavior was right and wrong. However, Paul believed it was crucial to view the law in its proper context. Just because a person knew the law did not mean they kept the law.

What was Jesus' role in changing Paul's and other Jewish Christians' understanding of the law?

Paul said that before Jesus, God's righteousness was revealed by the law. After Jesus, God's righteousness was revealed through faith in Jesus.

The law itself did not make a person right with God. A person's response to the law was the important thing. It was through the law that people learned what behavior was right and wrong to God. Love encapsulated all godly behavior. "Love," Paul concluded, "does no wrong to a neighbor; therefore, love is the fulfilling of the law." (NRSV, Romans 13:10)

Paul often used the word "justification." What does it mean?

It means "made right" or "brought in line with." So when Paul spoke of justification by faith, he meant the act of aligning one's self with God's command by belief, or faith, in Jesus.

GIFT OF GRACE

What did Jesus' death and resurrection prove?

Paul said, "But God demonstrates his own love for us in this: While we were still sinners, Christ died for us." (NIV, Romans 5:8) Paul pointed out that Jesus' life paralleled Adam's in some ways. Through sin, Adam brought condemnation to the world. Through the unselfish act of dying on a cross, Jesus took away the condemnation. In this way, God showed the world undeserved love and compassion—God showed the world grace.

According to Paul, how were people supposed to respond to God's grace?

Paul told people not to allow their passions to rule them, but to obey God. Paul understood the hold such passions had on people. He described his own struggle with passions this way: "For in my inner being I delight in God's law; but I see another law at work in the members of my body, waging war against the law of my mind and making me a prisoner of the law of sin at work within my members. What a wretched man I am!" (NIV, Romans 7:22–23)

What did Paul say would help people respond to God's grace?

The Holy Spirit. Paul said God sent the Holy Spirit to help people in their weakness. "What then are we to say about these things?" Paul questioned. "If God is for us who can be against us?" (NIV, Romans 8:31)

LIVING ACCORDING TO GRACE

What was Paul's advice on getting along with other people?

Paul encouraged the believers to live peaceably with others. That meant not seeking revenge when wronged, and not being haughty. Also, Paul encouraged believers to think beyond their own needs, and consider the needs of others.

What did Paul say about suffering?

Paul said that suffering in the present was nothing compared to the glory revealed by God's word.

What did Paul say about judging others?

Paul said that judging other people was unacceptable. He elaborated, "Therefore let us stop passing judgment on one another. Instead, make up your mind not to put any stumbling block or obstacle in your brother's way." (NIV, Romans 14:13)

What did Paul say about obeying governing authorities?

In Romans, Paul was clear about how to deal with ruling bodies. He said, "Let every person be subject to the governing authorities; for there is no authority except from God, and those authorities that exist have been instituted by God." (NRSV, Romans 13:1)

What did Paul say about death?

Paul said death was the natural result of sin, but God provided the free gift of eternal life through faith in Jesus.

I CORINTHIANS

When did Paul write the first letter to the Corinthians?

Paul wrote the letter around 55 C.E. to address divisive issues among the Christians in Corinth. Paul was on his third missionary journey.

Where was Corinth?

Corinth was (and is) in Greece, which at the time of Paul's letter was part of the vast Roman Empire. Corinth was destroyed by an earthquake in 1858, but was rebuilt a few

The ruins of Corinth are in Greece. Corinth was one of the first places to which Paul spread Christianity.

miles away, and stands to this day. Ancient Corinth was ransacked by the Romans in 146 B.C.E. By 44 B.C.E., it was rebuilt as a Roman colony. It became a thriving, wealthy center of international trade. Paul helped establish the church in Corinth sometime during his second missionary journey, around 50 C.E.

How does I Corinthians begin?

Paul began the letter with the traditional greeting and thanksgiving to God.

CONFLICTS IN THE CORINTHIAN CHURCH

Why was there conflict among the Christians in Corinth?

Some of the Corinthians were confused about who the church leader really was. Paul wrote, "What I mean is that each of you says, 'I belong to Paul,' or 'I belong to Apollos,' or 'I belong to Cephas,' or 'I belong to Christ.'" (NRSV, I Corinthians 1:11)

How did Paul respond to this?

Paul pointed out that neither he nor the other church leaders were crucified for the people's sins. Only Jesus was. That made Jesus the church leader.

THE PARADOXES OF GOD

How did Paul describe God's wisdom?

Paul described it in terms of contrast. "Where is the one who is wise? Where is the scribe? Where is the debater of this age? Has not God made foolish the wisdom of the world?" Paul continued, "For God's foolishness is wiser than human wisdom, and God's weakness is stronger than human strength." (NRSV, I Corinthians 1:20, 25)

What did this mean to the Corinthians?

For the Corinthian believers, it was a humbling reminder that there was no room in the church for human ego or pride. Paul scolded, "For since there is jealousy and quarreling among you, are you not worldly?" (NIV, I Corinthians 3:3) Godly wisdom was to be valued over human wisdom.

THE INDIVIDUAL'S ROLE IN THE CHURCH

What did Paul say was the role of the individual in the church?

Paul said that each believer was a servant of Jesus. As such, individuals in the church are "stewards of the mysteries of God." (KJV, I Corinthians 4:1)

What did Paul say were characteristics of a good steward?

A good steward was trustworthy, humble, and generous.

269

How were some of the Corinthians not being good stewards?

One man had made a paramour of his stepmother. One believer took another believer to court.

What did Paul advise the Corinthians to do in order to become good stewards?

He advised them to "associate with anyone who claims to be a Christian yet indulges in sexual sin, or is greedy, or worships idols, or abusive, or a drunkard, or a swindler. Don't even eat with such people." (NLT, I Corinthians 5:11) Also, when it came to matters of the law, Paul advised them to settle disputes among themselves, and not take each other to court. Paul even pointed out that disputes should be avoided altogether. He reasoned, "Why not just accept the injustice and leave it at that? Why not let yourselves be cheated?" (NLT, I Corinthians 6:7)

Didn't Jesus eat with people like that?

Yes, he did. One theory as to why Paul contradicted Jesus' example is that there was a major difference between the sinners with whom Jesus associated and the sinners with whom the Corinthians associated. The ones with Jesus cared about his message. The ones with the Corinthian believers did not.

How did Paul describe the human body?

He described it as part of the body of Jesus Christ, and as a temple of the Holy Spirit.

PAUL ON THE ROLES OF MEN AND WOMEN

Did Paul approve of marriage?

Yes and no. Paul thought it was best if people stayed single like he did; once married, a person became concerned about not just God, but his or her spouse as well. Still, Paul conceded that it was "better to marry than to burn with lust." (NLT, I Corinthians 7:9)

That being said, Paul was angry about the way in which one believer satisfied his passion. Paul wrote, "It is actually reported that there is sexual immorality among you, and of a kind that is not found even among pagans; for a man is living with his father's wife." (I Corinthians 5:1) Both Roman and Jewish law forbade marriage between a man and his stepmother.

What was Paul's recommendation for dealing with this particular man?

Paul was not one to mollycoddle. He wrote, "Hold this man's conduct up to public scrutiny. Let him defend it if he can! But if he can't, then out with him! It will be totally devastating to him, of course, and embarrassing to you. But better devastation and embarrassment than damnation. You want him on his feet and forgiven before the Master on the Day of Judgment." (The Message, I Corinthians 5:5) Scholars continue to debate what Paul meant by this. The most common theory is that Paul meant for the believers to expel him from the church in the hopes that the severity of the penalty would prompt the man to mend his ways.

Did the believers expel the man from the church?

Based on Paul's extant writings, the outcome of the dilemma is unclear. Some scholars point to II Corinthians 2:5–6 to suggest that the man repented and was welcomed back in the church.

Did Paul approve of divorce?

No. He cited Jesus' teaching to support his stance on this.

What did Paul recommend that believers do if their spouses were not believers?

Paul said, "If you are a man with a wife who is not a believer but who still wants to live with you, hold on to her. If you are a woman with a husband who is not a believer but he wants to live with you, hold on to him." (The Message, I Corinthians 7:13) The benefit was that the Christian spouse might convert the non-Christian spouse.

Did Paul think that men and women were equal?

Yes—sort of. In that era, most women were second-class citizens. They did not have as many rights as men. Paul confirmed this bias with such statements as: "And man was not made for woman's benefit, but woman was made for man." (NLT, I Corinthians 11:9) And: "Women should be silent during the church meetings. It is not proper for them to speak. They should be submissive, just as the law says. If they have questions to ask, let them ask their husbands at home, for it is improper for women to speak in church meetings." (NLT, I Corinthians 14:34–36)

Still, he wrote also of how the genders complemented each other equally with such statements as these: "The husband should not deprive his wife of sexual intimacy, which is her right as a married woman, nor should the wife deprive her husband." (NLT, I Corinthians 7:3) He also repeatedly addressed the recipients of his letter as "brothers and sisters." So there were some apparent contradictions in Paul's views. It is possible that because the church was still forming, contradictions and changing views among its leaders were inevitable.

RESPONSIBILITIES OF BELIEVERS

Why was Paul concerned that some believers might thwart other believers' faith?

People from all walks of life became believers. For example, they had a variety of beliefs about what foods were acceptable to eat. Paul did not want these differences of opinion to encourage one believer to chastise another believer. Paul wrote, "It's true that we can't win God's approval by what we eat. We don't miss out on anything if we don't eat it, and we don't gain anything if we do." (NLT, I Corinthians 8:8) Faith, not food, was the key to life in Jesus.

How did being a Christian affect the daily lives of people living in Greece and Rome?

The nature of Christianity made it impossible for faithful followers to continue their lifestyles that glorified Greco-Roman influence. Participating in many areas of public life was incompatible with Christian beliefs. For instance, early Christians could not sanction theatrical presentations or athletic events because both were prefaced with sacrifices to gods. One such athletic event was addressed by Paul in his first letter to the Corinthians. Corinth was known for being the location of the Isthmian Games, something akin to the Olympic Games. Wishing to explain a faithful life using an analogy to which the Corinthian believers would relate, Paul wrote: "Remember that in a race everyone runs, but only one person gets the prize. You also must run in such a way that you will win. All athletes practice strict self-control. They do it to win a prize that will fade away, but we do it for an eternal prize." (NLT, I Corinthians 9:24–25)

What was one kind of food that Paul said was never acceptable to eat?

Food that was sacrificed to idols. In a city where the worship of Greco-Roman gods was prevalent, and temples to these gods were common sights, whether or not it was acceptable to eat food sacrificed to idols was a real concern.

What did Paul say about temptation?

Paul understood that believers might be tempted to partake of ungodly behavior, but offered this advice: "No test or temptation that comes your way is beyond the course of what others have had to face. All you need to remember is that God will never let you down; he'll never let you be pushed past your limit; he'll always be there to help you come through it." (The Message, I Corinthians 10:13)

What did Paul say about personal appearance?

Paul wrote about hairstyles. He said, "Any man who prays or prophesies with something on his head disgraces his head." Paul went into more detail for women. He continued, "but any woman who prays or prophesies with her head unveiled disgraces her head—it is one and the same thing as having her head shaved. For if a woman will not veil herself, then she should cut off her hair; but if it is disgraceful for a woman to have her hair cut off or to be shaved, she should wear a veil." (NRSV, I Corinthians 11:4, 5–6) There is no consensus for what Paul meant by these lines. Some people think that Paul meant women—then and now—should cover their hair in church, and men should not. Others think that Paul was making a distinction between men and women, but that the distinction applied to his day only.

SPIRITUAL GIFTS

How did Paul define spiritual gifts?

Talents people used to do God's work.

About what kinds of spiritual gifts did Paul write?

Paul wrote there are many kinds of gifts, but all of them come from God. Some of the gifts about which Paul wrote were leadership, teaching, assisting, and healing. To give the Corinthian believers a visual image of what he meant, Paul likened the church to the human body. The human body has many parts, but all of them work together for the benefit of the body. Likewise, Paul believed that each person in the church should use his or her skills in conjunction with the skills of other believers to benefit the entire church.

What quality was needed for any of the spiritual gifts to be of use?

Love. Without love, spiritual gifts were useless. Paul wrote, "If I speak with human eloquence and angelic ecstasy but don't love, I'm nothing but the creaking of a rusty gate." (The Message, I Corinthians 13:1)

How did Paul define love?

Paul's description of love in I Corinthians 13 is one of the most oft-repeated passages in the Bible. Paul wrote that love has these qualities: truth, kindness, faith, endurance, and hope. Paul balanced that with a list of things that love does not have: envy, boastfulness, arrogance, or rudeness.

THE END OF TIME

When did Paul think the end would come?

Paul believed that Jesus would come back during Paul's lifetime. When Paul reminded the Corinthian believers about some of the Israelites being killed for their sin while in the desert with Moses, he wrote, "All these events happened to them as examples for us. They were written down to warn us, who live at the time when this age is drawing to a close." (NLT, I Corinthians 10:11)

II CORINTHIANS

When did Paul write the second letter to the Corinthians?

Paul wrote it a few months after he wrote the first one in 55 C.E. In this letter, Paul defended himself from verbal attacks from people who questioned the validity of his authority, and the authenticity of his faith.

How does II Corinthians begin?

Paul began the letter with the traditional greeting and thanksgiving to God.

PAUL'S OPPONENT

Who was the one caused Paul pain?

Paul wrote, "Now, regarding the one who started all this—the person in question who caused all this pain—I want you to know that I am not the one injured in this as much as, with a few exceptions, all of you." (The Message, II Corinthians 2:5) The identity of the man is unclear. One theory is that Paul referenced the man who was in a relationship with his stepmother. Another theory is that the man was someone who attacked Paul verbally.

What was Paul's recommendation for dealing with the man?

Paul wrote, "What the majority of you agreed to as punishment is punishment enough. Now is the time to forgive this man and help him back on his feet. If all you do is pour on the guilt, you could very well drown him in it. My counsel now is to pour on the love." (The Message, II Corinthians 2:6–7) Presumably, the man was ostracized, and Paul recommended that the believers welcome him back to the church.

THE PARADOXES OF GOD, PART 2

How did Paul describe the new covenant?

Paul described it in terms of contrast. "He [God] has made us competent as ministers of a new covenant—not of the letter but of the spirit; for the letter kills, but the Spirit gives life." (NIV, II Corinthians 3:6) The new covenant—or the new promise—from God took away sins, and promised eternal life through the death and resurrection of

> ## What eye disease plagued Paul, according to some scholars?
>
> Some proponents of the theory that Paul suffered from an eye disorder believe that the disease was chronic ophthalmia. This condition is characterized by inflammation of the eyes. In severe cases, the swollen areas become discolored, engorged, and leak pus.

Jesus. The old covenant—or the old promise—was the set of laws prescribed in the Old Testament.

How did Paul describe the difference between Old Testament followers of the law and the believers of his day? Unlike Moses, who had to hide his face behind a veil when the glory of God passed by, for believers of the new covenant the veil is removed. Paul wrote, "And we, who with unveiled faces all reflect the Lord's glory, are being transformed into his likeness with every-increasing glory, which comes from the Lord, who is the Spirit." (NIV, II Corinthians 3:18)

How did Paul defend himself against those who criticized him?

Again, Paul employed contrasting images. "Through glory and dishonor, bad report and good report; genuine, yet regarded as impostors; known, yet regarded as unknown; dying, and yet we live on; beaten, and yet not killed; sorrowful, yet always rejoicing; poor, yet making many rich; having nothing, yet possessing everything." (NIV, II Corinthians 6:8–10)

What evidence did Paul provide to prove how authentic he was in his ministry?

He reminded them of some of the bad things he experienced while spreading the Gospel. At the beginning of the letter Paul wrote, "We do not want you to be uninformed, brothers, about the hardships we suffered in the province of Asia. We were under great pressure, far beyond our ability to endure, so that we despaired even of life." (NIV, II Corinthians 1:8) Later, he described the threats he faced in more detail:

"Five times I have received from the Jews the forty lashes minus one. Three times I was beaten with rods. Once I received a stoning. Three times I was shipwrecked; for a night and a day I was adrift at sea; on frequent journeys, in danger from rivers, danger from bandits, danger from my own people, danger from Gentiles, danger in the city, danger in the wilderness, danger at sea, danger from false brothers and sisters; in toil and hardship, through many a sleepless night, hungry and thirsty, often without food, cold and naked." (NRSV, II Corinthians 11:24–28)

What did Paul have that kept his ego in check?

Paul wrote that "to keep me from being conceited because of these surpassingly great revelations, there was given me a thorn in the flesh." (NIV, II Corinthians 12:7)

275

What was the nature of the thorn?

Paul does not say. However, theories abound. One theory is that the thorn referred to those who persecuted him. Another theory is that based on Paul's use of fraught language, the thorn referred to an emotional problem, such as bipolar disorder. Still another theory is that based on veiled references in his letters to the Galatians (4:13, 4:15, 6:11), the thorn to which Paul referred was an eye disorder.

GALATIANS

When did Paul write this letter to the Galatians?

Paul wrote the letter around the early to mid-50s C.E. in response to false teachings in Galatia. Paul helped establish the church in Galatia around 45 C.E.

Where was Galatia?

Galatia was a Roman province in the hilly north-central region of modern-day Turkey.

How does Galatians begin?

Paul began the letter with the traditional greeting and thanksgiving to God.

FALSE GOSPEL

Why did Paul criticize the church in Galatia?

He criticized them for turning to "another gospel," a teaching that did not mesh with Christianity (KJV, Galatians 1:6). Particularly, believers were told that they had to be circumcised and convert to Judaism before they became Christians.

What was Paul's response to the false teaching?

Paul wrote, "As we have said before, so say I now again, If any man preach any other gospel unto you than that ye have received, let him be accursed." (KJV, Galatians 1:9)

How did Paul defend his position?

Paul explained that the gospel he taught them was not from him, a human. The gospel he spread was given to him by divine revelation. Neither circumcision nor the adherence to any other Mosaic laws was required to become a Christian. Paul wrote, "For in Jesus Christ neither circumcision availeth anything, nor uncircumcision; but faith which worketh love." (KJV, Galatians 5:6)

Who did Paul give as character references?

Paul provided the Galatians with information regarding his conversion and his first meeting with church leaders, James, Peter, and John. Paul added that when those three

> ## Was there any conflict between Peter and Paul?
>
> **P**eter was Jesus' personal friend and major influence in the spreading of the gospel. Even so, Paul used the sharp edge of his tongue to criticize what he viewed as Peter's hypocrisy. A disagreement between Paul and Peter arose when Peter—who usually had no problem eating with Gentiles—held back from eating with Gentiles when certain Jewish leaders visited. Paul wrote that Peter feared offending "the circumcision group." (NIV, Galatians 2:12)

men "who seemed to be pillars, perceived the grace that was given unto me, they gave to me and Barnabas the right hands of fellowship." (KJV, Galatians 2:9)

TRUE GOSPEL

What did Paul say was a mark of a true believer?

Paul reminded the Galatians that they received the Holy Spirit by faith, not by works or adherence to the law.

Who did Paul use as an example of someone who lived by faith?

Paul cited Abraham's life. Paul wrote, "Just as Abraham 'believed God, and it was reckoned to him as righteousness,' so, you see, those who believe are the descendants of Abraham." (NRSV, Galatians 3:6–7)

What was the point of the law then?

He explained it this way: "Is the law, therefore, opposed to the promises of God? Absolutely not! For if a law had been given that could impart life, then righteousness would certainly have come by the law." (NIV, Galatians 3:21) He continued, "Now before faith came, we were imprisoned and guarded under the law until faith would be revealed. Therefore the law was our disciplinarian until Christ came, so that we might be justified by faith. But now that faith has come, we are no longer subject to a disciplinarian." (NRSV, Galatians 3:23–25)

Was Paul promoting lawlessness?

No. The law highlighted for people their many imperfections, their inherent inability to approach God because of his holiness. Without the law, people would not realize how far removed from God they were. The law, then, pointed out the need for the saving faith found through Jesus. Living by faith meant listening to the Holy Spirit. The Holy Spirit never encouraged people to participate in "fornication, impurity, licentiousness, idolatry, sorcery, enmities, strife, jealousy, anger, quarrels, dissensions, factions, envy, drunkenness, carousing,

277

and things like these." Paul added, "I'm warning you, as I warned you before; those who do such things will not inherit the kingdom of God." (NRSV, Galatians 5:19–21)

What did Paul tell the Galatians about spiritual gifts?

He told them—as he told the Corinthians—that there were different kinds of spiritual gifts, but that all gifts worked for the good of the entire church.

EPHESIANS

When did Paul write the first letter to the Ephesians?

Doubt exists about whether Paul wrote the letter to the Ephesians because scholars say the writing style is so different from his other letters. If Paul did write it, he did so between 60 and 62 C.E. as 'an ambassador in chains' while under house arrest in Rome. If one of Paul's companions wrote the letter, it might have been written as many as twenty years later.

Where was Ephesus?

Ephesus was one of the largest cities in the Roman Empire. It was a thriving port city until silt bottled up the harbor. Ephesus was located in modern-day Turkey.

What is the letter to the Ephesians about?

In his letters to the Romans, Corinthians, and Galatians, Paul wrote to quell dissension, and to explain points of belief that were confusing. In the letter to the Ephesians, however, Paul had nothing but praise for the church there. In the letter, Paul shared some of the same wisdom he shared in his letters to other churches. He wrote about spiritual gifts and the nature of grace.

How did Paul and his followers negatively affect an ancient form of souvenir sales in Ephesus?

Ephesus was famous for its temple to Artemis (also known as Diana), one of the Seven Wonders of the Ancient World. In the book of Acts, Luke told of an incident regarding Paul and the artisans who made little silver models of the shrine to sell. Demetrius, one of the artisans, rallied his colleagues to protest the work of Paul and his companions. While they were in Ephesus, Paul and his companions converted many people to Christianity. More Christians meant fewer Artemis worshipers. That meant fewer people were buying the silver models of the shrine. The artisans' protest became heated, but a riot was avoided. (Acts 19:23–41)

How does Paul's letter to the Ephesians begin?

Paul began his letter with the traditional greeting of praise and thanksgiving.

GOD'S BLESSINGS

How did Paul describe God's blessings?

Paul was effusive and enthusiastic about the bounty of blessings given to believers. Through Jesus, believers have adoption, redemption, forgiveness, and knowledge of God's will.

SPECIAL EQUIPMENT

What did Paul advise the Ephesians to wear?

He advised them to put on a spiritual armor, "the whole armor of God." (KJV, Ephesians 6:10)

How did Paul describe the armor of God?

Paul wrote, "Stand therefore, and fasten the belt of truth around your waist, and put on the breastplate of righteousness. As shoes for your feet put on whatever will make you

The ruins of Ephesus are located near the western coast of present-day Turkey.

279

ready to proclaim the gospel of peace. With all of these, take the shield of faith, with which you will be able to quench all the flaming arrows of the evil one. Take the helmet of salvation, and the sword of the Spirit, which is the word of God." (Ephesians 6:13–17)

Why did this analogy apply to the Ephesians especially?

One of the things for which Ephesus was famous was an enormous coliseum that sat 25,000 people. At first this open-air coliseum was used for theater productions, but later it was used for gladiator events. So in his analogy, Paul might have been likening the believers in Ephesus to gladiators. Or Paul might have been likening the believers in Ephesus to Roman soldiers. Both gladiators and soldiers were professional fighters.

PHILIPPIANS

When did Paul write the letter to the Philippians?

Around 53 C.E., during his second missionary journey, Paul went to Philippi to start a church there. Most likely, Paul wrote this letter to the Philippians several years after his visit, sometime between 60 and 62 C.E. At the time Paul wrote the letter, he was in prison in Rome waiting for trial. The church in Philippi was the first Christian church in Europe.

Where was Philippi?

Philippi was founded in Macedonia in 356 B.C.E. and was abandoned in the 1300s. The ruins are in present-day Greece.

Philippi was an important city in Macedonia, one of several Greek cities Paul worked on converting to Christianity.

What is the letter to the Philippians about?

This letter is a thank you note. In it, Paul thanked the Philippians for their spiritual and financial support.

How does Paul's letter to the Philippians begin?

Paul began his letter with the traditional greeting of praise and thanksgiving.

PAUL IN PRISON

According to Paul, what were the benefits of being in prison?

Paul wrote, "But I would ye should understand, brethren, that the things which happened unto me have fallen out rather unto the furtherance of the gospel." (KJV, Philippians 1:12)

What did Paul want the Philippians to do?

He wanted them to continue to live "in a manner worthy of the gospel of Christ." (Philippians 1:27) To do that, Paul said they should demonstrate love, humility, and selflessness. Paul encouraged them: "Do all things without murmuring and arguing, so that you may be blameless and innocent, children of God without blemish in the midst of a crooked and perverse generation, in which you shine like stars in the world." (Philippians 2:14–15)

What was Paul's advice for living that way?

Paul commanded, "Rejoice in the Lord always: and again I say, Rejoice. Let your moderation be known unto all men. The Lord is at hand. Be careful for nothing; but in everything by prayer and supplication with thanksgiving let your requests be made known to God." (KJV, Philippians 4:4–6)

What did Paul promise would be the result of living that way?

Paul assured the Philippians: "And the peace of God, which passeth all understanding, shall keep your hearts and minds through Christ Jesus." (KJV, Philippians 4:7)

What were Paul's plans for the future?

Paul planned to visit Philippi again. Until that time, however, Paul wrote that he planned to send his companions Timothy and Epaphroditus to them.

What were Paul's views on death?

Paul looked forward to death so he could receive his heavenly reward. Still, he acknowledged he had work to do on earth: "For I am in a strait betwixt two, having a desire to depart, and to be with Christ; which is far better: Nevertheless to abide in the flesh is more needful for you." (KJV, Philippians 1:23–24)

COLOSSIANS

When did Paul write the letter to the Colossians?

Estimates vary. The letter could have been written any time between the mid-50s C.E. and the early 60s C.E. It is doubtful that Paul ever visited Colossae, but he was interested in the development of the church there, as this letter attests. Paul wrote the letter to address divisive issues that had come up among the believers.

Where was Colossae?

Colossae was close to what is the modern-day town of Honaz in Turkey. Shortly after Paul wrote this letter, Colossae experienced an earthquake. A series of devastating earthquakes followed, and the area was abandoned.

PAUL'S WAY WITH WORDS

How did Paul describe Jesus?

He described him this way: "He is the image of the invisible God, the firstborn of all creation; for in him all things in heaven and on earth were created, things visible and invisible, whether thrones or dominions or rulers or powers—all things have been created through him and for him." (NRSV, Colossians 1:15–16)

About what did Paul warn the Colossians?

He warned them about false teachings. Paul explained that other philosophies held "empty deceit," but following Jesus led to freedom and eternal life.

What were Paul's recommendations for right living?

Paul suggested that the Colossians rid themselves of "fornication, impurity, passion, evil desire, and greed." (NRSV, Colossian 3:5) Instead, they should practice "compassion, kindness, humility, meekness, and patience." (NRSV, Colossians 3:12) In addition, Paul emphasized the importance of forgiveness and all-encompassing love.

I THESSALONIANS

When did Paul write the first letter to the Thessalonians?

Paul and his companions traveled to Thessalonica during Paul's second missionary journey. This letter, written around 50 C.E., was written shortly after Paul left Thessalonica. Paul wrote the letter to encourage the newly founded church and to clarify Christian beliefs.

The Christian presence in Thessaloniki (formerly Thessalonica) is still strong today. Seen here is the Eastern Orthodox Church of God's Holy Sophia.

Where was Thessalonica?

Known as Thessaloniki today, Thessalonica is located in Greece.

How did Paul encourage the Thessalonians?

He told them he was thankful for them, and told them he was impressed with Timothy's reports of their church.

What beliefs did Paul clarify?

Paul clarified beliefs about death. Paul wrote: "And regarding the question, friends, that has come up about what happens to those already dead and buried, we don't want you in the dark any longer. First off, you must not carry on over them like people who have nothing to look forward to, as if the grave were the last word. Since Jesus died and broke loose from the grave, God will most certainly bring back to life those who died in Jesus." (The Message, I Thessalonians 4:13–14) Paul continued, "The Master himself will give the command. Archangel thunder! God's trumpet blast! He'll come down from heaven and the dead in Christ will rise—they'll go first. Then the rest of us who are still alive at the time will be caught up with them into the clouds to meet the Master. Oh, we'll be walking on air!" (The Message, I Thessalonians 4:16–17) As in earlier letters, Paul's writing suggests he believed Jesus was coming back in his lifetime.

283

Did Paul tell the Thessalonians when Jesus was coming back?

No. Paul said the time was unknowable, but that it would come suddenly and unexpectedly.

II THESSALONIANS

When did Paul write the second letter to the Thessalonians?

Paul wrote this letter shortly after he wrote the first letter to the Thessalonians. He wrote the letter to clarify more issues of faith.

What beliefs did Paul clarify?

As evidenced from the substance of Paul's letters, believers in Thessalonica were allowing anticipation of Jesus' return to stop them from working and supporting themselves.

What was Paul's response?

Paul wrote, "Now, friends, read these next words carefully. Slow down and don't go jumping to conclusions regarding the day when our Master, Jesus Christ, will come back and we assemble to welcome him." (The Message, II Thessalonians 2:1) Paul continued, "Refuse to have anything to do with those among you who are lazy and refuse to work the way we taught you. Don't permit them to freeload on the rest." (The Message, II Thessalonians 3:6)

I TIMOTHY

Who was Timothy?

Timothy, whose name means "honoring God," was one of Paul's protégés. Timothy was the pastor of the church at Ephesus. According to Acts 16, Timothy's mother was a Jewish woman who became a Christian. Timothy's father was Greek.

When did Paul write the first letter to Timothy?

Paul wrote this, the first of his so-called pastoral letters, to Timothy around 63 C.E. Paul wrote it to provide Timothy with instruction on how to minister—or pastor—effectively.

Who was "the lawless one"?

Scholars continue to debate this. One theory is that the lawless one was a reference to the Roman general Titus, who demolished the Jewish temple in 70 C.E. Another theory is that the lawless one was a reference to the Antichrist.

> ## Do Paul's views represent the views of the church to the present day?
>
> Scholars continue to debate this. Some say that Paul's views apply to all times and all situations. Others say that Paul's views should be viewed in the context of society in first-century Rome. In that case, Paul might have been trying to change attitudes first. Then when slaveholders and tyrannical husbands received the Holy Spirit, changed behavior would be the natural outpouring of that blessing. Paul's views on women and slaves appear in several of his letters.

PAUL ON RUNNING A CHURCH

What was Paul's advice regarding teaching?

Paul advised Timothy not to get distracted by "myths and endless genealogies" that promote controversy and strife. (NIV, I Timothy 1:4) Instead, Timothy's instruction should come from "a pure heart and a good conscience and a sincere faith." (NIV, I Timothy 1:5)

What was Paul's advice regarding leadership positions?

Paul wrote to Timothy that a leader should be above reproach, married only once, temperate, sensible, respectable, hospitable, an apt teacher, gentle, selfless, and a good manager of his own household.

What was Paul's advice on praying?

Paul told Timothy to pray for everyone, including "kings and all who are in high positions." (NRSV, I Timothy 2:2) In this way, everyone might come to know Christianity.

What did Paul say were the characteristics of Christianity?

Paul gave a concise description: "Christ appeared in the flesh and was shown to be righteous by the Spirit. He was seen by angels and was announced to the nations. He was believed on in the world and was taken up into heaven." (NLT, I Timothy 3:16–17)

What did Paul want Timothy to avoid?

Paul told Timothy to avoid "profane myths and old wives' tales." (NRSV, I Timothy 4:7)

PAUL ON DEALING WITH PEOPLE

Did Paul's views on the roles of men and women change since his letter to the Corinthians several years earlier?

His views did not change. He wrote to Timothy: "Women should listen and learn quietly and submissively. I do not let women teach men or have authority over them. Let them listen quietly."(NLT, I Timothy 2:11–12)

What were Paul's views on dealing with elders? Widows? Slaves?

Paul told Timothy elders should be addressed with respect, widows should be honored and cared for, and slaves should honor their masters.

II TIMOTHY

When did Paul write the second letter to Timothy?

Paul wrote this letter of encouragement to Timothy around 67 C.E. By that point, Paul and Timothy had developed a deep friendship that is evidenced by Paul's salutation: "To Timothy, my beloved child." (NRSV, II Timothy 1:2) Paul wrote this, his last known letter, from prison in Rome. Timothy was still in Ephesus.

How did Paul encourage Timothy?

Paul encouraged Timothy by reminding him of the gift of God in him. "For," Paul added, "God hath not given us the spirit of fear, but of power, and of love, and of a sound mind." (KJV, II Timothy 1:7) In addition, Paul reminded Timothy of his background. He wrote, "But continue thou in the things which thou has learned and hast been assured of, knowing of whom thou has learned them; And that from a child thou hast known the holy scriptures, which are able to make thee wise unto salvation through faith which is in Christ Jesus." (KJV, II Timothy 3:14–15)

What was dangerous to ministering?

Paul told Timothy to avoid "wrangling over words," "profane chatter," and "senseless and stupid controversies." (NRSV, II Timothy 2:14, 16, 23)

What was beneficial to ministering?

Paul encouraged Timothy to be kind, patient, and peaceable in his teaching. Also, Paul told Timothy to be persistent.

How were some other teachers distorting the gospel?

Paul warned Timothy to avoid those "who concerning the truth have erred, saying that the resurrection is past already." (KJV, II Timothy 2:18)

What were Paul's concerns about the end times?

Paul wrote to Timothy that people would be on their worst behavior. "For men shall be lovers of their own selves, covetous, boasters, proud, blasphemers, disobedient to parents, unthankful, unholy, without natural affection trucebreakers false accusers, incontinent, fierce, despisers of those that are good, traitors, heady, high-minded, lovers of pleasures more than lovers of God." (KJV, II Timothy 3:2–4) Paul added, "For the time will come when they not endure sound doctrine; but after their own lusts shall they heap to themselves teachers, having itching ears." (KJV, II Timothy 4:3)

What was Paul's final request of Timothy?

Paul knew that he was about to be killed because of his faith. Rome nearly burned to the ground in 64 C.E. Emperor Nero blamed the Christians for setting the fire. Accordingly, he jacked up anti-Christian persecutions. Christians were thrown to hungry dogs, burned alive, and crucified. It was under this oppression that Paul wrote this letter to Timothy. Paul loved Timothy, and wanted to see him again. He wrote, "Do thy diligence to come before winter." (KJV, II Timothy 4:21). It is not known whether Timothy made it or not.

TITUS

Who was Titus?

Titus, whose name means "honored," was a Gentile believer. He became a trusted envoy and co-worker of Paul.

When did Paul write the letter to Titus?

Most scholars think that Paul wrote this letter between 63–65 C.E., during his prison time in Rome. At the time, Titus was responsible for the church on the island of Crete. As in his letter to Timothy, Paul wrote to Titus on how to minister effectively.

Where was Crete?

Crete was (and is) a large Greek island. Some 1500 to 2000 years before the time of Paul, Crete was the home of the Minoan civilization. Under Minoan influence, the arts flourished in Crete. The people excelled in architecture, statuary, painting, and metalwork. Around 1200 B.C.E., the Minoan civilization disintegrated. The reason for the demise is not known for certain, but theories include an earthquake and a tidal wave. The island became a haven for pirates and other criminals. Lawlessness was the law. The Roman army conquered the island in 67 B.C.E., and restored order. However, Crete's reputation as crime headquarters persisted through Paul's day. He warned Titus of the reputation by quoting a seventh-century B.C.E. poet, Epimenedes: "The people of Crete are all liars; they are cruel animals and lazy gluttons." (NLT, Titus 1:12) Today, Crete is a major vacation spot, drawing people from all over the world with its temperate climate, rich culture, and hospitable people.

PAUL ON RUNNING THE CHURCH IN CRETE

What was Titus' job?

Paul told Titus to appoint church elders, refute the opposition, and deal effectively with the people.

What was Paul's advice regarding leadership positions?

Paul's advice to Titus was similar to the advice he gave Timothy. Paul wrote that Titus should appoint leaders who are "blameless, married only once, whose children are believers, not accused of debauchery, and not rebellious." (NRSV, Titus 1:6)

What was Paul's advice for refuting the opposition?

Paul told Titus to make sure he and the other church leaders knew Christian teachings well, so they could set straight those who opposed them ideologically.

What was Paul's advice for dealing effectively with people?

Paul told Titus to encourage the older men to be temperate and serious, the older women to be temperate and instructive to the young women, the younger men to be self-controlled, and the slaves to be respectful and submissive to their masters.

How did Paul describe God's grace?

Paul wrote, "But then God our savior showed us his kindness and love. He saved us, not because of the good things we did, but because of his mercy. He washed away our sins and gave us a new life through the Holy Spirit. He generously poured out the Spirit upon us because of what Jesus Christ our Savior did. He declared us not guilty because of his great kindness. And now we know that we will inherit eternal life. These things I have told you are all true." (NLT, Titus 3:4–8)

In other words, our loving God appeared in order to save people. People did not have to earn salvation. God gave it to them. Accordingly, people who accepted God's salvation were baptized with water to represent their renewal by the Holy Spirit.

OTHER LETTERS

PHILEMON

Who was Philemon?

Philemon was a slaveholder who held church meetings at his home in Colossae. Paul wrote the letter around 60 C.E.

What is the letter to Philemon about?

In this, his shortest surviving letter, Paul requested that Philemon free his slave, Onesimus. At some point, Onesimus escaped from Philemon and went to Rome. In Rome, he met and was converted by Paul.

How did Paul try to convince Philemon to free Onesimus?

Paul used his considerable powers of persuasion and coercion. He was warm like the sun and forceful like the wind. He wrote, "For this reason, though I am bold enough in Christ to command you to do your duty, yet I would rather appeal to you on the basis of love." (NRSV, Philemon 1:8). Paul continued, "So if you consider me your partner, welcome him as you would welcome me. If he has wronged you in any way, or owes you in any way, charge that to my account. I, Paul, am writing this with my own hand: I will repay it. I say nothing about your owing me even your own self." (NRSV, Philemon 1:17–19)

If Onesimus was already free because he escaped, why did Paul bother to write Philemon?

Presumably, Paul wanted Onesimus to honor Philemon by going back to him. In exchange, Paul wanted Philemon to free Onesimus. If Philemon did that, then he could have Onesimus "no longer as a slave but more than a slave, a beloved brother," according to Christian belief. (NRSV, Philemon 1:16)

HEBREWS

Who wrote the letter to the Hebrews?

The author's name is never identified in the letter, nor is the name of the person or people he addressed. The author might be addressing a specific community, or all Jewish people. Tradition holds that Paul wrote the letter.

When was the letter written?

Most scholars say the book was written between 64 and 70 C.E. In 64 C.E. the Emperor Nero started persecuting Christians. And in 70 C.E. is the year the Romans destroyed the temple in Jerusalem, a fact the author of Hebrews most likely would have mentioned, given the context of the letter.

What is the letter about?

In the letter, the author described how the coming of Jesus made the old way of observing the Jewish faith no longer necessary. The author draws extensively on his knowledge of the Old Testament to form distinctions between the old way and the new way.

How did the author describe the differences between Judaism and Christianity?

Judaism/Old Testament	Christianity/New Testament
God spoke through prophets.	God spoke through his son.
Moses, God's servant, was faithful to God's call.	Jesus, God's son, was faithful to God's call.
Melchilzedek was the high priest for Abraham.	Jesus was the great high priest.
Aaron was the high priest for Moses.	Jesus was the great high priest.
Abraham obtained the promise God made to him.	God's heirs obtained a promise God made to them.
If perfection could be achieved through Levitical priesthood, there would not be a need for another priest later on. Perfection is not achieved through Levitical priesthood.	Jesus became priest, not through legal requirements but through the power of indestructible life.
There were many priests. Death prevented them from continuing in office.	Jesus is eternal, and always able to save those who approach God through him.
No one could enter the Holy of Holies except for the high priest, and he could do that only once a year (each and every year) to make special sacrifices. Even these special sacrifices could not perfect the conscience of the worshipper.	Jesus entered the Holy of Holies, not with blood of goats and calves, but with his own blood. This single act meant eternal redemption.

Judaism/Old Testament	Christianity/New Testament
Sacrifice with animal blood over and over.	Sacrifice with blood of Jesus one time.
Law cannot perfect those who approach altar of God. If law made people perfect, there would be no need for continuous animal sacrifices. In animal sacrifices, however, there is constant reminder of sin.	No animal sacrifices. Sacrifice of Jesus' body. Through Jesus, believers have confidence to approach altar of God.

Was the author saying that Abraham, Moses, and the other people in the Old Testament were wrong?

No, the author did not say the Old Testament people were wrong. He believed that their faith made them right with God.

How did the author describe faith?

He wrote, "It is the confident assurance that what we hope for is going to happen. It is the evidence of things we cannot yet see." (NLT, Hebrews 11:1)

What does that mean?

To understand that verse, it helps to read the two verses that follow it: "By faith we understand that the entire universe was formed at God's command, that what we now see did not come from anything that can be seen." (NLT, Hebrews 11:2–3) So Abraham and other Old Testament believers believed God's promises, even though they did not understand at first why God commanded them to do certain things.

What are some examples of Old Testament people obeying God even though they did not fully understand the reasons?

Abel's sacrifice was more pleasing to God than Cain's sacrifice because of faith. Noah built a boat big enough for thousands of animals because he had faith in what God told him. Abraham packed up his family and all he owned to move several hundred miles away because he had faith in what God told him. Abraham prepared to sacrifice his son Isaac because he had faith in what God told him. The author gave several examples, but acknowledged that he left out many because of time constraints. There were so many more "who through faith conquered kingdoms, administered justice, obtained promises, shut the mouths of lions, quenched raging fire, escaped the edge of the sword, won strength out of weakness, became mighty in war, put foreign armies to flight." (NLT, Hebrews 11:33–34)

What name did the author give this group of believers?

He called them a "huge cloud of witnesses," and he cited their faith as something to inspire the recipients of his letter. He wrote, "Therefore, since we are surrounded by such a huge crowd of witnesses to the life of faith, let us strip off every weight that slows us down, especially the sin that so easily hinders our progress. And let us run with endurance the race that God has set before us." (NLT, Hebrews 12:1–2)

How did the author conclude his letter?

He concluded his letter with advice on daily living, including this piece on hospitality: "Do not neglect to show hospitality to strangers, for by doing that some have entertained angels unaware." (NRSV, Hebrews 13:1)

JAMES

Who was James?

There are two possibilities. One was James the apostle. The other was James the brother of Jesus. If the author was James the apostle, the letter predates 44 C.E., because that is the year James was executed by Herod Agrippa. If the author was the brother of Jesus, the letter dates from the early 60s C.E. James, the brother of Jesus, was executed by local Jews around 66 C.E. The letter was written to believers outside Israel, particularly Jewish Christians.

What is the letter about?

In the letter, James warned about the dangers of gossip and wealth.

What did James say about suffering?

James wrote, "Consider it pure joy, my brothers, whenever you face trials of many kinds because you know that the testing of your faith develops perseverance." (NIV, James 1:3)

What did James say about faith?

James explained that faith was important because without it "he who doubts is like a wave of the sea, blown and tossed by the wind. That man should not think he will receive anything from the Lord; he is a double-minded man, unstable in all he does." (NIV, James 1:6–8)

Also, James explained that faith without works was not really faith at all. James wrote, "What good is it, my brothers and sisters, if you say you have faith but do not have works? Can faith save you? If a brother or sister is naked and lacks daily food, and one of you says to them, 'Go in peace; keep warm and eat your fill,' and yet you do not supply their bodily needs, what is the good of that? So faith by itself, if it has no works, is dead." (NRSV, James 2:14–17) James pointed out that even "demons believe—and shudder." (NRSV, James 2:19)

What did James say about manners of speech?

He advised the recipients of the letter to listen more than they talk. He wrote, "Let everyone be quick to listen, slow to speak, slow to anger, for your anger does not produce God's

---

What did James say about wealth?

James said wealth was temporary, like a flower in a field. He criticized those who loved the pleasure of wealth more than the pleasure of faith. "Adulterers!" he exclaimed. "You adulterous people," he exclaimed, "don't you know that friendship with the world is hatred toward God?" (NIV, James 4:4)

---

righteousness." (NRSV, James 1:19–20). He added, "How great a forest is set ablaze by a small fire! And the tongue is a fire." (NRSV, James 3:5–6) James pointed out that the tongue was a double agent. He wrote, "With it we bless the Lord and Father, and with it we curse those who are made in the likeness of God. From the same mouth come blessing and cursing. My brothers and sisters, this ought not to be so." (NRSV, James 3:9–10)

What recommendation did James make so the people could avoid these behaviors?

He told them to submit themselves to God. "Come near to God," he urged, "and he will come near to you." (NIV, James 4:8) Also, he encouraged them to pray. He wrote, "The prayer of a righteous is powerful and effective." (NIV, James 5:16)

I PETER

Who wrote the first letter of Peter?

Peter, Jesus' apostle, allegedly wrote this letter. Evidently, there were several copies of the letter, because the letter is addressed to people in Pontus, Galatia, Cappadocia, Asia, and Bithynia. He wrote the letter to address the concerns of a group of believers who used to participate fully in the culture of their country, but because of their new faith, found themselves marginalized and even abused. Most scholars think Paul wrote the letter in the early 60s C.E.

What was the letter about?

Peter told the believers that God would reward those who suffered for their faith. He wrote, "But rejoice that you participate in the sufferings of Christ, so that you may be overjoyed when his glory is revealed. If you are insulted because of the name of Christ, you are blessed, for the Spirit of glory and of God rests on you." (NIV, I Peter 4:13–14)

According to Peter, what was the benefit of faith?

Faith brings about "indescribable and glorious joy." (NRSV, I Peter 1:8). Also, faith brings about "the salvation of [their] souls." (NRSV, I Peter 1:9) Peter emphasized the role of prayer in an active faith. He wrote, "Cast all your anxieties on him, because he cares for you." (NRSV, I Peter 5:7)

What was Peter's advice on how to be an active believer?

Peter wanted believers to set all their hope on Jesus. He urged believers to resist the temptation to return to their previous ways. He wrote: "Therefore, rid yourselves of all malice and all deceit, hypocrisy, envy, and slander of every kind." (NIV, I Peter 2:1) The most important thing, however, was to "love each other deeply." (NIV, I Peter 4:8)

What was Peter's advice on dealing with antagonists?

Peter said that no matter what, be honorable. In doing so, your antagonists would see your honorable deeds and glorify God.

What was Peter's advice for believers who were marginalized?

Peter advised slaves to accept the authority of their masters, and for wives to accept the authority of their husbands.

Did Peter approve of slavery? Did he think that men were better than women?

Peter's statements were similar to those of Paul's. Like Paul, Peter believed that Jesus was coming back during his lifetime. He wrote, "Therefore be clear-minded and self-controlled so that you can pray." (NIV, I Peter 4:7) Many scholars think Peter did not approve of slavery, nor did he view women as inferior to men. Rather, he was focused on changing belief, not behavior. Behavior would follow—if Jesus didn't come first.

II PETER

Who wrote the second letter of Peter?

Some scholars say Peter wrote the letter. After all, the salutation of the letter says as much. However, some scholars say one of Peter's students wrote the letter long after Peter died. So the letter could have been written any time between the early 60s C.E. and the 90s C.E. The author, whoever it is, did not say to whom he was writing. The message reads like an open letter to believers everywhere.

What was the letter about?

In the letter, Peter encouraged believers to keep growing in faith, resist false teachings, and not be discouraged that Jesus was not back yet. Peter wanted the believers to review and remember what he said after he died. He knew his death was imminent: "I know that I'm to die soon; the Master has made that quite clear to me." (The Message, II Peter 1:14)

According to Peter, what should believers do in order to support their faith?

Believers should strive for goodness, knowledge, self-control, endurance, godliness, and
love.

A Christian tradition is that Jesus gave the keys to Paradise to St. Peter, who now mans the pearly gates, allowing entrance only to those who are worthy.

How did Peter know that Christianity was genuine, and not a fad?

He wrote, "We weren't, you know, just wishing on a star when we laid the facts out before you regarding the powerful return of our Master, Jesus Christ. We were there for the preview! We saw it with our own eyes: Jesus resplendent with light from God the Father as the voice of Majestic Glory spoke: 'This is my Son, marked by my love, focus of all my delight.' We were there on the holy mountain with him. We heard the voice out of heaven with our very own ears." (The Message, II Peter 1:16–18)

What was the difference between real prophets and false prophets?

Peter differentiated between the two this way: "First of all you must understand this, that no prophecy of scripture is a matter of one's own interpretation, because no prophecy ever came by human will, but men and women moved by the Holy Spirit spoke from God." (NRSV, II Peter 1:20–21) On the other hand, false prophets brought in "destructive opinions" and paraded their "bold and willful" ways. (NRSV, II Peter 2:1, 10)

Who did false prophets prey on especially?

New converts. Peter explained how false prophets did this. He wrote: "There's nothing to these people—they're dried up fountains, storm-scattered clouds, headed for a black

295

hole in hell. They are loudmouths, full of hot air, but still they're dangerous.... They promise these newcomers freedom, but they themselves are slaves of corruption, for if they're addicted to corruption—and they are—they're enslaved!" (NIV, II Peter 2:18–19)

What did Peter say to those who mocked Christianity because Jesus was not back yet?

Peter wrote, "Don't overlook the obvious here, friends. With God, one day is as good as a thousand years, a thousand years as a day. God isn't late with his promise as some measure lateness. He is restraining himself on account of you, holding back the End because he doesn't want anyone lost. He's giving everyone space and time to change." (The Message, II Peter 3:8–9)

I JOHN

Who wrote the first letter of John?

Most scholars believe that John, of "Matthew, Mark, Luke, and John" fame, wrote the letter late in life, maybe in the 80s or 90s C.E. Some scholars believe one of John's students wrote the letter.

What is the first letter of John about?

By this point in church history, Christianity was seen no longer as a branch of Judaism, but as a distinct and separate religion. So the earlier arguments about being circumcised or not, eating kosher food or not, etc., were moot. The conflicts John wrote about had to with congregations splitting over the whys and wherefores of Jesus' life and ministry.

Why was John the ideal person to write a letter defending the authenticity of Jesus' life and ministry?

He knew Jesus personally, and he said as much in the first part of the letter.

What single behavior demonstrated obedience to God's commandments?

The act of loving people. John mentioned love many times in this letter. He wrote, "Whoever says, 'I am in the light,' while a brother or sister, is still in the darkness. Whoever loves a brother or sister lives in the light, and in such a person there is no cause for stumbling." (I John 2:9–10) He wrote also, "Whoever does not love does not know God, for God is love." (NRSV, I John 4:8)

According to John, what was a mark of true faith?

Obeying God's commandments. John explained, "Now by this we may be sure that we know him, if we obey his commandments. Whoever says, 'I have come to know him,' but does not obey his commandments, is a liar, and in such a person the truth does not exist." (NRSV, I John 2:4)

II JOHN

Who wrote the second letter of John?

Most scholars agree that it was John the apostle who wrote this letter. He wrote it as a private letter to a friend or single congregation he expected to visit soon. The letter was written about the same time as the first letter of John.

What is the letter about?

The substance of this letter is like that of the first letter, only in condensed form. John warned the recipient or recipients of the letter about people who claimed to be Christians, but spread false beliefs about Christianity. Also, he emphasized the importance of love in Christian faith.

III JOHN

Who wrote the third letter of John?

Most scholars agree that John the apostle wrote the letter. The letter is addressed to a person name Gaius. The letter was written about the same time as the first two letters.

Who was Gaius?

Judging from the content of the letter, Gaius was a leader of a church. John did not say in the letter where he was writing from, or where Gaius lived. John praised Gaius for his faithfulness to Christian beliefs.

What is the letter about?

In the letter, John complained about a church leader, Diotrephes.

What did Diotrephes do that John did not like?

Diotrephes did not acknowledge John's authority. Also, he spread "false charges" against John and some of the others. John did not go into detail about the nature of the false charges. Also, John was displeased because Diotrephes did not welcome certain believers into his home, thus denying them the very basics of hospitality. Diotrephes threatened those who wanted to welcome the believers with expulsion from the church.

JUDE

Who wrote the letter of Jude?

Jude. At the beginning of the letter, Jude identifies himself as being the brother of James. Jesus had four brothers—James, Joseph, Simon, and Judas. Most scholars think that the Jude who wrote this letter was the Judas who was Jesus' brother. The letter was written around 60 C.E. Jude does not identify his locale. The recipients are identified as "all who are called to live in the love of God the Father and the care of Jesus Christ." (NLT, Jude 1:1)

What is the letter about?

In the letter, Jude explained that he believed it was necessary to write in order to encourage believers in their faith. Jude was concerned about "certain intruders" who mixed with the believers and spread false beliefs.

What false beliefs were being spread?

From the content of Jude's letter, it seems likely that one false belief making the rounds was that once saved, sinning was fine. Jude reminded the believers that God did not like sin, and that he punished those who persisted in sin. Jude cited the Israelites in the wilderness, and the people of Sodom and Gomorrah.

How did Jude describe those who spread false beliefs?

Jude wrote that "these false teachers, who claim authority from their dreams, live immoral lives, defy authority, and scoff at the power of the glorious ones" He continued, "They are like clouds blowing over dry land without giving rain, promising much but producing nothing." (NLT, Jude 1:8, 12)

What example did Jude use to illustrate that slander is never acceptable, even slandering someone who is evil?

Jude wrote about when the archangel Michael fought with Satan over Moses' body. Michael did not dare slander Satan, but instead exclaimed, "The Lord rebuke you!" (NLT, Jude 1:9)

Is that event described in Deuteronomy, the book in which Moses' death is recorded?

No. The struggle between Michael and Satan is not recorded in the Bible. Some scholars think Jude referenced a work called "The Assumption of Moses." However, the part of "The Assumption of Moses" that survives today does not describe that particular event.

REVELATION

Who wrote the book of Revelation?

The full title of the book is *The Revelation of John,* so presumably, a man named John wrote it. Some, but not all, scholars think the John in question was the apostle of Jesus. Most likely, the book was written during the reign of Domitian, who ruled the Roman Empire from 81–96 C.E. It was a time when Christians faced severe persecution. For practicing and preaching his faith, John was sent to prison on the Greek island of Patmos.

What is the book of Revelation about?

It is the blueprint of God's plan for judgment and salvation.

How does the book of Revelation begin?

It begins with John explaining that the revelation detailed in the book was given to him by Jesus.

What literary form does John use in the book?

He uses three forms: epistolary, prophetic, and apocalyptic. Epistolary means the book is in the form of a letter. Prophetic means the book deals with possible future outcomes regarding judgment and salvation. Apocalyptic means that the book deals with the unveiling of God's purpose, especially as it relates to end times.

What is the significance of John referring to Jesus as "the firstborn of the dead?"

The name is a celebratory acknowledgment of Jesus' triumph over death and sin by his resurrection.

What is the significance of God referring to himself as "the Alpha and the Omega?"

Alpha is the first letter of the Greek alphabet. Omega is the last letter of the Greek alphabet. God is the beginning and end of all things.

What was the first thing John saw in his vision?

He saw seven golden lampstands. Standing in the midst of the lampstands was a man.

What did the man look like?

He was "clothed with a long robe and with a golden sash across his chest. His head and his hair were white as white wool, white as snow; his eyes were like a flame of fire, his feet were like burnished bronze, refined as in a furnace, and his voice was like the sound of many waters. In his right hand he held seven stars, and from his mouth came a sharp, two-edged sword, and his face was like the sun shining full force." (NRSV, Revelation 1:13–16) The man said, "I was dead, and see, I am alive forever and ever." Most scholars believe the man was Jesus.

JOHN TAKES DICTATION FROM JESUS

To whom is the book addressed?

It is addressed to "the seven churches in the province of Asia" (NLT, Revelation 1:4)—in what is modern-day Turkey. These churches were in the cities of Ephesus, Laodicea, Smyrna, Philadelphia, Pergamum, Thyatira, and Sardis. The letters, though written out by John, are the words of Jesus.

Why did John write the letter?

God told him to: " Write down what you see, and send it to the seven churches…." (NLT, Revelation 1:11) Each church received a different letter, with content varying according to the spiritual well-being of the church.

What is the significance of the seven golden lampstands and the seven stars?

In the book, the man said the lampstands represented the seven churches referred to earlier. The seven stars represented the "angels" of the seven churches. One theory is that the angels were guardian angels of the churches.

What concerns did John address in his letter to Ephesus?

John, at Jesus' dictation, praised the Ephesians for their patience and work on behalf of their Christian faith. However, John chastised them for allowing their love to grow weak. He encouraged them to build that love again.

What concerns did John address in his letter to Smyrna?

John commiserated with the people of Smyrna for their suffering for their Christian faith. He told them that they would suffer still more, but not to be afraid. At death, they would receive "the crown of life." (NLT, Revelation 2:10)

What concerns did John address in his letter to Pergamum?

John called Pergamum "Satan's throne," because it was the region's center of Roman emperor worship. Also, Pergamum was famous for its enormous altar to Zeus. Amid an environment that was hostile to Christianity, the Christians in Pergamum maintained their faith. John praised them for this. Still, John scolded the Christians in Pergamum because there were some among them who dabbled in pagan worship.

What concerns did John address in his letter to Thyatira?

John praised the Christians in Thyatira for "thy works, and charity, and service, and faith, and thy patience." (KJV, Revelation 2:19) However, John criticized them because they tolerated a false prophet he likened to Jezebel in the Old Testament.

What concerns did John address in his letter to Sardis?

For the most part, John's letter to the Christians in Sardis was one of warning. John scolded them for being sleepy in their faith. "If therefore thou shalt not watch," Jesus told John to say, "I will come on thee as a thief, and thou shalt not know what hour I will come upon thee." (KJV, Revelation 3:3)

What concerns did John address in his letter to Laodicea?

John chastised the Christians in Laodicea for being "neither cold nor hot." (KJV, Revelation 3:15) In worldly things, the Christians in Laodicea were rich, but in spiritual things they were poor. The city was noted for its sheep with fine black wool and its manufacturing of medicinal eye powder. This comment was tailored especially for the Christians there: "I counsel thee to buy of me gold tried in the fire, that thou mayest be rich;

What is eschatology?

Eschatology is a fancy word for the study of end times.

and white raiment, that thou mayest be clothed, and that the shame of thy nakedness do not appear; and anoint thine eyes with eye salve, that thou mayest see." (KJV, Revelation 3:18) John dictated Jesus' encouragement as well: "As many as I love, I rebuke and chasten: be zealous therefore, and repent. Behold, I stand at the door, and knock: if any man hear my voice, and open the door, I will come in to him, and will sup with him, and he with me." (KJV, Revelation 3:19–20)

JOHN VISITS HEAVEN

What did John see in Heaven?

In a vision or in actuality, John went to Heaven. In Heaven, John saw a dazzling figure on a throne. Around the throne were twenty-four thrones on which were twenty-four elders clothed all in white and crowned in gold. Amidst all of this, were four living creatures who were part human and part animal.

Who were the twenty-four elders?

Theories vary, but one prevalent idea is that the twenty-four represented the new, complete church. That is, the twelve represented twelve tribes of Israel established by God in the Old Testament and the other twelve represented the twelve apostles commissioned by Jesus in the New Testament.

What was the significance of the living creatures?

The identity of the living creatures continues to stir debate, but the most widely accepted theory is that the living creatures represented all earthly beings. They sang God's praise nonstop.

What did the figure on the main throne have in his hand?

The figure had a scroll. It was rolled up and sealed with seven seals. No one was worthy enough to break the seals and open the scroll except for "the Lion of the tribe of Judah, the Root of David"—Jesus. In Revelation, he is also called "the Lamb."

What was the significance of the seven seals?

Each seal represented a divine judgment. The Lamb opened each seal, asserting his right to rule the world.

The first seal: A figure on a white horse appeared. The rider carried a bow and wore a crown, and "he rode off victorious, conquering right and left." (The Message, Revelation 6:2) One theory is that this figure was Jesus, and the white horse represented righteousness and the swift spread of the gospel. Another theory is that the rider and the white horse represented military conquest by earthly rulers.

The second seal: A figure on a red horse appeared. This rider "was off to take peace from the earth, setting people at each other's throats, killing one another. He was

What book by Sir Isaac Newton addressed biblical prophecy?

Sir Isaac Newton, in addition to being a great scientist and mathematician, was a deeply religious man. His *Observations on the Prophecies of Daniel and Apocalypse of St. John* was published posthumously in 1733.

given a huge sword." (The Message, Revelation 6:4) One theory is that this figure represented Satan, and the red horse represented the spread of evil and destruction. Another theory is that the rider and the red horse represented war.

The third seal: A figure on a black horse appeared. This rider held a set of scales. A voice in the midst cried out, "A quart of wheat for a day's pay, and three quarts of barley for a day's pay, but do not damage the olive oil and the wine." (NRSV, Revelation 6:6) Generally, this is interpreted to mean famine.

The fourth seal: A figure on a pale green horse appeared. The rider's name was Death. Hades followed him. They were given authority over one-quarter of the earth, "to destroy a fourth of the earth by war, famine, disease, and wild beasts." (The Message, Revelation 6:8) Generally, this is interpreted to mean death.

The fifth seal: John saw under the altar the souls of martyrs, those who died for the word of God. The souls cried out, "How long, Strong God, Holy and True? How long before you step in and avenge our muders?" (The Message, Revelation 6:10) The souls were given white robes and told to wait just a little longer.

The sixth seal: John saw terrifying things happen in the natural world. In addition to a great earthquake, the sun blackened, the moon took on the appearance of blood, stars fell to the ground, and the sky vanished. Every person, regardless of social status, hid in caves and among the clefts of mountains. They were terrified. Also, John saw four angels standing at the four corners of the earth holding back the wind. Another angel called out to the four: "Don't hurt the earth! Don't hurt the sea! Don't so much as hurt a tree until I've sealed servants of our God on their foreheads!" (The Message, Revelation 7:3)

The seventh seal: When the Lamb opened the seventh seal, there was silence in heaven for half an hour. Then John saw seven angels with seven trumpets standing before God. Another angel with a golden censer came and stood at the altar, and "he was given a great quantity of incense so that he could offer up the prayers of all the holy people of God on the Golden Altar before the Throne." (The Message, Revelation 8:3) The angel took the censer, filled it with fire from the altar, and threw it on the earth. The earth quaked amid thunder and flashes of lightning.

When the sixth seal was opened, how many people were sealed on their foreheads?

One hundred forty-four thousand. Some people believe this number is literal. Others believe it is symbolic. In contrast to this finite number, the next few verses describe a countless throng: "After this I looked, and there was a great multitude that no one could count, from every nation, from all tribes and peoples and languages, standing before the throne and before the Lamb, robed in white, with palm branches in their hands. They cried out in a loud voice, saying, 'Salvation belongs to our God who is seated on the throne, and to the Lamb!'" (NRSV, Revelation 7:9–10)

When the seventh seal was opened, what happened when the seven angels blew their trumpets?

The blowing of their trumpets signaled the final wrath of God.

- When the first angel blew his trumpet, hail, fire, and blood were hurled to the earth.

- When the second angel blew his trumpet, a fiery mountain was thrown into the sea. As a result, a third of the sea became blood, a third of the living creatures in the sea died, and a third of the ships on the sea were destroyed.

- When the third angel blew his trumpet, a star named Wormwood fell on one-third of the earth's rivers, rendering the water bitter. In the vision, many people died from drinking the water.

- When the fourth angel blew his trumpet, a third of the sun, a third of the moon, and a third of the stars were darkened.

- When the fifth angel blew his trumpet, an enormous plague of monster/locust hybrids was released on the earth. They were ruled by "the angel of the Abyss." In Hebrew, their king's name is Abaddon. In Greek, his name is Apollyon. Both names mean "destruction." This plague was the first of three woes.

- When the sixth angel blew his trumpet, a surreal cavalry was released. The horsemen "wore breastplates the color of fire and of sapphire and of sulfur; the heads of the horses were like lions' heads, and fire and smoke and sulfur came out of their mouths." (NRSV, Revelation 9:17) This was the second of three woes.

- When the seventh angel blew his trumpet, the twenty-four elders who sat on their thrones before God fell on their faces and worshiped God, singing, "We give thanks to you, Lord God Almighty, the one who is and who was, because you have taken your great power and begun to reign." (NIV, Revelation 11:17) Then the Ark of the Covenant was seen in God's heavenly temple. Thunder, lightning, hail, and an earthquake accompanied this. This was the third of three woes.

Did the people repent?

No. The Bible reads, "The rest of mankind that were not killed by these plagues still did not repent of the work of their hands; they did not stop worshiping demons, and idols of gold, silver, bronze, stone and wood—idols that cannot see or hear or walk. Nor did they repent of their murders, their magic arts, their sexual immorality or their thefts." (NIV, Revelation 9:20–21)

> ## What was the purpose of the three woes?
>
> The woes were unleashed as one last push to urge people to repent before the world ended.

THE SECOND SCROLL

Who gave John the second scroll?

A mighty angel who came down from heaven, "robed in a cloud, with a rainbow above his head; his face was like the sun, and his legs were like fiery pillars." (NIV, Revelation 10:1–2) When the angel spoke, seven thunders sounded.

What was the significance of the seven thunders?

The seven thunders revealed something to John, but just as he was about to write down what they said, another voice told John, "Seal up what the seven thunders have said, and do not write it down." (NIV, Revelation 10:4)

What did John do with the scroll?

The voice told John to eat the scroll. So John "took the little scroll from the angel's hand and ate it." (NIV, Revelation 10:10–11) A popular theory is that the sweetness represents the gentle relief given to believers, while the upset stomach represents the harshness of God's judgment on the unrepentant.

THE TWO WITNESSES

Who were the two witnesses?

John does not identify them by name, but some scholars suggest the witnesses might be Moses and Elijah.

What was the role of the two witnesses?

The Lamb told John that he would give the two witnesses authority to prophesy for 1,260 days. That is three-and-one-half years. Three-and-one-half years is half of seven. In the Bible, seven represents completeness and holiness. Three-and-one-half, then, represents chaos. While prophesying, the witnesses were to wear sackcloth, a sign of repentance.

What special abilities were the witnesses given?

God gave the witnesses the "power to shut up the sky so that it will not rain during the time they are prophesying; and they have power to turn the waters into blood and to strike the earth with every kind of plague as often as they want." (NIV, Revelation 11:6)

What did John say would happen when the witnesses finished prophesying?

John said that a beast will come up from a pit and kill the witnesses. The witnesses will not receive a proper burial. Their bodies will be gazed at and mocked by people all over the world. After three-and-one-half days, however, "the breath of life from God" (NIV, Revelation 11:11) would fill the witnesses and bring them back to life. The people who mocked them would be terrified at this reversal of events. The witnesses would be taken up to heaven, while those who mocked them would experience a great earthquake.

THE WOMAN, THE CHILD, AND THE DRAGON

What did the woman in John's vision look like?

Her appearance was glorious. She was "clothed with the sun, with the moon under her feet, and on her head a crown of twelve stars." Despite her regal appearance, her circumstances were dire. She was pregnant and cried out "in birth pangs, in the agony of birth." (NRSV, Revelation 12:1–2) Most scholars say the woman represents the Jewish nation from which Jesus came, and the twelve stars represent the twelve tribes of Israel.

What did the dragon in John's vision look like?

The dragon was red. It had seven crowns on its seven heads, and ten horns. His tail swept across the sky, brushing a third of the stars onto earth. Most scholars say that the dragon represents Satan. That he swept a third of the stars out of the sky is a symbolic representation of Satan's immense power.

What happened between the woman and the dragon?

The dragon stood before the woman, ready to devour her baby the minute it was born. The Bible reads, "And [the woman] gave birth to a son, a male child, who is to rule all the nations with a rod of iron." (NRSV, Revelation 12:5) Most scholars say that the baby represents Jesus, who was born out of Israel and came to rule the world. The baby was snatched from her and taken to God and his throne. The woman fled to the wilderness, to a place prepared by God.

WAR IN HEAVEN

Who fought in the war in heaven?

The archangel Michael and some other angels fought against the dragon and the dragon's angels.

What was the outcome of the war?

Team Michael won. The dragon—"that ancient serpent called the devil, or Satan, who leads the whole world astray"—was thrown out of heaven and cast down to earth. His angels were tossed out with him (NIV, Revelation 12:9).

The dragon described in Revelations had seven heads and ten horns. Scholars believe the beast represents Satan.

What did the dragon do then?

He pursued the woman who had the baby, but God gave her two wings so she could fly back to her place in the wilderness. She stayed there where she was nourished "for a time, times, and half a time." (NLT, Revelation 12:14) Generally, "a time" is thought to mean one year, "times" is thought to mean two years, and "half a time" is thought to mean half a year. So the woman stayed in the wilderness for three and a half years. The dragon became angrier with the woman, and went off to make war "against the rest of her children." (NLT, Revelation 12:17)

TWO BEASTS

What did the first beast look like?

The first beast came out of the sea, and had ten horns and seven heads. Each horn had a crown. On each head were imprinted blasphemous names. The beast was a leopard/bear/lion hybrid, and had all the wild, ravenous qualities of those animals. Generally, this beast is interpreted to be the Antichrist. This beast is described again in Revelation 17.

What did the second beast look like?

This beast came out of the earth, and had two horns. Generally, this beast is interpreted to be a false prophet.

What did the beasts do?

The first beast became the object of worship for the whole earth. The people said, "Who is like unto the beast, who is able to make war with him?" (KJV, Revelation 13:4) The beast spewed blasphemous and arrogant words against God. Also, the beast was allowed to attack the saints, or Christians, and conquer them.

The second beast misled humans by forcing them to worship the first beast and by performing "great wonders." (KJV, Revelation 13:13) Also, it made people, "both small and great, both rich and poor, both free and slave," be marked on the right hand or the forehead with the mark of three sixes. This mark is a direct contrast to the seals put on the foreheads of God's servants in Revelation 7.

Both beasts took orders from the red dragon.

THE VISION OF SEVEN ANGELS WITH SEVEN PLAGUES

What did John see in this vision?

Detailed in Revelation 15 and 16, in this vision John saw seven angels with seven bowls full of seven plagues.

What did the angels do with the plagues?

At God's instruction, the angels poured the plagues on the earth.

What kinds of plagues were there?

Painful sores, bloody sea, bloody rivers and springs, tortuously hot sun, darkness, the Euphrates River was dried up, and finally, the great cities of the earth fell amid lightning, thunder, earthquake, and hail.

Who experienced the plagues?

Those who had the mark of the beast, the three sixes.

THE GREAT WHORE

What did one of the angels show John in this vision?

One of the angels showed John "the judgment of the great whore that sitteth upon many waters: With whom the kings of the earth have committed fornication, and the inhabitants of the earth have been made drunk with the wine of her fornication." (KJV, Revelation 17:1–2)

What did the great whore look like?

She was clothed in purple and red. She was adorned in gold, silver, and pearls. In one of her hands she held a golden cup full of her sins. On her forehead was written, "MYSTERY, BABYLON THE GREAT, THE MOTHER OF HARLOTS AND ABOMINATIONS OF THE EARTH." (KJV, Revelation 17:5) The woman was drunk with the blood of the saints, and the blood of the witnesses to Jesus. She sat on the seven-headed beast first described in Revelation 13.

THE FALLEN CITY

What did one of the angels show John in this vision?

It was not so much what John saw as what he heard. He heard an angel sing a dirge about the fallen Babylon: "Babylon the great is fallen, is fallen, and is become the habitation of devil, and the hold of every foul spirit, and a cage of every unclean and hateful bird." (KJV, Revelation 18:2)

Why did Babylon fall?

The angel explained as he sang, "For her sins have reached unto heaven, and God hath remembered her iniquities." (KJV, Revelation 18:24) The angel said that Babylon was condemned for pride, extravagance, and evil deeds.

THE MARRIAGE OF THE LAMB

What did John hear after the angel sang?

John heard a throng of voices praising God. Also, the throng sang, "Let us celebrate, let us rejoice, let us give him the glory! The Marriage of the Lamb has come; his Wife has made herself ready, She was given a bridal gown of bright and shining linen. The linen is the righteousness of the saints." (The Message, Revelation 19:6–8)

What were the angel's instructions to John?

The angel told John to write down these words, "Blessed are those invited to the Wedding Supper of the Lamb." (The Message, Revelation 19:9) Generally, the marriage of the Lamb is viewed as the final, triumphant coming together of Christ and his people.

What did John see in his next vision?

Heaven opened, and he saw a rider on a white house come out of heaven.

What did the rider look like?

The rider was called Faithful and True. His eyes were like flames, and he had many crowns on his head. He was "dressed in a robe soaked with blood." (The Message, Revelation 19:13) Generally, the rider is viewed as being Christ.

What did the rider do?

He captured the beast and the false prophet and threw them "alive into the lake of fire that burns with sulfur." (NLT, Revelation 19:20) The people who had received the mark of the beast were destroyed as well.

THE DRAGON AGAIN

What happened to the dragon after the marriage of the Lamb?

The dragon, "that ancient serpent, who is the Devil and Satan" (NRSV, Revelation 12:9) was seized by one of God's angels, bound and thrown into a pit.

Did the dragon stay there forever?

No. According to John, the dragon was to be kept in the pit for a thousand years. In the pit, he could not deceive people. After the thousand years in the pit, he would be released for a while.

What happened to the dragon after he was released from the pit?

John saw Satan deceiving many people and recruiting them into his army. They surrounded "God's people and the beloved city," and tried to conquer it. However, the dragon was thrown into the lake of fire where the beast and the false prophet were tormented night and day. (NLT, Revelation 20:9)

THE BOOK OF LIFE

What was the vision like in which John saw the Book of Life?

In the vision, John saw a "great white throne." (KJV, Revelation 20:11) God was on the throne. John saw the dead standing before the throne. Two books were opened.

What were the two books?

One was the Book of Life. The other book is not named in the Bible, but became known as the Book of Deeds. According to John, "And the dead were judged according to what they had done, as recorded in the books." (NLT, Revelation 20:12) People whose names were not written in the Book of Life were cast into a lake of fire. This became known as the final judgment.

A New Heaven and a New Earth

What did John see in his vision of a new heaven and a new earth?

He saw the first heaven and first earth pass away into nothingness. In addition, John saw the new holy city.

What was the new holy city?

It was the New Jerusalem. John saw it come down out of heaven "like a beautiful bride prepared for her husband." (NLT, Revelation 21:2) This image is a vibrant contrast to the image of the whore of Babylon.

What was the role of the New Jerusalem?

God told John that the New Jerusalem was the home of God among men.

What did the New Jerusalem look like?

It had "radiance like a very rare jewel." (NRSV, Revelation 21:11) The gates were made of pearl, and the streets were made of gold. There was no temple in the city. There was no need for one, because God himself was there.

What else did God tell John?

God told John that the status quo was going to change. There was no more death, pain, or sorrow. Also, God told John that people who were faithful to God will inherit the water of life, while those who are not faithful to God will be cast into a lake of fire.

What was the source of the water of life?

It came from a crystal clear river that flowed through the center of the New Jerusalem.

After the Apocalypse, there would be a new Heaven and a new Earth. New Jerusalem would be the home of God among men.

311

How does the book of Revelation end?

It ends with Jesus' assurance to John that it was he, Jesus, who sent the angel to John with all of this testimony. Jesus concluded, "Yes, I am coming soon!" (NLT, Revelation 22:20)

WHAT DOES IT ALL MEAN?

What are some of the most common ways of interpreting Revelation?

Revelation is full of symbols, images, visions, and puzzling wording. For centuries, scholars and believers have tried to decipher the complex book. There are many ways of interpreting the book. Four of the most popular interpretation methods are Preterist, Historicist, Idealist, and Futurist.

Preterists interpret the book of Revelation against the backdrop of the Middle East in the first century. Adherents believe that John wrote about current and imminent events, and his intended audience was first-century believers. For instance, the Roman Empire was known as the City of Seven Hills, so in this view the seven crowns represent the Roman Empire. If Revelation was indeed written during the reign of Domitian, that means ten emperors came before him. These ten emperors might be symbolized by the ten horns. Likewise, Babylon in Revelation 18 is symbolic of Rome.

Historicists believe the book of Revelation is a symbolic representation of the church's history from the time of Jesus' apostles to the time of Christ's return. One theory that fits into the Historicist view is that the great earthquake described in Revelation 11 was a reference to the social upheaval wrought by the French Revolution.

Idealists believe that the events in Revelation are nonliteral symbols of events that apply to all people in all ages. In this viewpoint, Revelation does not apply to specific past or future events. For example, one theory that fits into the Idealist view is that the Beast is a symbol for the abuse of political power or exploitation of workers.

Futurists believe nothing in Revelation has happened yet, but that everything will happen just before Jesus comes again. Futurists believe that when Jesus comes, the dead who were believers in life will be resurrected, and believers who are living will be "raptured." The Jerry Jenkins and Tim LaHaye *Left Behind* book series is based on this ideology.

More About
the Bible

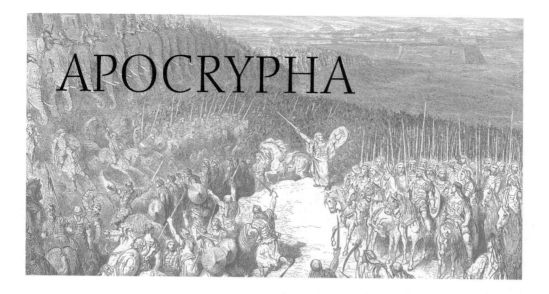

APOCRYPHA

What is the Apocrypha?

Today, the word "apocryphal" is a secular word used to describe something that is false or counterfeit. However, centuries ago the word meant something different. The root "apoc" means "hidden things." In the Protestant church, Apocrypha is the name given to a group of books written between 300 B.C.E. and 70 C.E. that were excluded from the Old Testament because they were not considered divinely inspired. Among the churches that do accept these books as divinely inspired, there is no consensus on the books that should be included.

What are the names of the most widely accepted books, and which churches accept them?

These are accepted by the Catholic Church:

- Tobit
- Judith
- Esther additions
- Wisdom of Solomon (sometimes referred to as Wisdom)
- Sirach (also known as Ecclesiasticus or The Wisdom of Jesus Ben Sirah)
- Baruch (which includes the Letter of Jeremiah)
- Daniel additions (includes Prayer of Azariah, Song of Three Jews, Susanna, and Bel and the Dragon)
- I and II Maccabees

The above books plus I Esdras, II Esdras (also known as the Prayer of Manasseh), and Psalm 151 are accepted by the Orthodox Church.

All of the preceding books, plus III Maccabees, IV Maccabees, and a few others, are accepted by some smaller Christian Churches in eastern Europe and Africa.

Why were these books considered "hidden"?

No one knows for sure. At any rate, the Catholic Church and some Orthodox churches kept some of the Apocrypha as part of their canon, and continue to do so to this day. However, these churches do not use the term Apocrypha. They refer to these books as being "deuterocanonical." While Protestants do not deny the usefulness of these books, they do not accept them as Holy Scripture.

BOOK OF TOBIT

What is the book of Tobit about?

Tobit is a novella. It has a little bit of a whole lot of stuff. It has prayers, romance, humor, a wild plot, and unforgettable characters.

Who was Tobit?

Tobit was the son of Tobiel of the tribe of Naphtali. Naphtali was one of the tribes that rebelled against the house of David, but Tobit expressed continual concern for Jerusalem. Tobit remained loyal to God, while most of his fellow countrymen did not. Tobit was married to Anna, and had a son, Tobias. Tobit was taken into captivity by the Assyrians, where he was put to work as an officer in the court of Shalmaneser.

Why did Tobit get in trouble with King Sennacherib?

Tobit got in trouble for burying dead people who had been tossed outside the city wall, and that included people the king put to death. When the king found out what Tobit had done, he confiscated all of Tobit's property.

Did Tobit ever get his property back?

Yes. Just a few weeks later, King Sennacherib's sons killed their father. Under the new reign, Tobit's property was restored to him.

What tragedy befell Tobit soon after his property was restored to him?

In what is one of the most unusual stories in the Bible, Tobit became blind. His blindness came about because sparrows defecated in his oculi. That's right. Birds pooped in his eyes. Tobit remained blind for four years.

Why did Tobit argue with his wife?

As the years passed, Tobit became sadder and sadder. One day his wife received a goat in payment for some weaving she did. When Tobit heard the goat bleat and found out from his wife how the goat came to be at their house, Tobit did not believe his wife. They argued. Tobit confessed his sins, and prayed to die: "So now deal with me as you will; command my spirit to be taken from me, so that I may be released from the face of the earth and become dust." (NRSV, Tobit 3:6)

SARAH IN MEDIA

Who was Sarah?

At this point in the book of Tobit, the scene shifts suddenly to Media, more than three hundred miles away from Nineveh. Sarah had been married to seven husbands, but each husband was killed by the demon Asmodeus. Significantly, the husbands were killed "before they had been with her as is customary for wives." (NRSV, Tobit 3:8) That put Sarah in an untenable situation.

Why was Sarah's situation so bad?

She had several husbands, but not a single child. In the ancient Near East, that was just about the worst thing for a woman. Furthermore, Sarah was an only child. If she did not have any children, her family would die out. In addition, Sarah's father's maid taunted her because of all of this.

What did Sarah do to try to remedy her situation?

At first she thought about committing suicide, but then she decided that would bring shame on her father. So then she prayed to God to kill her.

TOBIT'S AND SARAH'S PRAYERS

How do the stories of Tobit and Sarah come together?

Tobit prayed for death, and Sarah prayed for death. God heard their prayers at the exact same time. The archangel Raphael was sent to heal both of them.

What else happened that day?

Tobit remembered some money he had left in trust with a man named Gabael in Media. Tobit told his son, Tobias, to retrieve the money and use it to care for Anna after Tobit was dead. Tobit gave Tobias a solid deathbed talk, even though Tobit was not on his

317

deathbed. He advised Tobias to honor God, be generous to everyone, and stay away from wanton women.

Did Tobias go to Media as his father instructed?

Yes. First, he looked for someone who would help him find the way to Media. Tobias found Raphael, only he did not know it was Raphael. The two of them set off for Media. The family dog went with them.

ON THE WAY TO MEDIA

What happened to Raphael and Tobias on the way to Media?

God heard the prayers of Tobit and Sarah and sent the archangel Raphael to help.

When Tobias went to soak his feet in the river, a big fish jumped out and tried to eat his foot. Raphael told Tobias to pull the fish onto land and cut it open, saving the gall, heart, and liver for medicine. They roasted and ate some of the fish, and salted some of the fish to eat later.

When did Raphael and Tobias meet Sarah and her parents?

They met Sarah and her family that day because it was Raphael's plan all along that he and Tobias should stay the night at their house. At the house they had dinner, and after some discussion, it was decided that Tobias and Sarah would marry right then.

What are some other interesting facts about Raphael?

Raphael is also identified as the angel who moved the waters of the healing sheep pool, and he is the patron of the blind, of happy meetings, of nurses, of physicians, and of travelers. His feast day is celebrated on September 29.

Did the demon Asmodeus still plague Sarah?

Yes. When Sarah and Tobias retired for the evening, the demon was there. Tobias burned the fish pieces. The odor from the fish repelled Asmodeus so much that he fled to the outer edges of Egypt. Raphael ran after him and bound him hand and foot. Sarah and Tobias prayed a prayer of thanks, and went to sleep.

What did Sarah's parents think about their daughter's marriage?

They were surprised, but happy. Sarah's parents doubted Tobias would last the night, so during the night, they dug a hole in which to bury him come morning. When morning

What medicinal value did gall, heart, and liver have?

That is just what Tobias asked Raphael. Raphael replied, "As for the fish's heart and liver, you must burn them to make a smoke in the presence of a man or woman afflicted by a demon or evil spirit, and every affliction will flee away and never remain with that person any longer. And as for the gall, anoint a person's eyes where white films have appeared on them; blow upon them, upon the white films, and the eyes will be healed." (NRSV, Tobit 6:8–9) (See where this is going?)

came and they discovered that Tobias was alive, the filled the hole quickly so he would not see it.

TOBIT'S MONEY

Did Tobias retrieve his father's money?

Tobias sent Raphael to do it so he could enjoy his honeymoon. So Raphael retrieved the money Tobit had left in trust with Gabael. After some more celebrating, Raphael, Tobias, Sarah, and the dog headed back to Nineveh. Meanwhile, this whole time Tobit and Anna worried and grieved that they would never see their beloved son again.

What happened when the travelers arrived at Tobit and Anna's house?

Tobias and Raphael ran ahead to arrive at the house first. They had the fish gall ready. When Tobias saw his father, he smeared the fish gall on his father's eyes. Then Tobias peeled the white film from his father's eyes. Tobit exclaimed, "I see you my son, the light of my eyes!" (NRSV, Tobit 11:14) Then Tobit praised God and thanked him. The family celebrated Tobit's sight and Tobias' wedding.

What happened when Tobit and Tobias tried to pay Raphael for his services?

Raphael told them that he was an angel. Tobit and Tobias were stunned and afraid. Raphael comforted them: "Do not be afraid; peace be with you. Bless God forevermore. As for me, I was with you, I was not acting on my own will, but by the will of God. Bless him each and every day; sing his praises." (NRSV, Tobit 12:18)

How does the book of Tobit end?

The book of Tobit ends with the death of Tobias at 117, living in peace and prosperity with his family in Media. This all came about because just before Tobit died, he advised Tobias to take Sarah and their children, leave Nineveh, and go back to Sarah's parents in Media. Tobit warned Tobias, "For I believe the word of God that Nahum spoke about Nineveh, that all these things will take place and overtake Assyria and Nineveh. Indeed,

319

everything that was spoken by the prophets of Israel, whom God sent, will occur." (NRSV, Tobit 14:3–4)

BOOK OF JUDITH

What is the book of Judith about?

It is about the-ends-justify-the-means; Judith and the power of God versus the power of a human military. The story takes place during the reign of Nebuchadnezzar (605–562 B.C.E.), though the book was written a few hundred years later, perhaps in the first century B.C.E. In the book, Nebuchadnezzar and his Babylonian army have conquered Nineveh and the rest of Assyria. The book of Judith takes place in Nineveh, but it was a Babylonian province at that time.

Who was Judith?

Judith was a beautiful, wealthy, intelligent Jewish widow. She had a reputation for being devout, and she was—most of the time.

How does the book of Judith begin?

It begins with Nebuchadnezzar declaring war on Arphaxad, king of Media. Nebuchadnezzar asked neighboring nations for help, but they refused. That angered old Nebby. He defeated Arphaxad with his own army, then vowed revenge on the nations that did not help him: "Their wounded shall fill their ravines and gullies, and the swelling river shall be filled with their dead. I will lead them away captive to the ends of the earth." (NRSV, Judith 2:8–9)

Who helped Nebuchadnezzar organize the army?

The general of the army, Holofernes. Holofernes led the army and destroyed many of the targeted nations. Other countries got wind of this, and sent ambassadors to Holofernes begging for clemency. Holofernes traveled to some of those towns, where the people "welcomed him with garlands and dances and tambourines." (NRSV, Judith 3:7) Unmoved by their gesture of hospitality, Holofernes demolished their shrines and sacred groves.

What did the people of Judah think of all this?

The people of Judah had come back to Jerusalem recently, and gathered the sacred vessels to put in the temple. Now the people were afraid Holofernes would destroy them. So the people of Judah sent word to the neighboring towns, and instructed them to stand guard on the mountaintops. In addition, the people stored up food and other supplies just in case there was a long siege. Also, the people fasted and prayed to God.

What happened when Holofernes found out what the people of Judah did?

He got mad. He refused to believe Achior, an Ammonite, when he told him how God protected the people of Judah.

Does Judith ever show up in this story?

Yes. Just be patient.

Did Holofernes attack the people of Judah?

He began with a siege. He surrounded Jerusalem with his troops. The people of Judah ran out of water, and became discouraged. They wanted to surrender. Uzziah, one of the city leaders, encouraged the people to hold out for five more days, at which time, he assured them, God would rescue them. If God did not, Uzziah said he would agree to the surrender.

ENTER JUDITH

What did Judith do when she heard what was happening in Jerusalem?

She summoned Uzziah and the other city elders and scolded them: "What you have said to the people today is not right; you have even sworn and pronounced this oath between God and you, promising to surrender the town to our enemies unless the Lord turns and helps us within so many days. Who are you to put God to the test today, and to set yourselves up in the place of God in human affairs?" (NRSV, Judith 8:12–13) Eloquently, she

continued, "You cannot plumb the depths of the human heart or understand the workings of the human mind; how do you expect to search out God, who made all these things, and find out his mind or comprehend his thought? No, my brothers, do not anger the Lord our God." (NRSV, Judith 8:14) She encouraged the elders to wait for God's deliverance.

What else did Judith recommend?

She told the elders: "I am about to do something that will go down through all generations of our descendants." (NRSV, Judith 8:32) She refused, however, to tell the elders what she was going to do.

What did Judith do?

First, she humbled herself before God by putting ashes on her head and falling prostrate on the ground. She prayed to God. She acknowledged God's greatness and his mercy. She prayed for God's help.

Judith dressed and groomed herself to meet Holofernes. She would entice and then murder him to save her people. (*Judith and Holfernes* by Pedro Américo)

321

What did Judith do after she prayed?

She took a bath and put on perfume. She fixed her hair, put on a tiara, and put on her nicest clothes. She put on her fine jewelry. In short, "she made herself very beautiful, to entice the eyes of all the men who might see her." (NRSV, Judith 10:4) Then she went to find Holofernes.

What did Holofernes think of Judith?

He was charmed by her beauty.

What did Judith say to Holofernes when she met him?

She told the truth when she told Holofernes that she was a Hebrew, and that she worshiped God. However, she lied and told him that the people of Judah were planning to eat animals that were banned by their dietary laws. She assured Holofernes that once the people did that, God would abandon them. Judith said God would let her know when that happened, and then she in turn would tell Holofernes. Then Holofernes could march right into Jerusalem and seize the city.

How long did Judith stay in Holofernes' camp?

She was there for three days. On the third day, Holofernes sent for Judith. He said, "For it would be a disgrace if we let such a woman go without having intercourse with her." To that, Judith replied, "Who am I to refuse my lord? Whatever pleases him I will do at once, and it will be a joy to me until the day of my death." (NRSV, Judith 12:14) Judith meant one thing, and Holofernes heard another.

Did Judith sleep with Holofernes?

No. She encouraged him to drink. A lot. In fact, he drank so much, "he was dead drunk." (NRSV, Judith 13:2) When the two of them were alone, she cut off his head with his own sword. She took his head with her. Then she headed back to Jerusalem.

What did the people of Jerusalem say when they learned what Judith did?

She was met with some degree of surprise and celebration. She was praised for risking her own life to save the Hebrew nation. There was no discussion about her lying and murdering.

ESTHER (THE GREEK VERSION CONTAINING THE ADDITIONAL CHAPTERS)

Why are these chapters separate in the Apocrypha?

The original book of Esther was written in Hebrew in the mid-400s B.C.E. Many scholars say that the 107 verses that comprise the additions were added to Esther when the Greek translation came out in the 200s or 100s B.C.E., and thus are not canonical.

Why were the additions made?

Most scholars think that the additions were made to make the subtle story of Esther more dramatic. Also, the original Esther is remarkable in that God is not a character in it (though his influence is obvious). The additions make God a more explicit component.

What information do the additions contain?

- A dream Mordecai had in which he saw the possible destruction of the Jews. Mordecai dreamt: "Noises and confusion, thunders and earthquake, tumult on the earth! Then two great dragons came forward ready to fight, and they roared terribly. At their roaring every nation prepared for war, to fight against the righteous nation." (NRSV, Esther [Greek] 1:4-6)

- The letter King Artaxerxes wrote authorizing the slaughter of the Hebrews. The king wrote: "We understand that this people, and it alone, stands constantly in opposition to every nation.... Therefore we have decreed that those indicated to you in the letters written by Haman, who is in charge of affairs and is our second father, shall all—wives and children included—be utterly destroyed by the swords of their enemies, without pity or restraint.... " (NRSV, Esther [Greek] 3:18-19)

- Prayers offered to God by Mordecai and Esther. Mordecai prayed: "O Lord; do not destroy the lips of those who praise you'." (NRSV, Esther [Greek] 4:27) Esther prayed: "You know my necessity—that I abhor the sign of my proud position, which is upon my head on days when I appear in public. I abhor it like a filthy rag, and I do not wear it on the days when I am at leisure'." (NRSV, Esther [Greek] 4:44)

- More detail on Esther approaching the king. The author wrote: "She was radiant with perfect beauty, and she looked happy, as if beloved, but her heart was frozen with fear." (NRSV, Esther [Greek] 4:52)

- The letter King Artaxerxes wrote denouncing Haman and praising Mordecai and Esther. In part, the letter read: "But unable to restrain his arrogance, [Haman] undertook to deprive us of our kingdom and our life, and with intricate craft and deceit asked for the destruction of Mordecai, our savior and perpetual benefactor, and of Esther, the blameless partner of our kingdom, together with the whole nation." (NRSV, Esther [Greek] 8:24-25)

- Mordecai's dream explained. Mordecai exclaimed, "The two dragons are Haman and myself. The nations are those that gathered to destroy the names of the Jews." (NRSV, Esther [Greek] 10:7–8)

BOOK OF SIRACH

What is the book of Sirach about?

The full title is The Wisdom of Jesus, Son of Sirach. The book is known as Ecclesiasticus as well. This Jesus was not Jesus Christ. Jesus, son of Sirach, wrote this book sometime before 180 B.C.E. The book was translated from Hebrew into Greek by the author's grandson. The grandson wrote the prologue to the book.

What are some of the definitive verses in the book?

Some definitive verses include:

- "There is but one who is wise, greatly to be feared, seated upon his throne—the Lord." (NRSV, Sirach 1:8)
- "Let those who are friendly with you be many, but let your advisers be one in a thousand." (NRSV, Sirach 6:6)
- "Do not kindle the coals of sinners, or you may be burned in their flaming fire." (NRSV, Sirach 8:10)
- "How can dust and ashes be proud? Even in life the human body decays. A long illness baffles the physician; the king of today will die tomorrow." (NRSV, Sirach 10:9–10)
- "I take pleasure in three things, and they are beautiful in the sight of God and mortals: agreement among brothers and sisters, friendship among neighbors, and a wife and a husband who live in harmony." (NRSV, Sirach 25:1)

BOOK OF BARUCH (INCLUDES LETTER OF JEREMIAH)

Who was Baruch?

Baruch was Jeremiah's secretary. Scholars continue to debate whether Baruch was actually the author of the book.

What is the book of Baruch about?

The events described in it took place during the sixth century B.C.E., the years of the Babylonian exile. Baruch was in Babylon. In the letter, the author wrote a confession for the Jews in Jerusalem to use during worship. Also, the author included words of encouragement.

What are some of the definitive verses in the book?

Some definitive verses are:

"And you shall say: 'The Lord our God is in the right, but there is open shame on us today, on the people of Judah, on

A seventeenth-century Russian icon of Baruch.

324

the inhabitants of Jerusalem, and on our kings, our rulers, our priests, our prophets, and our ancestors, because we have sinned before the Lord.'" (NRSV, Baruch 1:15–17)

"O Lord Almighty, God of Israel, the soul in anguish and the wearied spirit cry out to you. Hear, O Lord, and have mercy, for we have sinned before you." (NRSV, Baruch 3:1–2)

"Take off the garment of your sorrow and affliction, O Jerusalem, and put on forever the beauty of the glory of God." (NRSV, Baruch 5:1)

"For God will lead Israel with joy, in the light of his glory, with the mercy and righteousness that come from him." (NRSV, Baruch 5:9)

The Letter of Jeremiah

Who was Jeremiah?

Jeremiah lived in the southern kingdom of Judah, and was a prophet during the reigns of King Josiah, King Jehoiakim, and King Zedekiah, until the Babylonian captivity in 587 B.C.E. This is the same Jeremiah who has a book to his credit in the Old Testament.

What is the Letter of Jeremiah about?

It is a letter written to the people of Judah as the first round of them are about to be forced into exile by the Babylonians. This letter dates from about 587 B.C.E., ten years before the Babylonians conquered Jerusalem. In the letter, Jeremiah pleaded with the people to avoid idol worship when they went to a foreign nation.

What are some of the definitive verses in the Letter of Jeremiah?

Some definitive verses are:

"Because of the sins that you have committed before God, you will be taken to Babylon as exiles by Nebuchadnezzar, king of the Babylonians. Therefore when you have come to Babylon you will remain there for many years, for a long time, up to seven generations; after that I will bring you away from there in peace." (NRSV, Letter of Jeremiah, Verse 3)

"So beware of becoming at all like foreigners or of letting fear for these gods possess you when you see the multitude before and behind them worshiping them." (NRSV, Letter of Jeremiah, Verse 6)

The Prayer of Azariah and the Song of the Three Jews

What is the Prayer of Azariah?

This collection of writings is additions to the book of Daniel. Azariah is the Hebrew name of Abednego. This first part of this apocryphal book is the prayer he says while in the fiery furnace. It is followed by the hymn of all three. The last part of the prayer is often called "The Song of the Three Jews."

What are some definitive verses from the Prayer of Azariah?

Some definitive verses are:

- "Do not withdraw your mercy from us, for the sake of Abraham your beloved and for the sake of your servant Isaac and Israel your holy one, to whom you promised to multiply their descendants like the stars of heaven and like the sand on the shore of the sea." (NRSV, Prayer of Azariah, Verses 12–13)
- "Deliver us in accordance with your marvelous works, and bring glory to your name, O Lord." (NRSV, Prayer of Azariah, Verse 20)

THE SONG OF THE THREE JEWS

What is the Song of the Three Jews about?

The Song of the Three Jews is a song sang by the trio when God saved them from harm while they were in the furnace.

What are some definitive verses from the Song of the Three Jews?

Some definitive verses are:

"Then the three with one voice praised and glorified and blessed God in the furnace: 'Blessed are you, O Lord, God of our ancestors, and to be praised and highly exalted forever.'" (Song of the Three Jews, Verse 29)

"Bless the Lord, winter cold and summer heat; sing praise to him and highly exalt him forever. Bless the Lord, dews and falling snow; sing praise to him and highly exalt him forever." (Song of the Three Jews, Verse 44–45)

BOOK OF SUSANNA

Who was Susanna?

Susanna was a beautiful, pious Hebrew woman living in Babylon during the time of the exile.

What is the book of Susanna about?

The book is considered to be an addition to the book of Daniel. In this addition, two dishonest elders frame Susanna for adultery when she refuses their advances.

How does the book of Susanna begin?

It begins by introducing the reader to Susanna and her family: "Her parents were righteous, and had trained their daughter according to the law of Moses." (NRSV, Susanna, Verse 3)

Was Susanna married?

Yes. Her husband, Joakim, was very rich and well respected among the people.

How did the trouble begin?

Susanna liked to walk in her garden. Sometimes she bathed there. One day, two associates of her husband saw her bathing and planned to rape her.

What was Susanna's reaction when the men came in her garden?

She was horrified. The men said to her, "Look, the garden doors are shut, and no one can see us. We are burning with desire for you; so give your consent, and lie with us. If you refuse, we will testify against you that a young man was with you, and this was why you sent your maids away." (NRSV, Susanna, Verses 20–21) Susanna cried, "I am completely trapped. For if I do this, it will mean death for me; if I do not, I cannot escape your hands. I choose not to do it; I will fall into your hands, rather than sin in the eyes of the Lord." (NRSV, Susanna, Verse 22)

Artist Giuseppe Bartolomeo Chiari's early eighteenth-century painting *Susanna and the Elders* captures the moment when the innocent Susanna is resisting the lascivious advances of two elders.

What did the two men do?

They told everyone that Susanna had a lover in the garden. Adultery was punishable by death, and Susanna's accusers had no problem with sending her to her death.

What did Susanna do next?

With her family and townspeople gathered around, she prayed to God for deliverance.

Did God deliver her?

Yes. "The Lord heard her cry. Just as she was being led off to execution, God stirred up the holy spirit of a young lad named Daniel, and he shouted with a loud voice, 'I want no part in shedding this woman's blood!'" (NRSV, Susanna, Verse 46)

Did Daniel's shout save her?

No. Daniel still had to prove that Susanna did not have a lover.

How did Daniel do that?

Daniel separated the two men and cross-examined them. The two stories conflicted. "When [the two conspirators] were separated from each other, [Daniel] summoned one of them and said to him, 'You old relic of wicked days, your sins have come home, which you have committed in the past.... Now then, if you really saw this woman, tell me this: Under what tree did you see them being intimate with each other?" (NRSV, Susanna, Verses 52–54) Daniel asked the same thing to the other conspirator. Their conflicting answers proved that the charges were trumped up.

What happened after the two men were proved to be liars?

Susanna's family and all the people praised God. Then, "acting in accordance with the law of Moses, they put [the two men] to death. Thus innocent blood was spared that day." (NRSV, Susanna, Verse 62)

BOOK OF BEL AND THE DRAGON

Who was Bel?

Bel was a Babylonian idol. Daniel's Babylonian name, Beltashazzar, means "Bel protects."

Who was the Dragon?

The dragon was an unidentified reptile to which the Babylonians attributed magic powers.

What is the book of Bel and the Dragon about?

The book is considered to be an addition to the book of Daniel. In Bel and the Dragon, Daniel proves that Bel is not a real god, and that the Dragon does not have magical powers.

How does the book of Bel and the Dragon begin?

It begins with a conversation between Daniel and the king. The king asked Daniel why he did not worship Bel. Daniel replied, "Because I do not revere idols made with hands, but the living God, who created heaven and earth and has dominion over all living creatures." (NRSV, Bel and the Dragon, Verse 5)

How did the king respond to Daniel?

The king said, "Do you not see how much he eats and drinks every day?" At this Daniel laughed, and said, "Do not be deceived, O king, for this thing is clay inside and bronze outside, and it never ate or drank anything." (NRSV, Bel and the Dragon, Verses 6, 7)

How did Daniel prove to the king that he was right?

Daniel came up with a plan. He "ordered his servants to bring ashes, and they scattered them throughout the whole temple in the presence of the king alone. Then they went out, shut the door, and sealed it with the king's signet, and departed. During the night the priests came as usual, with their wives and children, and they ate and drank everything." (NRSV, Bel and the Dragon, Verses 14–15)

How did Daniel prove that the dragon did not have magical powers?

The dragon was a reptile of some sort. As a living creature it did eat, but it was not magical. So Daniel came up with another plan. He "took pitch, fat, and hair, and boiled them together and made cakes, which he fed to the dragon. The dragon ate them, and burst open. Then Daniel said, 'See what you have been worshiping?'" (NRSV, Bel and the Dragon, Verse 27)

BOOK OF I MACCABEES

Where does the name "Maccabee" come from?

The name Maccabee is a derivation of Maccabeus. Maccabeus, or the hammer, was the nickname of Judas, one of Mattathias' sons.

What is the book of I Maccabees about?

The book is set between 175 and 143 B.C.E. When the Jews returned to their homeland after exile, they enjoyed a time of relative peace. However, by the time the second century rolled around, the situation had changed.

How does the book of I Maccabees begin?

It begins with a short history describing the rulers of the region from Alexander the Great to Antiochus IV.

What did Antiochus do that angered the people of Judah?

He attacked Judah. When he did so, he entered the sanctuary of the temple and ransacked it. A couple of years later, one of Antiochus' captains came and plundered the city, and captured many of the Judeans. Then Antiochus issued a decree saying that everyone in his kingdom, including the Judeans, had to drop their own customs and religions. The Jews faced severe persecution for not accommodating the widely accepted Greek culture and customs.

How did the people of Judah react?

The Jews were divided. Some thought accepting Greek culture and religion was fine. Others said it was not.

Who were the ones who did not obey Antiochus?

This group was led by a Jewish priest, Mattathias, and his sons. "But Mattathias answered and said in a loud voice: 'Even if all the nations that live under the rule of the king obey him, and have chosen to obey his commandments, every one of them abandoning the religion of their ancestors, I and my sons and my brothers will continue to live by the covenant of our ancestors.'" (NRSV, I Maccabees 2:19–20) So they rebelled with an assertive military campaign. The campaign became known as the Maccabean Revolt.

Were the rebels successful?

Many of them died because they refused to fight on the Sabbath. Later, however, they reclaimed the temple. Judas encouraged the people: "It is easy for many to be hemmed in by a few, for in the sight of Heaven there is no difference between saving by many or by few. It is not on the size of the army that victory in battle depends, but strength comes from Heaven." (NRSV, I Maccabees 3:18–19)

To celebrate the event, they established the Festival of Lights, or Hanukkah.

Did the rebels have any other plans for retaliation?

Yes. They made a treaty with Rome so the Romans would help them.

BOOK OF II MACCABEES

What is the book of II Maccabees about?

The book covers the same time period as I Maccabees. However, the focus is different. I Maccabees deals with military matters. II Maccabees goes into more detail about the many injustices and cruelties the Jewish people experienced at the hand of Antiochus.

How does the book of II Maccabees begin?

It begins with a letter from the Jews in Jerusalem to the Jews in Egypt. The letter explains why Hanukkah should become a regularly observed festival among the Jews.

Judas Maccabeus successfully led an army against Nicanor's troops. Nicanor was captured and beheaded.

Who became a Jewish priest by corruption?

Jason. He promised the king a lot of silver for the honor. In addition, Jason tried to shift the Jewish people toward the Greek way of life.

How does the book of II Maccabees end?

It ends with the Jews winning a decisive battle against Nicanor and his troops. Nicanor had been appointed by the king to be governor of Judah. "Nicanor and his troops advanced with trumpets and battle songs, but Judas and his troops met the enemy in battle with invocations to God and prayers. So, fighting with their hands and praying to God in their hearts, they laid low at least thirty-five thousand, and were greatly gladdened by God's manifestation." (NRSV, II Maccabees 15:25–26) When the battle was over, they cut off Nicanor's head. Then they agreed by public vote to observe the day every year. The day became known as Nicanor's Day, and was commemorated until 70 C.E., when the Romans sacked Jerusalem.

BOOK OF I ESDRAS

Who was Esdras?

Esdras was another name for the prophet Ezra.

331

What is the book of I Esdras about?

Esdras covers the same material as the book of Ezra: the return of the exiles and the rebuilding and dedication of the temple.

Book of II Esdras, or The Prayer of Manasseh

Who was Manasseh?

Manasseh (sometimes spelled Manasses) was one of the kings of Judah. God allowed the Assyrians to attack Judah because of Manasseh's apostasy. Manasseh was taken in shackles to Babylon. II Chronicles 33:12 reads: "While he was in distress he entreated the favor of the LORD his God and humbled himself greatly before the God of his ancestors. He prayed to him, and God received his entreaty, heard his plea, and restored him again to Jerusalem and to his kingdom. Then Manasseh knew that the LORD indeed was God."

What is the Prayer of Manasseh about?

This prayer dates from the first or second century B.C.E., and so was written several centuries after Manasseh lived. This prayer is an idea of what Manasseh might have said to God in his distress.

How does the Prayer of Manasseh begin?

It begins with acknowledgement of God's covenant with the Jewish people. The author said, "O Lord Almighty, God of our ancestors, of Abraham and Isaac and Jacob and of their righteous offspring; you who made heaven and earth with all their order.... " (NRSV, Prayer of Manasseh, Verses 1–2).

Did Manasseh confess his sin?

Yes. He said, "And now I bend the knee of my heart, imploring you for kindness. I have sinned, O Lord, I have sinned, and I acknowledge my transgressions." (NRSV, Prayer of Manasseh, Verses 11–13).

How does the Prayer of Manasseh end?

It ends with the author singing God's praises: "For all the host of heaven sings your praise, and yours is the glory forever. Amen." (NRSV, Prayer of Manasseh, Verse 15).

Why are I and II Esdras sometimes called III and IV Esdras?

Sometimes I and II Esdras are referred to as III and IV Esdras. The reason is that, in the Latin Bible, I and II Esdras refer to the Hebrew Bible's books of Ezra and Nehemiah.

> ## Why isn't this Psalm 151 with the other psalms in the Old Testament?
>
> Psalm 151 is not in the Masoretic Text, considered to be the authoritative Hebrew Bible (Old Testament) that was assembled by scholars at Talmudic academies in Babylonia and Palestine from the sixth to the tenth centuries C.E.

PSALM 151

Who wrote Psalm 151?

The psalm is written from the viewpoint of King David. However, scholars think the psalm dates from the third century B.C.E., several hundred years after King David lived.

What is Psalm 151 about?

In it, David (or the unknown author) describes his encounter with Goliath.

How does Psalm 151 begin?

It begins: "I was small among my brothers, and the youngest in my father's house; I tended my father's sheep." (NRSV, Psalm 151:1).

How does Psalm 151 end?

It ends: "But I drew his own sword; I beheaded him, and took away disgrace from the people of Israel." (NRSV, Psalm 151:7)

III MACCABEES

What is the book of III Maccabees about?

Despite what the title suggests, it is not a continuation of I and II Maccabees. Rather, it is a fictional story about Jews in Egypt under Ptolemy IV Philopator (221–205 B.C.E.). This was fifty years or so before the Maccabean period.

How does the book of III Maccabees begin?

It begins with an account of the Battle of Raphia, which took place on June 22, 217 B.C.E. The battle was fought because Antiochus had control of the area of what is now Syria. Ptolemy wanted control. The Jews supported Ptolemy.

What happened when Ptolemy visited the Jews in Jerusalem?

At first, the Jewish people were happy to see him. After all, he was the enemy of their enemy. However, when Ptolemy entered the temple to pay his respects, he said he wanted to go into the inner sanctuary as well. Upon being told that no one was allowed to go in there except for the high priest, and that only rarely, Ptolemy continued to insist that he be allowed to enter. The Jews became upset at Ptolemy's insistence. They did not want the inner sanctuary to be sullied, so they prayed to God to help them in this situation. Simon the high priest prayed as well. Then, "God, who oversees all things, the first Father of all, holy among the holy ones, having heard the lawful supplication, scourged him who had exalted himself in insolence and audacity. He shook him on this side and that as a reed is shaken by the wind, so that he lay helpless on the ground and, besides being paralyzed in his limbs, was unable even to speak, since he was smitten by a righteous judgment." (NRSV, III Maccabees 2: 21-22). Ptolemy recovered, but was not made humble by the experience. Instead, "he by no means repented, but went away uttering bitter threats." (NRSV, III Maccabees 2: 24).

IV MACCABEES

What is the book of IV Maccabees about?

Although the book takes place during the same time period as the Maccabean Revolt, it deals very little with the actual revolt. Mostly, the book deals with Jews who died for their beliefs at the hands of Antiochus and his men.

What was Antiochus' policy for dealing with Jewish people?

"The tyrant Antiochus ... ordered the guards to seize each and every Hebrew and to compel them to eat pork and food sacrificed to idols." (NRSV, IV Maccabees 5:2)

What happened to Eleazar the priest when he refused to eat pork?

He was tortured. The king's guards stripped Eleazar of his clothes and flogged him until his skin was in shreds. Through it all, Eleazar "remained adorned with the gracefulness of his piety." (IV Maccabees 6:2) Even after the flogging, Eleazar refused to eat pork. So the king's guards amped up the torture. They "burned him with maliciously contrived instruments, threw him down, and poured stinking liquids into his nostrils." (NRSV, IV Maccabees 6:27)

Did Eleazar cave in?

No. "When he was now burned to his very bones and about to expire, he lifted up his eyes to God and said, 'You know, O God, that though I might have saved myself, I am dying in torments for the sake of the law.'" (NRSV, IV Maccabees 6:27)

Was Eleazar's death the only one described in the book?

No. Several people's deaths are described in detail. All were tortured to death.

How does the book of IV Maccabees end?

It ends with a consolation: "But the sons of Abraham with their victorious mother are gathered together into the chorus of the fathers, and have received pure and immortal souls from God, to whom be glory forever and ever. Amen." (NRSV, IV Maccabees 18:23–24)

THE BIBLE AND ARCHAEOLOGY

What is archaeology?

Archaeology is the study of past cultures through the examination of physical aspects—in whole or in part—of that culture. Such aspects include buildings, tools, jewelry, textiles, documents, and burial sites. As a science, archaeology has existed only since the middle of the nineteenth century. The field evolved from a trendy, sometimes slapdash, hobby of the wealthy into a circumspect, disciplined field of study.

How has archaeology contributed to understanding the Bible?

Some discoveries led to new knowledge concerning dates. Other discoveries led to new knowledge concerning how the Bible was passed down over the years. Still other discoveries brought to light information about the way people lived in biblical times. Also, archaeology connects events in the Bible to events not recorded in the Bible.

What is an artifact?

An artifact is a manmade item that conveys (usually) information about a specific culture. Artifacts can be any number of years old.

What particular challenges do biblical archaeologists face?

Centuries of weather, building and razing, and living and dying have piled layers upon layers of sediment and debris onto the artifacts sought by biblical archaeologists. Much of the land where biblical cultures existed has been in constant use since ancient times. Because people live and work in these areas, many artifacts are simply inaccessible. Considering how many untold artifacts have been decimated by the effects of time or are physically inaccessible, it is safe to say that what artifacts have been unearthed are just a tiny fraction of what lies buried. So, although some peo-

Maresha (also known as Marissa) is a fruitful archaeological site in Israel where many artifacts have been uncovered. It is also believed to be the site of the first temple.

ple argue that the dearth of biblical artifacts suggests that the events in the Bible did not take place, it is worthy to consider the old saying, "Absence of evidence is not evidence of absence."

THE DEAD SEA SCROLLS

What is the most significant biblical archaeological find so far?

All finds are significant in one way or another, but the most significant find so far is that of the Dead Sea Scrolls.

What is a scroll?

A scroll is a roll of paper, leather, parchment, or other material that has writings or drawings on it.

What are the Dead Sea Scrolls?

These are a collection of hundreds of biblical and non-biblical scrolls and scroll fragments found in mountain caves of the Qumran area on the western shore of the Dead Sea. The first discovery, by a teenage Bedouin shepherd, occurred in 1946. That chance discovery sparked more exploration and further discoveries over the next decade.

Why are the scrolls important?

These scrolls and scroll fragments are significant for a couple of reasons. First, all thirty-nine books of the Hebrew Bible are represented, at least in part, except for Esther and maybe Nehemiah (though Nehemiah might be combined with Ezra). Before these discoveries, the oldest Hebrew Bible manuscripts in such complete condition dated to about 1000 C.E. The Dead Sea Scrolls predate that by about a thousand years, dating to the last century B.C.E. at least. Second, the Dead Sea Scrolls are crucial to understanding how the Old Testament was passed down through the years. After studying the Dead Sea Scrolls and comparing them with their younger counterparts, scholars determined that content was passed down with meticulous attention to detail, there being few differences and alterations in the texts. A few of the scrolls, however, suffered greatly from the deleterious effects of time and temperature. As a result, they survive in such fragmentary form that they are unreadable.

Who put all those scrolls in the cluster of caves, and why?

Around 152 B.C.E., a sect of Jewish priests split from the rest of the Jewish priests, and formed a monastic brotherhood headquartered in the desert. This new sect became known as the Essenes. Various translators suggest the word Essenes means "pious ones," "healers," "modest ones," or "silent ones." The prevailing theory is that around 68 C.E., the Essenes knew the impending raid by the Romans would end their way of life. Not

The Qumran Caves, located in the Judean Desert, are the location where the Dead Sea Scrolls were found by a shepherd in 1946.

wanting centuries of their work on script preservation and script copying to be looted, the Essenes hid the scrolls in nearby caves. Perhaps the Essenes thought they would be able to retrieve the scrolls at some point, but they never did.

From what are the Dead Sea Scrolls made?

Most of the scrolls are made of papyrus and parchment.

In ancient times, how was papyrus made?

Papyrus was made from the papyrus plant, a tall, reedy plant that grew in abundance in the marshes of ancient Egypt. Once gathered, the plant was cut into strips several inches long. The outer rind was stripped off, leaving the soft white pithy center. The pith was cut lengthwise into strips. The strips were moistened with water. The addition of water made the pith gummy. Then the strips were laid out side by side on a hard surface, the edges of the strips touching or barely overlapping. A second layer of strips was laid at a perpendicular angle across the first layer. Cloth was used to absorb the excess water. The gummy residue in the papyrus bound the strips together, and bound one layer to the next. To complete the binding of the two layers, they were pounded with a wooden mallet. Then the sheet was placed under a weight, and left in the sun to dry. Once dry, the papyrus sheet was trimmed around the edges, and its surface was smoothed with a pumice stone. The surface was then polished with shell, stone, or ivory. Then the sheet was attached to other sheets using paste made from flour. The resulting long sheets could then be rolled up into scrolls.

In ancient times, how was parchment made?

Making parchment was a lengthy, detailed process that required the skills of a professional. Parchment was made from the skin of a goat, calf, or sheep. The skin was washed carefully and soaked in water. To loosen the hair from the skin, the skin was soaked in a solution of lime and water. The skin stayed in this solution for one to two weeks. While in the solution, the skin had to be stirred several times a day. Then the skin was removed from the solution, and draped over a log or other hard, narrow surface. The hair was scraped off using a blunt, curved knife. After all the hair was removed, the skin was soaked in water for a couple of days to remove the traces of lime. After this soak, the skin was stretched with cords across a wooden frame. The skin was attached to the frame with adjustable pegs. The pegs were turned occasionally to pull the skin taut. While the skin was still wet, it was scraped on both sides to remove any remaining hair, bumps, or other things that made the skin less than perfectly smooth. The skin dried (and shrunk) in the sun. When it was dry, the skin was scraped again until it was the desired thickness. In the final step before it was ready for use, the skin was buffed with pumice stone to whiten the surface. Now the skin was parchment, and ready for use. A parchment maker was called a percamenarius. The making and use of parchment was popular into the eighteenth century.

Are all the Dead Sea Scrolls made of parchment and papyrus?

No. One scroll is made of copper. When the copper scroll was found, it could not be unrolled using conventional methods. So, over a period of two years, painstaking care was used to cut the scroll into thin strips so it could be laid flat and read. Once it was laid flat, researchers transcribed the text.

Does this scroll have biblical scripture on it?

No. The scroll contains an extensive inventory of gold and silver, and clues to its various locations.

Has the gold and silver been found yet?

No. Scholars continue to debate the coordinates of the exact locations. Some scholars think the treasure trove might not exist at all, or that it might have been found and dispersed in ancient times.

Where are the Dead Sea Scrolls kept now?

Various parts of the Dead Sea Scrolls have toured the world as part of temporary exhibits in museums. Most of the scrolls and scroll fragments are housed at the Israel Museum

The Israel Museum in Jerusalem houses the Dead Sea Scrolls.

in Jerusalem. In 2011, Google and the Israel Antiquities Authority collaborated in a digitization project that made portions of the Dead Sea Scrolls available for viewing online.

Other than the Dead Sea Scrolls, have other biblically related scrolls or scroll fragments been found?

Yes. Another important scroll fragment is the Rylands Library Papyrus 52, or the St. John Fragment.

What is the St. John Fragment?

The St. John Fragment is a tiny piece of papyrus. It measures 3.5" × 2.5" and came from a codex, or a collection of bound manuscripts. On the fragment is written part of the Gospel of St. John. The fragment was in a cache of papyri purchased for the University of Manchester (England) in 1920. The fragment is on display at the John Rylands Library at the university.

Why is the fragment important?

The fragment is important because it dates from somewhere between 100 C.E. and 150 C.E., making it the oldest known transcript of a canonical New Testament text. Of added interest is the fact that the fragment has writing on both sides. On one side, the fragment bears a portion of John 18:31–33. The other side bears a portion of John 18:37–38. The text is written in Greek.

What other documents are in the Rylands papyri?

The collection contains documents that span centuries and originate from several different countries. Included in the collection are private letters, business agreements, and religious texts. Not all of the documents in the collection have to do with the Bible. Another text that does have to do with the Bible is Rylands Papyrus 458.

What is Rylands Papyrus 458?

Rylands Papyrus 458 is a Greek translation of Deuteronomy. Today, the papyrus exists as a few bits and pieces. It is important because it is the oldest surviving Hebrew-to-Greek translation of an Old Testament document. It dates from around the second century B.C.E..

OTHER WRITINGS

In addition to parchment and papyrus, what were other substances used for writing in ancient times?

Some ancient writings have been found etched in stone and clay.

Where have biblically related writings on stone been found?

Some of the most significant biblically related writings have been found on steles.

What is a stele?

A stele is an upright slab of stone that has inscriptions on it.

Why are steles important to biblical archaeology?

Steles are important to biblical archaeology because several intact ones have been found. People recorded military deeds, civic events, and other major occurrences on steles. Steles are treasure troves of information.

What are some of the most biblically significant steles?

One is the Merneptah Stele. Others are the Mesha Stele and the Tel Dan Stele.

What is the Merneptah Stele?

In 1896, an archaeologist named Flinders Petrie discovered a stele in the ancient Egyptian capital of Thebes. This 10' × 5' granite stele dates from the 1200s B.C.E. dur-

The eight fragments of Rylands Papyrus 458 contain parts of a Greek translation of Deuteronomy.

ing the reign of Merneptah. This was roughly the same time that the judges ruled in Israel. The stele chronicles Merneptah's military victories. The last few lines of the stele deal with a military campaign in Canaan. One line translates, "Israel is laid waste and his seed is not."

Why is this find important?

The find is important because it marks the earliest known written reference to Israel outside the Bible. Scholars debate the context of the reference. Merneptah did not annihilate Israel. Perhaps Merneptah referred to a subset of the Israelite community. Perhaps Merneptah meant that the Israelites' granary was destroyed, not the actual people. Maybe he was exaggerating his exploits to make himself look better. Known as the Merneptah Stele or the Israel Stele, it is on exhibit at the Cairo Museum in Egypt. The Merneptah Stele is also known as the Victory Stele of Mernepah. Incidentally, although the stele known as the Rosetta Stone bears no information about events or people in the Bible, it was nonetheless crucial to deciphering the Merneptah Stele.

What is the Rosetta Stone?

Many people consider the Rosetta Stone the most important stele of all time. The Rosetta Stone took its name because it was discovered in 1799 by some of Napoleon's soldiers who were building a fort in the Egyptian village of el-Rashid, which translates as Rosetta. Dating from about 196 B.C.E., this 45" × 30" granite slab bears a decree about royal cult worship of Ptolemy V. The decree is written in three forms: hieroglyphic, demotic, and Greek.

How was the Rosetta Stone influential in helping researchers interpret the Merneptah Stele?

By the eighteenth century, hieroglyphs had been undecipherable for centuries. By using what they knew of Greek, scholars were able to decipher the meaning of hieroglyphs. This was the key needed to unlock the plethora of pictographs inscribed on untold numbers of Egyptian treasures, including the Merneptah Stele.

Have any other ancient Egyptian artifacts influenced biblical studies?

None has been as significant as the Merneptah Stele. Over the years, archaeologists in

Discovered in Egypt in 1799, the Rosetta Stone helped archeologists determine how to translate Egyptian hieroglyphs because it included that language along with Greek.

Egypt have found a plethora of artifacts relating to life in Egypt during ancient times. Egyptian tombs have yielded sarcophagi, jewelry, statuary, food, clothing, bones, and numerous other artifacts. Also, there are numerous written records from ancient Egypt. With all that recorded history, it seems as if there would be a record of Moses and the exodus. After all, the mass exit of several hundred thousand people who made up a large part of the Egyptian workforce was a major event. However, the ancient Egyptians left no record of it—if they did, it has not yet been found. Most scholars point out that there is a reason why the Egyptians did not record the event. In ancient times, it was customary to record, in art or script, only that which reflected favorably on the culture. Being bested by a ragtag group of slaves was not something the Egyptians wanted to memorialize.

What is the Mesha Stele?

Also known as the Moabite Stone, the Mesha Stele is a black basalt stone slab that dates from around 850 B.C.E., and was discovered in 1868 in Jordan. The stele measures about 44" × 27." The text is written in the Moabite language. In addition to bearing descriptions of several building projects, the stele bears an inscription describing how King Mesha paid tribute to the Israelites, but stopped suddenly. Now King Mesha of Moab was a sheep breeder, who used to deliver to the king of Israel one hundred thousand lambs, and the wool of one hundred thousand rams. But when Ahab died, the king of Moab rebelled against the king of Israel. So King Jehoram marched out of Samaria at that time and mustered all Israel. The inscription goes on to say that King Meshah seized the holy "vessels of YHWH," and that "Israel perished everlastingly." King Jehoram was ruler of the kingdom of Judah at this time.

Why is this find important?

This find is important because it marks the earliest known written reference to the God of Israel outside of the Bible. Israel did not perish everlastingly. As with the Merneptah Stele, most scholars believe the boast was the exaggeration of a warrior or the description of an interaction with a small group of Israelites. The Mesha Stele is on permanent exhibit at the Louvre in Paris, France.

What is the Tel Dan Stele?

This basalt stone stele is actually three fragments of a stele. It dates from the 800s B.C.E. Discovered in 1993 by archaeologists working in northern Israel, the Aramaic writing on the slab describes conflict between Hazael, King of Aram, King Joram of Israel, and King Ahaziah of Judah. In part, the stele describes Hazael's hand in the downfall of the House of David. II Kings 8 seems to confirm at least part of this with a description of a conversation between the prophet Elisha and Hazael: "Then the man of God wept. Hazael asked, 'Why does my lord weep?' He answered, 'Because I know the evil that you will do to the people of Israel; you will set their fortresses on fire, you will kill their young men with the sword, dash in pieces their little ones, and rip up their pregnant women.'" (NRSV, II Kings 8:12) Later, Elisha's prophecy is confirmed:

The Tel Dan Stele, which dates back to the 800s B.C.E., includes the earliest known reference to the House of David.

"The anger of the LORD was kindled against Israel, so that he gave them repeatedly into the hand of King Hazael of Aram, then into the hand of Ben-hadad son of Hazael." (NRSV, II Kings 13:3) Today, the Tel Dan Stele is part of the collection at the Israel Museum in Jerusalem.

Why else is the Tel Dan Stele important?

This find is important because not only does it refer to Israel, but it refers to the House of David as well. Most scholars agree that this is the earliest known reference to the House of David outside of the Bible.

Besides the Dead Sea Scrolls and steles, what are some of the more significant ancient written records that have to do with events or people in the Bible?

The Taylor Prism and the Cyrus Cylinder.

What is the Taylor Prism?

The Taylor Prism dates from about 690 B.C.E. This six-sided clay barrel is about 15" tall. The writing on it is in cuneiform, a system of writing made of wedge-shaped incisions. The text describes Sennacherib's entry into Judah. The Taylor Prism was named for one

Colonel Taylor, the British official who found the prism in the ruins of Sennacherib's palace in Nineveh (modern-day northern Iraq). The Taylor Prism is on exhibit at the British Museum.

Why is the Taylor Prism important to biblical studies?

It is important because it supports (with a few variations) an event in the Bible. The event described on the Taylor Prism is King Hezekiah's routing of the Assyrian king, Sennacherib, and his army. According to II Kings 18, the Assyrians descended on Judah and captured all the fortified cities. Hezekiah pleaded with the Assyrian king to remove his armies. Even after Hezekiah stripped his palace and the temple of gold and silver, and turned all of it over to Sennacherib, Sennacherib refused to leave Judah alone. Hezekiah prayed to God for help. The author of II Kings described what happened next: "That very night the angel of the LORD set out and struck down one hundred eighty-five thousand in the camp of the Assyrians; when morning dawned, they were all dead bodies." (NRSV, II Kings 19:35) Sennacherib went home and was killed promptly by two of his sons.

Another version of the Taylor Prism, the Sennacherib Prism, is part of the collection at the Oriental Institute in Chicago.

What is the Cyrus Cylinder?

Discovered in Babylon in 1879 via an expedition sponsored by the British Museum, the Cyrus Cylinder is a barrel-shaped clay cylinder about 9" tall. Covered with text written in cuneiform, the cylinder dates from about 539 B.C.E. The Cyrus Cylinder chronicles the military conquests of the Persian ruler, King Cyrus.

Why is the Cyrus Cylinder important to biblical studies?

The cylinder records the Israelites' return to Israel after the Babylonian captivity. Included in the cylinder's catalog of conquests is the seizure of the seemingly indomitable Babylonian Empire in 538 B.C.E.

Isaiah, a prophet active between 740 and 700 B.C.E., foretold the Babylonian Empire's demise in the so-called "Cyrus Oracle":

> Thus says the Lord to his anointed, to Cyrus, whose right hand I have grasped to subdue nations before him and strip kings of their robes, to open doors before him—and the gates shall not be closed: I will go before you and level the mountains, I will break in pieces the doors of bronze and cut through the bars of iron, I will give you the treasures of the darkness and riches hidden in secret places, so that you may know that it is I, the LORD, the God of Israel, who calls you by your name. (NSRV, Isaiah 45:1-3)

The Cyrus Cylinder, like the prophet Ezra, chronicles what happened after Persia conquered the Babylonian Empire. King Cyrus decreed that the Israelites be allowed to go back to their homes. In addition, Cyrus granted the Israelites permission to rebuild their temple in Jerusalem. The Cyrus Cylinder is part of the British Museum collection.

What is the Pilate Stone?

The Pilate Stone is a limestone block measuring about 32" × 27". It dates from around 26–36 C.E. In parts of its inscription can be read the name of Pontius Pilate. The stone was discovered in the 1960s by archaeologists excavating a first-century B.C.E. theater in the town of Caesarea (known now as Caesarea Maritima). The stone was in an unexpected place. The archaeologists found it built into a staircase, apparently repurposed during fourth-century C.E. renovations.

Why is the Pilate Stone important?

The stone is important because it connects Pontius Pilate to one of the areas where Jesus visited.

Dating back to around the time of Jesus, the Pilate Stone, discovered in the 1960s, significantly includes the name Pontius Pilate.

MORE THAN WRITTEN RECORDS

Besides written records, what other artifacts have contributed to biblical studies?

Another significant artifact that contributes to biblical studies is Hezekiah's tunnel.

What is Hezekiah's Tunnel?

When the people of Jerusalem faced an impending Assyrian siege, King Hezekiah, who reigned from 715 to 687 B.C.E., knew he had to do something to help his people. In those days, it was common wartime practice to stop up an enemy city's water supply. The Assyrians would have stopped up Jerusalem's water supply if they could, but Hezekiah came up with a plan to keep this from happening. Hezekiah had workers build a tunnel underground from the springs outside the city to reservoirs inside the city. The tunnel is roughly a third of a mile long. The building of the tunnel is recorded in II Kings: "The rest of the deeds of Hezekiah, all his power, how he made the pool and the conduit and brought water into the city, are they not written in the Book of the Annals of the Kings of Judah?" (NRSV, II Kings 20:20)

Why is this find important?

Hezekiah's tunnel was discovered in 1839 by Edward Robinson, a Bible scholar from the United States. This find is important because it is indisputably evidence showing where biblical events took place. In addition, it provides researchers with information about building methods in ancient times.

In addition to studying the tunnel itself, how do modern peoples know about the methods used in the tunnel's construction?

The Siloam inscription describes how the tunnel was built.

What is the Siloam inscription?

The Siloam inscription is a stone slab bearing text written in Hebrew. The stone dates from the time of Hezekiah, and was found by a boy (some accounts say two boys) playing in the tunnel in 1880. The inscription was mounted on the wall of the tunnel. Previous examinations of the tunnel had not revealed this, most likely because it was camouflaged by generations of grime. The inscription describes how workers began to dig simultaneously at both ends of the tunnel. Most likely, the idea was for the workers to meet in the middle. The sharp turn at the center of the tunnel suggests that workers did not meet in the middle as planned, but adapted the construction as needed. Today, Hezekiah's tunnel is open to the public.

What are some other existing ancient buildings connected to the Bible?

Other ancient constructions related to the Bible are the Burnt House and the Arch of Titus.

What is the Burnt House?

The Burnt House is the name given to a house in Jerusalem that was torched by the Romans in 70 C.E. This was the same fire that destroyed the temple. When Israeli archaeologists excavated the house in the late 1960s, they found it remarkably intact.

Why is the Burnt House important?

The house is important because it conveys much about what life was like in Jerusalem during the first century C.E. For example, many stone items were found, including stone pestles, grindstones, and ovens. Also found were jugs, bowls, measuring cups, and a weighing device. Scholars think these items suggest that the room was a perfumery. The most tragic find was the skeleton of a young woman who died when the building collapsed on her. Today, the Burnt House is a museum.

The Arch of Titus, which still stands in Rome, Italy, was built to commemorate the destruction of Jerusalem in 70 C.E.

347

What is the Arch of Titus?

The Arch of Titus is an enormous marble arch in Rome. It stands fifty feet high and forty-four feet wide. The Romans built it shortly after they destroyed Jerusalem in 70 C.E. The arch was built to commemorate that destruction.

Why is the Arch of Titus important to biblical studies?

The arch is important because of the wealth of information conveyed in the carvings on the sides. Scenes carved into the marble show Romans carrying off treasures from the temple. Depictions include the looting of the lampstand (menorah) and trumpets.

Clues in Burial Customs

What have researchers found out about life in biblical times based on items related to death?

Sometimes the most telling information about life is found in the arena of death. In the past century and a half, researchers have found literal treasures in Egyptian tombs, and figurative treasures in terms of information. While burial customs in Israel were not as elaborate as those in Egypt, researchers have nonetheless deciphered clues about life in ancient Israel. For example, much information has been gleaned from ossuaries.

What are ossuaries?

An ossuary is a container used to hold the bones of a deceased person or persons.

What are some of the most telling ossuaries archaeologists have found?

Probably the most famous ossuary found to date is the Caiaphas ossuary. A relatively recent discovery, the Caiaphas ossuary was found in 1990 when, during the course of a construction project, a bulldozer broke through a hidden tomb by accident. In the tomb was an elaborately carved limestone ossuary measuring about 14" high and 30" wide. In the ossuary were found the remains of a sixty-year-old man. Researchers saw an Aramaic inscription on the end of the ossuary. It reads, "Yehoseph bar Qypa." This translates into Joseph Caiaphas. Could this be the same high priest Caiaphas who interrogated Jesus before he was crucified? Most scholars think so.

Why is this find important?

This find is important because it is a tangible link to a key figure in the New Testament.

What else was in the tomb that construction workers found?

There were eleven other ossuaries. Most scholars agree that if the bones in the first ossuary are those of Caiaphas, then the bones in the other ossuaries belonged to members of Caiaphas' family.

Was there anything significant or telling about the other bones?

Yes. The bones of sixty-three bodies were found. Of these, nearly half the skeletons belonged to children under age five. This somber fact sheds light on mortality rates in first-century Israel. Sickness was common and destructive, even among the wealthy. Treatments and medicines were scarce and/or ineffective.

Where has other information about death been found?

A particularly gruesome find in 1968 gave scholars insight into the practice of crucifixion.

In a burial cave at Giv'at ha-Mivtar just outside Jerusalem, archaeologists found a tomb. In the tomb were several ossuaries. One ossuary contained the bones of a man scholars think was killed in his twenties. A large nail was stuck in one of the man's ankle bones. Apparently, the man was killed by crucifixion. Most scholars think the man was killed around the same time as Jesus.

Why is this find important?

Most of what is known about crucifixion comes from written records. This find is important because it provides visible clues about crucifixion. According to some written accounts, some victims of crucifixion were nailed to the cross. Analyses of this young man's bones led researchers to conclude that he was tied to the cross instead. This shifted the focus from injuries caused by nails to the problem wrought by being tied up—suffocation. In addition, because of the short length of the nail, researchers suggest that the man's ankles were nailed on the cross separately, one on either side of the upright beam. This suggests that the man's legs would have been in a position in which his legs were bent slightly at the knee.

PROOF OF KINGS

Is there any archaeological evidence of kings mentioned in the Bible?

Yes. There are many artifacts associated with the reign of the infamous King Ahab. I Kings 22:39 (NRSV) reads, "Now the rest of the acts of Ahab, and all that he did, and the ivory house that he built, and the cities that he built, are they not written in the Book of the Annals of the Kings of Israel?" Archaeologists believe they found the ivory house in Samaria, the capital city during Ahab's reign. On the site of the house—or palace— archaeologists found several small ivory carvings. The carvings represent figures considered by the Israelites to be idols. This setting dovetails with the biblical record of Ahab's idolatry and descriptions of his palace.

For decades, archaeologists searched for proof outside the Bible that King David existed. If he existed, archaeologists wanted to know if he was as major a ruler in real life as he was described in the Bible. The mention of the House of David in the Tel Dan Stele confirmed the existence of a ruler named David in that region. In 2012, a team of archaeologists announced that a site they had been excavating for the past several years was one of David's fortified palaces. Located in Khirbet Qeiyafa, an ancient town about twenty miles from Jerusalem, the site dates from the tenth century B.C.E.—the time of King David. If this was one of David's palaces, then the size and grandeur of the remains suggest that David was indeed a major figure. Among the ruins, the archaeologists have found thousands of animal bones (but no pig bones) and items suggestive of religion (none of which is an animal or human figurine). The presence of some clues and the absence of others suggest that this was the location of a distinctly Hebrew group.

THE MOST ELUSIVE ARTIFACTS

What key items from the Bible have not been found?

There is much in the Bible that has not been found. And over the centuries, some items have developed a mystique which lends to their desirability. One item that has not been found is the Ark of the Covenant. Another item is the cup Jesus is purported to have used at the Last Supper—the Holy Grail.

THE ARK OF THE COVENANT

What makes the Ark of the Covenant so desirable?

To the Israelites, it was the footstool of God. Its sacred walls held the Ten Commandments. Furthermore, it was made of gold and other precious materials.

What mystique has developed around the Ark of the Covenant?

The Ark of the Covenant steps out of the Bible narrative in the book II Maccabees, and into the realm of mystery. Some people believe the Ark of the Covenant is missing, and that no one knows where it is. Some people believe the Ark of the Covenant is not missing, but hidden so that only a few people know where it is. Another theory is that the Copper Scroll found with the Dead Sea Scrolls is not just any treasure map, but the map to the treasure of treasures—the Ark of the Covenant.

THE HOLY GRAIL

What makes the Holy Grail so desirable?

It is one of the last things Jesus touched. He instituted the practice of Communion as he drank from this cup.

What mystique has developed around the Holy Grail?

Since the early Middle Ages, stories have been written about the quest for the Holy Grail. Probably the most notable early tale is that of the quest by the knights of King Arthur's court. Throughout the ages, however, this theme has inspired numerous books and

An angel collects Jesus' blood in the Holy Grail in this seventeenth-century icon housed at the State Hermitage museum in St. Petersburg, Russia.

351

films. One of the most popular movies to deal with the search for the Holy Grail is *Indiana Jones and the Last Crusade*.

RELICS

What is the difference between an artifact and a relic?

An artifact is a physical piece of history that was made by humans. A relic is a physical piece of history that has the reputation of being associated with a known historic figure. The provenance is based on tradition. In the case of biblical relics, the relics are revered and prayed over by some believers.

What are some of the most famous relics related to the Bible?

Some of the most famous relics are the bones of John the Baptist. In 2010, archaeologists excavating an ancient monastery on a Bulgarian island known as Sveti Ivan (which translates to Saint John) discovered bone fragments and a tooth thought to belong to John the Baptist. The bones date from the first century C.E. The reason John the Baptist's name is linked to the bones is because the archaeologists found a box nearby bearing the name of John the Baptist and his date of birth.

Another set of bones thought by some to be from biblical times are those belonging to Mary Magdalene. According to centuries-old tradition, a few years after Jesus was crucified and resurrected, Mary Magdalene was imprisoned. After she was released, she and some other Christians were exiled by being put in a boat without sails, oars, or any supplies. It was a miracle that the boat drifted safely to the southeast shore of France. There, according to legend, Mary and her companions converted the people there. When she died, her bones were kept in a stone crypt. In the intervening centuries, thousands of people have paid homage to Mary's bones. Occasionally, a bone or two is taken on tour. As recently as March 2013, one of Mary's shinbones toured parts of the United States.

Other relics are the Chains of St. Peter. Legend has it that when Pope Leo I held the chain associated with Peter's imprisonment in Jerusalem next to the chain associated with Peter's imprisonment in Rome, the two chains fused together. The chains are kept in a clear case at the Church of Peter in Chains in Rome.

Are there any relics associated with Jesus?

Yes. Since the time of Jesus' crucifixion and resurrection, traditions have grown up around items associated with him. One such item is Jesus' foreskin. Known as the Holy Prepuce, the foreskin was venerated by believers for centuries. The problem was that across Europe, more than a dozen foreskins were being venerated. So in 1900, the Catholic Church forbade its congregants even to talk about the Holy Prepuce. Today, none is known to exist.

Does the Crown of Thorns still exist?

Some people think so. A thorny crown is held by the Cathedral of Notre Dame in Paris. Cathedral officials say that the authenticity of the crown cannot be substantiated. Still, the crown is presented occasionally for veneration by those who believe the crown is the one Jesus was forced to wear as he was being crucified.

What is the Shroud of Turin?

A shroud is a piece of cloth used to wrap a dead body. For centuries, people have been fascinated by the Shroud of Turin. The shroud bears the ghostly image of a crucified man. Many people believe this was the shroud in which the women wrapped Jesus after he died. However, controversy over the shroud's authenticity persists. Some think it is a medieval forgery. The Shroud of Turin is on display at the Cathedral of St. John the Baptist in Turin, Italy.

A Collectible Today, an Artifact Tomorrow?

Artifacts related to the Bible carry with them a certain gravitas. Perhaps it is because of their association with the Holy Book. Perhaps it is their great age. Still, not all items related to the Bible date to antiquity. Some are quite new. Since an artifact is manmade, since there is no age requirement to be an artifact, and since these items convey something about the culture in which they were made, these items might well be modern-day artifacts.

What are some of these modern-day collectibles/artifacts?

One popular item is the nativity scene. Dating back to at least the thirteenth century, nativity scenes (or "nats," as they are affectionately known by some collectors), or crèches, commemorate the birth of Jesus. Nativity scenes can be made out of almost anything, and be of almost any size. Figures in the scenes at least depict Mary and Jesus. More elaborate scenes depict Joseph, shepherds, wise men, livestock, and angels.

What are some examples of the types of nativity scenes?

While many nativity scenes go for a realistic look by featuring human figures as the major players, some do not. For instance, some nativity scenes depict the people as rubber ducks, gnomes, cats, or children.

Theories abound about the nature of the Shroud of Turin, which is the purported burial shroud that bears the image of Jesus.

353

Also, many nativity scenes are made of wood or ceramic, but not all are. Some are made of corn husks, felt, coal, or animal horn. The scenes come in different sizes. Some are miniature. Some—such as the inflatable yard set— are larger than life.

Besides nativity scenes, what other collectibles are related to the Bible?

People love things that belonged to famous people, especially Elvis Presley. In 2012, a British collector put his Elvis memorabilia up for auction. One of the items that sold was Presley's Bible, given to him in 1957 during his first Christmas at his Memphis home, Graceland. Presley read this particular Bible until his death in 1977. Notes in his handwriting fill the margins. Some passages are underlined. Originally, it was thought that Presley's Bible would sell for around $40,000. It actually sold for £59,000—roughly $95,000—to an anonymous buyer. Other items that sold included a pair of Elvis' shoes, and one of his movie contracts. A pair of his stained underwear did not sell.

In June 2013, a Bible that Albert Einstein gifted to an American friend sold at a New York City auction for $68,500. Einstein wrote in the Bible that the book "is a great source of wisdom and consolation and should be read frequently."

Are there Bible museums?

Yes. There are many kinds of Bible museums. Bible Walk, a museum in Ohio, features seventy life-size wax dioramas depicting scenes from the Bible. The Museum of Biblical Art (MOBIA) in New York City features art from ancient to modern times, all of which is inspired by the Bible. The Museum of Biblical History in Tennessee features replicas of biblical artifacts, including the Mesha Stele and the Taylor Prism. Both the Dunham Bible Museum in Texas and the Living Word National Bible Museum in Missouri have vast collections of rare Bibles and manuscripts, all of which help tell the story of how the Bible has changed over the centuries.

PAREIDOLIA

What is pareidolia?

Pareidolia is a theory that says human brains are wired to see certain patterns—such as the human face—in random objects.

What does pareidolia have to do with the Bible?

For centuries, stories have circulated about Christian images being seen in everyday objects. To some people, the images are religious due only to the brain's affinity for patterns. To other people, the images are signs from God.

Which tree common in the American South bears a Christian symbol?

The dogwood tree. Lore has it that long ago, the dogwood tree was taller and stronger than the pine and the oak. When people came to chop down a tree to make Jesus' cross, the tree cried at having to be used for such an ignoble purpose. Jesus heard the tree's cry, and promised it that, because of its compassion, it would never be used for such a task again. From then on, dogwoods did not grow tall and strong. Now they grow to be slender, delicate trees. In the spring, when the dogwood tree blooms with pink and white blossoms, each flower bears the marks of the crucifixion. Each flower has four petals, and thus resembles a cross. The tip of each petal looks torn and has a reddish-brown color, as if to suggest blood. The center of each flower resembles a crown.

Which common household pet bears a Christian initial?

The tabby cat. There are several legends about how the tabby cat came to have a mark in the shape of an "M" on its forehead. A Christian legend describes how, on the night Jesus was born, a cat climbed into the manger with him to keep him warm. Mary, the mother of Jesus, was appreciative, so she stroked the cat's head, thus marking it forever with M for Mary or Madonna.

Which common farm animal bears a Christian symbol?

The donkey. Most donkeys have a stripe of dark fur across their shoulders, and another intersecting stripe down their backs. The stripes form the shape of a cross. There are a couple of versions as to how the cross got there. One version of the story says that the donkey who carried Mary while she was pregnant with Jesus was blessed with the mark, and passed the mark to other donkey generations. Another version of the story says the donkey who carried Jesus when he entered Jerusalem the week before he died is the one blessed with the mark.

What sea creature bears a Christian symbol?

The sand dollar. The lore goes that four of the five holes in the sand dollar represent nail wounds in Jesus' hands and feet. The fifth hole represents the spear wound. On one side, the image of a flower represents the Easter lily. The image on the other side represents the poinsettia, the flower most associated with Jesus' birth. At the center of the flower is a five-pointed star, which represents the star that led the shepherds and wise men to Jesus. If shaken, the shell rattles. If broken open, the rattling items are found to be five tiny dove-shaped shells that represent the Holy Spirit.

Staurolites are natural crystal formations that can resemble crosses.

What item bearing a Christian symbol can be found only in a few areas of the world?

The fairy crosses. Usually, these small staurolite crystal formations are about one inch long. One characteristic of this particular crystal is that it is in the shape of a cross. Lore has it that these rocks were formed when Jesus died. The woodland fairies cried when they learned that Jesus had been crucified. When their tears fell to earth, they turned into stone crosses. These formations are found in small areas of the United States and Europe.

What item bearing a Christian image is really out of this world?

The Cone Nebula. The Cone Nebula was photographed in 2002 by Advanced Cameras for Surveys (ACS) on NASA's Hubble Space Telescope. NASA describes the nebula as having the appearance of a beast rising out of the sea, but others say the nebula bears the resemblance of a bearded man praying. The idea that the nebula resembles a man praying gave rise to its nickname, the Jesus Nebula.

Which biblical person's image was seen in the window of a bank?

Images of Jesus, the cross, and/or Mary have been seen in toast, wood grain, water stains, and other everyday objects. For instance, a week before Christmas Day in 1996, someone noticed what looked like a rainbow-hued image of the Virgin Mary on the windows

What are the largest and smallest Bibles in existence?

The smallest New Testament was made by scientists at the Massachusetts Institute of Technology (MIT) in 2001. They used a process called microlithography to create a New Testament that fits on the head of a pencil eraser.

The largest New Testament is the Waynai Bible, located in the library at Abilene (Texas) Christian University. This King James translation took Louis Waynai 8,700 hours over the course of two years to make. He used a homemade press. The Bible is 43.5" tall, and the spine is 34" thick. The book has 8,048 pages, and weighs 1,094 pounds.

of a Clearwater, Florida bank. The image attracted a few onlookers. Then the image attracted people from all over the world. Some people believed the sixty-foot image was a sign from God. Others believed the image was a stain of some sort. In 2004, someone vandalized the shrine by breaking the top window panes.

Is it only images from the New Testament that people see?

Maybe images from the Old Testament are seen, but images from the New Testament are more often reported. One notable example of an Old Testament image (or an image related to the Old Testament) being seen in an everyday item became popular thanks to an e-mail that went viral in 2008. The author of the e-mail explained how the dollar bill came to have several Jewish symbols on it. On the back of the dollar bill, the Great Seal of the United States is shown. The starry circle on the right hand side is in the shape of the Star of David. If the bill is turned upside down, a menorah can be seen near the feet of the eagle. The author explained that the symbols were placed there to honor Hayim Solomon, one of George Washington's aides. According to the e-mail, Solomon gave a significant portion of his wealth to shore up the bedraggled Continental army, thus changing the course of the war in favor of the Continentals. Critics of this theory agree that Hayim Solomon was a major player in the events of the Revolutionary War, but that his financial assistance was in the form of brokering bills of exchange (although he is thought to have made personal loans to indigent veterans). Also, the government website about official seals and documents (www.ourdocuments.gov) makes no mention of the symbols having a Jewish association.

What is the oldest extant publisher of Bibles?

Cambridge University Press. Opened in 1584 under the auspices of King Henry VIII, this publishing house published its first Bible, the Geneva Bible, in 1591. Cambridge printed its first translation of the King James Version in 1629.

THE BIBLE AND POP CULTURE

What is pop culture?

Pop culture, or popular culture, is the collection of attitudes, tastes, and images that reflect mainstream interests in the twentieth and twenty-first centuries, particularly in the Western hemisphere. Television, movies, music, books, and other media are influenced by this collection of ideas.

The Bible has a broad and varied history of influencing church doctrine and the morality of those who believe in the book's sacredness. The Bible's influence is so pervasive, however, that much of its content is entrenched in secular consciousness. Events, images, and people in the Bible pop up in all kinds of secular venues. Because the Bible's influence in secular society is so widespread, it would be impossible to describe them all here. Still, some biblically influenced pieces of pop culture panorama bear mention because of the enormity of their popularity or influence inside and outside religious circles.

THE BIBLE AND MOVIES

When was the Hollywood heyday for mainstream movies based on events in the Bible?

In the mid-twentieth century, movies based on biblical events were big business. Their appeal extended beyond religious circles. Big-name stars and lavish sets were the norm. Generally, these movies went more for dramatic effect than for strict adherence to the Bible. Costumes, for instance, looked vaguely biblical, but were couched firmly in 1950s fashion, including conical bras, sassy ponytails, and matte red lipstick for the women, and slick, pomaded hair and clean-shaven faces for the men.

Which Hollywood movie producer and director said, "Give me any two pages of the Bible, and I'll give you a picture"?

Cecil B. DeMille (1881–1959). DeMille was made famous by his creation of lavish movie epics, many of them about events in the Bible. One of the movies that was especially popular with the public was *Samson and Delilah* (1949). Victor Mature and Hedy Lamarr played the starring roles. *King of Kings* (1927) was a silent movie about the last weeks of Jesus' life. Most of the movie was filmed in black and white, which was the norm for that era. However, DeMille, who was noted for his creativity, filmed the scenes dealing with Jesus' resurrection using the new and expensive Technicolor.

Which of his movies did DeMille produce twice?

The Ten Commandments. DeMille made a silent version in 1923, and an extravagant, full-color sound version in 1956.

Besides being made by DeMille, what did *King of Kings* and the later version of *The Ten Commandments* have in common?

Actor H. B. Warner appeared in both films. In *King of Kings,* Warner played Jesus. In *The Ten Commandments,* Warner played Amminadab. Warner played the elderly druggist, Mr. Gower, in *It's A Wonderful Life* in 1946, just nineteen years after he played Jesus. Warner was fifty-two when he played Jesus.

How has DeMille's *The Ten Commandments* affected nearly sixty years of movie watchers?

Charlton Heston being cast as Moses proved a definitive pairing in moviemaking history. It is hard to imagine what Moses might have looked like without thinking of Heston. *The Ten Commandments* was not the only biblically based movie in which Heston appeared. In addition, he appeared in *The Greatest Story Ever Told* (1965). This time Heston played John the Baptist. Other noteworthy actors played in *The Greatest Story Ever Told*: Pat Boone played the angel at the tomb, John Wayne played the centurion at the tomb, and Sidney Poitier played Simon of Cyrene.

Charlton Heston's portrayal of Moses is considered iconic by many movie watchers. Whose portrayal of God is considered iconic by many movie watchers?

George Burns. In the movie *Oh, God!* (1977), Burns starred as God in this offbeat comedy about a reluctant modern-day Moses played by John Denver. The tagline for the movie is: "Anybody who could turn Lot's wife into a pillar of salt, incinerate Sodom and Gomorrah, and make it rain for forty days and forty nights has got to be a fun guy."

Which person appears in only four chapters of the Bible, but has inspired several films?

Samson. In addition to the handful of early black-and-white silent films made about Samson and his fatal flirtation with Delilah, the ill-fated romance received full-color treatment in later films. In addition to the Cecil B. DeMille version in 1949, there was a made-for-TV version. Made in 1984, *Samson and Delilah* once again featured Victor Mature. In the 1949 version, Mature played the long-haired, lovelorn strongman. In the 1984 version, he played the role of Samson's father, Manoah. Another made-for-TV version, *Samson and Delilah* (1996), featured model and actress Elizabeth Hurley as the sultry temptress.

What creative measures have some moviemakers used to tell the story of Samson and Delilah?

Samson and Delilah were cartoons in the thirty-minute animated video *Samson and Delilah* (1986). Linda Purl, of *Happy Days* fame, provided the voice of Delilah. Then, in 2009, the famous story was filmed as a lush opera featuring tenor Clifton Forbis as Samson, and mezzo-soprano Olga Borodina as Delilah.

Gregory Peck and Susan Hayward played another tragic biblical couple in which film?

David and Bathsheba (1951). One movie ad ran with this tagline: "For this woman, he broke God's own commandment!" Most of the time, movie producers of this era were not particularly strict about historical accuracy. For instance, throughout *David and Bathsheba,* Gregory Peck wore a Star of David emblem. The Star of David dates back to probably no earlier than the twelfth century C.E., some two thousand years after David's time.

How has Jesus' life been depicted in movies?

The life of Jesus makes for great drama. This is attested by the numerous film versions made of his life, including the aforementioned *King of Kings* and *The Greatest Story Ever Told.* One noteworthy version is *Jesus of Nazareth* (1977). Director Franco Zeffirelli already had the now-classic films *Romeo and Juliet* and *The Taming of the Shrew* under his belt when he made this made-for-TV miniseries. Zeffirelli's depiction of Jesus' life is noteworthy for its faithfulness to the way events are described in the Bible, and for its authentic-looking setting and costumes (although some criticize the casting of a blue-eyed man to play Jesus). The movie had a star-studded cast, including Laurence Olivier, Ernest Borgnine, Anne Bancroft, and Christopher Plummer.

Another noteworthy version is *The Passion of the Christ* (2004). Produced and directed by Mel Gibson, this film garnered three Oscar nominations. This movie deals with the last several hours of Jesus' life. When it was first released, the movie created a furor. Some people loved it because in it they saw a tribute to Jesus. Some people hated it because they saw anti-Semitic bigotry it. In a 2007 list compiled by *Entertainment Weekly,* this movie ranked as the most controversial movie of all time.

Strictly speaking, *The Last Temptation of Christ* (1988) is not based on the Bible, but on the novel, *The Last Temptation of Christ* by Nikos Kazantzakis. Directed by Martin Scorsese, the film sparked controversy due to what some saw as its blasphemous content. Some people objected especially to the scene where Jesus imagined what his life might have been like had he lived as a "normal" man with a wife and children. Like *Jesus of Nazareth, The Last Temptation of Christ* had a cast filled with Hollywood luminaries. Willem Dafoe played Jesus, and Barbara Hershey played Mary Magdalene. *Entertainment Weekly* ranked this movie the sixth most controversial movie of all time.

THE BIBLE AND SCIENCE FICTION

What do the Bible and *Star Trek* have in common?

The *Star Trek* franchise has legions of fans from all walks of life. *Star Trek* is not about the Bible specifically, but there is no end to the parallels between this famous sci-fi franchise and the Bible. The comparison has been made that starship captain Jean-Luc Picard is a Christlike figure because of his wisdom, compassion, and capacity for self-sacrifice. Likewise, the omniscient Q is likened to God. Other connections have less to do with personality traits of main characters, and more to do with coincidental connections. For instance, actor Jeffrey Hunter played Jesus in the movie *King of Kings* (1961). Three years later, he played Captain Christopher Pike in the original *Star Trek* series pilot (1964). Incidentally, Hunter was in his mid-thirties when he played Jesus, close to Jesus' actual age when he was crucified. Still, critics dubbed Hunter "The Teenage Jesus," a disparagement of his polished Hollywood good looks.

Another interesting commonality between *Star Trek* and the Bible is that while actor Leonard Nimoy is best known for his portrayal of the Star Trek icon Mr. Spock, Nimoy has played the role of another wise man. He played the role of the prophet Samuel in the made-for-TV movie *David* (1997). In addition, Leonard Nimoy is credited with using an ancient Hebrew sign to create the Vulcan salute.

What do the Bible and *Star Wars* have in common?

As with *Star Trek,* an array of parallels can be drawn between the Bible and the wildly successful franchise *Star Wars I-VI* (1977–2005). For instance, Anakin Skywalker and Luke Skywalker were portrayed in varying degrees as Christ figures. Anakin, like Jesus, was born of immaculate conception. Luke, like Jesus, was the chosen one, the special individual destined to bring peace and unity to the galaxy. The Force's similarity to the Holy Spirit prompted the spread of a joke based on liturgy. A clergyman intones, "May the Force be with you." Congregants respond, "And also with you."

Other bit of trivia linking the Bible and *Star Wars* have more to do with coincidences. For instance, in *Star Wars Episode I: The Phantom Menace* (1999) and *Star Wars Episode II: Attack of the Clones* (2002), actress Pernilla August played Anakin Skywalker's mother, Shmi Skywalker. With a sense of wonder, Shmi confessed that Anakin did not have a father. The same year she appeared in *The Phantom Menace,* Pernilla August played Mary to Christian Bale's Jesus in a made-for-TV movie called *Mary, Mother of Jesus.* Another Star Wars connection to the Bible derives from the fact that actress

How is the Vulcan salute derivative of an ancient Hebrew sign?

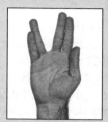

The Vulcan salute occurs when a person raises his/her hand and forms the shape of a "V" with the ring finger and the index finger. An ancient Hebrew sign still used today occurs when a Jewish priest spreads out both of his/her hands, thumbs touching. The priest creates a V-shape between the ring finger and the index finger on both hands. Both hands positioned like that create five distinct spaces. Usually, the priest accompanies the sign by saying the Aaronic, or Priestly, Blessing: "May the Lord bless you and keep you. The Lord make his face shine on you and be gracious to you. May the Lord turn his face toward you and give you peace."

Keisha Castle-Hughes played the Queen of Naboo in *Star Wars Episode III: Revenge of the Sith* (2005). The next year, Castle-Hughes played Mary in *The Nativity Story*.

What short-lived science fiction TV series featured a preacher named Book?

Firefly (2002). In the episode called "Jaynetown," the wise and kind preacher, Book, comes upon Sky, the waifish teenage girl who—because of cruel and debilitating government experiments done on her brain—vacillates between states of childlike fancy and high logic, evidenced by this conversation:

Book: What are we up to, sweetheart?
River: Fixing your Bible.

Book: I, um … what?
River: Bible's broken. Contradictions, false logistics—doesn't make sense.
[River is shown tearing pages out and marking through lines.]

Book: No, no. You—you—you can't …
River: So we'll integrate non-progressional evolution theory with God's creation of Eden. Eleven inherent metaphoric parallels already there. Eleven. Important number. Prime number. One goes into the house of eleven eleven times, but always comes out one. Noah's Ark is a problem.

Book: Really?
River: We'll have to call it early quantum state phenomenon. Only way to fit 5,000 species of mammal on the same boat.
[River rips out another page]

Book: Give me that. River, you don't fix the Bible.
River: It's broken. It doesn't make sense.
Book: It's not about making sense. It's about believing in something, and letting that belief be real enough to change your life. It's about faith. You don't fix faith, River. It fixes you.

363

The Bible and Television

How has the Bible influenced mainstream television in America?

The influence of the Bible on television cannot be overstated. Over the years, innumerable sitcoms, dramas, documentaries, and commercials have contained biblical content. Many shows on television, such as *7th Heaven* (1996–2007) and *Touched by an Angel* (1994–2003) have explicit biblically based content. The first show features a minister and his family. The second show features angels helping people. Some television shows are not about the Bible *per se*, but have scenes or episodes that contain marked biblical references.

Which long-running series featured a widower sheriff who raised his young son in a small North Carolina town?

The Andy Griffith Show (1960–1968). Andy and the other residents of Mayberry went to church a lot. They had the pastor over for dinner on Sundays. They talked among themselves about the meaning of the pastor's sermon. They sang hymns while sitting on the front porch. *The Andy Griffith Show* was so grounded in biblical teachings that it inspired creators of the Sunday school curriculums, "The Mayberry Bible Study" and *The Andy Griffith Show* Bible Study Series." The show had distinctly Christian underpinnings, but continues to draw religious and secular audiences all over the world.

Which long-running animated series features a character named Reverend Lovejoy?

The Simpsons (1989–present). Middle-class America with all its cultural trappings is satirized via the lives of Homer, Marge, Bart, Lisa, Maggie, and the other citizens of Springfield. References to the Bible are frequent occurrences throughout the long-running series. On April 4, 1999, the episode "Simpsons Bible Stories" focused entirely on the Bible. Reverend Lovejoy, encouraged by the fervent Ned Flanders, delivered a very long sermon one muggy Sunday. During the sermon, the Simpson family napped. Each family member dreamed of a scene from the Bible, adapted and parodied Simpson-style. Marge dreamed that she and Homer were Adam and Eve during the "Applegate" scandal. *The Simpsons* is the longest-running comedy television show in history. It has widespread secular appeal.

The late actor Andy Griffith (1926–2012), shown here receiving the Presidential Medal of Freedom in 2005, portrayed a kind and moral sherrif in the Southern town of Mayberry that was populated mostly by Christian citizens.

The Simpsons is not the only long-running television series to contain biblically based content. The late-night TV show, *Saturday Night Live!* (1975–present) has made a nearly forty-year career of spoofing every aspect of American life. A recurring trope on the series is the use of fake television commercials. One such fake commercial was for the "Myowling Bible" which aired in May 1987. According to the smarmy salesman played by actor Phil Hartman, the Myowling Bible was ideal for sharing with your cat. He promised, "Told with moving reverence but told in language even your cat can understand, the Myowling Bible will enrich your life—or nine lives, as the case may be." The camera switched back and forth from Hartman to a cozy domestic scene where an elderly lady sat reading with her cat. The watercolor illustrations featured human figures with cat heads.

Which sitcom features four scientist friends who try to figure out every aspect of life, including religion?

The Big Bang Theory (2007–present). Sheldon, the obsessive-compulsive super-genius of the bunch, resists his strict church upbringing, but his conversation shows his familiarity with the Bible. In the episode "The Large Hadron Collision," Sheldon (portrayed by actor Jim Parsons) becomes angry with Leonard (portrayed by actor Johnny Galecki) when Leonard invites Penny instead of him to go to Switzerland to see the Large Hadron Collider. In a fit of petulance and sour grapes, Sheldon initiates a game.

The cast of *The Big Bang Theory* includes (left to right) Jim Parsons, Johnny Galecki, Kaley Cuoco, Simon Helberg, and Kunal Nayyar. The TV comedy series sometimes makes clever references to the Bible.

Sheldon: All right. This game is called Traitors. I will name three historical figures. You put them in order of the heinousness of their betrayal. Benedict Arnold, Judas, Dr. Leonard Hofstadter.

Leonard: You really think I belong with Benedict Arnold and Judas?

Sheldon: You're right. Judas had the decency to hang himself after what he did.

Leonard: Come on, Sheldon. Can't you at least try to understand how much this means to me?

Later in the university cafeteria, Sheldon leaves a container with thirty pieces of silverware at Leonard's table.

In another episode, "The Werewolf Transformation," Sheldon was in a snit because his regular barber was in the hospital, and could not cut his hair. He tries to explain his extreme upset to his girlfriend, Amy (portrayed by actress Mayim Bialik):

Sheldon: I'm sorry. I'm looking for a barber, and I'm running out of time. My hair is growing at the rate of 4.6 yoctometers per femtosecond. I mean, if you're quiet, you can hear it.

Amy: What about Supercuts?

Sheldon: I tried it once. They do men's and women's hair in the same room at the same time. It's like Sodom and Gomorrah with mousse.

TELEVANGELISM

What is a televangelist?

The word "televangelist" combines two words: television and evangelist. An evangelist is someone who spreads Christianity, in part, by talking about the Bible. A televangelist, then, is someone who spreads Christianity by talking about it on television.

Who was the first televangelist?

Bishop Fulton Sheen. Sheen was already a respected teacher, priest, and author by the time he began a weekly radio show in 1930. The show, *The Catholic Hour,* proved immensely popular. In 1951, Sheen began a weekly television show, *Life Is Worth Living.* The show was praised by critics and viewers alike. In 1952, Sheen won an Emmy for his work on the show. The substance of the show consisted mainly of Sheen's talking about the roles of faith and religion in the workaday world. His use of technology to reach a much bigger audience paved the way for future televangelists, including Pat Robertson, Billy Graham, and Joel Osteen.

How has televangelism influenced the secular world?

Because untold billions of people all over the world have televisions, it stands to reason that a large portion of those viewers have seen all or part of a televangelist's show.

Whether or not viewers accept the religious message, they are aware of its existence. Also, some televangelists have, for a variety of reasons, appeared in mainstream news headlines, and have been the brunt of widespread secular jokes.

THE BIBLE AND MAINSTREAM MUSIC

How has the Bible influenced mainstream music in America?

The Bible's influence on mainstream music is incalculable. That could be a book in itself. From the Ecclesiastes-inspired Byrds' 1965 hit "Turn, Turn, Turn" to Lady Gaga's 2011 hit "Judas," mainstream music is packed with biblical ideas and images.

Which musical genre features many explicitly biblical pieces but attracts a wide secular audience?

Musicals and country music often feature biblical pieces.

Which British composer wrote music about Jacob and his twelve sons, and about Jesus?

Andrew Lloyd Webber. In *Joseph and the Amazing Technicolor Dreamcoat* (1968), Webber and lyricist Tim Rice envisioned the Old Testament account of Joseph and his family set to music and dance. Filled with buoyant, catchy tunes, the score also features somber moments, such as Joseph's song from prison, "Close Every Door." The show is filled with sight and sound gags, including the Elvis Presleyesque Pharaoh and the Parisian café setting for Joseph's starving brothers in the song "Those Canaan Days."

In the rock opera *Jesus Christ Superstar* (1970), Webber and Rice teamed up again to set the last days of Jesus to song and dance. Like *Joseph*, this musical is filled with memorable, bright songs which contrast dramatically with somber moments, such as when Jesus, left alone in the garden, sings the mournful "Gethsemane."

Webber and Rice are not the only ones to build musicals around the Bible.

Composer Andrew Lloyd Webber has penned scores for such popular Broadway musicals as *Joseph and the Amazing Technicolor Dreamcoat* and *Jesus Christ Superstar.*

367

Stephen Schwartz adapted John-Michael Tebelak's book *Godspell* to create a musical of the same name in 1971. *Godspell* features the parables of Jesus. Schwartz's music is supplemented by traditional Episcopal hymns.

Which hit musical from the 1950s featured characters named after people from the Bible?

Seven Brides for Seven Brothers (1954). From MGM's musical heyday, this movie features seven uncouth brothers who were given biblical names in alphabetical order. The oldest son was Adam. Then there was Benjamin, Caleb, Daniel, Ephraim, Frank, and Gideon, the youngest. Upon being introduced to the brothers, Jane Powell's character, Milly, remarks she does not remember anyone named Frank in the Bible. Brother Caleb explains, "There were no 'F' names in the Bible, so Ma named him 'Frankincense' because he smelled so sweet."

While the movie is not about the Bible *per se*, it does contain pointed biblical references. For instance, when Milly works to clean the cabin, do laundry, and prepare a good meal, she becomes appalled when Adam and his brothers continue in their messy, disruptive ways. She thumbs through her Bible looking for solace, and finds Matthew 7:6—"Give not that which is holy unto the dogs, neither cast ye your pearls before swine, lest they trample them under their feet, and turn again and rend you." That verse sets in motion Milly's plan to civilize the brothers.

Which hit musical chronicles the lives of an Orthodox Jewish man and his family?

Fiddler on the Roof. First a Broadway musical (1964), then a movie (1971), this story describes how Tevye, a dairyman, tries to instill traditional Jewish values into the hearts and minds of his daughters. Tevye finds opposition in the form of suitors who do not meet his idea of appropriate spouses for his daughters, and in the form of a tsar who orders Tevye's village vacated because its inhabitants are Jewish. Traditions rooted in Hebrew Scriptures (Old Testament), such as Shabbat, flesh out the story.

Which music-filled 1980s movie pits townspeople against each other over biblical interpretation?

Footloose (1984). Kevin Bacon stars as teenager Ren, who resists the conservative town's ban on dancing. When defending dance in a town hall meeting, Ren cites the Bible: "Aren't we told in Psalm 149—'Praise ye oh Lord. Sing unto the Lord a new song. Let them praise his name in the dance'?" Ren continues, "It was King David, King David who we read about in Samuel. And what did David do? What did David do? What did David do? [fumbles through pages of Bible looking for specific verse] 'David danced before the Lord with all his might—leaping and dancing before the Lord.' Leaping and dancing. Ecclesiastes assures us that there is a time for every purpose under heaven. A time to laugh. A time to weep. A time to mourn. There is a time to dance. There was a time for this law, but not anymore. See, this is our time to dance. It is our way of celebrating life. It's the way it was in the beginning [holds up Bible]. It's the way it's always been. It's the way it should be now."

THE BIBLE AND MAINSTREAM LITERATURE

How has the Bible influenced mainstream literature?

Much literature is derived from the Bible. Dante Alighieri's *The Inferno* (c. 1314) deals with Christian ideas of sin and eternal punishment. The protagonist of John Bunyan's *Pilgrim's Progress* (1678), Christian, reads the Bible, and feels ashamed of his sins, so he works through a physical and metaphorical wilderness to seek God's mercy and deliverance. Victor Hugo's *Les Misérables* (1862), one of the most significant novels of the nineteenth century, contains one of literature's most memorable Christlike figures in the person of convict-turned-martyr, Jean Valjean. The title of John Steinbeck's 1952 classic *East of Eden* is an allusion to the expulsion of Adam and Eve from Eden. The story itself is packed with biblical parallels, including two rival brothers who bear numerous comparisons to Cain and Abel. Some works, like Christopher Moore's *Lamb: The Gospel According to Biff, Christ's Childhood Pal* (2002), are derived from the Bible in a tongue-in-cheek manner. In this novel, Moore imagines the years of Jesus' life that the Bible left

An illustration by Gustave Doré for Dante Alighieri's *Inferno*.

out. Biff, Jesus' friend, describes the journey he and Jesus took to the East in order to find out what Jesus was supposed to do.

In the past fifteen years, two literary phenomena stand out for their worldwide mass appeal, and for sparking debate about the Bible and religion. What are they?

The first is the Harry Potter series (1997–2007) by British author J. K. Rowling (1965–present). Ever since the first book in the series (*Harry Potter and the Sorcerer's Stone* or *Harry Potter and the Philosopher's Stone*, depending on country of publication) was published, readers have pointed out similarities between it and the Bible. The most basic comparisons are that Harry can be seen as a Christ figure, Dumbledore as a God figure, and Voldemort as a Satan figure. In the series, the unforgiveable killing curse, Avada Kedavra, derives from the age-old Abracadabra. Abracadabra is an Aramaic word used to ward off evil and sickness (the Ancient Israelites believed in one God, but they were superstitious as well). For the word to have its desired effect, it had to be written over and over inside a triangle. On the other hand, some critics of the series charge that it is blatant in its anti-biblical content by its promotion of occultism.

The second series, written by American author Dan Brown, begins with the book *Angels and Demons* (2000). Although it was a best seller, it was the second book in the series, *The Da Vinci Code* (2003), that launched worldwide debate and discussion among those interested in history and religion. In this novel, symbologist Robert Langdon and cryptologist Sophie Neveu investigate a murder at the Louvre in Paris. In the process, they uncover long-buried secrets about the early days of Christianity, particularly Jesus' relationship with Mary Magdalene, and the potentially holy lineage of French kings. The third and fourth books in the series are *The Lost Symbol* (2009) and *Inferno* (2013). The immense popularity of *The Da Vinci Code* spawned a new subset of related books, including *Truth and Fiction in the Da Vinci Code* (2004) by Bart Erhman, *De-coding Da Vinci: The Facts Behind the Fiction of* The Da Vinci Code (2004) by Amy Welborn, and *The Divine Code of Da Vinci, Fibonacci, Einstein, and You* (2009) by Matthew Cross, Robert Friedman, and others.

Which best-selling series of novels depicts events related to the Rapture?

The Left Behind series (1995–2007). Written by Tim LaHaye and Jerry Jenkins, this series deals with the people who were "left behind" on Earth after the Rapture. New believers (Rayford and his daughter, Chloe) spearhead an effort to prepare people for the coming Tribulation. All the while, they have to deal with Nicolae Jetty, the new secretary-general of the United Nations, who, unbeknownst to most people, is the Antichrist. The series is based on a dispensationalist interpretation of the Bible, a set of theories regarding God's relationship with people, and the order and nature of events during the end times. The books in this series prompted rounds of debate on whether the events depicted were theologically accurate.

Which classic children's series is a secular fantasy wrapped in Christian allegory?

The Chronicles of Narnia (1950–1956) by C. S. Lewis. In the first book in the series, *The Lion, the Witch, and the Wardrobe* (1950), siblings Lucy, Edmund, Peter, and Susan walk through a wardrobe into the enchanted land of Narnia. There they meet the White Witch, who uses her dark powers to put Narnia in a state of endless winter. The lion, Aslan, is the rightful king. Though Peter betrays Aslan, much like St. Peter betrayed Jesus, Aslan saves him from the White Witch through his sacrificial death. Later, Aslan is resurrected and helps the children conquer the White Witch. Lewis was an atheist for much of his early years, but converted to Christianity in his thirties. Through his writings, he became a prolific and articulate defender of Christianity. *The Chronicles of Narnia* inspired animated and live-action movies, board games, video games, and action figures.

Which popular franchise geared towards girls includes a component with strong Hebrew Scripture influences?

One major pop culture phenomenon is The American Girl franchise. Introduced in 1986, the book series features girls from various times of American history. Over the years, the franchise grew to include dolls and a plethora of doll furnishings, clothes, and other accessories. In 2009, a new American Girl was introduced—Rebecca. This series features the life of young Rebecca in New York City in 1914. Her parents and grandparents were immigrants who brought with them from Europe their rich Jewish heritage. Jewish traditions rooted in Hebrew Scriptures, such as Shabbos and Passover, are integrated into each Rebecca book.

Besides novels, what is another form of literature influenced by the Bible?

Comics. Not only are there manga and other graphic novel versions of the Bible, but some mainstream comics are based on the Bible as well.

In the universe of Marvel Comics, Apocalypse is a powerful mutant bent on winnowing out humanity in order to bring mutants to power. To do this, he recruits other mutants, including some X-Men, who form his self-styled staff, Horsemen of Apocalypse.

What is "fan fiction", and how has the Bible influenced it?

Fan fiction consists of stories, poems, and other short works written by fans—not the original authors—of particular books or book series. Generally, fan fiction is written for other fans who have knowledge of the original work, whether fiction or non-fiction. Stephenie Meyer's Twilight series has a huge fan fiction component, as does J. K. Rowling's Harry Potter series. The Bible, too, has a large fan fiction component. As of September 2013, one of the most popular fan fiction Web sites, www.fanfiction.net, featured over three thousand derivative works based on the Bible.

Another Marvel Comics character who has origins in the Bible is Doc Samson, who made appearances in some of the Hulk comics. Originally, Samson was Banner's mild-mannered psychiatrist, but contaminates himself due to exposure to gamma radiation. As a result, he finds that—like Hulk—he waffles between normalcy and mutancy. Like the Samson in the Bible, Doc Samson's level of strength depends on the length of his (green) hair.

In the universe of DC Comics, Resurrection Man was formed when a hard-hearted scientist, Mitchell Shelley, formulates a technology to heal deadly wounds and enhance a person's natural abilities. After an accident, Shelley uses the technology on himself. Afterwards, Shelley develops amnesia, so he no longer remembers his former selfishness and ambition. He feels a pull to help people instead. In addition, Shelley has the ability to come back to life. Each time he dies, he comes back with a new superpower. As he searches for answers to his purpose, he is pursued by agents from Heaven and Hell, each of whom has claims on his soul.

THE BIBLE AND SPORTS

How has the Bible influenced sports?

During the early years of the United States, it was illegal in most areas of the United States to play sports on Sunday. This was in obeisance to the Fourth Commandment, "Remember the Sabbath day by keeping it holy." (Exodus 20:8) Over the years, this observance fell out of practice in most areas of the country. Still, the Bible continues to influence sportsmanship and the lives of athletes in and out of the sports arena.

One major way the Bible has had long-lasting influence on sports culture has been with the establishment of the YMCA (Young Men's Christian Association).

How has the YMCA influenced sports culture?

Originally a London institution formed by George Williams, the first YMCA in the United States was formed in Boston in 1851 by Thomas Valentine Sullivan. The purpose of the organization was to meet a social need, that of providing a safe place for young men who might otherwise succumb to dangerous and unhealthy pastimes on the city streets to pray and participate in Bible study. By the 1860s, YMCAs were being built that included affordable housing for single men. In 1869, the first YMCA with a gymnasium was built.

Over the ensuing years, the YMCA continued to grow by providing men with opportunities for self-improvement through higher education classes and sports. Eventually, the YMCA's ministry embraced women, too. Today, the YMCA continues to use Christian ideals to help families from all walks of life build healthier lives.

What is Muscular Christianity?

The concept has been around since the time of Paul, who compared the Christian life to athletic discipline. The concept did not take hold in the United States until the YMCA was established. Muscular Christianity is the idea that Christian principles go hand in hand with physical strength and athletic skill.

How is the YMCA associated with the invention of basketball?

In 1891, James Naismith, a physical education teacher at the YMCA Training School in Massachusetts, came up with an indoor winter game whereby players had to throw a ball into a peach basket attached to the wall. That was the beginning of basketball. The effects of basketball on American culture and cultures around the world are incalculable.

What other sports organizations are influenced by the Bible?

The Fellowship of Christian Athletes (FCA) is a group founded in 1954 with the purpose of encouraging coaches and athletes of all ages to change the world using Christian ideals. Today, the FCA is the largest Christian sports ministry in the world. Also, Upward Sports, founded in 1995, focuses on teaching children how to be athletes and good citizens. Upward Sports is the world's largest Christian sports league for youth.

FOOTBALL

Which Heisman Trophy winner attracted national attention not only for his prowess as a quarterback, but for publicly demonstrating his Christian faith?

Tim Tebow.

Which common football practice did Tebow adapt to demonstrate his faith?

Many football players use eye black to deflect glares. When Tebow was in college, players began to write short messages on their eye black. Some players wrote their zip codes, their mothers' names, or their girlfriends' names. Tebow wrote Bible verses on his eye black. The practice of writing on eye black was banned by the National Collegiate Athletic Association (NCAA) in 2010.

Tebow's habit of going down on one knee and bowing his head in prayer led to the minting of the word "Tebowing." The term became so widespread that the online purveyor and protector of world data, The Global Language Monitor, declared it a real word in 2011.

Football player Tim Tebow became famous for bowing his head and praying on one knee during games, a gesture that came to be called "Tebowing" in American popular culture.

Which NFL kicker credits his faith in God for his professional success?

St. Louis Ram Greg Zuerlein sustained a potentially career-ending sports injury just before his senior year in college. It was during his recuperation that Zuerlein, a life-long Catholic, redoubled his prayers, and realized that God—not he—was in control of his career.

WRESTLING AND MIXED MARTIAL ARTS

Which professional wrestler's Christian persona was eclipsed by another wrestler's megalomaniacal persona?

In World Wrestling Entertainment (WWE), Steve Austin's persona, "Stone Cold" Steve Austin, defeated Jake "The Snake" Roberts in 1996. Roberts, whose wrestling persona was a Christian, was mocked by Austin, whose wrestling persona was not. Austin taunted, "You sit there and you thump your Bible, and you say your prayers, and it didn't get you anywhere! Talk about your psalms, talk about John 3:16. Austin 3:16 says I just whipped your ass!" This spawned a marketing frenzy of Austin 3:16 merchandise, including T-shirts, posters, bobbleheads, bumper stickers, and Christmas ornaments.

Has the Bible influenced mixed martial arts?

Yes. People who oppose mixed martial arts on religious grounds say the sport condones violence and pride. However, some people say that mixed martial arts does not go against religion. Rather, religious proponents of the sport say it provides competitors with a chance to practice courage and glorify God with the talents God has given them. The popularity of mixed martial arts has grown exponentially in the last fifteen years, leading to the manufacturing of T-shirts stating "Jesus didn't tap." This phrase refers to the gesture used to indicate submission to an opponent. Also, some churches sponsor mixed martial arts events to attract young, potential converts to Christianity.

STOCK CAR RACING

Has the Bible influenced stock car racing?

Yes. Stock car racing began as an illegal activity. Because making, selling, and buying alcohol was illegal in many parts of the southern United States during the early half of the twentieth century, some daredevils took to transporting moonshine from place to place in their souped-up cars. That was not easy. The roads were curvy and steep, and there was the constant threat of being caught by revenuers. Eventually, that moonshine running was the beginning of the National Association for Stock Car Auto Racing (NASCAR). Today, NASCAR is a wildly popular (and legal) spectator sport. A secular sport, its popularity has long since exceeded the boundaries of the South. Now it attracts fans from all over the world, and from all walks of life.

What ministry was inspired by NASCAR?

In 1988, minister and NASCAR fan Max Helton organized Motor Racing Outreach (MRO). Today, MRO is a nationwide ministry that serves racecar drivers, their families, and race fans. Part of their ministry consists of family-oriented worship events at various tracks on the racing circuit. Longtime racecar driver Darrell Waltrip serves on the MRO's board of directors.

VIDEO GAMES

How has the Bible influenced video games?

As in other pop culture arenas, the world of video games contains biblical imagery. One recent example appears in the game Bioshock Infinite®. Before the game was released in March 2013, its religious content was in the news. Developed for PC, Xbox 360, and PlayStation 3 by Irrational Games, this first-person shooter follows ex-Pinkerton agent Booker DeWitt as he and a teenage girl he rescued named Elizabeth flee their pursuiers in the floating city of Columbia. High fantasy and American history mix with Christian theology in a game that has drawn both praise and criticism from the public. During the game's development, one of Irrational Games' employees (a devout Christian) became so offended at one part of the game that he wrote a letter of resignation when he saw the direction the game was taking. A lengthy discussion between Irrational Games' creative director, Ken Levine, and the employee (who did not quit) prompted the writers to rewrite the game.

THE BIBLE AND FASHION

How has the Bible influenced mainstream fashion?

The Bible has specific mandates about clothing. One appearance-related item about which the Bible is specific appears in I Corinthians 11:15. It reads, "but that if a woman has long hair, it is her glory. For long hair is given to her as a covering." Today, some conservative religious groups take this to mean women should not cut their hair. In Leviticus 19:19, God told the Hebrews, "Do not wear clothing woven of two kinds of material." Today, some conservative Jewish groups interpret these verses to mean that it is wrong to wear clothing made of shatnez, which is any linen/wool blend. Observant Jews hire shatnez testers to ensure their clothes do not contain the prohibited fabrics. These are a couple of examples of how the Bible still influences some modern-day believers. The Bible has influenced mainstream fashion as well.

What was the "WWJD" trend?

During the 1990s, WWJD bracelets became popular. WWJD stands for "What Would Jesus Do?" The bracelets made their first appearance in Holland, Michigan in 1998. Youth pastor Dan Seaborn had a few bracelets made for the teens at his church. Then Seaborn and brothers Mike and Ken Freestone collaborated on how to manufacture and

The abbreviation WWJD, meaning "What Would Jesus Do?" has appeared on everything from bumper stickers to this hot air balloon.

distribute the bracelets to a wider audience. The bracelets caught on, not just in Christian circles, but on the secular stage as well. The bracelets proved so popular that buttons, hats, and other merchandise followed. Seaborn had been inspired by Charles Sheldon's 1896 book, *In His Steps*. In this book, a pastor challenges the people in his church to ask themselves "What would Jesus do?" before they made any decision.

Popularity of the WWJD slogan prompted a flurry of more "What Would" merchandise, including the books *What Would Jesus Eat?* (2005) by Don Colbert, and *What Would Jesus Deconstruct?* (2007) by John D. Caputo. Some of the merchandise did not have to do with Jesus at all, but simply borrowed from the wording. This category includes the reality TV show *What Would Ryan Lochte Do?* and the book *What Would Google Do?: Reverse-Engineering the Fastest Growing Company in the History of the World* (2011) by Jeff Jarvis.

What other fashion statement trended in the 1990s?

Birkenstocks. Birkenstocks have been around for more than two hundred years, but in the 1990s their popularity soared. In reference to their plain, old-fashioned appearance, these sandals came to be known by the nicknames "Jerusalem Cruisers" and "Air Jesuses".

So the Bible influenced a fashion trend. What about *haute couture*?

U.S.-based couture designer Monique Lhuillier revealed her Bible-inspired line the spring of 2011. With the Garden of Eden as her inspiration, Lhuillier designed a score of elegant garments. Hand-painted flowers, garden colors, and airy fabrics prevailed. One blue formal was trimmed in silky, pleated petals, suggesting either water or a rare flower. Another formal was red— as red as a ripe apple—and featured untold yards of wispy red fabric in its skirt. The garments are made with such fine materials and such expert craftsmanship that it is not unusual for Lhuillier's gowns to sell for thousands of dollars each.

Has the Bible influenced everyday fashion?

Yes. In July 2013, former Victoria's Secret model Kylie Bisutti launched a new clothing line for men, women, and children called God Inspired Fashion. The line combines trendy styles with scripture. Every garment in the line is imprinted with a word or sentence from the Bible. For example, available for purchase is a pair of women's skinny jeans with I Peter 5:7 written on one leg: "Cast your anxiety on him, for he cares for you." Bisutti's line consists of casual clothes priced comparably to stores at the mall. T-shirts, for instance, sell for around $25, and jeans sell for around $80.

THE JESUS FISH

How did the fish symbol come to represent Jesus and Christianity?

The Greek word for fish is *ichthys*. Early Christians made an acronym from this phrase: Iesous Christos Theou Yios Soter. This means Jesus Christ, Son of God, Savior. When early Christians were being persecuted, the fish became a secret symbol among them. The image of the fish continues to be a symbol of Christianity today, even to the point of sparking a bumper sticker fad in the 1990s. The fish symbol on bumper stickers spread to other things, such as key chains, T-shirts, and jewelry.

The Jesus fish reached full pop culture status when it was the focus of a *Seinfeld* episode. In this episode, "The Burning" (1998), Elaine (Julia Louis-Dreyfus) discovers that her boyfriend, David Puddy (Patrick Warburton), is a Christian. She finds his faith unsettling, especially his uncharitable assertion that she is going to Hell. She becomes so upset that she changes the Christian rock presets on his car stereo, and removes the Jesus fish from the back of his car. What happens next?

The symbol of the fish represents Jesus. This came about because the Greek word for fish, *ichthys*, can be an anagram for "Iesous Christos Theou Yios Soter," which means "Jesus Christ, Son of God, Savior."

377

Elaine: David, I'm going to Hell! The worst place in the world! With devils and those caves and the ragged clothing! And the heat! My God, the heat! What do you think about all of that?

David: It's gonna be rough.

Elaine: You should be trying to save me! [she slaps his chest]

David: Don't boss me! This is why you're going to Hell.

Elaine: I am NOT going to Hell. If you think I'm going to Hell, you should care that I'm going to Hell,even though I'm not!

David: You stole my Jesus fish, didn't you?

Elaine: Yeah, that's right! [Elaine uses her forefingers to make pretend horns on her head and snarls at David].

THE BIBLE AND THE U.S. GOVERNMENT

What does the Constitution say about the Bible?

The Constitution does not say anything about the Bible specifically, but it does have something to say about religion. After the designing dads penned the Constitution in 1787, they added some amendments, the first of which reads, "Congress shall make no law respecting an establishment of religion, or prohibiting the free exercise thereof; or abridging the freedom of speech, or of the press; or the right of the people peaceably to assemble, and to petition the Government for a redress of grievances." Exactly what that means has been argued ever since.

What happens when individuals or groups disagree about what the First Amendment means?

The Supreme Court has the right of judicial review. That means the Supreme Court has the right to examine laws to determine if they are constitutional. When individuals or groups do not agree on the meaning of the Constitution, they can take the issue to the Supreme Court. To this day, cases about the Bible and religion are being heard.

What have been the specific focus of these cases?

Sometimes the cases have to do with prayer in public schools or other public forums. Sometimes the cases have to do with religious groups meeting at schools. At other times, the cases have to do with specific biblical concepts. For instance, in 1980 the Supreme Court heard the case *Stone v. Graham*. In this case, the Supreme Court invalidated a Kentucky law that required the Ten Commandments to be posted in every public school-room in the state. Those who agreed with the Supreme Court's ruling believed the Kentucky law had an obvious religious purpose. Those who disagreed with the Supreme Court's ruling countered that having the Ten Commandments posted was appropriate because they were a foundational component of Western law.

Another case, *Board of Education of Westside Community Schools v. Mergens,* dealt with a Bible study club at a public high school. In 1984, Congress passed a law affirming that student religious groups had the right to meet in public high schools under the same auspices as other extracurricular activities. In 1985, Bridget Mergens, a student at Westside High School, sought administrative approval to have a Christian Bible Club at school. Administrators denied her request because they said she did not have a faculty sponsor. Mergens took her case to the Supreme Court where, in 1990, the case was decided in Mergens' favor.

Which key event in the federal government relies on the use of a Bible?

Most presidents have used a Bible to be sworn in. For his second inauguration, President Barack Obama used two Bibles. One was a Bible Abraham Lincoln used for one of his inaugurations. The other was a Bible that belonged to Martin Luther King, Jr.

Is the same bible used for every inauguration?

No. Some presidents have used family bibles or bibles given to them as gifts. For both of his inaugurations, Bill Clinton used a bible given to him by his grandmother. Sometimes the Bible has been opened to a certain verse or passage. When Gerald Ford was sworn in, his Bible was open to Proverbs 3:5–6—"Trust in the LORD with all your heart, and do not rely on your own insight. In all your ways acknowledge him, and he will make straight your paths." Wishing to emphasize the separation of church and state, John Quincy Adams did not swear on a bible, but a book of law. Theodore Roosevelt did not swear on any book at all.

How is the Bible used in other government forums?

The Bible is often used in courts of law. Before testifying, a witness places his/her left hand on a bible, and swears to tell the truth, the whole truth, and nothing but the truth, so help me God. However, this practice is not mandated by law in all places. People who do not believe in the holiness of the Bible are not required to swear on it.

THE BIBLE AS A SOCIAL CATALYST

Movies and fashions are one thing, but what about entrenched belief systems and social mores?

Since the founding of the United States, the Bible has helped shape the course of events. Many people, now and back in the early days of the country, have searched the Bible for moral guidance. People arrive at different conclusions as to what a verse, chapter, or the whole book means. Now, as in the past, these differences can lead to conflict. Conflict arises, too, between those whose decisions are shaped by the Bible, and those whose decisions are not.

In what three significant epochs in American history has the Bible has played a key role?

There have been three Great Awakenings. The 1730s and 1740s saw the first Great Awakening, a time in which religious fervor spread throughout the country due to a significant increase in itinerant preachers. Jonathan Edwards' fiery 1741 sermon, "Sinners in the Hands of an Angry God," epitomizes the emotional and intellectual tone of the era. The major theme of this Awakening was acknowledgment of one's sins and fear of God's judgment.

A second Great Awakening occurred between 1790 and 1840. This Awakening differed from the first in that the ministers of this era focused on trying to improve one's self and society. This massive shift in thinking led to the first great wave of social reform in the history of the United States. Effort, time, and money went into improving the lives of the poor, the mentally and physically ill, and those in prison. Also, a strong antislavery belief grew out of this Awakening.

The third Great Awakening occurred between the late 1850s and 1900. It was a time of rapid social change. People were moving from the country to the city in greater numbers. Factories were popping up everywhere, as were slums. The extravagant lifestyles of those made rich through railroads and other industries stood in startling contrast to the starved, barren lifestyles of the working poor. Social aid groups were organized to help the poor with health care, education, and housing.

What was one of the major problems the third Great Awakening sought to address?

Alcoholism was rampant, especially among men. Wives and children were affected greatly by the damages done by alcoholic husbands and fathers. Women took up the cause, and started what became known as the temperance movement. In 1873, some women formally organized into the Women's Christian Temperance Union (WCTU). Through prayer and protest, the women of this group hoped to close saloons, and thus bring an end to alcoholism in their homes.

What games have been inspired by the Bible?

Many board game classics have a biblical version. These include Cranium: The Bible Edition®, Apples to Apples: The Bible Edition®, Bible Taboo®, and Scattergories: The Bible Edition®.

Who was Carrie Nation?

She was one of the most vocal and active members of the WCTU during the organization's early years. Having had an alcoholic husband, she knew firsthand the damages it wrought on domesticity. She said she was doing God's bidding when she took to carrying an axe to destroy saloons.

Which fast-food restaurant chain ties the Bible into its products?

The fast-food restaurant In-N-Out prints the book and verse number of certain Bible scriptures on some of its packaging. The shake cup has the citation "Proverbs 3:5." The beverage cup has the citation "John 3:16." The hamburger bag has two citations: "Nahum 1:7" and "Revelation 3:20."

What are the most frequently tweeted Bible verses?

Sources differ as to which verse is most frequently tweeted. However, Jeremiah 29:11 and Philippians 4:13 are consistently in the running for first place. Jeremiah 29:11 reads, "For surely I know the plans I have for you, says the LORD, plans for your welfare and not for harm, to give you a future with hope." Philippians 4:13 reads, "I can do all things through him who strengthens me."

Glossary

Anonymous—Term used to designate that the authorship of a written work is unknown.

Apocrypha—In the Protestant church, this is the name given to a group of books that were excluded from the Old Testament because they were not considered to be divinely inspired.

Apostle—One of the original twelve men Jesus sent out to preach the gospel. The twelve were Simon Peter, James, John, Andrew, Philip, Bartholomew (aka Nathanael), Matthew (aka Levi), Thomas, James the son of Alpheus, Thaddaeus (aka Judas, but not Judas Iscariot), Simon the Zealot, and Judas.

Archaeology—The study of past cultures through the examination of cultural remnants.

Ark of the Covenant—A box made of wood and overlaid in gold that was built to store the tablets on which the Ten Commandments were written. It was carried by the Israelites as they traveled in the wilderness. First mentioned in the book of Exodus.

Artifact—A physical piece of history.

Assyrian Captivity—The term used to describe when the people of the northern kingdom, Israel, were conquered by the Assyrians.

Baal—A god worshiped in ancient times by various peoples, including the Canaanites.

Babylonian Captivity—The term used to describe when the people of the southern kingdom, Judah, were conquered by the Babylonians.

Beatitudes—The teachings Jesus offered when he gave his Sermon on the Mount. Appeared in the Gospels of Matthew and Luke.

Before the Common Era (BCE)—Refers to all events that happened before the birth of Jesus.

Bitumen—A black, tar-like substance.

Canon—In biblical studies, the writings widely accepted as eligible for inclusion in the Bible.

Catholicism—The word "catholic" means "universal." In the early days of the church, the entire Christian church was referred to as the Roman Catholic Church. Today, the word Catholic still carries the idea of the universal church, but refers also to a Christian who adheres to the tenets of the Roman Catholic Church as opposed to the tenets of the Protestant church.

Christianity—The religion that evolved, in part, from the belief that Jesus died on the cross to save people from sin and that he was resurrected on the third day after he was crucified. Adherents to the Christian faith are called Christians.

Circumcision—the surgical removal of the foreskin on a penis. Circumcision was practiced the Israelites and other groups of people in what is now the Middle East.

Cities of Refuge—At God's command, the Israelites set aside six towns where a person who killed another person by accident could seek refuge until a proper trial could be arranged.

Codex—Old manuscripts in book form, as opposed to being in loose scrolls.

Common Era (CE)—Refers to all events that happened after the birth of Jesus.

Court of the Tabernacle—The courtyard surrounding the Tabernacle and the location for the altar. Appeared first in Exodus.

Covenant—A formal agreement.

Crucifixion—In ancient Roman times, crucifixion was a form of capital punishment in which the condemned person was attached, arms stretched out to the sides, to a cross-shape frame, either by nails or by ties. In this position, the person's own body weight worked against him and caused undue pressure on the lungs. Usually, death came about because of suffocation.

Cubit—A unit of measure equivalent to about eighteen inches. It was usually calculated by the distance from a person's elbow to the tip of the fingers when extended.

Day of Atonement—Known now as Yom Kippur, this is the holiest day in the Jewish year. The Israelites observed this day once a year when the high priest entered the sanctuary of God to offer sacrifices for all the people. Appeared first in Leviticus.

Dead Sea Scrolls—After having been hidden in caves near the Dead Sea for centuries, these scrolls were discovered in 1946. They are one of the most significant archaeological finds ever because they predate other biblically related scrolls by at least one thousand years. In addition, by comparing these scrolls with their younger counterparts, scholars have been able to determine the meticulous care with which scribes passed down information.

Decalogue—Another name for the Ten Commandments.

Diaspora—Refers to the Jews who settled in other countries following the destruction of the Temple by the Romans in 70 C.E..

Disciple—A follower of Jesus.

Documentary Theory—The theory that Genesis, Exodus, Leviticus, Numbers, and Deuteronomy derived from four independent sources.

El—A Hebrew name for God.

Festival of Booths—Known also as the Festival of Tabernacles, this is an annual observance in which the harvest is celebrated for seven days. Appeared first in Leviticus.

Festival of Trumpets—Known now as Rosh Hashanah, this is an annual observance for celebrating the new year. Appeared first in Leviticus.

Festival of Weeks—Known now as Shuovot in Judaism, this is an annual observance for celebrating the harvest. In Christianity, the holy day is known as Pentecost, the commemoration of the Holy Spirit's descent upon the apostles. Appeared first in Leviticus.

Gabriel—An archangel of God. Delivers messages for God. Appeared first in the book of Daniel.

Gemara—In Judaism, the collection of writings containing interpretations of laws and stories.

Gospel—The word means "good news." Also refers to the books of Matthew, Mark, Luke, and John.

Hanukkah—The Festival of Lights. A Jewish celebration commemorating the re-dedication of the Temple following its desecration by Greeks in the 100s B.C.E.

Hebrew—In Judaism, a name used to designate descendants of Abraham. Also refers to the ancient language of the Jews.

Heresy—An idea that is contrary to the accepted ideas of the church. A person who disseminates such ideas is called a heretic.

Hesed—A Hebrew word without an exact equivalent in English, but is something akin to loving-kindness.

Holy Spirit—Powerful, mysterious, and ineffable part of the Trinity. Followers of Jesus believe it helps them live according to the gospel.

Illuminations—A style of illustrating that became popular in the Middle Ages. The style is characterized by religious themes, intricate patterns, and the use of many colors.

Immaculate Conception—Refers to the mystery surrounding Mary, the mother of Jesus, becoming pregnant even though she was a virgin.

Incense Altar—Made of wood and overlaid in gold, this is the altar where the Israelites offered incense to God. Appeared first in Exodus.

Intertestamental Period—The time between the last event recorded in the Old Testament and the first event recorded in the New Testament: about 400 years.

Jews—Originally, the term designated people of Judah. Now, the term designates people of the Jewish faith.

Judaism—The monotheistic religion founded in the Old Testament.

Judges—The seventh book in the Bible. The name refers to the judges put in place by God to administer justice among the Israelites.

Lectionary—A schedule for reading scripture.

Leprosy—A skin ailment referred to frequently in the Bible.

Lord's Prayer—A short prayer Jesus used as a model to teach his disciples how to pray. Appeared first in the book of Matthew.

Manna—White flakes sent by God to feed the Israelites when they traveled through the wilderness. Appeared in Exodus.

Mantle—A cape or cloak.

Mark of Cain—Refers to a mark of an unspecified nature that God gave to Cain following Cain's murder of his brother, Abel. The mark gave a person protection.

Maskil—A musical term of uncertain meaning.

Mercy Seat—Also known as the atonement cover, this was the lid of the Ark of the Covenant. Appeared first in Exodus.

Miktam—A musical term of uncertain meaning.

Mishnah—A collection of laws in Judaism used in addition to the Tanakh.

Mummification—An embalming process involving drying out and preserving the corpse.

Muscular Christianity—The idea that Christian principles go hand in hand with athletic skill and physical strength.

Nazarite Vow—A vow made by some Israelite men and women who wished to set themselves apart for God's service.

Nephilim—A race of giant people. Appeared first in Genesis.

New Testament—The New Testament is the second part of the Bible. It is made up of twenty-seven books and recounts the arrival of Jesus, his life on Earth, and what happened in the years right after his death and resurrection.

Old Testament—The Old Testament is the first part of the Bible. It is made up of thirty-nine books and includes the creation of the world and the formation of Israel. For Christians, parts of the Old Testament point to the coming of Jesus. In Judaism, the Old Testament is used, but the New Testament is not. In Judaism, the Old Testament is called the Tanakh.

Ossuary—A container for the bones of a deceased person.

Papal Indulgence—In the early Roman Catholic Church, the pope sold forgiveness of sins. This is one of the practices that led some people to seek reforms in the Church.

Papyrus—A reedy plant that grew in marshy areas of Egypt. Used to make a paper-like product.

Parable—A story with a lesson to it. Jesus used parables to teach his disciples.

Parchment—A thin material made of treated animal skin. Parchment was used like paper is today.

Pareidolia—The theory that the human mind is wired to find patterns and images in everyday things.

Passover—An annual holy day in which Jews remember how God passed over their households when he killed all of the firstborn in Egypt. Appeared first in Exodus.

Pentateuch—In Christianity, the term for the first five books of the Old Testament.

Pentecost—This took place fifty days after Jesus' resurrection and is considered the birthday of the church. It is when the Holy Spirit came to the followers of Jesus. Appeared first in the book of Acts.

Percamenarious—Someone who makes parchment.

Pharisees—A group of influential community leaders in Jerusalem during the time of Jesus. Appeared first in the book of Matthew.

Pitch—A sticky substance formed from the resin of certain plants.

Pharaoh—In ancient times, the title of the king of Egypt.

Plague—In the Bible, any number of diseases or illnesses that spread to many people.

Polyglot—A book in which the text is presented alongside translations of that text.

Pop Culture—Short for popular culture. The collection of attitudes, tastes, and images that reflect mainstream interests in modern times.

Prophet—One through whom God reveals His word.

Protestant—Refers to a Christian who is not a Catholic.

Protestant Reformation—A movement in the 1500s in which people who were dissatisfied with the way the Roman Catholic Church operated sought reform and ultimately broke from the Roman Catholic Church.

Proverb—A wise saying. Many of them are found in the Old Testament book of Proverbs.

Psalm—A song. Many of them are found in the Old Testament book of Psalms.

Pseudipigrapha—This collection of writings includes the Apocrypha plus other writings.

Q document—Q stands for the German word "quelle," which means "source." A theoretical document that some scholars think the Gospel writers referred to when writing their accounts.

Relic—A physical piece of history that has the reputation of being associated with a famous historical person.

Sabbath Day—God told the Israelites that they should rest on this day of the week. Appeared first in Genesis.

Sabbath Month—The Day of Atonement and the Festival of Booths occur during this month.

Sabbath Year—God told the Israelites that after working the land for six years, they should allow the land to rest in the seventh year. Appeared first in Leviticus.

Sackcloth—A rough fabric, sometimes made of goat hair.

Sadducees—A group of influential priests in Jerusalem during the time of Jesus. Appeared first in the book of Matthew.

Secular—Refers to the parts of society that are not religious.

Selah—A musical term of uncertain meaning.

Septuagint—This is the name given to the first Greek translation of the Hebrew Bible, or Old Testament.

Sermon on the Mount—A sermon Jesus delivered in which he described the Beatitudes, or blessings. Appeared first in the book of Matthew and is also in the book of Luke.

Shatnez—Hebrew word referring to any fabric made of the prohibited linen and wool blend.

Sheol—In Old Testament times, there was no concept of Heaven. Instead, it was believed that once a person died, he or she went to a dark, shadowy place known as Sheol.

Shroud—A piece of fabric used to wrap a corpse.

Stele—An upright stone slab bearing inscriptions.

Synoptic Gospels—Matthew, Mark, and Luke: so called because this trio of books concerns the same events and people.

Tabernacle—Also known as the Tent of Meeting, this was the tent the Israelites took down and reassembled every time they settled somewhere new in the wilderness. The Tabernacle was the place for worshiping God. Appeared first in Exodus.

Talmud—A collection of laws used in Judaism in addition to the Tanakh.

Ten Commandments—A collection of laws given to the Israelites by God. Appeared first in Exodus.

Torah—In Judaism, the first five books of the Tanakh, or Old Testament. Tradition holds that the Torah was written by Moses.

Transfiguration—Jesus appeared bathed in light. He spoke with Elijah and Moses. The event represented the ultimate fulfillment of Old Testament prophecy about the nature of Jesus. Appeared first in the book of Matthew.

Urim and Thummin—Akin to dice, these were used by the Levitical high priest to determine God's will.

Yahweh—A Hebrew name for God.

Year of Jubilee—God told the Israelites to make every fiftieth year the Year of Jubilee. This was a year in which all debts were to be forgiven and all slaves freed. Appeared first in Leviticus.

Versions of the Bible

The following is a list of some of the important versions of the Bible. This is not a complete and exhaustive list, but it highlights many of the significant translations and editions.

THE TANAKH, OR HEBREW BIBLE

Mikraot Gedolot (1526–1527): Known as the "Great Scriptures" and "Rabbinic Bible." Based on Masoretic texts.

Old JPS Tanakh (1917): An English translation of the Hebrew Bible based on the King James Version.

Koren Jerusalem Tanakh (1962): Generally viewed as the most authentic Hebrew/English Tanakh.

JPS Tanakh (1985): Modern English translation of the Hebrew Bible. Based on Masoretic Texts.

Stone Edition of the Tanakh (1996): Modern English translation. Features charts, maps, and other items useful for study.

Jerusalem Crown Bible (2001): An English translation based on the Aleppo Codex.

Koren Classic Tanakh. A Hebrew-language-only Tanakh with charts, maps, and other items useful for study.

Tanakh Sinaim. A Hebrew-language-only Tanakh that uses a plain, easy-to-read font.

THE KING JAMES BIBLE AND RELATED VERSIONS

King James Version (KJV) (1611): Sponsored by King James I of England, this version set the standard for all English translations to come. Noted for its lyrical, poetic language.

Young's Literal Translation (YLT) (1862; revised 1887, 1898): Translator Robert Young sought to correct inaccuracies and inconsistencies he found in the King James Version. He came up with a literal translation that preserves the tense and word usage of the original Greek and Hebrew manuscripts.

American Standard Version (ASV) (1885; revised 1901): The ASV represents the first major attempt to revise the King James Version. While this translation retains much of the formal elegance of the King James Version, the syntax reflects more modern usage.

Revised Standard Version (RSV) (1946 New Testament, 1952 Old Testament; revised 1971): A revision of the 1901 edition of the American Standard Version (ASV), the RSV sticks close to the ASV, but incorporates modern English phrasing.

New English Bible (NEB) (1961 New Testament, 1970 Old Testament): The first British Bible to be translated from the original Hebrew, Aramaic, and Greek since the King James Version.

The Living Bible (LIV) (1962 New Testament, 1971 Old Testament): A paraphrasing of the American Standard Version. Noted for staying as close to original manuscripts as possible, all the while using language that is understandable to people who are not familiar with the Bible.

New American Standard Version (NASV) (New Testament 1963, full Bible, 1971; revised 1995): Revision of the American Standard Version (ASV) of 1901, which was inspired by the English Revised American Standard Version New Testament (1891). Noted for its updated, more colloquial language, while maintaining faithfulness to the original manuscripts.

New King James Version (NKJV) (1982): Language and grammar updated from the King James Version, but retains the elegance of the KJV.

New Revised Standard Version (NRSV) (1989): An update of the 1952 edition of the Revised Standard Version. Noted for its facile language and use of newly available manuscripts in its translation.

Twenty-first Century King James Version (KJ21) (1994): Updates some of the archaic phrasing, punctuation, and grammar of the King James Version, while retaining enough of those qualities to allow the original beauty of the language to shine through.

English Standard Version (ESV) (2001): Reflects the stellar literary quality of the King James Version and the Revised Standard Version, all the while incorporating clear, mainstream English.

THE NEW INTERNATIONAL VERSION AND RELATED VERSIONS

New International Version (NIV) (1973 New Testament, 1978 Old Testament; revisions 1984, 2011): Made up of scholars from all over the world, the Committee on Bible Translation has met every year since 1965 to ensure that subsequent revisions of the NIV reflect the most current biblical scholarship. The translation is done from the original manuscripts. This is the best-selling modern English translation.

New International Readers' Version (NIRV) (1996): A thorough simplification of the New International Version. Perfect for children or those learning English as a second language.

CATHOLIC BIBLES

Douay-Rheims Bible (1609 New Testament, 1610 Old Testament): The Catholic answer to the English-language Protestant Bibles being published in the 1500s. Translated from the Latin Vulgate, it features elegant language similar to that in the King James Version.

Jerusalem Bible (JER) (1966): Based on the French Bible de Jerusalem of 1956, this Roman Catholic Bible features elegant phrasing.

New American Bible (NAB) (1970; New Testament revision 1986): Twenty-five years in the making, this is the first complete American Catholic Bible translated from the original Hebrew, Aramaic, and Greek. The text reflects post-Latin Vulgate scholarship.

The Way: The Catholic Living Bible (1973): Based on the 1962 edition of The Living Bible, while incorporating books found in Catholic Bibles but not in Protestant Bibles.

New Jerusalem Bible (NJB) (1985): Updated version of the Jerusalem Bible.

Other Significant Versions

Good News Translation (GNT Bible) (1976): A clear and simple modern translation using modern English.

English Version for the Deaf (EVD) (1978 New Testament, 1986 Old Testament): Uses simple syntax to make translating into sign language easier. The simple syntax makes it a good choice for children or adults with limited reading skills.

New Century Version (NCV) (1978 New Testament, 1986 Old Testament): Based on the International Children's Bible (ICB), this version features simple, accessible phrasing.

Simple English Version (SEV) (1980): Written at an elementary school reading level, the SEV uses a vocabulary of 3,000 words.

Contemporary English Version (CEV) (1991 New Testament, 1995 Old Testament): Written at an elementary school reading level, this version features footnotes that explain the cultural complexities in the Bible.

The Message (1993 New Testament, 1994 Psalms, 2002 complete Bible): Noted for its engaging, direct, accessible language.

Holman Christian Standard Bible (1999): Noted for its up-to-date English usage for English speakers and readers around the world.

Common English Bible (CEB) (2011): Substitutes words that are hard to understand with words that have a natural, conversational tone.

Works Consulted

BOOKS

Abanes, Richard. *Reflections on Easter and the Forty Days of Lent*. Hachette Book Group USA, 2008.

Ancient Civilizations, 2500 BC–AD 500. Time-Life Education, 1998.

Auer, Chris. Illus. Rick Johnson. *The Legend of the Sand Dollar: An Inspirational Story of Hope for Easter*. Zonderkidz, 2005.

Barzun, Jacques. *From Dawn to Decadence: 1500 to the Present: 500 Years of Western Cultural Life*. HarperCollins Publishers, 2000.

Borland, Hal. Illus. by Anne Ophelia Dowden. *Plants of Christmas*. Thomas Y. Cromwell, Jr. Books, 1969.

Brown, Dale M. *Mesopotamia: The Mighty Kings*. Time-Life Education, 1995.

Chaikin, Miriam. Illus. by Erika Weihs. *Menorahs, Mezuzahs, and Other Jewish Symbols*. Clarion Books, 1990.

Coogan, Michael D. ed. *The New Oxford Annotated Bible, 3rd ed. With the Apocryphal/ Deuterocanonical Books*. New Revised Standard Version. Oxford University Press, 2001.

Currie, Robin and Stephen Hyslop. *The Letter and the Scroll: What Archaeology Tells Us about the Bible*. National Geographic, 2009.

Deluxe Then and Now Bible Maps. Rose Publishing, 2008.

Draper, Charles W. ed., Chad Brand, ed., Archie England, ed. *Hollman Illustrated Bible Dictionary*. Holman Reference, 2003.

Fee, Gordon D., and Robert L. Hubbard, Jr. *The Eerdman's Companion to the Bible*. Wm. B. Eerdmans Publishing Company 2011.

Freedman, Russell. *In Defense of Freedom: The Story of America's Bill of Rights*. Holiday House, 2003.

Gardner, Joseph. *Who's Who in the Bible*. Reader's Digest Association, 1994.

Hakim, Joy. *A History of US: Liberty for All? 1800–1860,* 2nd ed. Oxford University Press, 1999.

Halley, Henry H. *Halley's Handbook*. Zondervan, 2007.

Hemming, Heidi, and Julie Hemming Savage. *Women Making America*. Clotho Press, 2009.

Jacobs, A.J. *The Year of Living Biblically: One Man's Humble Quest to Follow the Bible as Literally as Possible*. Simon and Schuster, 2007.

Kimmelman, Leslie. Illus. by Ora Eitan. *Dance, Sing, Remember: A Celebration of Jewish Holidays*. HarperCollins, 2000.

Knight, George. *The Holy Land: An Illustrated Guide to Its History, Geography, Culture, and Holy Sites*. Barbour Publishing, 2011.

Lang, J. Stephen. *1001 Things You Always Wanted to Know about the Bible*. 2010.

MacGregor, Jerry and Marie Prys. *1001 Surprising Things You Should Know about the Bible*. Baker Books, 2002.

Manchester, William. *A World Lit Only By Fire: The Medieval Mind and the Renaissance: Portrait of an Age*. Little, Brown and Company, 1992.

Maynard, Jill. *Illustrated Dictionary of Bible Life and Times*, Reader's Digest, 1997.

Miller, Stephen M. *The Complete Guide to the Bible*. Barbour Publishing, 2007.

Nicolson, Adam. *God's Secretaries*. Harper, 2003.

Parris, John. *Mountain Bred*. Citizen-Times Publishing Company, 1967.

Pirotta, Savior. Illustrated by Helen Cann. *Christian Festival Tales*. Raintree Steck-Vaughn Publishers, 2001.

Reed, Jonathan L. *HarperCollins Visual Guide to the New Testament: What Archaeology Reveals about the First Christians*. HarperCollins, 2007.

Robinson, George. *Essential Judaism: A Complete Guide to Beliefs, Customs, and Rituals*. Pocket Books, 2007.

Rogerson, John. Ed. *The Oxford Illustrated History of the Bible*. Oxford University Press, 2001.

Ryan, Donald. *Complete Idiot's Guide to Biblical Mysteries*. Alpha, 2000.

Smith, Charles Merrill and James W. Bennett. *How the Bible Was Built*. Wm. B. Eerdmans Publishing Company, 2005.

Spangler, Ann. *Praying the Names of God: A Daily Guide*. Zondervan, 2004.

The Visual Dictionary of Ancient Civilizations. Dorling-Kindersley, 1994.

Vos, Howard F. *Nelson's New Illustrated Bible Manners and Customs*. Thomas Nelson, 1999.

Wilke, Richard B. *Disciple: Becoming Disciples Through Bible Study*. Abingdon Press, 1993.

Wilkinson, Philip. *DK Illustrated Book of Mythology*. Dorling-Kindersley, 1995.

Index

Note: (ill.) indicates photos and illustrations.

Amalekites, 67, 85, 113
Amaziah, King, 128
American Girl dolls, 371
American Revolution, 21, 357
Amminadab, 360
Ammon, 180
Ammonites, 35, 100–101, 320
Amnon, 121
Amon, King, 128
Amorites, 58, 94–96, 129
Amos, 2, 5, 180–82, 181 (ill.)
Anakites, 31
Ananias [and Saul], 257
Ananias [Saphira's husband], 254
Andrew, 201, 214
The Andy Griffith Show, 179, 364
Angelico, Fra, 203
angels, seven, 308–9
Angels and Demons (Brown), 370
angels' visit to Lot, 36–37
anger of God, 70, 157, 161, 164
animals on Noah's ark, number of, 32
Anna, 238, 316–17, 319
Annunciation, 203 (ill.), 236
anointing oil, 74
Antichrist, 284.310, 312, 370
Antioch, Syria, 259–260
Antioch, Turkey, 259–260
Antiochus IV Epiphanes, 175, 329–330, 333–34
Apis, 62
apocalypse, 160, 176, 311
Apocalypse [character], 371
Apocrypha, 5, 7–8, 10–14, 18, 315–334
Apollyon, 304
apostles
    acts of the, 251–264
    busy, 255–56
    difference between disciples and, 200–201
    and end of life of Jesus, 224, 231–32

extra description in John, 249
and the first church community, 254
first meeting Jesus, 233
at Gethsemane, 225
illustrations of, 200 (ill.), 253 (ill.)
James as one of the, 292
and Jesus's betrayal, 226
and Jesus's crucifixion, 228
Jesus's interaction with after resurrection, 251
John as one of the, 243, 297, 299
New Testament writings connected to the, 10
Peter as one of the, 293
recruiting, 219–220
Revelation from time of, 312
saint meaning Jesus's, 256
Thomas as one of the, 250
and trouble with Jesus's disciples, 253
twelve, 201, 302
and the wedding in Cana, 245
appearances, Paul on, 272
Apples to Apples: The Bible Edition, 381
Arabian Peninsula, 126
Aram, 131, 343–44
Aram-naharaim, 40
Arch of Titus, 347 (ill.), 347–48
archaeology, the Bible and, 335–357
ark, Noah's, 32 (ill.), 32–33, 363
Ark of the Covenant
    bringing into Canaan, 92
    bringing to Jerusalem, 136
    illustration of, 72 (ill.)
    in the Tabernacle, 71–72, 74, 78
    in the wilderness, 82, 86
    missing, 76, 350
    retrieving, 119

stolen, 112
Arnold, Benedict, 366
Arphaxad, 320
arrangement of the Israelites' camp, 82
Artaxerxes, King, 138–140, 323
Artemis, 278
artifacts, elusive Biblical, 350–53
Arumah, 100
Asa, King, 128
Asenath, 49
Ash Wednesday, 223, 231
Ashdod, 112
Asher, 43
Asherah, 96, 99–100, 131
Asia, 275, 293, 300
Aslan, 371
Asmodeus, 317–18
Assyria, 29, 134, 183, 320
Assyrian Empire, 134–35
Astarte, 96
Athaliah, Queen, 128–29, 129 (ill.)
Athanasius, 10
Attila the Hun, 175
August, Pernilla, 362
Austin, "Stone Cold" Steve, 374
author of the Bible, 4
Azariah, 169, 315, 325–26

B

Baal, 96, 99–100, 129, 131–33
Baal-zebub, 133
Baannah, 118
Baasha, King, 128
Babel, Tower of, 34, 34 (ill.), 190
Babylon
    conquer of, 191
    Cyrus Cylinder discovered in, 345
    exile in, 138–39, 166, 169–170, 173, 175
    fall of, 171, 309
    importance of, 135
    in exile, 324–26